Menlove

The Life of John Menlove Edwards

with an appendix of his writings

by

JIM PERRIN

with a Foreword by Stephen Z. Edwards

ERNEST PRESS

First published in Great Britain 1985
by Victor Gollancz Ltd.
This edition published by The Ernest Press 1993
© Jim Perrin 1993

British Library Cataloguing in Publication Data
A catalogue record for this book is available
from the British Library

ISBN 0-948153-28-8

NOTE

The quotation from the *Hippolytus* of Euripides that appears on page iv is
translated by David Grene and is taken from *Greek Tragedies Volume I*
edited by David Grene & Richmond Lattimore, © 1942 by the University
of Chicago. It is reprinted by permission of the University of Chicago
Press.

Typeset by Parker Typesetting Service, Leicester
Printed by St Edmundsbury Press

CONTENTS

Many a time in night's long empty spaces
I have brooded on the causes of a life's shipwreck.
I think that our lives are worse than the mind's quality
would warrant. There are many who know virtue.
We know the good, we apprehend it clearly.
But we cannot bring it to fruition.

(from the *Hippolytus* of Euripides)

I will not cease from Mental Fight,
Nor shall my Sword sleep in my hand,
Till we have built Jerusalem
In England's green and pleasant Land.

(from the Preface to Blake's *Milton*)

This climbing. Perhaps, really, one was never made for it. I have a conceit
that I was even made for more than that: more than to satisfy extremely one's
own pride. It would be nice to feel that one could have possibilities of
interacting in an expansile manner, contacting with life beyond and outside
of ourselves. No. I do not particularly want to make things quail before me:
the satisfaction of seeing them bow the head is charged too much with
despondency. They all bow their heads and their eyes are averted. My chest
heaves up and down again, alone. Then one must strike an attitude, clench
the muscle of the jaw. How can one? One does not know what it is all about.
I wanted a friend, not this. I wanted understanding, not this. I hoped we
might help each other to pierce the partitions: how can one do that while one
holds oneself so, clenching the muscles of the jaw and of a fine appearance,
getting blunted.

Menlove Edwards

FOREWORD

I AM VERY glad to have the opportunity of writing a foreword to the sad story of my brother's life. Jim Perrin's patient, exhaustive and sympathetic research has brought to mind not a few things which I had forgotten, and much that I had not known about Menlove. One can see now that the six years which separated us were, in fact, a great barrier in those early days when I was growing into manhood and he was still a small boy. But I have many memories: of long days out on sea or lakeshores or on hills, of kettles boiling on wood fires and sandwiches eaten by mountain streams, of bathes in bitterly cold tarns or in deep, clear water on rocky coasts.

In the years before the war Menlove often used to visit us at Stokesay and Bullinghope. He would come for Christmas, especially when my mother and sister came too. But my move to Staindrop in 1942 put a considerable distance between us, and the problems of travel in wartime made our contacts much less frequent.

In these years too, his difficulties all too evidently increased, and communication of any real feeling or meaning became more and more difficult. He never spoke of his homosexuality, and our knowledge of it must have come through a gradual realization over a long period. As far as Mother, my sister and I were concerned, it made not the slightest difference to our love and sympathy for Menlove. This very real bond of affection for him remained to the end, and until that came we each in our different ways did whatever we could to help him, though this became more and more difficult as his mental stability declined.

Reading this story, one begins to comprehend something of the desperate sadness and isolation he endured. I always felt that in Menlove there was a deep and essential goodness, which I still remember with gratitude. His early years seemed so full of great possibilities, his end the more tragic for the frustrations which caused it. Jim Perrin's insight and careful study has given a sadly moving picture of a tragedy, and I am indeed grateful to him for his labours, for the care and skill of his writing, and for the deep understanding he has shown of Menlove.

STEPHEN Z. EDWARDS

HARLECH, APRIL 1984

INTRODUCTION

THE LIFE OF Menlove Edwards has about it something of the quality of tragic myth. Although he is not well known to the general reader, no name resounds more clearly from the history of the intensely insular world of British rock-climbing than his. He has been acclaimed as father and prophet to the modern sport, as one of its greatest innovators, the most significant pre-war explorer of new routes up the rock faces of this country, and the finest of climbing essayists. All of these claims can be argued with justice.

Apart from his importance as a rock-climber, his adventures on water were extraordinary. He swam down the Linn of Dee when it was swollen by melting snow. He rowed across the Minch to the Outer Hebrides, alone, in a small open boat, in midwinter. These exploits, and others like them, went virtually unpublicized and in that lay part of their attraction for him. They were personal Everests on the largest scale, undertaken at odd moments in an honest, private, busy life – and they were more hazardous and enterprising than many other feats which easily attract sponsorship and catch the public eye.

The physical adventures apart, he attempted to live his life with the uncompromising integrity handed down to him through his family, which held strong religious and humanitarian beliefs. His aim in his professional work as a clinical psychiatrist was to alleviate mental suffering, and there are numerous testimonies to his success in this. But his theoretical writings on psychology, which ran counter to the Freudian and Adlerian bias of the profession in the thirties, and which he considered to be the central achievement of his life, were rejected.

He was a homosexual who preached openness and tolerance at a time when the laws against deviation from the sexual norm were harshly punitive. And he was a conscientious objector—in a society bent on war—who made a massively principled silent stand for his cause. The isolation this brought him, allied to the sadness in which the love-affairs of his life ended and the rejection of his work, broke him down into insanity. The story of his last years is almost unbearably painful, relieved only by the great kindness shown him by relatives and friends.

This book was written partly out of that desire to vindicate his subject which is at once the biographer's plainest virtue and his most insidious vice.

The desire is an essential part of the compassionate affection which under-pins good biography, but at the same time it can distort perspectives, lead to an uncritical acceptance of the data at the writer's disposal, and lure him into too close an identification with the character he describes. I have tried, probably not with complete success, to avoid these faults. My object throughout has been, by presenting as full a picture of Menlove as is possible from the limited material available, to achieve a better understanding not only of the pain but also of the achievement and purpose of his life. For despite his apparent failure and defeat, Menlove left also a legacy of victory and hope. That a human spirit could bear witness and endure, right up to the point at which it was broken by intransigence, incomprehension and inhumanity, is a cause for gratitude and a reason for the study of that life. I believe Menlove has a wider significance for us today than that of the important but limited questions he tackled in his own time. If he was a moral crusader, he was a quiet, understated and ineffectual one. He had no gift of making common cause. Yet there are qualities about him, of individuality and moral courage, which stand as examples to us all.

This is not the first book to have been written about Menlove; *Samson: The Life and Writings of Menlove Edwards* was published privately in 1960. It printed a selection of his poetry and prose, together with notes and a short biographical memoir by Wilfrid Noyce and Geoffrey Sutton. In writing the present book I am greatly indebted to Sutton and Noyce for their assembling much valuable material which might otherwise have been lost. Noyce's compassionate intent, in putting together the tribute *Samson* was intended to be, deserves full recognition. But though *Samson* is an interesting book, and well meant, its editors were working under constraints which rendered it less than satisfactory in certain aspects. Noyce, for example, could obviously not speak frankly of his relationship with Menlove (and probably many of his generation will still be uneasy about its being treated thus). Apart from the personal embarrassment it would have caused Noyce, homosexuality was still illegal in Britain in 1960, so that part of Menlove's life is distorted, and an element of concealment is apparent. Sutton, too, had his influence in giving the book a slant towards the New Criticism and ideas about social alienation current in the late fifties. This produced some stimulating the-orizing, but perhaps worked against the painstaking accuracy which is the basis of biographical writing. Factually, *Samson* has to be treated with caution. For all that, it was a pioneering and a brave work, without which this book would have been much less complete.

Some indication needs to be given of the present volume's biographical method. The chief point to be made is simply that it is a work of biography, and not one of social or literary criticism. I have used the techniques of the latter here and there when dealing with Menlove's own writings, but only in order to bring out their biographical importance, and the extent to which they reflect back into his life. In a sense, this begs the question of the real quality of some of Menlove's essays and poems, and especially in the case of the poems gives the greater emphasis to his lesser work. With the essays, similarly, it has meant that "Scenery for a Murder" receives detailed attention whilst the more accessible and less biographically relevant writings of "A Great Effort" and "End of a Climb" are given little or none. No value-judgement is intended, and those who wish to enjoy the supple range particularly of the latter's prose, with its natural transitions from easy recall to exalted intuition, and its profound insights into process, motive and character, will find it included along with "Scenery for a Murder" and other essays and poems in the appendix.

Briefly, on the question of his work's relative merit, I think the claims made for Menlove as a literary figure in *Samson* ("one of the most original and exciting styles in English prose between the wars", "three or four love lyrics worthy to become permanent in the language") are inflated. Menlove is an important figure within the genre of mountain literature, and very probably its finest essayist. His prose-style is idiosyncratic, gains its fluency from free association of ideas, but it is often gratuitously quirky. It has to be said also that there is not enough of his work for any more major claims to be made for it, though what he did write is almost all of high quality (and everything of general and abiding interest is contained here either in the appendix or in the main body of the text). His poetry is inescapably minor, all too often stilted and infelicitous in its diction, and over-dependent on stock, unclarified symbols. Taken apart from the life, it would be of little worth; considered as a comment on the life, it is of immense value.

As a further point about biographical method, here and there I have used novelistic techniques to recreate scenes. The biographer must make use of what means he can to invoke the presence of his subject's personality and the contexts of the period. Whilst I have stopped short of what Menlove "must have thought" or "would have said", they have tempted me, and I would concede that in another guise they might have their uses. You need only compare Boswell's initial reports of Johnson's conversations, as given in his journals, with their finished versions in the *Life* to realize how important a role a strictly-focused imagination plays in biographical writing. Its use requires no apology.

A final point on method: I have quoted very extensively, not only from Menlove's poems and essays but also from prose-fragments and letters, in the belief that the subject of a biography should be allowed, as often as possible, to speak for himself. Particularly with the later diatribe-letters it may be thought that they should have been edited down, but to convey the sheer intensity and extent of his final delusion, they have been left complete.

In my own life, Menlove Edwards has meant a great deal. As a young climber, camping in the Llanberis Pass in the early 1960s, only a few years after his death, his routes—climbs like Brant and Slape, Rift Wall and Shadow Wall—were the touchstones of an aspiring style of living, paradigms of the intricate, effortful and perilous journey. Their ascents were polished for me by the resonance of phrases from his essays: "Climbing, climbing up the back of my mind trying to find a way out"; "My mind made up, it only remained to go, not always an easy thing to do"; "We will each make a little image from what we like to see of ourselves in the mirror of the hills"; "With the right direction of effort the mind of man can accomplish almost anything". It was as a rock-climber and the best of writers about rock-climbing that Menlove first registered on my consciousness. His humorously ironic outlook on that sport coloured my view of it from the outset and has remained with me ever since. He taught me the lesson that in many ways this serves as a model for the wider conduct of life, and there have been times when that has been of the greatest value: "perhaps if I shouted and sang . . ."; "the secret of life is in detachment from it"; "then with the whole organism great force must be exerted . . ."

It is more than ten years since I first thought of writing this book. The earliest attempt was discarded, the question asked of me whether I thought it should be written, the project shelved on the advice of one of Wilfrid Noyce's closest friends until those whom its revelations could hurt were dead; and not just for that, but because my own perception of the task was unclear. The Menlove I now see and have written about is not the simple hero of the spirit I knew ten years ago. He is much more clearly a victim of social circumstance, as courageous and unfortunate in his social endeavour as he was unique in his activities on water and rock. I hope that I have come somewhere near the true picture of him in this book, and that in giving him to readers thus he might find at last in their judgement the honest understanding denied him in his life. One of the men who did act most kindly towards him throughout the terrible last years wrote, fifteen years after his death, "I still wonder sometimes if we *could* have saved Menlove, given more love and understanding."

Perhaps so, but the *we* would have needed to be many, and the one without the other not enough.

ACKNOWLEGEMENTS AND SOURCES

Scholarly books being beyond the interest and means of most publishers and readers, I have kept the annotation in this volume to a minimum. Most of the sources are credited in the text, and dates given where these can be firmly established, but I have not thought it necessary in a general biography to give any more detailed information. Keen students, whether they be putative future PhD's in mountain literature from American universities or individuals pursuing the subject for their own interest, should be able to glean enough from text and acknowledgements to find their way back to most sources.

The assistance I have been given in writing this book has been enormous, and I am both grateful for it and moved by it. Without advice, permission to use Menlove's writings, encouragement and information from Menlove's brother and sister, the Reverend Stephen Z. Edwards and Nowell Hewlett Johnson, the task would assuredly neither have been undertaken nor completed. As mentioned in the introduction, the work which Wilfrid Noyce and Geoffrey Sutton put into *Samson* has been vital, both in stimulating my interest in the subject and providing a basis for research. The late Alec Keith provided lengthy and detailed accounts of schooldays and gave me free access to his journals and correspondence. Sir Jack Longland guided me expertly through the history and politics of mountaineering in the thirties. It would be impossible to assess each contribution, but the list of those who have helped is as follows: Roy Beard; Peter Biven; Robin Campbell; Stuart Chantrell; John Cleare; Ralph Collinson; David Cox; The Climbers' Club's Journal Editor and Archivist (the archives are now held at the University College of North Wales, Bangor); Dr Stephen Darbishire; Ed Drummond; the Reverend Stephen Z. Edwards; Norman Elliott; Sir Charles Evans; Livia Gollancz; Robin Hodgkin; John Jackson; Nowell Hewlett Johnson; Arfon Jones; Dr E. Wyn Jones; Dr Jim Joyce; Philip Judson; Alec Keith; B. H. Kemball-Cook; Rudolf Loewy; Sir Jack Longland; Charles Marriott; Nea Morin; Colin Mortlock; David Murray-Rust; Ken Pearson; Bill Peascod; Tony Shaw; Janet Adam Smith; Bill Stallybrass; John Stevenson; Selby Walmsley; Michael Ward; Ken Wilson. I offer my apologies to anyone whom I may have inadvertently omitted.

For reading through and commenting on various aspects of a draft of the main text, I have to thank David Cox, David Craig, the Reverend Stephen Z. Edwards, Sir Charles Evans, Terry Gifford, Robin Hodgkin, Philip Judson and Sir Jack Longland. In time-honoured phrase, many of this book's virtues are truly theirs, its vices all my own.

I am especially grateful to John Beatty for taking the time and trouble to prepare a portfolio of modern photographs of Menlove's climbs, and only regret that there was space to use so few of them.

My publisher, Livia Gollancz, earns my thanks for keeping faith long after the point at which hope could justly have been abandoned.

Finally, the debt I owe to Doris Vening for producing a coherent typescript from illegible scrawl, and for bearing with endless weeks of preoccupation and absent-mindedness on my part whilst working on the task, is axiomatic.

J.P.

DOLWYDDELAN 1984

PREFACE TO THE SECOND EDITION, 1993

It is nearly ten years now since this book was finished. I wrote it in the January and February of 1984, over an intense six week period broken only by the necessary relief of a lecture tour to my beloved and humane Ireland, and at the end felt less delivered of a burden than almost broken by it myself. The last pages of the manuscript (those were pre-word processor days) are tearstained, the biographer's pretence of objectivity slipping from me.

Several reviewers of the book picked up on the challenge to the reader in the last pages, and particularly on the idea that there is an internal logic, coherence and insight in Menlove's final diatribe-letters and that we are all in a sense inculpated in a defeat like his (and I still view it as that, though I would nowadays give increased weight to the pathological reasons for his breakdown).

In defence of that challenge, I would adduce a comment made by the *New Statesman*'s reviewer of the book, that it "forces the reader to think of a world where the story might have ended differently". That was certainly my intention. And I hold to the view that the splintering criticisms of human behaviour voiced in those terrible last cries of rage and despair have a relevance and validity that justified their inclusion.

As a technical point, the whole book is an example of what Robert Gittings defines – the term is not pejorative – as "impure" biography, by which he means life-writing which goes beyond simple narrative to have designs on the reader's moral and humanitarian outlook. The overt challenge at the end, both as literary device and in the periods of its prose, was based on Johnson's discussion – the passage is well-known to students of life writing – of the whore's half-guinea in his *Life of Savage*, which is the greatest example in English of "impure" biography, or perhaps even of biography itself.

Most of those who noticed the book were extraordinarily generous in their comments on it – to a far greater extent, surely, than it deserved. I was, and am, grateful for the attention bestowed on it by a wide range of publications, from the *Gay Times* to the *Church Times*, from *Country Life* to *New Socialist* and the *London Review of Books*. The tolerance of an older generation towards open treatment of a subject it found difficult and even embarrassing – Menlove's homosexuality – was particularly heartening. In accepting it they have, I think, shown something of the same spirit and courage which Menlove displayed in that astonishing sermon he delivered in Stokesay Church in 1935. Which prompts me to take the opportunity given by this second edition to thank again Stephen Edwards, Menlove's brother, for the crucial help and unremitting support he gave me throughout the writing and publication of the book. Without his help and that of his wife Ruth – a most lovely and gracious woman who died two years ago – it would not have been finished.

Writers should, I think, be wary of entering *caveats* against their reviewers. At publication, the work becomes its own justification, and should stand alone. But one extended review, privately published long after the book had appeared, did to this author sound a note of curious personal animosity, discord and dishonesty. Its psychotic distortions of my argument, manipulation and misquotation of my text, rendered it to my mind unworthy of a detailed reply. But for the record, and briefly, its charge that this book is a celebration of sacrifice and death will, I hope, be seen as ludicrous by those who read my text.

I wrote *Menlove* – at a time when I viewed with dread political developments in this country – as a plea for tolerance and proper love, no matter what form the latter may take. And I wrote it also as a *paean* to its subject's humour, modesty and integrity – all of them qualities insufficiently regarded in our society. There is no glory, to my mind, in the way that society's false and martial gods of power, vanity, materialism and deceit sacrifice such as Menlove who stand out against them.

Many factors in the years since 1984 increase my anxiety about the operation of society. Even within the last few weeks events like the election of a British National Party councillor in Tower Hamlets and the vicious xenophobia of speeches at the 1993 Conservative Party conference – both of them a part of Thatcherism's vile legacy – draw in further the shrinking boundaries of social kindness. And the AIDS epidemic which has spread since *Menlove*'s first publication inevitably predicates an intolerance of response towards social minorities. If *Menlove* were to be written now, I fear that I would have sketched a bleaker hinterland for the action to take place against.

But my hope remains that this account of an honest, difficult life's being made more widely and cheaply available can help us even a little farther in extending tolerance and lovingkindness towards everyone worthy of it by virtue of their common humanity in our society. And though I cannot speak for his living of it, the pain of writing Menlove's life would then have been worthwhile.

CHAPTER ONE

The Childhood Background, 1910–1923

A CURIOUS ASPECT of researching this biography has been the number of unconnected, fragmentary jottings which turned up, always in black ink and Menlove's spidery, unpredictable scrawl, usually on the Rodney Street-headed notepaper of his thirties psychiatric practice. One such reads simply thus:

> I was born the fourth and last child of two overworked parents at a country vicarage on flat, black soil.

It probably dates from 1937, when Menlove was twenty-seven. The country vicarage was that of Crossens, near Southport in Lancashire, where Menlove was born in June 1910, son of the Reverend George Zachary Edwards, and his wife Helen. These few words, on a scrap of torn paper now brown with years, written by a young psychiatrist, are an extraordinarily telling document: "fourth and last child", "two overworked parents", "flat, black soil". The heavy emphases set up a funeral toll which almost implies that right from the outset this was a life pre-judged, pre-ordained, and desolate. Whether it was, or need have been so, it is part of the task of this book to explore.

John Menlove Edwards was generally known to his family and friends as Menlove. The name was common enough in south-west Lancashire during the early years of this century, and to this day one of the major thoroughfares of Liverpool is called Menlove Avenue. The family into which Menlove was born came in part from Lancashire and in part from Leicestershire. "Nobility of character, responsible leadership, being well-informed, seemed to be the chief qualities the family set store on. They were interesting and versatile, known as keen church supporters and concerned with good causes," noted a one-time neighbour of theirs. The tradition of serious-minded Church-of-England socialism was very strong. Menlove's great-grandfather had been Alfred Hewlett, who was for more than 50 years vicar of the parish of Astley, near Leigh in Lancashire, where he was known as the

"Spurgeon of the North". (The reference nowadays is probably abstruse: Charles Haddon Spurgeon [1834–1892] was a Baptist preacher, author, and controversialist. Much love and admired, he was perhaps the most famous preacher of the mid-Victorian period. His oratory combined unconventional appeals to social conscience with shrewd comment on contemporary life, and the expository style of an older generation of Puritan divines.)

The figure of Alfred Hewlett, and the example of his good works for over half a century in the mining parish of Astley, remained a potent force amongst his descendants. It is clearly exemplified in the career of at least two of his grandsons: Hewlett Johnson, who was to become the so-called "Red Dean of Canterbury", and Hewlett's cousin George Zachary Edwards, Menlove's father.

George Zachary's father, who was Alfred Hewlett's son-in-law, had been vicar of Enderby in Leicestershire. He had died in 1884 at the age of forty-five, leaving George, then twelve, as the eldest son of a family of nine. Poverty and hard work were in consequence the twin themes of George's youth. His own education was held in abeyance until his younger brothers and sisters were settled in life. Only then could it be finished in order for him to follow in the family tradition and be ordained an Anglican clergyman. It is hardly surprising that the experiences of his youth and the model of his grandfather Alfred Hewlett's pursuit of factory, educational and housing reform in the Manchester area should have quickly begun to find expression in his work. He was a pioneering socialist churchman in the years before the Great War. Nowell Hewlett Johnson, Menlove's sister, wrote of her father that:

> He was very concerned about the young working-class lads of that period who left their home villages in search of work, and the problems of those who couldn't find work and drifted on the roads, which could often lead to them becoming habitual tramps, drunkards or criminals.
>
> Twice he disguised himself as a tramp, and in company with a real "man of the roads" spent a fortnight on the road, visiting doss-houses at night and getting to know at first hand the terrible conditions of those days. He spoke at meetings and succeeded in getting many improvements made in local towns. In his own parish of Crossens he was very much beloved.

These were the days when the safety-blanket for the poor against starvation and utter destitution was the workhouse, with all the degradation, dependence and segregation of husband from wife which that entailed. Hatred and fear of "going to the workhouse" was endemic amongst the working class, particularly in the North of England. George Edwards' work during the all-too-brief years of his ministry should be seen against the background of an economy still staggering away from the Great Depression of the 1880s, and the social evils attendant upon it. The height of George's interest in Poor Law reform seems to have been reached in 1910, coincidentally the year of Menlove's birth. A newspaper cutting from that year laconically captions a picture as being of "the Rev G. Z. Edwards, vicar of Crossens, who has been on the road, and a real tramp whom he picked up on his travels, and for whom he is now getting up a subscription. Mr Edwards is on the left of the photograph."

The subscription did raise enough money to send his companion to Canada, and was thus more directly successful than another production of the same year, a 32-page pamphlet with introduction by the Rector of Birmingham, entitled *A Vicar as Vagrant*. Again, the background is important. Agitation against the punitive and inhumane Poor Law which, with very little revision, dated from 1834, resulted in one major attempt at reform early in the twentieth century. In 1905 a Royal Commission was appointed to investigate, and in 1909 it issued two reports, differing in detail and extent, entitled Majority and Minority. Both agreed on the need for abolition of the Boards of Guardians, which controlled the workhouses and administered Poor Law relief, and transfer of their powers to County or Borough Councils; both insisted on the need for expert and official handling of Poor Law work. The implementation of either measure was defeated by the apostasy of the erstwhile socialist John Burns, and the Boards of Guardians were not finally abolished until 1929, by which time their role had been well undermined by the development of Old Age Pensions, National Insurance, and the beginnings of a welfare state. This is the broader context into which George Edwards' pamphlet was launched.

A Vicar as Vagrant is the account of two fortnights he spent on the road, going round the doss-houses of Lancashire, begging, sleeping rough, finding out about the so-called charitable institutions of the time and the conditions they perpetuated. It could be described as a proto-*Road to Wigan Pier*. The underlying conviction is radical, working from a passionate sense of basic human rights, and although the style in which it is written occasionally resembles that of Dickens at his most rhetorical or sentimental, even in its worst excesses the sense of a strong and committed intellect lurks behind it. The bantering, playful tone of much of Menlove's writing is far removed from that of the following extract, in which George Edwards describes the "penny sit-up" in Shepherd Street, Preston:

Its only recommendation is its cheapness; but how dearly you buy that cheapness! For one penny you buy the privilege of entrance—this admits you to a room about twenty-five feet long by eighteen feet broad.

You enter it in the evening, when the day is done. Already there are some twenty or twenty-five men there. The room is literally bare, with nothing in it, nothing! No fireplace, no stove, no hot water pipes, no sink, no water, no beds, no chairs, no blankets, no mattresses—nothing, nothing whatever for the furnishing of the room except a small, very small oil lamp, very dimly lighted, and four long wooden kneelers about two inches off the floor sloping upwards towards the back. Two of these at either ends of the room, and the other two running right down the middle of the room back to back. What are they for? This surely is not a house of prayer? No, these are pillows, wooden pillows, and presently the floor of this room will be covered with bodies lying feet to feet in two double rows down the length of the room.

When your food is eaten there is nothing to do but lie down on your length of the floor, some six feet by two feet, and then if your limbs ache with lying down on the hard boards sit up, and if you are privileged to have one of the select spots against the wall, you can lean against that if you will. If you are wet through you sit or lie in your wet rags till they dry, that is all!

Think of it! Ten, twelve, fourteen hours thus. Thirty to sixty men thus, night by night, in misery, wretchedness, filth of body, and starvation. The conversation is in the dull, hopeless undertone of exhausted men, except when it flashes forth now and again in the tone of revenge, hatred and bitterness against us who have condemned them to this. It is always heavily laden with oath or blasphemy, and is of begging, pinching, roguery, trickery, beastiality [sic], at the best of the criminal courts, their prisoners and judges. The leaden weight of exhaustion and despair is only lifted when a man is dead drunk.

And so these men try to settle themselves to sleep. Sleep? Were human beings, God indwelt, ever meant thus to rest, in dirt, in degradation, in depression indescribable?

No clean horse-box with freshly-strewn straw, this! No well-drained pig-stye with abundance of bedding, warmth and food, this! No rat-hole, this, where father, mother, and baby rats may live together and seek their meat from God!

But a vermin-infested room, bare of aught but men's bodies clad in rags—bodies which are not washed or groomed or cleaned from one twelve-month to another, except when forced to go to casual ward or gaol. Bodies which are half-starved, emaciated, lean. Bodies which carry the germs of horrible disease, yet which are untended, uncared for. Bodies which, because they are so poor, so poor in rich life blood, are thereby fit and proper food for the tramp's, the dirty beggar's worst enemy, lice.

Little crawling, clinging, biting lice, which breed in twenty-four hours in the seams of your clothes next your skin, and live upon you—biting, biting, feeding, feeding, like the gnawing worm of hell.

The atmosphere! Figuratively speaking, you could cut it with a knife! You yourself sleep next to an old decrepit man, who cannot always control his bodily actions; his trousers stink, stink; you will carry the stench in your nostrils for a week. Sixty thus, and if not quite thus, all unwashed, all with the smell of the unwashed. Add to this, rank tobacco smoke of all blends, some unknown even to connoisseurs, such as "kerb-stone twist" (old chews), old cigar ends, "o.p.s." (other people's stumps), and old dried tea leaves. Add to this foul breath, some very foul, add also the stale atmosphere of the room itself when empty, and remember scarce any ventilation during the night except the occasional opening of the door into the yard, and you may think you imagine what you never will, till you experience it.

Thus the poorest of the poor live by night in Preston, thus the local authorities allow them to live, thus we Christian men through our ignorance, our party strife, and our fear of businesslike reform suffer it, and shame on us all.

It is the cause of this great national evil of needless degradation I wish to fight; not any one result, disgusting though it be. Yet be it known in Preston that the "Penny sit up" is a Lancashire disgrace—to the soul and spirit of man, and not a cause for pious rejoicing.

Obviously a man who, even for the short space of a fortnight, could set out on the road, starve, freeze, beg for food and money, experience at first hand conditions such as those described here, was taking a very serious view of his duty as a Christian minister to intercede specifically on behalf of the poor. And what supports him in the quest for knowledge about those for whom he accepts the responsibility for spiritual care, his pamphlet makes clear:

Shall the poor ever cry in vain? Shall this drift downwards never cease? Where, where is the man today who, to the tens of thousands of vagrants and casual labourers of our land, shall be as an hiding place from the wind, as a covert from the tempest, as rivers of water in a dry place, as the shadow of a great rock in a weary land?

For George Edwards there was a firm, although probably not an easy, answer to these questions. A part of Menlove's tragedy, when it came to his turn to intercede on the complex and emotionally loaded issues which he chose, was the lack of clear connection with either fellow-humanity or a strong and simple faith.

Nowell related one story about her father which further revealed his character. It concerns a confrontation between George Edwards and the Board of Guardians of an Ormskirk workhouse on which he sat. The Chairman of the Board had delivered a lengthy and perhaps rather complacent speech and report, in which he denied that the human squalor and misery being brought to public notice in other work-houses by Poor Law reform campaigners could ever exist in their institution. When he had made his concluding remarks, George Edwards stood to address the Board: "Gentlemen, I have slept in our house of charity, and can bear witness to the unimaginable human degradation that such a place entails. I would now like to lead you to visit the establishment under our care."

This is the strong and authentic voice of Menlove's father in 1910, vigorous, challenging, zealously idealistic. Photographs taken of him at this time show a man of powerful physical frame, the features pronounced, high-browed and with large, kindly eyes. There is more than a passing resemblance to Alfred Hewlett in the face. It is the family face, the features recognizably shared by Hewlett Johnson and by George Edwards' three sons.

George married a woman by the name of Helen Dawes. Her mother was German, the maternal grandfather having been personal physician to Frederick the Great. Helen's mother's marriage had been arranged. One afternoon she was told to go and put on her best clothes, as she was to meet her fiancé. A month or two later she was married, and returned with her husband to England. She bore seven children, five girls and two boys, all of whom were scholastically brilliant and most of whom, the unhappy example of their parents before them, remained unmarried. One of the daughters, Mary, was the first woman to be awarded an MA by an English university; another, Lily, gained a DLitt., and but for ill-health would have been presented to Queen Victoria.

Photographs of Helen's father show an excessively well-groomed or even dandified man glaring at the camera with suspicion and surly arrogance. His behaviour towards his own household is said to have been abominable. Helen, Menlove's mother, shared the family's academic gifts. She could read well in Latin and Greek, and spoke French and German fluently. She was a determined, handsome girl who pursued the career of an art teacher—an acceptable outlet for a young lady's talent amongst the professional classes of those days—at the Royal College of Art until her marriage to George Edwards. Extant drawings and paintings by Helen Edwards display an uncluttered, imaginative approach allied to considerable technical skill. In her choice of partner, Helen certainly fared much better than her mother, but she seems nonetheless to have had a far from easy time of it, even in the early years of the marriage. There is a jotting of Menlove's, on the Rodney Street notepaper, to the following effect:

> Holiday abroad. Mother always walked off her feet. Everybody told father to do less, but he would plan it out beforehand on the map, and would hate not to complete it.

Nowell provides the following gloss on this fragment, which dates from a time, after Menlove's father's death, when Menlove and his mother lived together in a Liverpool flat: "This quotation refers to their very early married life, before any children were born and when my father took a chaplaincy in Switzerland." Stephen further recollects that during this period Helen paid for her accommodation by selling sketches, as only the chaplain's board and lodging was provided. Perhaps the most striking feature of the note, though, is the very marked degree of sympathetic identification on Menlove's part with his mother.

The marriage of George and Helen Edwards produced four children, all of whom were born during their father's incumbency at Crossens. Stephen Zachary was the eldest, born in December 1904. The brunt of expectations of the first-born son lay upon him. He was to follow his father into the church and became, variously, curate at St Helens and vicar of Stokesay, Bullinghope, Staindrop, Coniston, and Preston, near Cirencester, before he retired to Harlech, where he and his wife still live. He is a large, kind man, his features unmistakably like those of Menlove. He was to introduce Menlove to the sport of climbing—an activity from which he himself retired after his marriage. Nowadays, apart from continuing parish work, his chief interest is in birds, flowers and the natural world around him.

In December 1906 his sister, Nowell Mary, was born; Helen's artistic abilities were passed on to her in good measure. She married her father's cousin, Hewlett Johnson, in 1938, some years after the death of his first wife, went with him to China and Russia, and served as a Justice of the Peace. After his death she continued, despite crippling arthritis, actively to pursue social work from their home in Canterbury. A gracious and wholly delightful woman of extraordinary physical beauty in her youth, she died in 1983. George Hewlett, known as Hewlett, was two years her junior, and was killed in tragic circumstances in 1933. Lastly came Menlove, born on 18 June 1910.

The vicarage at Crossens, which was home to the growing Edwards family, was a large house, quite plain, but elegant in an early Victorian manner. It was surrounded with garden, one part of which was given over to an orchard where apple-blossom and daffodils flowered in spring and where the fruit ripened abundantly each autumn. Beyond the vegetable garden were fields and a slow-moving stream; separated from the house by lawns was the church. There was a long drive lined with London Pride. Outside each window of the house George Edwards had placed a large tree-stump to enable the children to climb in and out. On fine days he would get up at four a.m. to garden.

Life here in Edwardian England had many of the characteristics of traditional English pastoral. The religious festivals—Easter, Whitsun, Harvest Thanksgiving and Christmas—were dutifully and joyfully observed. At such times the church would be decorated with flowers or with fruit, and on the green in front of it the processions assembled, the Morris Dancers circled and leapt, the May Day sports were contested. There is an odd juxtaposition here between the traditional version of pastoral with its limiting stock symbols, and the more politically complex issues with which George Edwards was otherwise engaged in his ministry. It is a pattern which recurs in Menlove's later life.

Those more complex issues certainly intruded themselves on the consciousness at least of the elder children through the person of their nurse. Although the Edwards family was quite poor, it had a maid, Betty, and a nurse, Polly. For best, Polly dressed in exquisitely hand-embroidered aprons. All the children, but especially Menlove, adored her. She could recount tales of being woken before five a.m. and carried half-asleep on her father's back to the cotton mills at the age of five, working there until noon, and then being so tired that she, and many other small children like her, slept throughout afternoon school. She was perhaps thirty-five at the time of Menlove's birth, for Stephen recalls conducting her funeral service, after she had died at about the age of eighty, in the mid-1950s. Her testimony suggests that the provisions of Althorp's 1833 Factory Act were still not fully implemented in sections of the Lancashire cotton industry as late as the 1880s. There, in the heart of the family, she was a living witness to social history and conscience.

In 1912, when Menlove was only two, the family moved from Crossens to Ainsdale, a large new village on the coast just north of Liverpool. It was a dreary place in comparison to the one they had left. To the east were suburban villas built on the Lancashire Mosses, the little remaining agricultural land being given over to potato fields, where the black, peaty soil lay bare. The church—a temporary mission building of recent date—was situated to the east of the village. To the west beyond an area where much new building had taken place, a large expanse of sand-dunes led to the sea-shore, from which you could look out west over Liverpool Bay to the hills of Wales. In a very few years' time these sand-dunes were to be put to a use which would imprint itself indelibly on Menlove's mind. For this was one of the main sites used by the army in the Great War for training in the digging of trenches. So many of the men whom Menlove's childish, wondering eyes watched at their strange games were condemned by the strategic blunders of Douglas Haig to die in the mud of Ypres, Passchendaele, or the Somme.

A determination dourly to exploit those sent to serve them seemed to prevail amongst some of the parishioners. Stephen recalls one old lady who lived alongside the railway line and sent begging letters on ever-more-fantastic pretexts to the new vicar and his wife, always concluding with "God is Love". Helen was finally reduced to a state of exasperation by her, and sent Stephen with the curt reminder that "God is Truth".

The parish was not an easy one for Menlove's father. There was controversy as to whether a new church, to be built at the west side of the village, was needed, yet without it his work was doubly hard. He and his wife were slowly worn down by continual over-exertion. "Mother used to weep sometimes in despair at the visiting in Ainsdale. People were so rude and unfeeling," wrote Menlove, at a later date. The compensations now had to be looked for in family holidays, of the general pattern of which Stephen supplies the following reminiscence:

I suppose the seeds of Menlove's early climbing, and my own too, were set in those early holidays that followed a pattern which every decent holiday I have ever had has followed too. We used to take a boat across the lake, to get the necessary impedimenta out to some favourite spot, some solitary place. There a camp would be made for the day, a fire would be lit, a kettle would be boiled, and the day would be spent in pottering round, looking for flowers, and birds and nests, or climbing the hill or exploring the coast.

Swimming was a great thing, to bathe every day of the holiday an ideal not to be left short by one single day. In all this Father was the moving spirit, sowing in us the seeds of endeavour, hoping for great things of this sort from us. He took us up Helvellyn once. When we got to the top he sent me off to find the source of a stream which flowed down to Thirlmere, and was most displeased when I came back without having found it. I found it years later; it was far too far to send a child of that age without any sort of guidance. I imagine he made similar suggestions to Hewlett and Menlove as they grew up . . .?

Other memories are of time spent at Torver, by Coniston, where the family took out a boat and improvised a sail and mast from a rug and borrowed hay-rake, which worked splendidly until the latter broke.

In 1914 the family took their holiday in the Lake District, enjoying themselves in their usual manner. And then something happened, adventitiously, the consequences of which were to reverberate through each member of the family's life from that time onwards. The account is Stephen's:

> In all our holiday activities, Father was the moving spirit. August 1914 found us, one day, enjoying our usual pleasures. Father was desperately anxious about the war, then either begun or just about to begin. I was then nine. We were taking a picnic in a little wooded bay with lovely rocky points opposite to the Ullswater Hotel at Patterdale.
>
> After lunch Father sent me across the lake, all by myself, in the rowing-boat to fetch the paper, which did not arrive till mid-day. When I came back I found a scene I remember vividly to this day. Father was lying on some sort of stretcher, looking very pale, and everyone around him was in great distress. He had picked up a good big piece of driftwood, put it in the fork of a tree, then used the fork as a lever to break the wood. It broke, and he went over backwards. His shoe caught in the roots of the tree and held his foot tight. The result was a compound fracture of leg and ankle which never healed properly.

A local doctor set the leg but failed to diagnose the broken ankle. Whilst the Father convalesced, Stephen was taken into the household of Mr Yates, a teacher at Holmwood, his preparatory school, which proved an unhappy time for him. Nowell and Hewlett went to stay with Hewlett Johnson and his first wife, Mary, in Altrincham, Cheshire, where he was vicar. Menlove stayed with his parents.

Back at home in Ainsdale, George Edwards resumed his arduous rounds of visiting and supervision, but he was in great and continuous pain. Eventually this become intolerable and he was forced to go into hospital in Liverpool. He was operated on by Robert Jones, an orthopaedic surgeon of great skill who was to be knighted for his services to the profession during the Great War. The broken ankle bones were discovered and the leg set again, though it remained permanently stiffened and painful. At about this time the onset of Parkinson's Disease became apparent. Perhaps the strain of years of over-exertion had triggered it off, or perhaps it was the intense pain he endured from his injury. For two years he attempted to continue about his work, but the task was an impossible one and eventually his will could sustain him no longer. In 1917, at the age of forty-three, he retired on a clergyman's small pension—a third of a living, which itself in those days only amounted to a little over £200—to Formby, where he was to spend the last sixteen years of his life.

The accident placed the family in straitened financial circumstances.

According to Stephen "we were always desperately hard-up. The cast-off clothes of friends came our way, and so on . . ." At a slightly later time Stephen remembers feeling at least some resentment that they "could not play golf, nor tennis, nor anything else in the local clubs of a pretty well-to-do neighbourhood". He adds the rider that "to go off to climb and to do as a matter of course things that the other fellows would never dream of doing gave one a sense of superiority that undoubtedly helped us through a very difficult time". It is a comment that belongs to a period of their life perhaps ten years after their move to Formby, but it probably defines pretty exactly *one* of the building blocks of Menlove's character.

Helen Edwards, in addition to tending to her husband and children, now had to return to her old profession. She took posts as art mistress at several private schools in nearby, exclusive Birkdale. The pressures upon her were heavy, and she was often nervously and physically ill. Over several years she underwent a series of operations for glandular trouble in her neck. She was always run down and tired. Menlove recollects his childhood in the following way:

> I never really remembered anything but a home very saddened by suffering, and a mother very overburdened. During all those years I had no great purpose; in fact I cannot remember anything sensible at all. I was shy, but in a family like ours you could keep away easily and there was no need to try to say anything.

It is notable how negative are Menlove's comments upon his childhood. There is no chiaroscuro about his versions; they are almost wholly shade. Yet the lighter aspects did exist. Nowell considered that "our childhood was a happy time, though always overshadowed after Father's accident". The house at Formby was detached, quite small for a family of six but large-windowed and light. At the bottom of the garden was a workshop, where Hewlett busied himself with all kinds of boyish experiments involving mechanical devices. He and Menlove both attended Holmwood preparatory school (which had the reputation of being one of the best in the north of England), and were inseparable. They escaped much of the direct burden of expectation which the father imposed on Stephen, and delighted in the surroundings of their home. A lane ran beside the house on Freshfield Road, and across it were fields and a stream. In front of them, over more fields, was the railway, and beyond it pinewoods, sand-dunes and the sea. Stephen had been sent away to St John's, Leatherhead—a school for sons of the clergy—where his fees of £23 a term were paid for by Hewlett Johnson's sister, Mary.

There was still the annual month's holiday, on which the parents always came. Until he became too ill even for this, George Edwards was pushed along by the children in his bathchair on their minor expeditions and to church. He maintained a supervisory role, directing the boys into solitary explorations and endeavours. On one such holiday, taken in the Isle of Man in 1920, he suggested to Stephen, then thirteen, that he should find a companion and walk round the island by the shore, a formidable proposition to a boy of his age. Nonetheless, Stephen incurred his father's disappointment by not acting upon it. It would be remarkable if Hewlett and Menlove escaped completely from these neurotic projections of personal desire on the part of their father (so reminiscent of the father in *To the Lighthouse*), but no specific accounts exist. The holidays must have been marvellous times, though. During this one of 1920 they stayed at Port St Mary, then a tiny fishing village, and walked and climbed around the coast, rambled over the gorse-covered hills, visited the then-ruined Celtic village of Cregneish, discovered St Patrick's Footprint in a stone on the clifftop which looked out to the Calf of Man, and climbed the 150-foot sea-stack of the Sugar Loaf.

Each day they swam. Menlove had just recovered from an operation for appendicitis and used mainly his arms, which built up powerfully in consequence. Nowell describes their activities:

> We had many exciting bathes in tempestuous seas, when we would come out all covered in cuts from being thrown up and down on the rocks.
>
> I remember too going in a rowing boat a mile or two from Port St Mary towards Port Erin, to an area called the Chasms, where there were exciting caves in the cliffs, through which you could take a boat. We calculated we could swim through the caves, leaving our boat to float on the tide, and catch it when we emerged on the other side—and we did! I still remember the swell in the caves, being right up against the walls one moment, and right down in green, lighted water the next.

An earlier year they spent on Anglesey, in the hope of giving the father the complete quiet and rest which, it was thought, might effect a cure from Parkinson's Disease. They stayed first at Trearddur Bay on Holy Island, and at that time Stephen and Nowell boarded at school. But their accommodation became too costly as the summer season drew on. Stephen and Nowell rejoined them at Easter to stay for the summer term, and they moved to an isolated farmhouse—Skerries View—near Cemaes Bay, on the north coast. It was a glorious place. At night the beam of the lighthouse shone on the bedroom wall. They swam in the sea every day, watched birds on the shore, collected shells and flowers and went everywhere barefoot. But on Sundays, they wore shoes to church.

The year did nothing to halt their father's decline, and at the end of it, not without regrets, they returned home to Formby. George Edwards' condition steadily worsened. He was now shaved, washed and dressed by Nowell. The whole family took turns at nursing and feeding. He could still walk, in a shambling, lurching fashion. Sitting at table he would fall forward. His mouth had to be wiped; he had to be helped from room to room; he couldn't turn the pages of his book. On many evenings Menlove would sit attentively next to him just to do this when he was reading, and to keep him upright. On holidays he could no longer be left, so the children explored on their own, day after day. Stephen tells of "a splendid holiday at our Great Aunt Mary's in Lyme Regis, when I had just taken School Certificate. We could go off by ourselves by then, and we explored that coast, the Undercliff, Golden Cap and so on to our heart's content. I remember how cross our aunt was when we returned at the end of one particularly long day with Menlove so tired that I had to carry him."

Inevitably the Father's disability tightened their sense of group identity. A neighbour of the time recalls that "the brothers and sister sat a few pews in front of us in Formby parish church. We knew the brothers as Stalky & Co and Menlove as Beetle." (This was the time when Kipling's novels were popular.) The same neighbour also remembered that Hewlett and Menlove would play trains with the hymn books, sending them sliding along the backs of the pews to fall off into the aisles—for which activity Nowell and her mother were forever scolding them.

Menlove had grown into a sturdy, pretty boy with brown curls and a ready smile. He was good-natured and peace-loving. Nowell remembers how "Stephen and Hewlett used to squabble and fight. When Menlove came along he would put things right somehow." Ralph Collinson, a contemporary at Holmwood, gives an interesting insight into Menlove's physical development towards the end of his schooldays: "My main memory of him during schooldays was the immense strength of his wrists and hands. I was two years older than him, and am no weakling, but for fun he would hold me and others by our wrists and challenge us to wriggle out. We never could!"

Unselfishly, Stephen worked in a bank for four years to help support the family prior to going to Cambridge in 1926. Nowell spent three years at the nearby Southport College of Art and then went to the Royal College of Art on a scholarship, a friend of hers called Topsy coming to live in the house to help the mother in term-time. Hewlett had left Holmwood in 1922 to attend the Merchant Taylors' School at Crosby, and the following year Menlove won a place as Foundationer at Fettes College, a Scottish public school just outside Edinburgh. He was thirteen, and it was to be his first time away from parents and home.

CHAPTER TWO

Schooldays, 1923–1928

So MENLOVE CAME from a close family group of high idealism and sound
Christian virtue, where the Father, leaning on family tradition, became
increasingly stern and hopeful of high achievement for his children as his
own potency failed. The Mother was the family's real support, and both she
and her daughter were necessarily gentle and sympathetic in their behaviour
through the presence of an invalid. From this sphere of solicitous women,
and from the company of his admired elder brother Hewlett, the thirteen-
year-old Menlove was sent several hundred miles to the hard life of a
Scottish public school. And understandably, he was unhappy:

> He was a very gentle and charming small boy when he went there, and he
> hated it. For three days before he went back he could only sit about in
> sheer misery, and the first one or two years the tears would trickle down
> his face throughout the day.

He very early learned to conceal his emotions, and lose himself in the
traditional outlets of hard work and harder play. Thus a schoolfellow's
memories:

> To say that he was very unhappy all his time at school is absolute
> nonsense. Like the rest of us he was homesick on returning, but like the
> rest of us he got over it in a short time. Life sometimes was miserable. No
> one was happy when, after a miserable game of rugger in the rain, he came
> in and had to wash off the mud in cold water, after waiting till the bigger
> boys had used it first—and a lesson was to come—not well prepared—
> with a master one did not like. And then putting on a wet muddy jersey
> and shorts the next day. But there were warm days in the summer when
> we lay on our rugs eating cherries, surreptitiously, and watching their XI
> making a mess of things, or our heroes doing well. I should say Menlove
> was rather the same as the rest of us, sometimes frightened and miserable,
> but usually happy enough.

Roy Jenkins, in a review of the biography of Iain Macleod, referred to Fettes as a "minor Scottish public school". In Scotland and the North of England at least, it was regarded as a major public school in the English style. According to one Old Boy, the only real signs of Scottishness were porridge morning and evening, kilts and a pipeband in the OTC. Sir William Fettes, a rich Edinburgh merchant who died in 1836, had left his estate "to form an endowment for the maintenance, education and outfit of young people whose parents have either died without leaving sufficient funds for that purpose, or who, through innocent misfortune during their lives, are unable to give suitable education to their children". The trustees of the estate eventually went ahead with the building of Fettes College, to a design by David Bryde, in 1863. In the regulations, three categories of boys were to be provided for: Foundation Scholars, who must be boys who have spent the previous three years at least in Scottish state-aided schools and who, in addition to getting their board and tuition free, receive a small sum each term to help in buying clothes and books; secondly, Foundationers—those whose parents had died or were unable "through innocent misfortune" to give their sons the education they had intended. These received no grant of money but, so long as they had a Scottish sponsor, did not need to have resided in Scotland for the previous three years. Qualification for both these categories was through a competitive examination in Latin, Greek, and the usual school curriculum subjects. The third category was that of normal fee-paying boys. In Menlove's time there were about 50 boys "on the foundation", and the school roll mustered about 250.

The college was built on a fine site on the northern outskirts of Edinburgh, seen to best advantage from the Queensferry Road. The schoolhouse is a huge piece of Victorian neo-Gothicism in the style of a French château; a tall central spire, flying buttresses, tracery, gargoyles, etc. There are extensive grounds, in which, in Menlove's time, were four boarding houses, the sickbay, tuckshop, and swimming bath. On the north side, huge playing fields extended to the Queensferry Road, and there was nothing between the school and the Firth of Forth but fields and a few woods, until Granton in the east, with its gas works and harbour. The north-east winds blew unimpeded from the Firth, a constant feature of school life. The boarding houses were surrounded by large expanses of grass, with clumps of trees here and there in which birds and squirrels nested. On a winter's morning, the sun would rise behind Arthur's Seat, silhouetting the spectacular basalt crags, the castle, and the spires of the old town against a red sky.

Physically and academically it was a very tough school, with a reputation for rugby and scholarship at Oxford and Cambridge. One former inmate has it that:

... life was hard. It has often been said that to anyone educated at Fettes there would be no hardship in going to gaol. The cold was all-pervading, and though there was central heating in college, it did not come on till eight and went off again at nine. So we got up and went to bed in the freezing cold, with the wind whistling in from the Forth through the open windows in the winter.

Schooldays were long. The boys rose at seven, and were in school at seven-thirty after a cold shower and, if there was time, a cup of cocoa. An hour's school was followed by chapel and breakfast, school continuing from nine-forty-five till one. Each afternoon there were games from two to three-thirty, school from four to six, and after tea prep. from seven-thirty to nine, then prayers and bed from nine-forty-five to ten-thirty according to age. Free time was to be filled in by reading the novels of Sir Walter Scott, for whom most pupils seemed to conceive an intense dislike. Food, in these days of lingering austerity after the First World War, was poor, porridge being a staple of the diet, and the boys were always hungry. Another Old Boy intoned the daily intake as follows:

> Breakfast the best meal of the day. Porridge, a hot dish, roll and butter, tea or coffee. Lunch: soup and meat or meat and pudding. Tea: bread and butter and tea. Supply your own jam, and an egg or meat-paste if times were good.

The two most important things in the school were rugby and Classics; for the former Menlove could raise little enthusiasm, but as far as work went he had little difficulty. Of all the boys who entered the school on the foundation in his year he was placed the highest, and he got into the Upper VI very early in his career. Work, according to his contemporaries, came easily to him, and he was thought a very good prospect for getting a scholarship to Oxford or Cambridge. In addition to his school work, he read widely, and by the end of his third year at Fettes had read the whole of the *Decline and Fall of the Roman Empire*. (It is amusing to speculate how he would have justified to his masters the preference for Gibbon rather than Scott.) Of Menlove's own feelings about the place, we have only two fragmentary impressions, the second of them recorded on the Rodney Street notepaper during the brief years of near-happiness in his later life. The first tends to confirm his sister's view that his schooldays were at least a little unhappy:

> They throw about my mother's old dictionary. She gave it to me at home with kindness. She rebound it herself in green cloth, and then somebody

threw it across the classroom. It fell spread out on the floor, with leaves crushed, and my misery fell with it and dissolved unhappily into tears. School. They're so hard at school. I must never let myself want affection.

This is a recollection which repays careful scrutiny. It was written probably a dozen years after the event, and yet it conveys with extraordinary immediacy his unhappiness, isolation, and duality; there is the consciousness of his mother's kindness, the slipping of the mask of restraint, and the oddly-prompted final thought as though in that prop lay everything.

Of the atmosphere of the school itself he wrote:

Reading down the old Fettes College lists. The brick damp corridors of the asylum with the smell of food and the great bare corridors with the stair-rails sweating and greasy to the touch. The cold stone as we leant out of the windows and looked down the long stiff lines of trees, the drive, the waving of leaves a long way from us, and in the distance, hills, promises, and the puff of dirty smoke from a train.

My mind's gone all quiet—all quiet.

Also written at a later date, there will be an inevitable element of re-interpretation through experience in all this, but it is still a haunting and significant little vignette. There is the sense of physical repulsion and recoil occasioned by his immediate surrounding. Between his present situation and the distant hills, with their promises, the sobering touch of cold stone at a window bars the way. The stiffness of the trees bears comparison with the use of tree-symbolism in his poetry, where it is frequently a homo-erotic reference to young men. But everything beyond the window is far off, unreachable, and the entire set of images concludes with the "puff of dirty smoke from a train", and the symbolic possibilities that phrase contains.

By the end of his third year at Fettes Menlove had committed himself to an ideal which led him in a direction entirely counter to the one he was expected to follow. He had resolved to become a medical missionary. In consequence his course of study had to be changed:

He decided that as he was going in for medicine he should go on the Modern side and got himself transferred to the Modern VI. The Modern side at Fettes in those days was to a large extent where the men who couldn't cope with the Classics ended up. It was full of hearties, good at rugger and other games, who were destined to go into father's business or some such, and it was not renowned for its standard of work. So it was a great disappointment to the headmaster and his housemaster when

Menlove, with such a rosy academic career in front of him, as they saw it, chose to spoil it all by "going Modern".

For the time and environment this must have been a striking case of individual thought. The many objections which would have been raised must have required considerable effort of will effectively to be silenced.

Alec Keith, later Orthopaedic Surgeon at Glasgow Royal Infirmary, and a lifelong friend of Menlove's, gives the following lengthy account of him from this time onwards:

What went on in VI Mods I never really knew, but I suspect that Menlove, with a little gentle guidance from H. G. Newman, read what he liked. I don't remember him doing any science, which would have helped him in medicine, but maybe he did. He sometimes helped me with my Latin and Greek translation, but it was never very satisfactory, for he could never see the difficulties that got in the way of the less gifted. I found the same thing later when I climbed with him.

At games he did well enough to get by but I cannot remember him playing rugby at all, which is queer because we must have played in hundreds of games together. I suspect he worked as a forward in the middle of the scrum, keeping out of sight and trouble, and he was probably in the bottom half of Little Side—4th XV, if there had been such a thing. At cricket I remember him as a steady medium-pace bowler in the House XI, who could go on for ever, and a stodgy but fairly sound batsman a bit down the order. He was a much better cricketer than I was, and got his 3rd XI colours. He got into the Hockey XI, which was a considerable feat. Hockey was played for a few weeks at the end of the Easter term after rugby was finished, and the Hockey XI was made up very largely of rugger bloods. Anyone not in the XV who got into the Hockey XI did so on merit and had to be good, and it was at least a little out of character for Menlove to make the effort and show how good he was. Something must have urged him to compete. He played hockey at University later so maybe he liked the game or felt he could use it to out-perform the rugger-enthusiasts. The thing he was best at was swimming. He loved the baths and bathing and in our second year won the Junior Anderson swimming race. Usually the winner of this went on in a year or two to win the Senior Anderson for older boys, but though he tried Menlove never did. He never developed enough speed because he never did a proper crawl using a scissors kick rather than a paddle. The race was a sprint, but if it had been longer or an endurance test Menlove would have had it I'm sure.

Menlove and I often went together on cross-country runs—the worst bind at school, done on days when the rugby fields were unplayable, or one hadn't got a game. We plodded round four or five miles in the country between the school and the Forth, now totally built up. He and I had much the same attitude towards them, running just fast enough to keep from getting cold, and moaning to each other all the way round.

It wasn't really until the last term that he and I could have been said to have become firm friends. All Foundationers were in College so we were in the same house and in the first year had next-door cubicles in our dormitory, so we were thrown together for a start. Douglas Wilson and I both came from Aberdeen, had been to school together there, and were friends too. Menlove, because of his superiority at lessons, got a study before us, so when our turn came Wilson and I shared. But Menlove and I went for Sunday afternoon walks together exploring the shores of the Forth and, as we believed, Stevenson's House of Shaws. We went to school matches and so on together and saw a good lot of each other. And in our last summer term every Sunday after chapel we spent the evening—as many other boys did—walking together over the playing fields and round the green walks; talking, I suppose, of the future, and what we were going to do. Menlove's resolution to be a medical missionary was strong.

As you can appreciate, all this was fifty years ago, and my memories have necessarily become a little dim. One incident I remember, à propos of something else, is of Menlove being found out of bed by his Housemaster and being beaten then and there with a slipper, and how he argued vigorously and at length about the injustice of it all, as he considered he had a legitimate excuse. Apart from this, and the difficulties he made for himself by his choice of scholastic work, he was never in trouble with authority. And we were lucky in our house in that there was no bullying and none of the homosexual troubles which did occur in another house in my time, and that the relations between junior and senior boys were good, and between boys and housemasters. Menlove did not always respect or believe in authority, but he did not fight it, and I think he liked H. G. Newman, and did respect Mr Ashcroft, the headmaster. I don't remember him moping about, but just behaving as any other boy might do.

Another contemporary remembers him as:

a boy of medium height but exceptionally powerfully-built, little attracted by the conventional successes of work and play, declining leadership that could have been his for the asking in favour of pursuing advanced studies of human nature and behaviour.

Other gleanings are that he was "small, red-faced", "rather remote and sensitive", "ultra-socialist and something of a misogynist". The official school line, in the school magazine obituary, had it that "J. M. Edwards was a most able boy, who came to college in 1923. He was shy and retiring, and never really adapted himself to the common life of the place." His favourite subjects at school were English and History, and he won a prize for an essay on Stevenson, in which he shows a particular interest in Hugo and Fielding. And that, more or less, is the sum of our knowledge of his school life.

The family still forgathered in their favourite summer haunts during the long vacations. The children's Godfather, the former Rector of Birmingham, Denton Thompson, was now the Bishop of Sodor and Man, so holidays in the golden summers of the 1920s were taken at Ramsey or Port St Mary, where the energetic and enterprising Edwards children were assured of a friendly reception and the opportunity for endless play and adventure. Always the water was the focus, the sea and coast an entrancing world to be thoroughly investigated in all its potential. It is against this early familiarity, gained through group endeavour, with powerful natural forces that Menlove's later undertakings need to be seen. The feats of the grown man were extraordinary. Our understanding of his habituation to their medium through unrestrained childhood experience, encouraged by the father, in no way lessens their personal scale of achievement.

The hills, too, began to intrude on his consciousness during schooldays. A fragment survives in which he recalls the feelings they aroused in him. The account is written much later, and dwells on the uncomplicated delights of first acquaintance. The sensuality of response which it reveals is nonetheless very characteristic of Menlove throughout his life; as is the yearning remembrance of being in company with someone; of not having been alone:

> I remember when I was still at school walking over the hills and watching the short grass bend in the wind. We lay on the slopes and gazed up at sky together. We were gay and not at strife among hills then. The wind moved over the brow of the hill and the stones nestled down closer among the grass. We wore shorts and the knees were strong against the air. The neck sprang free with the shirt blown wide open. Yes and our heads were packed with a pulse, a fullness of glory of ourself, and far too full for sense.

Whilst the above glimpse is very generalized, Selby Walmsley, a contemporary of the Edwards brothers who lived near their home in Formby, gives a more specific account of Menlove's earliest excursions into the mountains:

Back in the mid-twenties or so, Stephen, Menlove, my brother Cyril and myself used to go to Langdale every New Year, staying at Middlefell Farm for four or five days for some winter walking and scrambling. Rock-climbing as such had not then captured us, but the early probings in that direction had begun. We pottered round the base of Gimmer, doing the odd pitch and then coming down again after probably getting stuck. We were in our early twenties and Menlove only in his teens. I remember the weather was always rough and snowy. Menlove was at this time a shy, immature youth with a cherubic countenance, bright rosy cheeks and a crop of close, curly hair. He appeared to be sturdy, but a planned day's excursion via Wrynose Pass and Swirl Howe to Coniston Old Man had to be abandoned at Great Carrs because Menlove collapsed with the cold and exposure. It was a frightful day of high wind, soft snow and blizzards, and the conditions were pretty tough for all of us. However, we managed to get him back without too many ill effects, and he was ready for more the next day.

Towards the end of his time at school Menlove had begun to write poetry, and a rather forlorn little correspondence exists between him, on holiday at Port St Mary in the summer of 1927, and a vanity-publishing house, A. H. Stockwell of Edinburgh. Stockwell's reader commented on the poems that "some of them are quite clever, though considerable revision and embellishment would be necessary before publication", and offered to publish 1,000 copies of them in pamphlet form on payment of £19. 10s. 0d.—a very considerable sum in 1927. Not surprisingly Menlove seems to have refused their terms, whereupon the publishers lowered their asking price to "a contribution of ten guineas". When Menlove rejected this also, they rather peevishly wrote back that "with regard to magazines, we should like to point out that the market for single poems is really very limited indeed".

The condition of Menlove's father was steadily worsening. He began to resort to faith-healers. Nowell remembers accompanying him to one such session in London. Helen went too, but was sceptical, worn out by many such occasions, whilst Nowell was riven by the desperation and guilt attendant upon a desire to believe which worked against all the evidence of feeling and sense. Stephen's memories are of special diets tried on the advice of a Mrs Herriott of Gower Street, and he recalls with particular relish the delicious walnut and honey bread which figured large on them.

In 1928 Menlove won the Begg Memorial Prize, a scholarship from Fettes valued at £60 per annum, tenable for five years and usually awarded to a pupil going to Oxford or Cambridge. Menlove disregarded the convention

and chose to study medicine at Liverpool. Hewlett was already there studying sciences with the intention of going on to Cambridge to take Holy
Orders. No doubt the affection between him and Menlove partly dictated
the latter's choice, but probably also Menlove desired to be near his family
again, and to be able to help his mother financially. Intending to devote his
life to medical work in India, he applied to the Church Missionary Society
for a grant. (There were no mandatory local authority grants to university
students until the 1950s.) He was awarded £100 per annum on the understanding that he would work as a doctor in a CMS hospital for a number of
years after completion of his training.

In July of 1928 his ruminations about the future with Alec Keith during
their Sunday walks by the Firth of Forth were finally brought to an end. He
left Fettes, and in October of that year enrolled as a student of medicine in
Liverpool University.

CHAPTER THREE

"There was once a man who desired glory . . ."
1928–1931

BETWEEN THE WARS Liverpool University was a grimy collection of Victorian redbrick clustered together in the area north of where the Metropolitan Cathedral now stands. Its medical school, thanks to the gifts and influence of the same Sir Robert Jones who had operated on Menlove's father, had one of the best reputations in the country.

Menlove initially involved himself very little in student social and sporting life, although he did play hockey together with Hewlett in the University first XI. There is some very slight evidence to suggest that Hewlett found his devoted younger brother's company a little irksome during the first years of college. Both lived at home and travelled each day the few miles from Formby into Liverpool. Home life gave Menlove the opportunity to retreat into a privacy which had been lacking for him at Fettes. He was conscientious about his work, driven on by an insecurity bred of those high expectations held out for him by his family. His devotion to his parents was genuine, and many impressions survive as proof of this:

> Menlove had endless patience helping Father as he grew older, sitting by him turning over his pages and helping him, feeding him at meals. He was a great help to Mother and me, very sympathetic as he grew up. Always working terribly hard, never keen on going out socially and could never be got to learn to dance, or go to a party. He was, however, a great favourite, and I remember a friend of mine saying he was "the best of the lot", though both Steve and Hewlett were gay and handsome, getting on with everyone. But Menlove was a favourite because of his sympathy and thoughtfulness, and his great kindness. He was very unselfish.

Menlove probably started to climb in the Lake District with Hewlett and the Walmsley brothers, Cyril and Selby. Photographs which Stephen dates to a family holiday in 1928 or 1929 in Pembroke exist of Menlove leading quite difficult pitches on the sea-washed limestone slabs at Giltar Point, near Tenby. Selby Walmsley remembers being with him on Gimmer Crag in

1929 or early 1930, but the earliest record of his climbing dates from June of
the latter year. Stephen, now at Cambridge, had joined the university
mountaineering club there and attended Easter meets at the Climbers' Club
hut of Helyg in 1929 and 1930. In the summer of 1930 he organized a trip with
two university friends, Bill Lancaster and Tommy Wyatt, to Pralognan, in the
Vanoise region to the south of Mont Blanc. Menlove was invited along and as a
preliminary joined Stephen and Hewlett at Helyg for a few days at the end of
June.

Helyg lies in a grove of trees between the A5 and the Afon Llugwy in the
Nant y Benglog. Just across the stream is the bulky vegetated mass of Gallt yr
Ogof. More elegantly, Tryfan stands face-on a little down the valley, with all
the grander hills around Llyn Ogwen massed behind it. In the 1930s, for all
the intellectual and sporting glitter of its habitués—Longland, Wager,
Greene, Auden, Kirkus, Hargreaves, Watkins, Shipton, Smythe all stayed
here—it was rather a seedy place. George Borrow's description of it as a
"miserable hovel" was still not wholly inappropriate. Sooty oil lamps offered
poor illumination to its grubbier recesses. Cooking was carried out on primus
stoves. It was a male preserve and it showed it, by a cavalier unconcern for any
of the dictates of tidiness or hygiene. The log-book was filled with interfac-
tional sniping over responsibility for mouldering rubbish in the grate or
excreta in the incinerator. A bus, a rattling green boneshaker of a Crosville
Foden diesel, passed to and fro each day between Bangor and Betws y Coed,
whence the branch line ran to Llandudno Junction and the main coastal
railway. On the evening of 26 June Menlove alighted from this bus to begin, on
the following day, his recorded climbing career. In the hut-book, immediately
succeeding accounts of the first ascents of Clogwyn Du'r Arddu's Great Slab
Route and Dinas Mot's Nose Direct by Colin Kirkus, there is a note in
Stephen's hand of Menlove's first two known days' climbing:

> June 27th. Girdle traverse of Idwal Slabs. Met ferocious-looking and
> evil-smelling goat by the ashtree. [Stephen remembers Menlove standing
> by ready to catch if it jumped off.] The said animal disappeared too fast to
> see its route. Idwal Buttress to follow. SZE and JME (non-member) June
> 28th. Morning spent wandering round Alt yr Ogof [sic]. A fine pair of
> falcons [peregrine?) have a nest somewhere in these rocks. They screamed
> about us for half an hour and were well worth seeing. Many corpses were
> strewn about, including several pigeons. One was a homer and ringed. SZE
> and JME.

As an entry to the sport this is solid, sober, and undistinguished. As a
lead-in to many of the later preoccupations of Menlove's climbing it is slightly

George Edwards, Menlove's father

Helen Edwards, Menlove's mother

Menlove, Hewlett, Nowell and Stephen, 1923

Menlove, 1927

One of the first climbing pictures of Menlove, on sea-cliff limestone, location and date unknown

Stephen, Tommy Wyatt and Menlove on path from Pralognan to Refuge de Polset. Vanoise, August 1930

more revealing. For Gallt yr Ogof and the quite similar cliffs of Clogwyn y Geifr were soon to be regarded virtually as Menlove's territory, mornings spent wandering in such places as the hallmark of his activity, and humorous meetings such as that with the goat entirely typical of a man who, in his best years, punctured the pretensions and broadened the comedy, variety and interest of a sport still very much in a seriously self-regarding state of adolescence.

Stephen's memories of the 1930 Alpine holiday—understandably after more than 50 years—are fragmentary: of the snowy day when he and his two Cambridge friends walked down to Pralognan to purchase another ice-axe, leaving Menlove alone with the caretaker of the *refuge* in which they were staying. When they returned it was nearly dark and he was missing, having gone out alone to climb the nearby rock peak of the Aiguille Doron—which was used by the French Air Force for target practice, its rock much shattered in consequence. When Menlove arrived back after dark he was soundly berated by Stephen, who felt responsible for his younger brother.

On another day, whilst they were ascending a rock-ridge, Menlove's rope came undone on one pitch, and the party jokingly wondered whether to show more concern for Menlove or the rucksack he was carrying, which contained their food. Yet another day was spent climbing the snow peak of the Dôme de Polset, above Modane, after which they lazed around eating delicious strawberry ices.

After these introductory experiences, the rapidity with which Menlove established himself, along with Colin Kirkus and Jack Longland, as one of the three great pioneers of Welsh rock-climbing in the 1930s—and the greatest innovator amongst them—is astonishing. His first new route immediately followed the Alpine holiday of July, and was on Lliwedd in August in company with a fellow student at Liverpool University, Sandy Edge. Jack Longland was on the cliff on the same day. Looking down from the route he was on, he saw a climber breaking out on to the right wall of Shallow Gully, and thought how slow and clumsy he was in his movements. But the young climber painstakingly worked his way up and finished the pitch. Ochre Slab, on the East Buttress of the cliff, cannot be claimed as anything more than a pleasant and neat diversion up a little facet slab on the gully-side, giving a good alternative to the scrambling and scrabbling necessary to surmount a demoralizing section of Shallow Gully. As a gesture, it held considerably more significance. The first point to be made is that in 1930 Shallow Gully most emphatically would not have been considered any place for two novices. It is a Severe rock-climb, over 1,000 feet in length. The generation previous to Menlove's looked upon it as one of the harder climbs in Wales, and its first ascent had been made by two of the most gifted performers of the first decade of the century, Herbert Reade and Geoffrey Winthrop Young. Lliwedd itself was still regarded as a cliff for experts. (At this time the number of people who had led climbs on Clogwyn Du'r Arddu could still be numbered on one hand.) If you were a beginner, you stuck pretty religiously to the Milestone Buttress or the easy ways up the Gribin Facet and the Idwal Slabs. The East Face of Tryfan and the climbs on Glyder Fach or Craig yr Ysfa were there for you after your apprenticeship had been served, and should you ever aspire beyond those, there, lording it over Cwm Dyli, in all the pucker and frown of its 1,000-foot faces, was Lliwedd, preserve of the élite. Although comparisons are very difficult to make, there was probably as much *cachet* attached to Shallow Gully in 1930 as there is today in Extremely Severe routes on the Anglesey sea-cliffs such as Wendigo or Tyrannosaurus Rex. For two novices to compound their presumption in being on a Lliwedd Severe by adding a significant new variation of their own because they found the normal way tedious was strikingly bold and original.

Menlove's initial enthusiasm for climbing expressed itself in one direction through the foundation, on 25 November 1930, of a club at the university. It came about through a meeting of climbing friends who were all then Liverpool students. Hewlett was elected chairman, Menlove agreed to act as secretary, and a committee was appointed of Messrs Edge, Geary, Hancox and Stallybrass, with a Miss Wilkinson to provide the female representation. The annual subscription was to be 3s 6d., and on 8 December they met again to adopt a constitution. The usual run of club activities were mooted: term time meets at the nearby sandstone outcrop of Helsby; trips farther afield in the vacations; lectures to be given by prominent climbers; a pool of equipment and guidebooks, and a log-book to be kept of all club enterprises. "University days," Menlove commented later, "frisky, comparatively." There was one thing about this club which marked a radical departure from established precedent and that, quite simply, was its name. It was firmly, clearly, and constitutionally to be called "The Liverpool University Rock-Climbing Club". No other such club existed in the country at that time. (The Fell and Rock Climbing Club came close, but still hedged its bets rather in the matter of title.) Indeed, the sport of rock-climbing then had no separate entity, for it existed under the aegis of mountaineering. It was a part of mountain-craft. Any text-book you cared to read told you that rock-climbing amongst our British hills, although admittedly at times pleasurable enough in itself, and very definitely a sphere where responsibility and mature judgement were required, was really only a part of the training, and a very small part at that, for the problems posed by those more sublime ascents of the Alpine (perhaps even Himalayan, though these were probably beyond the pale) giants which were surely the summit of any sound man's aspirations.

You will, I hope, forgive the element of parody here, but this was pretty well the received wisdom on the subject, and a point of view perpetuated by most of the contemporary mountaineering authors. Yet in 1930 the Edwards brothers quietly weighed up the mountaineering establishment's considered and authoritative dictum, shrugged their shoulders, and gave a name so precise in its definition that it is still unacceptable to most clubs whose year-round activity centres on rock-climbing. (Even the present-day climbing club at Liverpool University has rejected the lead and tamely calls itself the Liverpool University Mountaineering Club.)

There is a social point to be taken into account here as well which may, given Menlove's socialist background and tendency, have had some bearing on the choice. Mountaineering was very definitely a sport of the professional and upper-middle classes in 1930. It required time, for the venues were far away; education, for the natives of the climbed-in mountainous regions spoke French, German or Italian; and money,* for travel and to pay guides. The Alpine peaks were pretty much analogues for their ascensionists' situations in society during this period; mountaineering was capitalism and privilege geographized. There was a process of democratization beginning, particularly in the Peak District of Derbyshire where its representatives were working-class men like Frank Elliott and Eric Byne, but not until after the next war was there sufficient social change for it to be consolidated. In the context of 1930, the Liverpool University Rock-Climbing Club was revolutionary.

Its first meet was held at Helyg from 17 to 23 December 1930. Eight members attended. (Miss Wilkinson was absent, most probably because Helyg, and the Climbers' Club, were male domains at that time. The Liverpool Club's discouraging attitude towards women was, however, to run it into trouble later, the grant and university authorization being withdrawn because of discrimination. Bill Stallybrass, a member of that first committee, recalls that it "was supposed to be open to members of both sexes, but Menlove used considerable ingenuity, not always successfully, to discourage women from joining our meets".) On this December meet, most of them reached Helyg by bus. The scene can be imagined as it ground up the hill, engine labouring and gears crashing, out of Capel Curig into the Nant y Benglog. The weather was poor—low cloud and

---

* Two riders should be added here: the Cambridge University Mountaineering Club, inspired by Longland, had been pursuing the frowned-on practice of guideless Alpine climbing since the mid-twenties, and the strength of sterling against continental currencies in the inter-war period made for cheaper travel.

rain—and the conversation probably lagging by now, four hours' journey from Liverpool. These young, fresh-faced, future professional men are pressing their faces to the steamy windows, wiping away the condensation, peering at the misty shapes of the hills, measuring reputation, dream and ambition against streaming crag or half-glimpsed rocky ridge. Snow is down to 1,000 feet and every hillside veined with white cataracts. The bus pulls up by the stone wall around Helyg and a colourful, cheerful troupe unload. Bill Stallybrass probably leaps out first, a dapper figure, resplendent in check breeches and a Norfolk jacket which once belonged to his father. He is the best climber of the group apart from Menlove, a rip-roaring character who will hustle them down to the pubs in Capel Curig that night to play the piano and exercise a voice which can make a bawdy song sound like a Gregorian chant. In his later life he is to join the Oxford Group movement, besiege his friends with religious tracts every Christmas, and end up teaching modern languages at Sandhurst. Now, he's simply the group extrovert. Hewlett Edwards and Sandy Edge follow him; two big curly-headed fellows, Sandy loose-limbed and gangling, Hewlett surprisingly neat in his movements. As the others, clad in old jackets fastened with blanket pins, balaclava helmets, and clinkernailed boots at 17s 6d. from Timpsons, clatter down the steps, Stephen Darbishire comes out of the hut to meet them. He has arrived earlier on his Manx Norton, having driven up from Penmaenmawr—where his parents own the quarry. Self-assured, leather-jacketed and well-groomed, he was to achieve fame in motor-cycle racing and be placed second in the Junior and third in the Senior Isle of Man Tourist Trophy races. He greets the group boisterously and they turn to seek the shelter of the hut. Unobtrusively, almost shyly, Menlove's short, powerful figure, wearing baggy moleskin trousers and hobnailed shepherd's boots, joins on behind to follow them down to the cottage as the bus, winding heavily up through the gears, draws away along the road.

Their first morning at Helyg dawned grey and raining, with glimpses of snow here and there beneath the skirt of cloud. It was not a day for climbing. Menlove was up early, fretting around the hut, fishing for a partner whilst the others lay in their bunks feigning sleep. Eventually, won over by his enthusiasm, Keith Geary stumbled out of bed and he and Menlove set off up the valley to climb on Glyder Fach. An hour and a half later, having scrambled along the Heather Terrace and cut round the back of Tryfan, they found themselves at the foot of the cliffs. The rock gleams silvery with moisture, cloud hunts relentlessly up and down the gullies and the ledges are sprinkled with snow. The two hardest routes of the day on the cliff are Lot's Groove and the Direct Route. The former looks uninvitingly steep and glistens with slime. The account of its first ascent, which they read in the hut-book the previous evening, lingers in their memories: "unutterably severe climbing ... the hardest pitch in the Ogwen district—Belle Vue Bastion and Javelin Buttress are comparative walks! The name that seems best is Lot's Groove, because there is no looking back!" Discretion prevails, in view of the weather conditions. In the snow and the grease they settle for the Direct Route. For a contemporary view of the climb, we can turn to Dorothy Pilley: "This climb has a distinct *cachet*. In the books it is classed as 'exceptionally severe'. It goes up the middle of the steepest crag in the Ogwen district ..." Admittedly, this is an opinion formulated at a time which pre-dates Menlove's ascent by seven or eight years. The modern guidebook opinion is more modest: "It remains a grand piece of mountaineering on perfect rock which is sometimes very steep and always demanding." But a great deal of climbing is in the mind, a great deal of the difficulty is imagined. Reputation and grade are quite as formidable obstacles as any real difficulties of strenuousness or technique which a route may possess. On a wet and wintry day in December 1930, was Glyder Fach's Direct Route any sort of place for a novice in hobnailed boots to be aspiring to lead? One of the jottings on Rodney street notepaper gives an oblique answer.

Have you ever watched a beginner on the Slabs? A most instructive little psychological study. He puts his foot on a hold which he doesn't like and then does his very best to prove to himself that he's right in not liking it. He fidgets about but he doesn't succeed in getting the foot to slip off. So he develops a tremor and tries to shake it off. Still it stays firm so in desperation he gets on to it, lies down flat against the rock and with a yell of triumph pushes. With the right direction of effort the mind of man can accomplish almost anything.

This apparently slight humorous sketch is a most profoundly considered statement upon the nature of rock-climbing. In miniature, its argument is that of Freud's essay "Beyond the Pleasure Principle", but it goes beyond that in identifying an element of arrogance in the participant; the desire to be right in an assessment of the extent of his abilities precluding their free exercise. Logically, this was a nonsense and from the very outset Menlove saw it as such. In the *moment* of climbing experience, he sensed an opportunity to pare away the mind-clutter which weighs against effective action. Coming from a society where such clutter, in the form of myth and taboo, was institutionalized and even statutory, he found in climbing a way to cut through it and not have to compromise his personal integrity in so doing. Right out in the open and through direct personal action he could say:

"Look—reputation and tradition are just so much hot air. It is the integrity, ability, and commitment of the individual within a situation which matters. Let us look for ourselves and see what we can see." For the moment, in the simplicity of a winter's day on Glyder Fach, what he could see was the Direct Route as a perfectly feasible proposition for a strong beginner in a good pair of hobnailed boots. So they climbed it and, well-pleased with the discovery, he and Geary picked their way down to the foot of the cliff by Main Gully and plodded damply back along the Heather Terrace to the road, and Helyg.

The rest of their companions at the hut, having sat around all day in desultory conversation over games of cards and endless cups of tea, watching from behind windows as the rain incessantly fell, made room for them as they trudged in. Boredom found a new focus for its wit. Jokes were bandied about. The wet clothes came off and were hung above the fire as they sat by it in pyjamas and were handed steaming mugs of tea. The room was vibrant with an uneasy respect. Modestly, the stocky, brown-curled figure by the fire played with the questions, refused all heroic inflation, and quietly laughed it all down; but not without retaining for himself a due quota of pride. The following day, he and Geary went to Lliwedd, climbing a new and superior start to the Far East Arete in the belief that the whole route was new. A. B. Hargreaves, who repeated their line of ascent the following spring, summed it up as "fairly severe, more from the character of the rock and the exposure than from any notable technical difficulties". The weather was again foul, rain falling daylong to wash away the remnants of snow. To the remarks made on Lliwedd earlier in this chapter it need only be added that there are few more unpleasant places to climb under wet conditions. The rib and groove structure and predominantly limiting holds make for a style of climbing heavily reliant on friction—and on this cliff in the rain, friction is something it lacks.

The twentieth of December was sufficiently fine to tempt the Liverpool climbers out in strength. Sunshine after two days' enforced inactivity brought an exuberance to the team. Stephen Darbishire was up early in the morning to race his Norton along the straight outside Helyg before there was any traffic about. Soon the whole club was out, walking along the road towards Ogwen. Hewlett and Sandy Edge turned off the road beneath Tryfan for routes on the Milestone Buttress. Menlove and Geary headed up into Cwm Idwal to climb on the East Wall of the Slabs. Again, he was heading for the preserve of the expert, trying out the ground even though it was in the poorest condition. Despite the waterfall flowing down it, he climbed Kirkus's Grooved Wall route of the previous year and then, espying some unclimbed rock, proceeded to add a new route of his own—Route V.

As with Ochre Slab on Lliwedd, it is not a particularly good climb; the importance again lies in the gesture. Having made it, Menlove was quite content to continue up to Glyder Fawr in company with Stephen Darbishire, and wander his way up the Central Arete, an old and straightforward classic leading to the top of the mountain. That unclimbed rock was now becoming a passion the activities of the following day confirm. Menlove and Sandy Edge went back up to Glyder Fach and added a new finish to the Direct Route—one which nowadays often sees more traffic than the original, of which it is really an evasion. The last day of the meet Menlove spent on Tryfan, soloing up the North Buttress—not the approved practice for an inexperienced twenty-year-old—before joining forces with Edge and Warner for an ascent in nails of Owen Glynne Jones's "unjustifiably severe" Terrace Wall Variant.

On the following morning they waited for the bus in a slow, steady drizzle and rode to Betws y Coed. Menlove must have felt well pleased with his week as he sat in the train taking him down the Conwy Valley. He had emerged as beyond doubt the club's foremost climber. In doing so, he had crept from under the shadow of his elder brother Hewlett and had to contend with the considered judgement of his teachers and contemporaries, who continually opined that Hewlett—the tall, lithe, charming and handsome Hewlett, with his neat movements— was far more natural a climber than Menlove. Whether or not this was so is beside the point, for really the idea of "natural climbing" is that everyone should conform to a particular style in movement on rock—an approved style of self-consciously languid and balanced perfection which achieves its complete expression in the mountaineer who, covertly acknowledging his own inability to master anything more technical, is content to flow up a moderately difficult on the East Face of Tryfan so long as the wind does not blow too hard against him. It is, of course, the rock-climbing-as-training-for-the-Alps or school-as-training-for-life mentality at work again. It was a judgement which had no understanding of, or relevance to, the direction of Menlove's interest, and is as hackeneyed and vaporous as the prose of most of its upholders. Leaning back in his third-class carriage seat as the train clacked along towards the coast, Menlove could have afforded to smile gently to himself at the absurdities his campaign had begun to expose.

After the week at Helyg, it was back to the festivity of a Christmas at home. Roy Beard remembered visiting the Edwards family at about this time from his home in Southport.

> The general impression was one of cleanliness and pride. It was obvious if you looked closely that they were living on a stretched income—worn carpets and so on—but there was no meanness about their poverty. The

women kept rather in the background, hovering round the Father, who was terrifically alert mentally despite his disability. The three sons were all quite different. Stephen was the hospitable extrovert, Hewlett was pleasant and ordinary, whilst Menlove was rather an introvert, and often quite content to ignore the company and sit in a corner by himself in order to read.

Some of Menlove's own notes occasionally reveal amusing aspects of domestic life:

The foul pair of trousers, moleskin quite imperishable . . . I kept them in a drawer for a long time, but that wasn't nice for the other clothes. My mother, not knowing the stuff they were made of, tried to burn them. Slightly charred and dirtier than ever they disappeared under cover of some other things in the dustbin.

(Stephen adds that they were brown and the dye ran, so that after a wet day out Menlove's lower half would acquire a deep sun-tan.)

In the spring of 1931 he bought himself a motorbike in order to get out to Helsby and Wales more easily at weekends. Stephen Darbishire went as pillion passenger to Helyg with Menlove on one such weekend in March:

He was a desperate motor-cycle pilot. I recall a terrifying ride back from Snowdon, the owner and pillion passenger taking each corner in a different way on the same machine. It finally ended in a heap of laughing humanity in the middle of the road outside the office at the Pen y Gwryd.

On the Saturday they climbed, in the inevitable rain, Piton Route on the Holly Tree Wall. Darbishire's memory runs this:

It was a wet day and he was attempting to climb the then-celebrated Piton Route in boots for the first time. After he had stood on my head for about ten minutes, it was realised that the absence of the expected pain was due to the fact that there were hardly any nails in his boots.

Alan Hargreaves arrived at Helyg that night. Hargreaves, commonly known as AB, was one of the most amusing characters of his day. A tiny, fiery, bristling man of trenchant wit and vigorous vocabulary, he had kept company with most of the leading climbers of the time on many of their most important ascents. He was a key figure in climbing at the turn of these decades, and he has the following recollection of Menlove's entry into the sport:

As it happened Menlove's beginning as a climber—his first two or three years—coincided with my own little heyday, and I did quite a lot with him during that time.

We first met at Helsby when he was a Liverpool University student and was rapidly accomplishing all the harder climbs lately done by Kirkus and Hicks. At that time I had just come to live in the Lake District and I invited him to join me for a weekend there, so that he could see what the bigger crags were like. He came, and the first day among other things we did Tophet Wall Direct, which in those days ranked quite high. When I suggested that he should put rubbers on, he said, "Oh no, these will do," pointing to his almost brand new pair of boots studded with things like marbles. Nevertheless, to my surprise, he followed up quite easily.

The next day we went to Pillar, and I thought I would take him down a peg or two, nails and all, by performing Walker's Gully. But as it happened, it was wet when we got to the top pitch—always a hard place for me—and I dangled on the thread two or three times, and was unable to get up. So being the gaffer I said, "Sorry boys, now we've got to go down." (Like many another party.)

But Menlove said, "Let me have a go," and when I agreed to this, he promptly shot up quite easily. I have always remembered this as something quite remarkable, considering it was just about his first climb of any consequence. What a novice!

The outcrop-climbing mentioned at the beginning of AB's account is significant. Helsby is a bluff of red sandstone with exposed rock varying in height from 20 to 50 feet, above the village of that name eight miles north-east of Chester. It is safe to say that the standard of climbing there at the end of the twenties and beginning of the thirties was higher than anywhere else in the country. Colin Kirkus and Ted Hicks were the acknowledged experts, and the climbs they were ascending on the crag were, in terms of their technical difficulty, quite considerably harder than any Welsh route of that time with the possible exception of Longland's Javelin Blade. The Flake Crack, Eliminate I and Morgue Slab were the ultimate test-pieces on a crag where the climbing was characterized by a steepness beyond contemporary accepted limits, by a rock-type the reliability of which was always under suspicion, and by occasional sections of great delicacy. The predominant style of climbing there laid emphasis on finger-strength and gymnastic ability. Although only a short outcrop, there was an air of gravity about it. Because the rock was fragile, most climbs were initially done on a top-rope. The seriousness of leading them was good preparation for the longer but less technical run-outs on the hardest Welsh climbs. To add to the respectful manner in which the place was treated, fresh in memory would have been the death of C. W. Marshall on the cliff in the spring of 1928. He was a well-liked and competent climber, and the first custodian of Helyg, who had died after a fall whilst attempting to lead the Flake Crack—a long and strenuous layback high above the ground.

This, then, was Menlove's climbing nursery and here he harnessed his natural physical strength to the demands of technique. It became his habitual venue for fine evenings, weekends when he was not in Wales, or occasional afternoons when there were no lectures. Colin Kirkus was helpful to him at this time, and his tutelage and attention gave Menlove much confidence. At later dates, he always spoke gratefully of Kirkus, and the two were to be brought more closely together by several shared adventures and by Menlove's association with Kirkus's young cousin Wilfrid Noyce. For the moment, it is worthwhile considering the very rapid boost which the nature of climbing at Helsby and the friendly encouragement of Kirkus must have given to Menlove's climbing, making his entry into the sport all the more immediate and dramatic.

Back to Wales and the spring of 1931; another Liverpool University meet was held at Easter, once again using Helyg as its base. The general level of ability in the club, benefiting from Menlove's example and training on Helsby, was rising, so that his own ascents stand out less remarkably than on previous occasions. They were nonetheless considerable, for in the week of 9 to 16 April he led Belle Vue Bastion and soloed the Very Severe Long Chimney on Tryfan's Terrace Wall; he made a probe at what was later to become Grey Slab on Glyder Fawr's Upper Cliff (a line he had noticed on his ascent of Central Arete the previous winter); and he repeated Purgatory, Longland and Wager's Lliwedd route of 1928 which was then the most difficult on the cliff. A. B. Hargreaves rated it thus:

> . . . the hardest single pitch on the mountain. The first pitch of Paradise, if done in boots, as it first was, and should be always, is quite difficult enough for most people; but Purgatory is of a different order, demanding a mastery of the special boot technique required by the peculiar Lliwedd rock, which is possessed by very few.

Apart from the speed with which he established himself as fully capable of the hardest climbs, one thing which becomes apparent from this time is his habit of returning again and again to the same piece of rock, thoroughly working over the ground, repeating routes many times. He very quickly developed a stock repertoire of climbs and itinerary of cliffs which provided a basis, an essential foundation, to all his other climbing. It is as though he needed that reference point, needed to know it thoroughly and the security it gave. Although he did new climbs in a great number of places, he is not one of climbing's ubiquitous pioneers. He did not leave major ascents on many of the important cliffs throughout the country after the manner of Kirkus, Whillans, Boysen or Littlejohn. He is much more of the type which needs, as regards rock-climbing, to study exhaustively the ground on which it operates. (Joe Brown is of the same ilk.)

He was getting to know the ground quickly, however, and beginning to wander into the obviously unclimbed spaces between established routes. Idwal he liked. The walk to it was easy, and further assisted, on occasions when the unreliable motorbike was not available, by an old fixed-gear bicycle which Bill Stallybrass had deposited at Helyg. Roy Beard describes its use:

It had a light frame, light wheels, dropped handlebars and a fixed gear. On the level it was passable, on a slight downhill slope it was all right, but there was no chance of free-wheeling, no rest, no nothing; and uphill the thing was an absolute brute. We used to use this to get to Ogwen Cottage by hedgehopping. One of us would go off and ride for ten minutes, then (gratefully, in my case) place the bicycle on the side of the road, and walk on. The second man came along at a rapid pace and if it was Menlove it was a damned rapid pace, picked up the bicycle, mounted it and rode on for another ten minutes, propping it up against the wall, and so on. That was how we got to Idwal when we had no other transport, which was most of the time, for motor-bikes were always breaking down, and cars were far too expensive.

Menlove's immediate favourites in Wales, judging from the frequency of his visits to them in his first year's climbing, were Lliwedd and the East Wall of the Idwal Slabs. The nature and reputation of Lliwedd have been discussed above. As to the East Wall, Menlove's own Cwm Idwal guide of 1936 provides a pithy assessment: "not the leading ground for climbers just starting, nor for those apprehensive or unsteady". Nevertheless, on almost every one of his early visits to Wales Menlove was to be found climbing its routes, and adding new ones of his own. His climbing seems to have matured very rapidly, even in terms of the way he personally assessed it. For instance, on 17 May 1931, with Stephen Darbishire and Sandy Edge, Menlove thought to contrive a route between the Three Pinnacle Start to Craig Aderyn Route and Rocker Route on the West Buttress of Lliwedd. It was a large area of uncharted rock, 1,000 feet high. In the late sixties several routes were enthusiastically described here. Menlove's brief description notes that "It is only fair to add that the followers were throughout disgusted with their leader. It might be called Broken Buttress; we did our best." It was omitted entirely from his later guidebook.

Similarly with a new series of variations on Route I on the East Buttress, which he climbed in July; in his guidebook they were quite summarily dismissed: "there is a variation here of no great importance". For the clearest indication of his maturity and sure grasp of the essentials of the sport, we should look to his assessment of Lot's Groove on Glyder Fach, then thought to be the hardest route in Wales or even the whole of Britain, of which he did the second ascent at the end of a wet week's climbing in July: "Technical difficulty, of course, very high throughout, but by no means unjustifiable. No prodigious feats of strength but constant muscular tension. After the week's rain the actual crack was unpleasantly damp."

This is surely extraordinarily judicious coming from a climber of just turned twenty-one who has climbed what is reputedly the country's hardest route? There is no attempt at debunking or building up his own reputation at the expense of Kirkus's. It is merely a cool assessment of the climb, in contrast to both previous mentions of the route in the Helyg log (Hicks and A. B. Hargreaves top-roped it again shortly after the first ascent), which had been at least a little overblown.

On 11 July, the day after the Lot's Groove climb, Menlove, Sandy Edge and Stephen Darbishire climbed Javelin Buttress and then Hicks' fine and unrepeated Holly Tree Wall Girdle, to which they added two significant variations. The first of these was a more difficult first pitch which was to provide the substance of Menlove's later route Balcony Cracks. The second was a better finish, up a line which was later claimed as a first ascent by A. J. J. Moulam, described as a separate route, and named the Rampart. Together the variations made the Holly Tree Wall Girdle into a much harder and more considerable climb, and perhaps set Menlove's imagination back to work on a project at which he had already nibbled, and which was to give him his first truly classic Welsh climb.

In fact, each of the next three days produced a very good new route. On 12 July, after a wet morning, he wandered up to Idwal and soloed up the Sub-Cneifion Rib, a 410-foot Very Difficult about which the modern guidebook enthuses in the following terms: "An elegant stairway to the delights above . . . positively idyllic."

The thirteenth of July saw Menlove teaming up with Stewart Palmer and acting on the cue given by Hicks' route to climb the East Wall Girdle, one of the classic expeditions on rock in Snowdonia—a gently rising traverse, entirely natural in character, unlike many other climbs of this type—which starts from the foot of Tennis Shoe and finishes, 500 feet higher, by the top pitch of Kirkus's Grooved Wall. It was done in boots, and in the rain. On the following day Menlove and Palmer motored over to Cwm Silyn, in the hills above the Nantlle Valley. Menlove had visited the place a fortnight previously, climbed the Overhanging Chimneys of Trwyn y Graig on a wet day with Edge and Darbishire, and noted the remaining possibilities on the Great Slab of Craig yr Ogof. The route he and Palmer climbed there on 14 July, Outside Edge, is probably the best of its grade in Wales. It is only Very Difficult, yet goes into situations normally reserved for climbs of a much higher standard. The style is delicate—open slab work at a steep angle, in positions of great exposure above the overhangs of the Ogof Nose. It was a fitting climax to the holiday. The next day the following note appeared in the log book at Helyg: "Foully wet, some rain every day this fortnight; usually much rain. JME." Menlove had gone home to dry out.

Weather-wise, 1931 was one of the bad years. It rained constantly from January to August, keeping the climbers off the bigger crags, holding back the development which had begun so promisingly in Wales in 1927 and continued through 1929 and 1930, with a brief pause for the wet summer of 1928. It seemed to have very little dampening effect on Menlove's enthusiasm, however, for he climbed almost continually throughout July and August in the post-examination period of student life. He was not at home for very long after returning from Helyg. A meet of the Liverpool club had been arranged at the Robertson Lamb hut of the Wayfarers' Club, in Langdale in the Lake District. Menlove and Bill Stallybrass did a number of the standard routes on Gimmer, Gable, Scafell and Pillar in the still-falling rain. One day they went to Dow Crag. Menlove set off to lead Roper's 1920 route in Easter Gully, the Black Wall. The rock was slimy with lichen and streaming with water. He knew little or nothing of the climb's reputation. Nor, at that time, did many other climbers. Roper had been one of those occasional meteoric figures who burn through the atmosphere of the climbing world and are gone, leaving little behind them but the glowing presence of one or two routes for futurity. In Roper's case, the two routes—Black Wall and Great Central Route, both on Dow Crag—were very formidable propositions in their day. Kirkus had already fallen off the easier pitch of Great Central Route. Black Wall had seen no further ascents in ten years. Today it is graded Hard Very Severe. Menlove set out on it in his nailed boots on a wet day, climbed up for 20 feet thoughtfully, climbed a little farther with difficulty, and ground to a halt by an overhang, unable to continue or retreat. Stallybrass had to make a rapid ascent of the nearby Black Chimney and lower a rope in order to rescue him, to an accompaniment of mutterings from climbers on nearby routes that "here was a chap who had not yet reached maturity of judgement". Menlove left the Lake District to return to Wales with his tail, for the first time, quite distinctly between his legs.

Arriving at Helyg on 31 July, hoping to meet Hewlett, he found the cottage empty, and so he walked down the road to the Milestone Buttress, where he soloed up the first section of Wall Climb. An easy ledge traverses round to the right at its top, but there was an alternative to this which he had looked at previously, a sharp-edged overhanging crack no more than 20 feet in length, but of ferocious appearance. He climbed it, and commented that "it overhangs a little and is unutterably adolescent, but it quite graces Tryfan". When Hewlett and Stephen Darbishire investigated the find the following March, they made the following note: "The above climb was attempted on a rope. GHDE met with success but SBD, owing to a slight error in his technique, was pleased to have the rope around him . . . we fear for the sanity of the discoverer!" Fearing for his sanity or not, Hewlett followed him up two new climbs on Glyder Fach the following day (Dr Alan Sutcliffe-Kerr, who joined them, remembers "following him up a first ascent of Chasm Rib, a Severe on Glyder Fach, while I was still in the tyro stage, on a very wet day when I positively enjoyed being on the receiving end of small stones and patches of moss dislodged by his gardening efforts"); and the second ascent of Kirkus's route on Craig yr Ogof's Great Slab the day after, on which latter Menlove made a quite independent left-hand variation of his own.

Hewlett left for home and Colin Kirkus arrived at Helyg that night. A. B. Hargreaves speculated, in his obituary of Menlove, about their partnership on the climb which this chance meeting produced:

I have often wondered what happened [when] Kirkus and Menlove joined together for . . . Chimney Route on Clogwyn Du'r Arddu. That must have been a most interesting party—a complete contrast of styles and temperaments, with Kirkus (rather the senior) suffering a most embarrassingly efficient and thrusting second. No wonder that between them they forced the "rickety innards".

Given the first ascent team—established star and young pretender— Chimney Route was obviously destined for a huge reputation, and it was held to be the hardest of the Clogwyn Du'r Arddu routes for several years. Nowadays, unrecognizably cleaned and sound, it seems very straightforward on a dry day at its Very Severe grade. But the wet conditions which Kirkus and Edwards encountered make a much greater difference than on most routes. Menlove's description is well worth quoting:

To the right of Pigott's is an obvious, deep crack, narrowing halfway up and then overhanging a bit. The route follows the crack throughout.

The whole climb is very severe and exposed, with one move based on [a] sod of doubtful stability. Opportunities for lateral deviation are strictly limited throughout. Gardening operations were carried out incessantly by the undaunted leader, for which reason he saw very little of No 2 beneath the sods. The cracks were greasy throughout and the leader wore stockings. Stances and belays are good, though not extravagantly so towards the top. The rock is excellent, bar the obviously rickety innards of the last overhang. There is no impurity except the piton, and that will be found quite susceptible of removal by even the weakest purist.

After finishing the route they met up with A. B. Hargreaves and Alf Bridge, who had been on Pigott's Climb. Kirkus had to go back to Liverpool, so the muddy and bedraggled Menlove joined forces with the other two and walked over to Dinas Mot, where they made the second ascent— the first without assistance from a second's shoulder—of Kirkus's Direct Route on the nose. Sitting on top of the cliff, they indulged in mischievous imaginings: "Would it not be nice magically to substitute that crack's pitch for its easy prototype on Hope, and watch for the results," cackled AB. In a thoroughly good humour, they arrived back at Helyg to find preparations for a rescue on Craig yr Ysfa in progress. The three of them set off straightaway. AB: "I still have a recollection of [Menlove] staggering up Pen Helyg under an enormous load of blankets and food." From the col above the cliff, they saw a light near the Amphitheatre and started traversing across the cliff face towards it. Inevitably, they got into difficulties, were forced to descend, and eventually arrived at the scene of the accident. The climber they had come for was dead. Menlove and Alf Bridge between them carried the body down to the road in Cwm Eigiau, their powerful shoulders working together in the torchlight AB used to guide them. After leaving the body in the care of the local police, they walked back over the Carneddau, reaching Helyg at eight a.m., where they slumped and slumbered on the turf outside. Alf Bridge had a vague memory of the arrival of General Bruce, and his savage onslaught against the massed ranks of carrion-seeking gentlemen of the press, before sleep overcame all.

Menlove stayed on at Helyg for a few days more. On 6 August he returned, with Sandy Edge and Andrew D'Aeth, to the Nose of Dinas Mot and climbed Western Slabs, a lovely open climb on the righthand edge of the buttress: "On the first pitch it is customary to start by going up to the right and scratching about a bit, before coming down to start again." Sandy Edge retired after the first pitch, protesting that Helyg food was about to mount up his gullet and choke him, whilst Andrew D'Aeth retreated from the second pitch, so Menlove was left to complete the climb alone.* To restore D'Aeth's confidence, however, Menlove then led him up the Direct Route, and followed this with what he described as "a pleasant girdle traverse of the Nose, at about Difficult standard", and later as "a nice Difficult with good rope-technique, but the technique is not absolutely simple, and one should remember when explaining it to the other man that a cord around the neck of a good knave is better than a ship's hawser about the belly of an ass".

In the present guidebooks, the Girdle Traverse of the Nose is graded Very Severe.

On 7 August, a final day's climbing produced two new pitches on the East Wall in Cwm Idwal, both done solo. Under very wet conditions, he had attempted to solo Hick's Rowan Tree Slabs, and not surprisingly had been repulsed: "So retired in disgust to gardening and grammar, i.e. two new pitches between the upper part of Grooved Wall and Ash Tree Wall."

Rain now intervened in earnest. The only available activity was to study the fauna of Helyg: "Saw Helyg Rat (?) in morning. All afternoon we heard its plaintive notes as it called to its young. No kill. 7.35 p.m. Colossal bang from trap, followed by painless shattering and speedy cremation of one very small mole." Or again, more curiously: "We were worried by a smell in the land so that we bolted and barred the larder door. But the din rose and rose and suddenly the sausages burst through with a crash in packets of six and it took twelve strong men of us to take and put them in the fire . . . there was a sort of green haze oozing out of the chimney and we took to the hills."

His mood became resigned to the vagaries of climate: "Ascended Tryfan by North Buttress under the usual conditions of heavy rain and mist. Torrential downpour has not yet ceased. We feel that our end is nigh." After another day or two of sitting it out in Helyg, chafing at the tedium of hut-life, finishing the stock of reading-matter and the store of food, he returned to Liverpool with a clear ambition in mind for what would be the most prestigious and public ascent of the day, and one which would firmly establish his climbing reputation.

This is a fitting juncture, before we come to this climb and the preparations for it, to look back over Menlove's novitiate and draw what conclusions we can from it. People's memories over a space of 40 or 50 years become indistinct. Until the record begins to be written, we are dealing not with facts

---

* The condition this climb was in for its first ascent may be deduced from the fact that, five weeks later, Colin Kirkus retreated from the second pitch and was forced to climb instead the West Rib, which nowadays is considered much the more difficult climb.

but probabilities, and these we compound with assumptions. The probability is that Menlove started to climb regularly and seriously on the outcrop of Helsby in the spring of 1930. His physique and his intellectual drive, both of which were extremely powerful, quickly allowed him to excel at the outcrop, and brought him to the notice of several of the day's leading climbers, who treated him with varying degrees of notice, condescension, and regard. Colin Kirkus and AB seem to have been especially helpful and kindly. Most probably through them he first heard of the important climbs of the time in Wales and, to a much lesser extent, the Lake District. In the space of an extremely concentrated year's climbing, he had managed to work his way through a good number of these: Purgatory, Belle Vue Bastion, Lot's Groove, Nose Direct. Only the vicissitudes of an exceptionally wet spring and summer had so far prevented him from making ascents of the new climbs on Clogwyn Du'r Arddu, but they were not to wait long. His own explorations had been rather scrappy at first, and of no great dificulty, but by the beginning of August he had contributed at least four classic routes to the Welsh repertoire: the East Wall Girdle, Sub-Cneifion Rib, Outside Edge, and Western Slabs. All four, in character, are delicate, airy, sound and delightful. If there were an exact science whereby character could be defined by the climbs it chooses to pioneer (the suggestion is not quite so absurd as it might appear, and will seem less so as his climbing career goes on), then Menlove's at this time could be thought stable, balanced, open and bravely straightforward.

As to his position relative to the other great pioneers of the time, it was still a little uncertain. In 1931 the revolution in Welsh climbing which had begun in the late 1920s had rather stuttered to a halt. Hicks, after a good season in 1929, had faded, and anyway always gave place to Kirkus. Jack Longland, the astoundingly gifted young university climber from Cambridge, although he had added Javelin Blade in 1930, which in retrospect seems the hardest pre-war route of its type, had graduated more into Alpine and Himalayan mountaineering circles and ceased to climb regularly in Wales. Kirkus was the man to whom most people now looked up as the leading climber of the day. It is easy to imagine the twenty-year-old Menlove, on a summer evening in 1930, sitting below the rocks of Helsby, which glow warmly red in the light of a sun setting out over Liverpool Bay. He is watching the slight figure of Colin Kirkus composedly, perhaps slightly awkwardly on occasions, dealing with the problems of, say, Wood's Climb. Kirkus is at the height of his powers, yet he stops at those difficult moves into the base of the groove—just as Menlove did a few minutes previously. He moves up, feels the holds, and moves down again. Just as Menlove did. And then he starts to climb, leaning his body out to the right, running his feet up, reaching up just a trifle hurriedly for those holds in the groove. "This is the man whose routes in Wales are beyond the capacity of ordinary mortals. Yet they are on rock, the same at this, and ... did he really do those moves any better than I did?" muses the watcher, before he turns his gaze out west to where the hills of Snowdonia are a faint band of darkness on the farthest horizon.

All this is speculative. To come back to facts, during the middle part of August 1931 Menlove was staying at home and going each day to the gymnasium beneath the Adelphi Hotel in Liverpool. Here he worked long and vigorously at circuit training aimed at improving balance and strengthening muscles. (Circuit-training for climbing was almost unheard of at the time, although Graham MacPhee, also based in Liverpool, was a devotee and may have given Menlove the idea.) One particular exercise he had devised was specifically designed to build up the muscles used in laybacking. After working out in the gymnasium he often went across the Mersey to Helsby, and one afternoon he led the Flake Crack—the first-ever lead of it, for since Marshall's death three years previously whilst attempting a lead it had been held in awe, and was considered not justifiable without the protection of a rope. As a layback, it is a very hard climb still, with the most difficult move being the actual reach for the top hold. To fall off from a layback position at that point, 50 feet up above steep ground and a very bad landing, could only have resulted in serious injury or death. Menlove's progress up the climb, according to observers, was smooth and unhurried. On the very last move, his hand on the finishing hold, he turned and smiled his pleasure to the terrified audience.

By the end of August, the weather had improved. Menlove paid a brief visit to Wales with Andrew D'Aeth, in the course of which he made second ascents of Rake End Chimney, thought to be one of Kirkus's hardest routes, and Hicks' very thin climb, Rowan Tree Slabs: "The last traverse was the hardest bit—a swing on small handholds to a distant foothold. Very delicate ... parts were wet and added much to the amusement." In company with Marco Pallis, the explorer and Buddhist scholar, Menlove then travelled up to Wasdale. Bill Stallybrass recalls meeting them at the top of Pillar on 29 August. Menlove and Marco had just climbed Route One, one of H. M. Kelly's classic harder routes on the cliff. Marco then set off for a walk and Menlove joined forces with the Stallybrass brothers to climb the slightly more serious Route Two. It had not rained for ten days, the rocks were as dry as could possibly be hoped for, and the weather was perfect.

The next day was a Sunday. Bill Stallybrass returned from an early morning bathe in Ritson's Force to be told that Menlove and Marco were on their way up to Scafell, to the Central Buttress, and wanted him to join them.

Central Buttress of Scafell was a focal point in climbing mythology at the time. Most of the Lake District faction still believed it to be the hardest climb in Britain. Put up in 1914 by Siegfried Herford, it had a commanding presence, took a fine line up the middle of the most impressive crag in the Lakes, involved some complex rope-work, human pyramids and the like, and was treated by everyone who climbed it with the very greatest respect. And rightly so, for it still is a powerful climb. Stallybrass now takes up the story:

I caught up with Menlove and Marco in Hollow Stones, where Alf Bridge, Maurice Linnell, and Alan Hargreaves had camped for the night, fearing that there might be a queue for "CB". Maurice and Alan were on the Oval, and Alf, resplendent in a red shirt, was already at the foot of the Flake.

(The Flake Crack is the crucial pitch of Central Buttress, and the one on which aid was then invariably employed.)

As we watched, he gripped the edge of the Flake, put a foot against the wall to start a layback, and slipped. Somehow he managed to hold on until he found a foothold—an extraordinary feat of strength. A few pungent words floated down to us. Then he started to put loops over the chockstone and completed the climb by the standard method of bringing Linnell up and over his shoulders.

Our party was soon on the Oval. As last man on the rope, I was carrying a spare 100-ft line. In my haste to catch up with the others, I had left my rubbers behind and was climbing in stockinged feet. At the foot of the Flake, Menlove quickly arranged some slings, called to Marco and me to change places on the rope and brought me up to him. Our whole performance was hair-raisingly chaotic. For some reason, I was still carrying the spare line. I gripped hold of Menlove's shoulders and we both swung out from the rock. He seemed to be only very loosely tied-in. My strength was by then running out. I seized hold of a spare rope which Menlove had secured to the chockstone and lowered myself until I could jam my body into the crack and take a rest. Menlove meanwhile was making fresh arrangements with the rope. Suddenly he called out: "I'm going to have a go!" Next moment he was laybacking steadily up the crack, unbelayed, and was soon at the top. It was an astonishing feat of courage after witnessing Alf Bridge's near-disaster. Marco and I both had ignominiously to be hauled up like sacks of coal.

Later Menlove admitted somewhat shamefacedly that he had been determined to do the climb unaided, but had felt obliged at least to make a show of giving me a chance to climb over him in the orthodox manner.

On hearing of the climb, Kirkus immediately wrote to him in the following terms:

Dear Edwards,   31 Aug 1931
    Congratulations on CB. It was a most marvellous achievement to lead the Flake Crack direct. Herford did it on a rope without, but even he failed to lead it throughout. I have sometimes thought of it, but I expect I would have funked the beastly thing when I got under it. To do it straight off without exploration was a most marvellous feat. Three cheers for the Climbers' Club!
    I did the continuation of our Clogwyn Du'r Arddu climb on Sunday with MacPhee. It was straight-forward chimney climbing, not very hard—nothing like the rest of the climb in difficulty. The nasty-looking block we saw was loose as the devil, but we managed to back up outside it without much trouble. The pitch above is an amusing 70-ft. chimney, deep-cut, dead safe, and not more than mild VD.
    We also did another short new climb, about 200 ft., near righthand end of E. Buttress. Had some fun with it.
    Could you tell me how you did the Flake Crack? Did you layback all the way from below the chockstones, or could you get on the chockstones without?
                                    Yours ever
                                    C. F. Kirkus

What kindly and appreciative character this letter reveals on the part of Kirkus! There is no arrogance or competitive edge to it, merely heartfelt congratulation, a request for information and a modest account of his own activity—which here includes, incidentally, the ascent of Pedestal Crack, the most technically difficult of his Clogwyn Du'r Arddu routes to date. It is the letter of a man unthreatened by competition because he climbs for the simple pleasures to be derived from the sport. Menlove obviously treasured it, for it is one of the very few papers of this nature which pass down through his estate.

As to the ascent of Flake Crack, this was a very considerable achievement. The team which had just failed to climb it was one of the strongest which could have been assembled at that time. All three of its members had very distinguished climbing records; all three would have been ranked amongst the top men of the day. Bridge's failure would necessarily have had some psychological effect on Menlove's party, for Bridge was reputed to be the most powerful of climbers, an immensely strong man who would have been thought as likely as anyone to succeed on this kind of route.

Menlove, Marco Pallis and Bill Stallybrass, by contrast—and through the disorganized impression they presented, with Stallybrass shoeless and the peculiar antics at the chockstone—must have seemed raw recruits, perhaps even a little presumptuous in being on what was reputedly the hardest route in a region which still, quite unjustifiably by now, regarded itself as being in a higher state of rock-climbing development than Menlove's usual scene of activity, Wales. Yet Hargreaves, Bridge and Linnell must have considered that the youthful team pressing hard behind them had a good deal of talent at its disposal—AB climbed regularly with Menlove and Stallybrass and had been impressed by both of them. Menlove, as well, was at the height of his form. He had been climbing almost every day for two months, training hard, and this route was at the centre of his ambitions. Despite the apparent chaos, he was psychologically prepared for it and right under a very critical public eye he brought it off. As a leading climber he had arrived.

A week later he underlined the fact with the first ascent of a ferocious crack near the top of the Direct Route on Glyder Fach. The Final Flake, along with the very different Javelin Blade climb done eighteen months earlier by Jack Longland, now ranks as the hardest pre-war pitch in Wales. Menlove's assessment of it was ". . . steep and exposed, probably Very Severe. It was done on a rope before leading; and, as it seems unavoidable to depend to some extent on strong fingers, this is probably an advisable precaution." Kirkus, in his guidebook, summed it up as follows:

> A layback of extreme severity, demanding both strength and skill in a high degree. For this reason a prior inspection on the rope is advisable before leading.

The modern technical grade given to the pitch is 5b, the adjectival grade an unequivocal Hard Very Severe.

CHAPTER FOUR

"But louder sang that ghost, 'What then?'" 1931–1934

THERE IS SOMETHING to be said for wholehearted commitment to a single course of action with a clearly defined aim. If nothing else, involvement in the struggle to reach the goal obviates the necessity for rational assessment of the course. Throughout the summer of 1931 Menlove had sweated, trained and climbed to establish himself amongst the leading climbers of his day. By the end of that season only Colin Kirkus was likely to be considered his peer, and the modest, gentle Kirkus was quite happy to concede to Menlove the palm. In one way, this is the end of Menlove's progress as a climber. For a year or two there was a certain amount of posturing, of exacting the tribute which was the just reward of the efforts he had made. Thereafter, his very marked climbing abilities he dismissed, preferring instead with a curious humility to exalt and encourage others whose attainments neither would nor could ever equal his own. This is to anticipate. The singular fact to be considered for the present is that Menlove will never again climb so intensely as he did in this summer of 1931.

The likely reasons for the hiatus which occurs in Menlove's climbing career between the late summer of 1931 and his next intensive phase of exploration in the spring of 1933 are four in number, each one of them for a time either sapping the energy at his disposal or waylaying his attention. In no particular order of importance they are: his work as a medical student; complexities arising in his emotional life; a crisis of conscience connected to a lessening of religious faith; and a vague dissatisfaction with the sport itself. There are two extracts which look retrospectively at his state of mind during this early period of his climbing. The editors of *Samson* put them together with several others under the title of "False Gods" and suggested they were "fragments of an unfinished article". They are extremely revealing, although Menlove's usual habit of self-disparagement should be acknowledged in them:

Napoleon would have made a fine climber. La Gloire, fame, he wanted, without worrying about what place it should stand on. Fame, glory, power, for his own person. If it were customary that it should come by arms and blood then arms and blood be it. If climbing were the fashion then climbing. He would have kept in better condition, too, that way, and he would have been good at it. The precise mixture of obstinacy, hatred of being beaten, inability to keep a sense of balance, and withal a certain considerable shrewdness and a very considerable feverish sort of energy.

The mixture of disapproval, joking (note the comment about balance) and admiration, awareness of the negative values implicit in the stance combining with a knowledge of its necessity to the individual who adopts it, is notable, and the next passage opens it out more fully:

There was once a man who desired glory more than he desired any other thing. But he found that honest glory was not easily come by, and if come by was too easily lost. But the feeling, in his memory, was still he thought the finest and best feeling he had ever experienced. A sport called rock-climbing promised him all the glory that he desired, and though requiring great energy it was very immediate and was certainly much easier in this sense than anything he had yet come across. It was an impersonal struggle making personal relationships much easier. He was modest at first: admiring with the oil of youth, skin red like the morning. With success his face and his muscles became full and strong, and his hair waved in the wind of the mountains. He got together a resolute band of adherents determined at all costs by turning a blind eye and by many other sacrifices to retain that glory. Where he had been restless he was now restful.

Though he stood still the world was restless around him and did not want his happiness. The advancing edge of it went on without him, continued, caught him up and passed him, and in doing so took a number of short cuts that he did not approve: and again the glory had departed. But in fact many had been there before him and the place was well-known, and that particular glory had in fact departed many years ago.

He pretended, forgetting his duty to his fellow. He thought; made passes with his hand over his head in various ways signifying doubt. And he went home and sang:

"Israel, Israel, thy high places, and in thy temples the moneychangers: they worship false gods, and the glory is departed."

So he sang to his own god and his voice heard around him was very beautiful like a sound in the wilderness. It was so beautiful that it was some weeks before he began to realise that he had been stupid again.

Still, climbing had advantages, though it was not all that he still liked to think it was. And as the years went on this man died and his friends with him. And the progression of events continued.

What is being talked over here is much more than the common feeling of dissatisfaction with a goal once it has been reached, but in an assessment of Menlove's state of mind during 1931 to 1932 it fits for the present to leave it at that, because we are seeking an explanation both for a period of relative inactivity, and for other aspects of his behaviour at the time.

The practical reasons for the temporary departure from climbing are strong, and best dealt with first. His work as a medical student demanded time and attention, and had been neglected for some months. He needed to get back to a routine of study. Although his capacity for work was never in any doubt, he does seem to have found it difficult at university. He complained that he did not find it easy to remember the lectures and text-book material, and felt oppressed by the assumption on the part of his family that he would perform brilliantly. Of himself, he held constantly to the view that he could never achieve more than moderate academic success. Nevertheless, throughout the autumn of 1931 and spring of 1932 he settled willingly back in to a regular pattern of attending lectures and revising past work for coming examinations.

Putting aside for the moment a temporary discontent with the nature of the sport and the fundamental necessity of getting down to a sustained bout of study, there is a strong probability that the period in question was one of emotional difficulty for Menlove. Whereas Stephen and Hewlett were both sociable and popular with the girls they met in their everyday life, Menlove had the problem of coming to terms with the fact that, physically and emotionally, he was attracted to people of his own sex. In 1931 the social and moral strictures upon homosexuality were harshly proscriptive. Not until the 1967 Sexual Offences Act were physical relationships between consenting adult males made unpunishable by law. In the 1930s they were very definitely thought to be a crime. In addition to his guilt in the eyes of the law, Menlove's religious background would further have increased his anxiety. The Church's attitude towards homosexuality was unambiguous. As late as 1953 Dr John Fisher, Archbishop of Canterbury at the time that Hewlett Johnson (with whom Menlove was then living) was Dean of that diocese, stated unequivocally: "Let it be understood that homosexual indulgence is a shameful vice and a grievous sin from which deliverance is to be sought by every means." We shall see in the next chapter that Menlove was to attempt to argue for tolerance and understanding of those whom society labelled inverts or deviants. For the present, we need to grasp the context in which Menlove had to contend with the awakening of erotic feelings towards his own sex. If we look back on Menlove's early life, whilst we may have little success in the attempt to accord its patterns and events with theories about the genesis of homosexual behaviour, of which probably none would gain widespread support,* we can at least say that the situations which may have stimulated or confirmed his bias were balanced by those which would have intensified the feelings of guilt consequent upon it. Menlove's eldest brother by this time was a curate in St Helen's, and although Stephen throughout his life acted in a manner of exemplary kindness and understanding towards Menlove, he belonged to a church the teaching of which could only have exacerbated the sense of guilt. Menlove himself was destined for medical missionary work and supported by the CMS. Father, grandfather, great-grandfather, second cousin, were or had been churchmen, and Hewlett was to be one too. If he could not reconcile his position by the most strenuous intellectual efforts, the alternatives were repression or a loss of faith. All this was coming about at a time when a young man looks out for a companion with whom to share his most intimate thoughts, fears, and ambitions. For Menlove, any such close friendship was to be of the most temporary kind, and the loneliness he endured dreadful to think of: "I'm not frightened of being alone, but I do not like not being anything else ever."

Very few writings survive from this period. There is one jotting which sounds to be that of a much older man than the twenty-one-year-old Menlove, but it can fairly certainly be dated to the autumn of 1931:

Look at that young person, young and beautiful walking in the Quad. Look. Three times—no, four times—in the last two years I have seen that person, what eyes, what skin. For two hours in the library once I sat opposite and watched those lips and those hands while studying, then I asked for a cup of tea together and I was refused. I was refused, but it did not matter so much for there was a smile for me of a kind that I cannot resist and there would be another chance, I thought; but there has been no other chance for the next three times.

It is noteworthy that Menlove does not refer to the gender of "that young person" in this passage. It is not a coyness on his part, but an act of self-protection and an indication, even in his most private writing, of the pressure he felt at this time towards concealment. The same quality is encountered in the following poem, which is also quite revelatory of

---

* "Perhaps it is as useful—or as useless—to talk about the 'causes' of heterosexuality as it would be to talk about the 'causes' of homosexuality." Leonard Barnett, *Homosexuality—Time to Tell the Truth*

Menlove's state of mind. Entitled "Recquiescat", it was written on the death of Kit D'Aeth, brother of one of Menlove's regular climbing partners, who was lost in Baffin Island when his compass ceased to function and he died of exposure amongst the ice:

> For us all is drifting endless
> To aims inknown and in an unknown being,
> In Time untimed, a Time, yet trendless.
> Is Fact the all, not seeing?
>
> We shift our brain to here and there to know
> And train and train our same old light
> Upon a captious craft. And so
> Our living is a bar to our sight.
>
> He in his life saw nothing dim:
> To him his life was sea and brine,
> An active living, free and fine,
> And death was free for him.
>
> He saw no fault in death to man,
> But saw more strength than most men can,
> He saw a pathway for immensity,
> Looked into eyes of Eternity.
>
> The sun's bare gleam was wrought and milled
> From actions playing over Fate,
> But night lies stilled by Truth fulfilled
> In paths secure and straight.
>
> There stands his soul in Avalon,
> Stands at the gateway to his past,
> From life's everted carillon,
> To see his self of God at last.
>
> His valley glists with golden mist,
> And on its side the shade is grouped,
> The dim enclosed, the silence stooped
> To him, his evening kissed.

By any objective standards of judgement this is an embarrassingly bad poem, affected, uncertain in its metre, rhythmically flat, banal in imagery, and far from accessible at times in its meaning. It is also very derivative from Tennyson. To dismiss it in that manner is to miss the point, for although it purports to be an elegy it tells us far more about its author than its ostensible subject. The latter is idealized beyond recognition, and serves as little other than a vehicle on to which are projected the author's yearnings for the solace, security and truth of death, which itself offers a welcome contrast to the uncertainty, hindrances, and futile efforts of the writer's experience of life. The penultimate stanza, with its odd echo from Ben Jonson ("The very thought everts my soul with passion"), glibly resolves the conflict between these two opposed states of being—life's tribulation and contingency and death's vision of Infinity and Eternity—by a romantic and mystical union with God, though more through the Blakeian notion of recognition of an innate deity than the traditionally theistic viewpoint.

The real oddity within the poem is its final stanza. It seems to be misplaced, is possibly of later date, and is much more opaque than the others in meaning. Its being appended as a form of envoi may imply that it represents something missing from, and vital to, the body of the poem, which appears to be complete without it. The sensuality of the first line and occurrence of the verbs "stooped" and "kissed" suggest a physical element. The "valley" of the first line is also a recurrent sexual symbol in Menlove's poetry, reaching its most overt expression in the lines:

> I knelt, then rich my gown I broidered, my cheeks
> Befitted him, and my head was hot, always,
>   for the valley.
> (From the poem entitled "I'll Tell You How")

That this stanza should prove so difficult of interpretation whilst the rest of the poem is relatively simple probably stems from what Menlove had to say here, and whether he felt he could say it openly. It is a fair working assumption that along with its rather vaguely apprehended images of farewell it contains a physical celebration of the young man—that there is a homo-erotic element here. Twentieth-century male poets had on occasion managed to write this type of poem—Wilfred Owen's "Futility" is a case in point—but it would even so have been masked by a sufficient pretext—war, in Owen's case. Menlove, with no such excuse, would have needed to code and suppress the sensual element of his celebration, and did so successfully enough to enable the casual reader to understand it as no more than a traditional, if slightly confused, group of stock images of death and farewell.

With this background material in mind—and it should be remembered that the attitudes under discussion cannot be seen to have clarified until after 1933—it is fitting to turn from a consideration of personality back to the practicalities of his climbing, and examine the new preoccupations and directions in that from the autumn of 1931 onwards. That it became more desultory and sporadic has already been hinted at, but it did not cease altogether, and the few visits he did make to Wales are a significant pointer to a new area of interest.

On 18 October 1931, with Selby Walmsley, he first visited the north side of the Llanberis Pass—an area with which Menlove was to become inextricably associated. Here, from an article in the 1934 *Climbers' Club Journal*, is his general comment about the first of the cliffs on which he climbed:

> The Llanberis Valley has produced a very good bit of rock in the cliff opposite Dinas Mot. It is variously called the Castle, Columnar Cliff, and some long Welsh name that I have forgotten meaning something fine and central in Welsh legendry that I just cannot place. Haskett Smith writes of this place with his usual acumen. "It is somewhere in this neighbourhood that we must look for the mysterious precipice of which Edward Llwyd wrote two hundred years ago as being strikingly columnar in structure ..." It is very striking. In another publication it was rightly advertised as "an excellent spot for the artist, gardener, or master plasterer". These last two are in reference to the fact that much of the structure shows a regrettably low degree of cohesion, especially with regard to the plants: not just dank, like the Devil's Pasture: it goes in for horticulture of a larger scale.

The route they discovered was Holly Buttress on Dinas Cromlech, nowadays graded Very Severe, but rather easier at that time because of the abundant and robust vegetation which grew upon it: "The name was due to the fact that, being the first climb on the cliff, they did not realise that there were prickly things to push through on nearly all the routes up it."

Menlove spent a further day wandering around the hillside of Esgair Felen, out of which juts Dinas Cromlech, in November, complaining petulantly to his companion "why must it rain?" as he pried amongst the hillside's many rocky bluffs to discover where the best rock for climbing lay. In December he made three further climbs on Dinas Cromlech, including two which are certainly amongst the most popular climbs in Wales today—Spiral Stairs and Flying Buttress —the latter climbed solo whilst on an LURCC meet at Helyg which lasted from 17–23 December. The name of the former route is not the one it was originally intended to bear. Menlove wanted to call it Sodom, but the Climbers' Club guidebook editor of the day (G. R. Speaker, who a contemporary notes "was something of a prig") jibbed at this, and it was changed to something more bland and respectable. The temptation to read much into this is obvious—it may have arisen from no more than a response to the names of Kirkus's Glyder Fach routes on the opposite side of the mountain. Kelly's routes on Pillar were also commonly known as Sodom and Gomorrah. On the other hand, it is unwise wholly to discount the possibility of Menlove testing out reactions here, trailing his coat at conventional sexual mores—particularly as we shall see shortly that this was possibly the time when the first of the serious love affairs of his life began.

To come to the LURCC meet, it appears that he had in the course of a year become perhaps a little impatient with his fellow members' more limited abilities. Of the Adam Rib in Cwm Du on Mynydd Mawr he had to say: "Quite a pleasant climb; though easy, it is steep and admirably loose." Roy Beard, who seconded him that day, has a different version:

> The first thing that I ever climbed in Wales . . . was the Adam Rib in Cwm Du. To this day I can remember very little about that climb except being jerked several feet into the air to induce me to make a start, for as far as I could see there was neither handhold nor foothold to be made use of.

Bill Stallybrass has a more general impression formulated about this time:

> . . . it became more accurate to describe him as a grass and heather climber. The simple enjoyment of climbing a classic route was sacrificed as being unworthy of a tiger. One of his affectations was to treat with lofty scorn any route that was considered "popular".

The very esoteric Adam Rib, originally climbed by Archer Thomson and consigned thereafter to more or less perpetual neglect—unfairly, incidentally—is certainly not as easy as Menlove suggests. A good severe is the most accurate grade. Its attraction for Menlove probably lay in its distance from the fashionable venues, and the exploratory nature of any visit to the crag on which it lay. It was certainly the latter urge which stimulated him to return three times during this meet to his new-found "Columnar Cliff", on two of which occasions he was alone. Whether this was out of desire, or a lack of willing partners to go to a piece of rock which did not accord with the mountaineering requirements of the day by leading to the top of a mountain, we do not know, but either are possible explanations.

Menlove's absorption in the north side of the Llanberis Pass cliffs did give rise to a good deal of comment throughout the thirties, some of it amusingly reactionary, and most of it viewing the activities as markedly novel.

In the course of this December meet, the other cliff which Menlove seemed to find initially alluring was the unspeakable Creigiau Gleision ("the younger") above Llyn Cowlyd. Stallybrass had recently visited the place and returned enthusing about its potential. It had the advantage of being an easy walk from Helyg, and on his first visit there Menlove picked off the only worthwhile climb on the cliffs—Anvil Cracks. He went back the day after this ascent for further exploration:

> Dec 20th. Wet. Creigiau Gleision the younger again visited in hopes of amusement. Nothing else over 50 ft, however, was found to be worthy of trial. Beyond Castle Buttress there are high cliffs, but until the forces of detrition, sunshine, and much weed killer have made themselves manifest, they would seem to be superfluous. Incidentally, after finding this we discovered the most unpleasant existing route up this side of the mountain.

After this experience he obviously found it necessary to redeem his faith in Welsh rock, and a subsequent day found him back on the East Wall of the Slabs, with its clean and pocketed rock, making an ascent of Heather Wall, accompanied again by a relative beginner. Compared to the meet of only a year before he was beginning to seem remote. His growing stature in the climbing world might explain this, or the rapid rate at which his skill was outstripping that of all his contemporaries. His attitude towards his fellow university students had become one of gentle mockery, as in this passage describing an attempt by Sandy Edge on the Holly Tree Wall Original Route:

> In the crack above the Holly Tree. Sandy was a strong young chap and he struggled furiously. First few feet . . . rests because you can't hand all your weight on a three-finger handhold without getting weary—poor chap had to have tea without sugar—his fingers were too tired to squeeze the sugar tongs and I couldn't be fagged to do it for him, but that's a digression. Sandy on the HT. In the course of time he learnt to do the first bit and then there was the next bit. He jammed a hand back in the crack and one foot, and then cautiously edging up the arm helped by the other hand, still stretched full out, he just reached a tiny hold, tightened up all his muscles to move the foot up, but he couldn't, the foot was jammed, the boot stuck, nothing doing. I won't say how often that happened: and at last worn out

he could stand it no longer. He reached down a hand and pulled hard at the heel of his boot. No. It wouldn't come, so desperate he reached down also with his other hand and pulled his best with both. Then the boot came out, and Sandy flew outwards and downwards: there was a terrific jerk on the rope . . . then a dead weight . . . not a sound. I called "Sandy, Sandy." There was no answer. What had happened? Was he injured, dead, perhaps pierced by the HT? But it wasn't that. He was all right: swinging quietly in the air: happy to be resting.

Once the meet was over, he did not return to Helyg for six months, and the only contact he had with climbing during this time was a brief excursion to the Waverley Hotel in Fort William at Easter organized by the Wayfarers' Club, a long-established and august body of mountaineering devotees mostly resident in the Liverpool area. The list of those who attended this meet reads like a *Who's Who* of thirties climbing: Bridge, Hargreaves, Linnell, Kirkus, Longland, Hicks, Pallis, Waller, Spencer Chapman, Bicknell, were all present. Longland made his notable winter ascents of Tower Ridge and the North-East Buttress. What Menlove did, no one can remember. He may, one of those present suggests from distant memory, have gone off by himself to Skye.

Menlove's main contribution to climbing in the first six months of 1932 lay in the preparation of a guidebook to the East Wall and Holly Tree Wall of Cwm Idwal. It appeared in the first issue of a new publication entitled *The British Mountaineering Journal*, and was to form the basis of his 1936 guidebook to Cwm Idwal. Some discussion of the Kirkus' vs. Edwards' guidebook strategies will come later in the book. For the present, it can be said that these two interim guides show Menlove's typical style already well developed. It is based on good, clear topographical writing, allied to an impressionistic sense of the feel of climbing on the cliff and generally understated or even affectionately deflating accounts of individual routes. It was an enjoyable style for those who could be bothered to read the sections in full and use them as the author intended. For those who wished merely to extract, and who relished the heroic accolade, it must have been a disappointment. What it did demonstrate more than anything else was the closeness of the author's knowledge of these cliffs, and the soundness of his judgements upon them. It is surprising how quickly with Menlove we come to accept and expect this surety of touch and maturity of vision with regard to his climbing. The guide is the work of a twenty-one-year-old and the product of a year's acquaintance, yet there is no axe-grinding or skimping. The knowledge is thorough, the judgement fair throughout, and not a trace of exaggeration or hyperbole anywhere.

His examinations in June over, Menlove returned to Helyg after an absence of many months and attempted to take up again on the rock where he had left off the previous year. He, Stallybrass and Walmsley went to Dinas Mot and attempted the Nose Direct. Menlove was very much off form, Stallybrass quite well on form. The former's failure became the latter's success. The party repaired to the Tyn y Coed hotel for celebration or consolation, as best suited the case, and afterwards wrote the following joint account:

> Dinas Mot, Nose Climb. Below the corner at the top of the 2nd pitch the leader found himself in such a position that he was unable to advance and unwilling to retreat. The doughty second, however, sped rapidly to his assistance, finished the pitch and heaved with a will upon the rope. Thence the party looked at the traverse of the Direct Finish and went up the easy finish, using combined tactics where possible.
>
> The party then ascended the Cracks climb, the leader leading, the second was second and of course the third, third. We have just been to the Tyn y Coed so please excuse.

Most climbers suffer variations in form and enthusiasm throughout their life and Menlove, as one of his best-known essays, "A Great Effort"*, clearly shows, was no exception. There are not always tangible reasons for such vagaries, but nevertheless Menlove's enthusiasm during the six weeks of sunshine which he spent in Wales this summer does seem to have been surprisingly lacking, despite considerable inducements to climb. From 19 to 26 July, for example, both he and Colin Kirkus were staying at Helyg, Kirkus without a climbing partner, yet Menlove could not be tempted on to the rock. His sole record of a week's holiday is "many bathes and much new water covered".

If we put together all the evidence we have, it does suggest an explanation which is tentative, but at least plausible, for this inactivity. We know that Menlove had several significant love-affairs in his life. By a process of elimination we may surmise that his first relationship began late in 1931 and continued through most of 1932 to end, or rather tail off slowly, in the early part of 1933. During late 1931 and for some time in the summer of 1932, Menlove was in Wales quite frequently with a non-climbing companion and doing nothing much other than sunbathing, swimming and so on. For a brief time, particularly in the spring of 1933, his devotion to these pursuits seems to have verged on exhibitionism. Sandy Edge remembers Menlove lying naked on the Luncheon Boulder at Cwm Silyn one March day, and David Cox adds the following reminiscence:

---

* Reproduced in the Appendix p.280

I met Menlove for the first time, on my first Oxford University Mountaineering Club meet at Helyg in March 1933. This was memorable, because at about 10 pm (in March) a man walked into the hut stark naked and dripping wet, and borrowed a towel; he had just arrived from Liverpool and had gone down to bathe in the stream before bothering to come into the hut. It emerged presently that this was Menlove . . .

Now nude bathing was very much the norm of the time. (David Cox himself has some smiling reminiscences of mixed bathing in this manner with the Mallory sisters in Llyn Du'r Arddu, and in Llyn Cwm Ffynnon during Geoffrey Young's Easter Parties at Pen y Pass: "Oh, the convention was that the women stayed at one end of the lake, you went round to the other, and you just didn't look." Jack Longland too recalls that "nude bathing was very normal. At Quy, near Cambridge, with Geoffrey Young we used to stand up naked and still if women appeared at the other end of that beautiful long pool. There were usually some pretty well-known homosexuals in the swimming party—or at least fashionable bisexuals—but that wasn't the point of the exercise.") Nevertheless, Menlove's fondness for appearing unclothed in public situations at this time was sufficiently marked to attract the written notice which suggests that it was beyond normal bounds, and it could possibly have had an erotic element in it.

Whether or not this tentative suggestion that Menlove's first love-affair took place at this time is correct is perhaps not unduly important. At this distance, nothing can be ascertained. But love-affair or not, it is very odd that Menlove should have spent so much time in North Wales with apparently so little urge to climb. He was virtually the top climber of the day, and in various indirect ways proud of the fact. Most of the other climbers of his day would have given a great deal for the opportunity to spend four or five weeks in Wales at a time when the average annual holiday was a fortnight. His inactivity could almost be seen as the absence of some vital force. Or more tenuously, the refusal as established top performer to maintain his drive perhaps paralleled his failures to embrace those other areas which might have both complemented and threatened his status and self-image: the Alps, and scholarship. This is for the future; for the present, we might hope that there were some uncomplicated sunlit moments of pleasure for him to store up against the bleak years to come.

By the beginning of August, Menlove's companion had left. Still not interested in climbing, he spent most days swimming in the sea or across any available lake: "Observed JME crossing the Llyn with lusty stroke." One day he and Kirkus "played at white horses off Llanddwyn Island".

Roy Beard recollects a similar day in the same spot:

> For a man who was such a good climber and so physically fit he had an
> inordinate love of sweet cakes, and one of our relaxations, when he had a
> motorbicycle, used to be to go to Llanddwyn Island and bathe on my part,
> swim on Menlove's—vast great feats, out towards the Cormorant Island
> and back again in perilous seas, or so they seemed to me. Having reached
> land we ate the sweet cakes which we had brought across the dunes; there
> was no road to Llanddwyn in those days.

Llanddwyn is a narrow promontory spearing out into Caernarfon Bay
from the West Coast of Anglesey, the Cormorant Island a jagged reef
something over 100 yards out to sea from the tip. The channel between the
two is scoured by strong currents and the promontory lies in the face of the
weather. It would be a very frightening proposition to swim out to the
Cormorant Rock with any sort of sea running.

As August progressed, Menlove became more and more lethargic, content
with ever-smaller diversions:

> Aug 13th. Rat trap set cunningly. One small rat found dead in it.
> Aug. 14th. Rat trap cunningly set. One small rat died therein.
> Aug. 14th (Afternoon). Trap boiled, baited, and a bit bent. Found later—
> one small rat dead upon it. Helyg is now a scene of feverish haste,
> preparing for battle. Who knows . . .?

A few more days of putting things off, gorging himself with food, and
finally on 17 August, he forced himself into a climb. You can hear the joints
creak in his description of it—Procrastination Cracks on Glyder Fawr's
Grey Wall, still considered to be one of the harder Very Severes in the
Ogwen area:

> The leader, in his depraved, dilapidated and diseased condition, thought
> it was Very Severe but both cracks were very wet and gardening would
> make it nicer. The rock is excellent, no vegetation need be used if it were a
> bit more gardened, and anyhow 'tis but mud even now and only a thin
> layer. The problems are of varied type and continuous interest in a long
> and tortuous pitch. No problem that the cliff really offers is attacked
> where it threatens to become energetic or nasty.

In Menlove's 1936 Cwm Idwal guide he downgraded it to Severe. In the
1974 guidebook it appeared at Hard Very Severe. Thereafter, food and

indolence for another week, until the arrival of W. R. Reade and Geoffrey Bartrum, two of the grand old pioneers of Welsh climbing whose heyday had been in the first decade of the century. A rapport seems very quickly to have been established between Menlove and these two much older men. They certainly revitalized his interest in climbing, and the kindly regard they showed to a man who much of the time craved little more than that in his dealings with the world is one of the most heartening things in this story. They provided him with a sense of history and continuity, of belonging to a lengthy tradition. They were friends of Geoffrey Winthrop Young's and introduced Menlove to that charmed circle. They responded to and drew out the sense of the inherent comedy in human actions which was so characteristic of Menlove in his brighter days. They brought to his attention specific new areas for exploration, and keenly supported his interest in others he had already found. Reade, of course, was one of the most distinguished early Welsh pioneers. Here is Geoffrey Young's sketch of him:

Of the new figures associated with ... the beginning of Pen y Pass, W. R. Reade has perhaps not received the credit due to him, and which his self-effacement avoided. His was a steady influence, bridging the generations and the years. Lean and bony and hard-featured, with a short crop of greying hair and a smile that warmed the heart, he had much of Franz Lochmatter in his make-up: the same short body and long steely legs tapering to small feet, the same tentacular movement on rock, with the same composure and tranquil independence of others. He was only interested in new climbs: Jordan on the Pillar, the Central Cracks on Lliwedd, the outside route on Crib Goch pinnacle, with a mute preference for disappearing down the Llanberis Pass with anyone he could persuade to join him in explorations on the Columnar crags. As often happens with his type of mountaineer, probably a good deal that he did went unrecorded because he felt it to be incomplete. Geoffrey Bartrum had joined him, and shared in many of his pioneer climbs. While Reade's unobtrusive influence did much, both before and after the First World War, to advance younger climbers in Liverpool and the north, Bartrum, through the years and the Second World War, acted as genial counsellor in the south ...

Theirs was a long partnership, of imperturbable good humour. I realised it first when I watched them from the Lliwedd Bowling Green, worming up the slabs below, by what is now called Reade's Crack. It happened that Conor O'Brien and I twice worked out new routes, one up these slabs and another up the outside of the Crib Goch pinnacle, only to find that the pair had been before us, and that we had made two more of what Archer Thomson called "second first ascents".

Reade and Bartrum's arrival roused Menlove from his lethargy sufficiently for him to make the long slog up to Glyder Fawr's Upper Cliff, in company with Frank Reade, WR's twelve-year-old son, with whose charge Menlove had been entrusted for the day. Paying scant attention to the established pieties, which decreed that beginners were taken on safe and easy known routes, Menlove embarked on the first ascent of a route at which he had probed the previous year. Perhaps he had noticed, on his ascent of Procrastination Cracks the previous week, that the line of Grey Slab was dry at last. Here is the modern guidebook assessment:

> This long narrow slab is a route with classic qualities, and should not be treated too lightly. Its rough, textured surface is deeply indented with holds, but these are only thinly spread, and the top pitch is a bold lead, particularly the upper stretch, where water is often encountered when one is thoroughly committed.

For a long time, this climb was notorious for having the two longest consecutive pitches on any British rock-climb—120 feet and 150 feet respectively. It has always been considered a good Severe—Hard Severe is the present-day grade. It was Menlove's third route since the previous December, done in company with a young boy. To whom, according to Menlove, he turned round when he was at the top of the 150-foot pitch and shouted down: "Lean out from the wall and walk up it. I'll pull." When telling the story, of which he was immensely proud, he used to say that Frank enjoyed the ride.*

As a sign of pure independence of spirit and confidence in his own powers as a climber, it really is striking. It naturally drew upon him a considerable amount of disapprobation. Reade's comment is not on record, but I suspect the gesture won his sneaking regard. If so, he showed it in a comical manner. Reade was the man who, in 1898, had ascended the Devil's Kitchen for the first time as a normal rock-climb. He now introduced Menlove to the place. (Jack Longland notes that "WR was essentially unselfish and generous. He was always anxious to egg young climbers on to go beyond the remarkable routes he had earlier done.") In the intervening years between his ascent and 1932, the only other features to have been climbed on these very extensive cliffs were three obvious gully lines. The cliffs had an evil reputation. The rock was held to be rotten, which it often is. It was thought to be wet and vegetated, which is also true; and it was generally dismissed as not being for

---

* It has emerged recently that Menlove's was in fact a "second first ascent", the climb having been done by a Rucksack Club party two months previously.

those of sound mind: which is to take a stance something akin to a belief in sympathetic magic. The great buttresses at the head of the cwm have a strong atmosphere. To this day it is easy to understand the supposed reaction of the landing party from a ship in Conwy Bay, sent to find the source of the clouds which always boiled over the mountains, who are said to have glimpsed the dark cleft in these plutonic rocks, seen the cloud welling up out of it, and fled in abject terror, believing they had seen the very kitchen of the devil.

Realizing that the gully era was long gone, Reade set his young friend on to one of the buttresses—the largest and most central of them, that between the Devil's Kitchen and the Devil's Staircase:

> W. R. Reade and G. Bartrum tried to make a poor young innocent climb the nasty buttress between the Devil's Kitchen and Staircase. He found just exactly how horrid it was and screamed for help: the two aforesaid wandered slowly round, hit him on the head with the rope, let him tie on, and played him up the last 70—80 ft. Rewarded him with four small squares of chocolate.

That was not the end of the saga; after a day recuperating, Menlove returned:

> The aforesaid innocent was now made to lead it. Done unroped in preference to the weight necessary otherwise. Encouragement and threats from WRR and GB above.
> Standard—Severe, possibly Very Severe considering the nasty nature of both rock and grass—latter probably preferable—also the exposure, which becomes considerable towards the top.

An almost symbiotic relationship developed from this point onwards between Menlove and the Kitchen cliffs. Whether or not he saw in these buttresses and damp grooves, which patently would never become fashionable, and were built of fissile rock and unregenerate grass in equal measure and vying in their states of decay, an objective correlative to his own condition of mind, we cannot know. Did he equate their rottenness with his own feelings of guilt about his homosexuality? Was there some degree of auto-suggestion in his attraction to them—subconscious acceptance of the received opinion that he who climbed here could not be of sound mind? It seems a fanciful idea, but the fact of the obsession, right down to his last holiday in Wales only a few months before his death, remains. One or two new routes here would be understandable, but so many and spread over 25 years constitutes an enigma. In some sense, Menlove surely found in these cliffs a dark mirror held up to his own character, into which the climbs done here were glimpses taken at times of stress. Consider the following short extract:

> The rock: it knows what I feel. It might feel the same itself. Some great force, a force partly of its own making, has trodden on it, scarred it, planted heavy grass to wave on it, and left it there to carry on and forge yet more of the same force.

(A similar identification with the rock and mountain landscape occurs in the poem "You rock, you heaviness".) There are few places in the Welsh mountains with a more intense feel of the plasticity of all substance under natural forces than the Kitchen cliffs; few places so carved, riven and groined by geological movements; few places where the evidence of immense powers at work is so manifest. The possibility of the suggestion remains open, and even gains slight support from the fact that, in his happiest days, he did not go near the place.

Much of this pertains to the future. For the present, Reade and Bartrum departed, leaving Menlove to ponder on rats. Two more were caught before A. B. Hargreaves arrived and took things in hand. Menlove was hustled down into the Llanberis Pass by the little man. To revenge himself upon this enthusiasm he chose to climb on what is, under normal conditions, undoubtedly one of the most unappealing rock-faces in Britain—Craig y Rhaeadr. Its central wall is steep, seamed with overhangs, a uniform muddy-brown in colour, and offers itself up to the attention of a substantial waterfall. Menlove and AB took a line by a pedestal on the left of the face, traversed a ledge directly in the line of the waterfall, and finished up the groove on the right by a pitch 180 feet in length.

> It was expressly arranged that the climb should be done by leading through, but owing to the distribution of difficulty JME was able—with some low cunning—to snaffle the titbits. All present thought it was very nasty of him, and so a public apology—If an umbrella is carried it will enable more than the few—
> It will be found that if touch is lost at the top it will be simple to go round to the bottom of the cliff and see what no 2 really is doing.

Menlove duly made his apology by accompanying AB to Cwm Silyn the next day and seconding him on Kirkus's Upper Slab climb, which Hargreaves led in stockings and Menlove followed in his hobnails. It seemed to leave Hargreaves in a quandary as to which was preferable—to have Menlove as a second, or to have him hogging the lead:

As a second he was bad—at any rate to me. I don't mean consciously and deliberately, but one felt that he was thinking, "Why is that little man being so slow up there, making such a fuss about the wind and the rain? I could be doing it much better" (and he was quite right). But clearly he was far more interested in new possibilities round about for future reference than the responsibility of seconding up existing climbs.

Menlove was not always quite so bad a second as Hargreaves here suggests. He was probably less than wholly attentive because he had considerable faith in AB's ability as a leader. It should be remembered that at this time, when protection techniques were rudimentary or non-existent, great store was laid on the responsibility of the second to his leader. (Menlove neatly parodies this in a passage given below.) AB's judgement would then have sounded far graver than it does now. One point he raises which is unquestionable, though, is that of Menlove surveying the pioneering possibilities round about. The outlook from the Upper Slab is on to the vegetated, broken, and shadowy Western Cliffs of Cwm Silyn, and in a few months' time Menlove returned to climb two routes upon them.

Menlove's indolence won the day following the Upper Slab climb—AB tersely records their activities in the hut-book as "'nowt". But AB did not allow another day to elapse without some exercise. In Ivan Waller's Alvis they drove down to Cader Idris and "revelled in the joys of—vegetation", climbing the Great Gully of Craig Cau, and observing at close quarters the famous Pencoed Pillar climb of the early pioneers: "a nasty looking place—no harm in trying it, (in crampons, perhaps?)". Not even Menlove returned there.

The rest of his climbing for 1932 was negligible. December was cold, with snowfall early in the month. He climbed the line of High Pasture on Glyder Fawr, describing it in his first ascent note as "... the long grass slope immediately to the right of Central Gully. We believed that it had not been done or at least not recorded and certainly feel that it should be noted as belonging to that order of climb which, while thoroughly easy and straightforward, have some points of entertainment value, and are not entirely lacking in motif. It is well worth doing when it is very cold and icy and when nothing difficult is wanted, and possibly a little practice in easy grass work. Even motoring gloves need not be removed and an ice-axe may add something of difficulty to the work encountered."

During a third December meet of the LURCC at Helyg, he climbed the Central Gully of Glyder Fawr under snow and ice conditions with Roy Beard, and made "various other expeditions of a like nature". The newly-opened youth hostel at Idwal Cottage provided a focus for the small

Liverpool group's social activity, the warden hospitably entertaining them with strange combinations of food—plum pudding and pickled onions most notable amongst them. One of the fellow students on this meet was a young man, also a member of the Wayfarers' Club, who, like Roy Beard, was studying architecture and was later to set up a successful practice in Liverpool. His name was John Sheridan, and in the course of those few days at Helyg he and Menlove made plans for the first of the latter's important marine adventures. Shortly after Christmas, on Menlove's motorbike, they rode up to Arisaig in North-West Scotland, with the intention of hiring a boat there and rowing across the twelve miles of open water to the island of Skye. Perhaps fortunately, no boat was forthcoming in Arisaig and they were forced to ride the eight miles north to Mallaig, whence the crossing to Skye was no more than five miles, and in a more amenable direction, going with the south-easterly gale which had blown up rather than across it as would have been the case from Arisaig. In Mallaig they did manage to get a boat, and set off for Skye, landing in a rock inlet between Calligarry and the Aird of Sleat. The exploit was described in detail by Menlove in the 1935 *Wayfarers' Club Journal*, and is well worth quoting in full. It is entitled "Little Fishes":

"In the Wayfarers' Club everybody is fashioned by both nature and training to be almost imperishably tough and durable. It is said that a member can be left out for 48 hours in a thunderstorm without commencing to look sodden; snow is resisted in a like manner for a period almost as long. This is probably due, as already hinted, to the possession or acquisition of a quite extraordinarily hard skin or exterior. The thing is done, of course, to act as a protection during the usual round of Wayfaring ambitions which can, as we know, lead one into the most unpleasant and hazardous procedures. The toughened epidermis is of great assistance in disregarding this unpleasantness itself, and, in short, once acquired it is undoubtedly a factor of much value in all sorts of conditions that a Wayfarer is likely to meet with in life.

"All this is not in doubt, but for some of us it remains unhappily true that our resistances tend frequently to flag a little. Especially in the winter does this happen; there comes a time when we weaker brethren find our skins to cry aloud against the eternal tirelessness of hard weather on the hills and our muscles to grumble against the cold calculating force of gravity as we move up, or even, alas, down the slope. Climbing is not so bad perhaps as walking, but what comfort is there out on the rocks in the rain. We curse the day that put us in this fine modern exacerbation of self-assertion. Then out of the sublime depths of our racial and our personal past there rises to comfort us a vision of water: a swelling rolling hand that supports us without effort, lifts us without strain. Wayfaring over a motion of water. It would be so much better.

"It was water that took us to Arisaig. Technically speaking, we went there on a motor-bike but, more accurately—after Fort William—there being much water on every hand and the roads good and wet, our motion was that of skidding over to Arisaig. It was a large bike and had a very special kind of pillion seat, with springs which held up to 13 stone. We had a rucksack with over 3 stone of luggage in it and, as I was driving, my friend carried this. We had made Fort William the day before, direct from Liverpool, and I was very tired and sore when we reached Arisaig. I wanted a rest. The whole drive had been made infinitely more awkward by my friend, who, though a supple athletic figure of not much over 10 stone, did not seen happy on the palatial pillion seat and was very unsteady. This is rather beyond the main narrative, but I mention it to illustrate the truth of my previous remarks. Out of the subliminal past rose irresistibly to us the vision of water. We wanted a boat and preferably with a supple seat. We had no cushions, but we could pad it with sweaters, and we had anyhow this overmastering urge to float, to be rocked on the cradle of the deep for a time, and rocked very gently.

"It appears that man is destined in all his efforts to a high degree of disappointment. We could get no boat, and we had to walk all over Arisaig trying to find one. In our lodging we had a wretched little wooden chair in a wretched little room and we had to sleep on the floor of the same room. The dining table was not a big one and accommodated only two legs and one small set of eatables at a time. Meal after meal we had to break up our fried egg on the table and then take a pair of grim Scotch sausages on to the floor. It was the New Year season. Can it be wondered that an urge at first somewhat locally inspired in us spread its insistence up the back even to the jaws? During the brief, uneasy snatches of sleep that we dragged out in the difficult chains of the night, we dreamt always of the sea and of the soft waves of ocean.

"But the boat eluded us. We went first to John Macdonald, a grey-haired veteran of the clan. He said no, but *old* John Macdonald next door had a boat that might not be in for the winter. He himself had a nice boat, but it was probably *old* John Macdonald we would want. Oh yes! A good boat, but it was up for the winter of course. And it did not come out as quickly as that. The Macdonalds of Arisaig are no chickens: they are tough old sea-dogs and they speak slowly round the point. We had not quite realised, indeed, at this stage, that all the inhabitants of Arisaig were Macdonalds. True, we did later find one or two young Campbells about the place, but for dwelling purposes it was apparently felt that these folk should keep their houses over at Back o' Keppoch. The Macdonalds of Arisaig, loyal always to the ancestors, mystified the heathen also by keeping to a standard system of family names. Not absolutely rigid indeed, for in their love of originality and variety these dear old men called some of their children John and others John Duncan (Dinkun). They themselves of course had one of these names and usually rejoiced to hand on this variation to the first male child and sometimes also those following. With all this wealth of terminology at their command these Macdonalds were not, it seems, entirely satisfied with their system of nomenclature. They must needs add the soubriquet 'young' or 'old' in certain cases. It is hardly necessary to add that once a Young Macdonald always a Young Macdonald. They were true to their system. In the same way (we were able to verify this by personal observation) a Macdonald might be able to become Old Macdonald really very early in life, in fact as soon as such further definition might be considered desirable. Thus it came that either name might be applied to the elder couple, or the second or third generations of sons who were living with them—each or all. Again accuracy was added to accuracy by specifying John Duncan Macdonald (the Duncan sometimes omitted for brevity), son of John Macdonald, or, it might be, John Duncan. Sometimes they added John Macdonald, Up or Down, the Street, and these terms, being used properly as names, were applied according to individual custom and desire rather than the precise slope of any other question. Actually it happens there is only one real street in Arisaig and that goes down in two places near the middle. Yet even with this array the painstaking seamen occasionally found that precisely the same name might occur more than once, applied to different persons, in so large a community. They therefore accented sometimes the first, sometimes the last and sometimes the Duncan part of the complex. After relation of all this detail and accuracy of definition, it says much for the Macdonalds that the strongly individual strain of the Scot still shone through. Undismayed by technicalities and terms and true to the whimsical caprice that has made the Highland character famous, they refused to accept the dull monotony of accenting always the same name in the same individual.

"I mention all this because the system did aid us greatly, once we understood it, in finding the next person required. One simply went from door to door asking. Owing to the fact that frequently there were two or more separate families in each house, it was as well to take the precaution of asking again at the back door after being repulsed at the front. It is rather an amazing tribute to Highland hospitality that they always knew at once whom we wanted. 'John Macdonald?' they would say, 'No, it is Jóhn Macdonald here, it will be John Macdónald you are wanting.' All this, interspersed with a great variety of detail as to parentage and clan, with age, as to young or old, and dwelling place, as to next door, or up or down the street. The phrase 'next door' is a good-sounding one that was often found useful and answered well to most situations in Arisaig. It is not intended as having any definite meaning other than perhaps to indicate that the person referred to was not one of the Campbells of Back o' Keppoch. True to their staunch name, if ever a Macdonald did mean Campbell of Back o' Keppoch, he said so straight out and no mincing.

"As for the boats, there were a few out on the loch, for, winter or summer, storm or fine, these grand old men went down to the sea in boats and sailed out over the water engaged in the staple industry of Arisaig, namely winkle fishing. The winkles, we gathered, were tough little brutes to capture. They lived under the water at high tides and the men carried their lives in their hands as they had to scramble over the treacherous, weed-laden rocks of the lower tide levels. Winkles also, we heard, delight in a full moon and the moon being new just then, and the tide in at midnight, we found that the trade was for the time being stagnant and the boats mostly out of use. The nights were quiet at Arisaig pending a fresh bout of winkles.

"But for staying out over the nights none of the boats could be had, even for much money, neither on the first nor the second day of asking. Love does not wisely enter the consideration in Scotland. Thus, as the mists of evening folded frostily over the water, in grim silence we prepared ourselves for another night sleepless on the cold stone floor. Extinguishing our solitary candle we laid us down gently upon our backs and as our heads touched and balanced on the hard surface, at once there came again the dull rhythmic thuds of the wee Highland bairn as he made his joyless play in the attic over our heads. Night had come.

"A storm got up that night. The wind stiffened to a strong gale, setting from the south-east, towards the islands. We put on our heavy coats and sat down to an Arisaig breakfast with the wind howling. It looked like rain and we told each other to be prepared against a spot of weather. We did not want to be out walking in it, not in Arisaig, so we put on our sadly inadequate leggings and urged ourselves on to the motor-bike. Every muscle gave a little shriek of dismay and then settled down stiffly into position. The eight miles to Mallaig went unspoken and there we got a boat. At first we did not know why we should be allowed to take it. We bundled straight in and round the pier. The boat was lazy in the little harbour waves: too old it seemed, and sodden, to rise to them; indeed on looking again at it we saw that the boat-builder of Mallaig had known what he was about. There were also three oars and all had bent in their time and bent widely, beneath the stress of circumstances. If they bent any more they would certainly break across. The seats were thin and hard. Then the wind took us and we got among waves. John Sheridan was in the stern and spread his ample oilskins to keep out the white horses. They came and climbed up his shoulder, then with a gurgle of displeasure slid along the length of the boat, spilling a little over the edge. We baled them out again. Two fishing boats came out after us, but we sent them back about their business and continued in the direction of Skye, though trying to make south round the end of Sleat, rather across the waves. The waves got larger and the boat more full. We had to let direction go and content ourselves with keeping reasonably well above the waves. The sky was a dirty, dull colour, and even the bubbles of the white horses took on the grey. The only relief was the dead white line of spray breaking on the Skye coast. We kept straight on, seeing no harbour and the white grew bigger and less even. John went in front, and the wind took the stern and swept us broadside in the wash, with the waves curling over. We spotted a ten-foot cut channel through the rocks just as we were on them and, with a hectic jerk, shot through into a natural harbour.

"We stayed on Skye. It was a barren land containing whisky, which they called Highland hospitality, and it is true that if once they say 'd'ye taste?', they make you go right through with the bottle. In three days we tottered off Skye leaving our boat behind us. When we reached Mallaig there was a grey pall hanging over the island, peering dimly through the storm mist and we had forgotten something of our mere muscular and cutaneous discomfort. The pall had the appearance of a tall, thin bottle lying on its side and showing evidence of a bad spill at the Point of Sleat end. As it looked across at us there was no love in its eye. It had all that quality of casuistic cunning that characterises the Highland cat at his courting.

"We pushed the bike off and, as the rain streamed down, we were yet glad and spat out little snatches of song from under our single pair of goggles. Happily we were still unaware that our fine bike was destined to break down and die long before we reached the warm, soft Southland."

It should be said that to take to sea in an open rowing boat in a winter's gale is an unusual and hazardous enterprise, the scale of which is very much played down in this essay. Implicit in the portrayed stance of the fishermen of Arisaig is the considered opinion that what Menlove and John Sheridan were planning either could not or should not be done. By their own lights, the fishermen were right, as is most evident in the happening upon a ten-foot channel through the rocks on the Skye coast, which was both fortunate and fortuitous. It does seem that any argument based on reason and security would elicit from Menlove the most strenuously testing response. He had as much faith in such accepted beliefs as he did in the idea that winkles delighted in a full moon. What adventures like rowing to Skye in midwinter and the swimming exploit of the coming Easter represents is the desire for rational proof—untainted by fear, prejudice, or feelings of inadequacy masquerading as the voice of reason. Menlove was not going to believe that a thing was impossible until he had seen for himself, and it has to be said that on this occasion he was quite lucky to emerge unscathed, and sufficiently convinced for the moment not to want to row back to the mainland. Another element is undoubtedly the *kudos*, the feelings of superiority, ensuing from proving the established authorities wrong. Possibly also the venture was suggested by the Scottish adventure novels of Robert Louis Stevenson, which Menlove had read avidly as a schoolboy at Fettes.

One final point to be made about "Little Fishes" is that its first four paragraphs hint at an awareness of Freud's thanatological and Jung's archetypal writings, but it would be unwise to make too much of this here because, whilst the date of the events described is known, the date of composition may have been considerably later, at a time when Menlove was involved in psychiatric studies which would have included reading analytical psychology and psychoanalytical writings. More typical of Menlove's thinking at the end of 1932 and beginning of 1933 is the sub-Tennysonian poem "Night Conquest", too long and tedious to be given in full here, but which the following stanza serves to represent:

> Weary, weary is the spraying wave,
> Weary of its flying:
> Let us hasten to the grave
> Where the long light is dying.

At this point, having sketched in Menlove's sceptical and probing attitude towards most forms of received opinion, the likely effect on his religious beliefs should be pondered. There is a very interesting verse statement which sheds light on these, written in the few months before the Skye boat trip:

> I have been compassed by a strange divinity
> And strangely is my share of Godship made a sign
> Around me. Manoah my father was a saint
> Of uprightness, and him my honoured mother filled
> With gentleness in good content, and held his love
> In piety. For all the furbished practice of
> Their time took virtue in them. I was their chance
> Of greatness sent by God that they in duty vowed
> Me back to Him, and to the Lord they blessed me with
> Their care, and so I took my vows upon myself

And in the confines of my young ideals sought Heaven
Within itself in clear confidence. I knew
My parents and I knew them good: their life a great
Establishment, well worthy of the past. I too
Would rightly use it and inspire to be inspired.
And then the stirrings of great passion grew
In me, and massive strength on fountain spurts of power,
So I was moved to look and see myself to house
A devious motive in a splendid frame and saw
My vows too straight for me, and all the scattered
Particles of world call for the welding principle
Of power. New resolve, new opportunities
And this my mightiness is ready, that
It yearns to see myself significant.

These fluent alexandrines are central to an understanding of Menlove's character. I take them to be largely autobiographical in content, although they come from a dramatic monologue clearly inspired by Browning and written in the biblical character of Samson. The extract touches on Menlove's experience at several points. The fondly drawn relationship between the narrator's parents echoes that between Menlove's own, as do their individual characters and the burden of expectation they place on their son. In respect and obedience to the latter, the son pledges himself to the pursuit of high religious ideals—as did Menlove in his undertaking to the Church Missionary Society. From this situation, there arose in him powerful urges needing examination, which led to the discovery of "A devious motive in a splendid frame" and made the vow he had taken "too straight". The concluding near-rhymed heroic couplet resolves the quandary by stating a new purpose, albeit in a different direction. If there is an egotism here, it is of the man who wants to think well of himself rather than the one who has naturally assumed that stance. Looking at events in Menlove's life during early 1933, the meaning of the lines reflects increasingly clearly upon them.

At the end of the second chapter it was stated that Menlove had applied to the CMS for a grant, and been awarded £100 per annum on the understanding that he would accept the role of doctor in CMS missions for a number of years after completion of his training. His application had required sponsors, one of whom had been Hewlett Johnson, his father's cousin and at that time Dean of Manchester. In January 1933, in response to questions from the CMS about his intentions and plans after qualification, he was forced to express some doubt about his calling to missionary work. This put him in a potentially invidious position, for if he did decide to withdraw from his undertaking to the Society, it could have rendered his sponsor liable for the financial aid which had been given to Menlove. Menlove was in a severe dilemma, and he momentarily resolved to give up medicine—which does not anyhow seem to have been a course of study which he greatly enjoyed. Hewlett Johnson promptly rounded on him and, with the sound sense which that great and good man displayed throughout most of his life, urged him to get on with his work and finish the course, and not waste his four and a half years of study. Not only that, but also to do it with an easy conscience, since it was understood by all concerned that the original application had been made in good faith.

After a brief period of vacillation, in which he insisted that any burden of repayment should fall upon him, and in which he also proposed the novel fund-raising project of a canoe-trip down the River Euphrates, he seems to have appeased his pangs of conscience sufficiently to allow him to get on with his work. At this stage, he had not progressed far along the path which was to lead him into a position of agnosticism, but he had moved away from Anglican orthodoxy. The religious feeling in both the "Samson" and the "Recquiescat" poems, for example, is closer to Blake than to conventional Church of England teachings. It is interesting, but by no means conclusive, to speculate on this progression of thought in Menlove. What effect did the climbing have upon it? In the most simple way, it would have turned him away from an orthodox religious practice by working against regular Sunday attendance at church once the habit of weekends spent in mountainous venues had been established. (The psychochemical effects of frequently-stimulated adrenalin, as discussed by the American climbing writer Doug Robinson, may also have their place here. But this is hypothetical.) The chances are that it was no more than one natural direction in which an independent-minded, intelligent and sceptical young man of that time could have gone.

It obviously weighed on his mind, and could even be seen as surfacing in the single new climb he did in the period before Easter 1933. This route, on Dinas Cromlech, was the second and last new line he pioneered with Kirkus and was one of the poorest of Menlove's career. Its quality is so low that it has virtually been written out of the modern guidebook, but Menlove and Kirkus seem to have found it entertaining enough:

It would be tedious to describe in detail the types of turf to look for *en route*. The name is Nebuchadnezzar's Crawl; Neb's Crawl for short. It will be remembered that, during a period of mental aberration, this old gentleman went on his belly seven years with the beasts of the field, size not specified, and his face he buried in the grass. There was an amusing incident on the Crawl when we got into a corner and then got out again.

The identification with the two biblical figures of Samson and Nebu-chadnezzar within a few months is worth mentioning—both were religious outcasts, one through his lust and the other through his heathenism. Whether Menlove's choice of them was conscious or subconscious is almost beside the point. Assuredly, he would have been aware of their significance.

At the beginning of the Easter vacation Menlove paid a brief visit to Wales, on his first day making solo ascents of two particularly unpleasant climbs on the Western Cliffs of Cwm Silyn and in the evening an ascent of Devil's Pasture, where "the climber may feel the full joy of lying in long grass at his ease". The following day, with a complete novice from an Oxford University Mountaineering Club meet at Helyg, he went to his favourite "Columnar Cliffs" and added two further new routes at the steep left hand end of the cliff—one of them Very Severe. Both climbs struggled with the usual holly trees; they "were done in rubbers and shorts, but it should be noted that more protection would be advisable". After these ascents, Menlove left Wales and motored north to meet his old friend from Fettes, Alec Keith.

Alec had organized a visit to Maggie Gruer's house, Thistle Cottage, at Inverey, up the Dee Valley from Braemar and south-east of the Cairngorm high summits. Maggie Gruer was as much a legend amongst pre-war Scottish climbers as Ma Thomas was to the sixties generation in the Derbyshire Peak District, and shared the same characteristics: fierce blue eyes, diminutive size, iron-grey hair and a savage contempt for all Tories. She had a fine, bubbling sense of fun and a fund of stories relating to the district and her lodgers. Her two-up, two-down cottage was open only to climbers, and Maggie was reputed never to turn one away from her door, no matter how full the house was. Janet Adam Smith, in her book *Mountain Holidays*, describes the typical scene:

> At whatever hour you arrived (and I never gave her any notice), whatever the wetness of your clothes, Maggie would show no surprise. She would set you down at once by the fire—if necessary ordering "twa chappies frae Dundee", themselves now dry, to make room for the newcomer—pour you out a strong black brew from the teapot simmering on the range, and crack a couple of eggs on the frying-pan which, in Thistle Cottage, was seldom off the fire. No fuss, no excitement, no bother about "seeing your room"—you were warmed inside and out before you had time to realise that the walk was over. Then, with the kettle on again for the hot-water bottles, Maggie would let the talk play over the doings of the countryside.

For this holiday she had let to Alec Keith a bothy next to the byre, which contained two double beds and a small porch which served them as a kitchen. Breakfast was given in the kitchen of the house, and lunches provided to take out with them for the day. Three others attended, apart from Menlove. They were Bruce Nicol, Stewart Slessor and Monty McConnachie—the last two being doctors' sons from Fraserburgh and joint owners of the boat in which Menlove made his attempt in 1935 to sail to Norway. Here is Alec Keith's version of the events of this holiday:

"We all settled in pretty well, the only problem being the beds, and that was solved by Menlove as the visitor and myself as his host getting one and the others sharing the other one. On our first day we set off on one of our usual expeditions, this time to the Shelter Stone of Loch Avon and then, if time allowed, on to the plateau between Cairngorm and Ben MacDhui, up this latter, then down again to Loch Etchachan. It wasn't always easy to get the key to the locked gate at the foot of the Derry road and we had to walk from there to Derry Lodge, up Glen Derry, up Coire Etchachan, round the Loch and down to the Shelter Stone. Not Menlove's idea at all. We had lunch at the Shelter Stone and then Menlove changed the plans by proposing a climb; Castle Wall was the line he chose, on the snowed-up rocks to the right of Castle Gates Gully. Stewart and Bruce stuck to their original plan, and Monty went up Castle Gates Gully. Menlove and I had an ice-axe between us and the only rope in the party. Afterwards we glissaded down to Loch Etchachan and met the others at the top of the Coire.

"Next day Menlove and I went to do a climb in the East Coire of Lochnagar. We set off on his motorbike and I found this a very frightening experience. In my view, Menlove had very little understanding of or sympathy for machinery; I was an inexperienced pillion passenger, and the combination was uncomfortable. Halfway to Glen Muick we were stopped by a locked gate, and had to walk from here by the head of the Gelder Burn to the foot of the Black Spout. Here we stopped in a snowstorm for lunch, which had been provided by Menlove and was raw Pemmican out of the tin and chocolate. We then started off up the Black Spout, with Menlove leading on hard snow. This soon became boring and the view straight down the gully a little frightening, and when Menlove asked if I would prefer to try the rocks I said yes. We moved on to the right wall of the gully and did the climb now known as Black Spout Buttress. There was a good deal of snow to be cleared off the holds and a good deal of poorish rock too and I was frightened most of the way up, but Menlove enjoyed this part of the day and put up with my fear and ineptitude without complaint. We got to the top without incident and went down the ordinary way by the ladder to Conachraig and the bike. We were rather late in getting back to Inverey and the others were a trifle worried.

"The party had now become split into two, which I'd been a little afraid of—Menlove and I, and the three others, though Monty went home either this day or the next. At any rate, on the day after Lochnagar Menlove and I set off to look at the boiler plate slabs on the Devil's Point whilst the others went to climb Cairn Toul. We got as far as the shoulder of Cairn a Mhaim and looked at the Devil's Point but then gave up. I don't quite know—we were neither of us very keen to go on but I'm sure if I'd said 'let's go' we would have done so. At any rate, we strolled down again to the Derry and the Linn of Dee, and turned off the road to look at it. Menlove treated it as just another natural rock feature whereas we always treated it with awe as the place where Byron was almost drowned. We read the inscription on the tablet to the two people who fell in and were drowned there and I made some remark to Menlove about the dangers of falling in and the need for care. He promptly replied by jumping across the narrow part of the Linn below the bridge once or twice to show me how silly I was, and said then that he thought he could swim down it. I believe this was when the idea first entered his head. I argued a little, pointing out that the Linn was very full and strong with melting snow and rain, but he said that was an advantage if anything, as there would be enough water to let a body float over any snags sticking up from the bottom. After a while we gave it up and ambled back to Inverey.

"The following day was damp and not very cold, with low cloud over the surrounding hills. It didn't look like a day for climbing and when someone asked what we should do Menlove said it was a perfect day for the Linn and that he would swim down it. There was a considerable uproar at this to begin with. Stewart and Bruce couldn't believe he was serious. I knew he meant it and thought he would do it. We tried every argument except, looking back, the one that might have succeeded, namely to say, 'All right—go and do it, but we we're not coming with you.' In the end we gave in and made a solemn journey to Braemar to buy a new film for Bruce's camera, so that we could record the event. Then back to Maggie Gruer's so that Menlove could change and collect the rope which he had agreed to put on so that if anything did go wrong it would be easy for us to get him out of the water without getting into trouble ourselves. Menlove put on a rugger jersey and a pair of shorts and with the sacrifice duly dressed we set off on the sombre journey up the Linn. I suppose we all believed that he would get away with it or we would have made a more vigorous protest.

"I don't know if you have seen the Linn of Dee? The Scottish Mountaineering Club guide describes it as a place 'where the river rushes through a narrow channel only three or four feet wide cut in the schistose rocks, afterwards opening out into a series of great circular pools.' The description in *Samson* gives no idea of the thing at all and in fact a feature of the bit that Menlove swam down is that it is straight and not twisting. Also, the River

Dee above the Linn is already quite big, having received its first major tributary, the Geldie Burn, at the White Bridge, and flowing down a wide strath from there it keeps a width of thirty or forty yards for about four miles. The narrow channel into which all this water is compressed at the Linn is deeply undercut, and the width below water level greater than that at the surface. It starts above the bridge and at the bottom opens out into a circular pool with high black vertical walls. There is no way a swimmer could get out of this but the next pool, five yards or so lower down, is less steep and has a ledge jutting into it. Menlove showed us where he was to go in, just above the bridge, and where he intended to come out, on this ledge. The Linn was in spate, with a lot of meltwater and perishing cold.

"He tied one end of the rope to his waist and the other to a birch tree, since cut down, went up as far as the rope would let him, and then jumped in. He came down very fast, though all we could see was the rope as it slithered across the slabs and mercifully didn't catch on anything. Soon he was in the first whirlpool and we caught a glimpse of him struggling against the far wall. He was spun one complete circuit and on the next swam down with the current and managed to get on the ledge without help. He was slightly winded and had one or two bruises and superficial abrasions, but otherwise was unhurt.

"We lost no time in getting back to Maggie Gruer's for Menlove to change and for us to celebrate, but we somehow had a terrible sense of anti-climax and this fell rather flat. Perhaps because Menlove chose to say so little about it. All we could gather was that he had tried to swim the whole way down to make sure of keeping head first and not getting tumbled over. Also, he told us that the worst thing was that when he dived in the wet rope formed coils and he went through one of them and, during his circuit of the first whirlpool, had a struggle to keep it away from his neck. Using it must have added to the risk considerably and Menlove knew that.

"We spent the afternoon in a desultory way. First of all we went to the Linn of Quoich, but Menlove pointed out that this was a much more dangerous affair with a long vertical fall at one place. On the way back we stopped for another look at the Linn of Dee, and went down the south bank a bit. Menlove suggested a bathe in the lower pool known locally as the snaw-bree, and for some idiotic reason we agreed."

Leaving Alec's account of the holiday for the moment, it should be noted that there is a perfectly clear account of swimming the Linn of Dee in Arthur Hugh Clough's poem of 1848, "The Bothy of Tober-Na-Vuolich" (Bk 3 11.158–169), with which Menlove may well have been acquainted. There are two brief passages by Menlove himself about the swim. The first is an isolated jotting, the second from a letter:

I straightened myself up a bit, twitched the rope free and shouted "Are you ready?" They had been ready and waiting for some minutes, but I could not jump except under the eye of immediate moral compulsion. Then I fixed the plan of action in my head and overbalanced carefully into mid-stream. I have always been amazed at the strength of water. But what stand out to me, in the Linn, are the sudden strong fragments of feeling in me that answered the terrific command under the water.

You don't know the Linn? Well, next time you are up by Braemar make a point of taking the trip down the Linn waters, some day when it is fairly full up with a little of spate splashing it. "So short," you may say. But—do you want it long? Do you want that long, long trudge up Etchachan or away up the Lairig Ghru. Up beyond the shelter of the pines, where the sun hits you or the grey rain treads you down? No. Jump into the Linn straight from your car, let the stream take you down in its arms awhile then jump out again.

The tone of the two versions is well contrasted, the first factual and analytical, the second combining preference and bravado. The second applies equally well to his climbing, of course—"'So short,' you may say. But—do you want it long?" What the feelings were in the first is good ground for guesswork. The desire for death? The urge to survive? And if the latter, was it the need strongly to feel that in contrast to a usual overriding sense of dullness and melancholy in life which drove him on?

To take up with Alec Keith again, the holiday in Scotland was not quite over for Menlove. Alec invited him back for a few days at his parents' home in Turriff, north of Aberdeen:

I had another agonizing journey on the back of his motorbike. The visit—indeed the whole holiday—was not a great success. My mother could make nothing of him and he wasn't easy, being silent to the point of being tongue-tied. We spent one day doing some short climbs on the summit rocks of our local mountain, Bennachie. He disappointed me by turning down two possible routes which I suggested to him, but I couldn't make out if he thought they were impossible or if he couldn't be bothered. He liked to make his discoveries for himself. One day we played golf, which he did with a scythe-like hockey swing, but the contest was too unequal to be much fun. He also asked me to stop calling him Pow, which was his nickname from school. (Our housemaster was J. S. Edwards, nickname Pow, so naturally Menlove became Pow, or Pow Minor if there was any doubt in the matter.) All in all, it was rather a relief when he went home.

He spent very little time at home before taking leave of revision for his finals in favour of another three days at Helyg. As previously mentioned, above Helyg rises the extensive but generally broken and vegetated cliff of Gallt yr Ogof, round which Stephen and Menlove had wandered on the latter's first visit to Wales. Despite its proximity to Helyg, for climbing purposes it had been almost completely disregarded. It is split into two sections by a wide, slanting break, above which the cliff is wet, black and forbidding, its most prominent feature being the tall cave from which the Welsh name derives. This is always wet, being the line of a small watercourse, overhangs severely, and was not climbed until the long, dry summer of 1959, when Joe Brown took advantage of its abnormally dry state to make an ascent. Menlove and a fellow LURCC member by the name of Pixton made an attempt on it in the course of his first day at Helyg. They were inevitably repulsed by water, grease, and loose holds. Even today the route is hardly ever climbed under normal conditions, though it has become one of the most popular hard Welsh ice-routes. They called the cave Jonah's Whale, because it had spewed them out of its belly after a long period of time, and consoled themselves with a distinctly steep and airy little climb up its right-bounding rib:

A neat little climb ... spread out up there, to watch the evening sun in the long days.... Care should be taken not to drop off with fright if a large falcon swoops at you. Rumour has it that on the first ascent a stern struggle took place up there between man and beast locked in a death grip, high up among the clouds, and that there was much bloodshed and much scraping of nails before the great bird eventually had its indescribably nasty neck wrung.

(The peregrines still nest hereabouts.)

Having been on the cliff for most of the day, it was nearly dark by the time they were descending from it. The shepherds had set light to the heather on the hillside and the sight of it had a powerful effect on Menlove:

The flames that made their great red scars against the dying sky, and the smell of fire—and it gave one that queer plucking memory of things that does catch at one now and then, aside from the highway. Fantastic life. We had no grudge against the heather; it had borne us well. The crackling noise was a funny thing to call beautiful; and the bunches of flame made only curious shapes on the dark hill for a time. What is it in life that is so curiously alive, and that is so curiously dying? What is it in change that is so very still and so old? The sky was much too darkly coloured to be black.

This is one of the best pieces of natural description in Menlove's writing, but it isn't simply that. It centres much more on primordial memory and the unconscious responses of the mind which were soon to be Menlove's professed area of interest.

That evening, as Menlove was drying out his clothes, sodden in the tussle with the whale, in front of the Helyg fire, A. B. Hargreaves, Hewlett and Rennie Bere arrived from Liverpool, and the former had his usual galvanizing effect on Menlove. With typical efficiency (for Hargreaves was extremely thorough and painstaking in his approach to climbing) AB had obtained from Kirkus a full description of the as-yet-unrepeated Great Slab route on Clogwyn Du'r Arddu. He appointed himself as manager, Menlove as leader, and Hewlett as last man—an important position on a traversing route. Bere was put down as third man for ballast, a role he was conscientiously to fulfil. Early in the morning they departed for Llanberis and the walk up to the cliff. Kirkus's first ascent account does much to explain the feeling of awe in which this climb was held amongst the climbers of the time:

> The traverse was very severe. There was one sloping hold where my rubbers would not grip at all, so at last I took them off and managed to get across in my stockinged feet.
>
> I found myself on a tiny grass ledge, looking rather hopelessly up at the grim face above. I had crossed on to a higher part of the cliff and was already about 100ft. above the bottom, with the overhang below me. I started up [a] narrow slab. It was far more difficult than it looked, and wickedly rotten. I threw down every other hold. A thin ribbon of grass ran all the way up on the right, looking like a long and ragged caterpillar. I thought that even this might be safer than the rock and plunged into it; it began to peel off and slide down. I left this moving staircase very hurriedly, and took to the rocks again. Below my left feet the rocks dropped, sheer and unclimbable, for 200ft. Macphee called up that I had run out nearly all of the 120-ft. line. There was no stance in sight . . .
>
> . . . the corner was a 20-ft. wall of literally vertical grass. I made a mad rush at it. I had to climb up more quickly than the grass fell down.

No doubt Kirkus's story had been told many times and was running through their minds on the hour-long walk to the foot of the cliff. They traversed round under the silvery, crack-seamed walls of the East Buttress, pausing to look up at Kirkus's climbs of the last two years—the Curving Chimney, as it was then known, and the Pedestal and Terrace Cracks, AB perhaps questioning Menlove about the Chimney Route he had done with Kirkus, to which Menlove's puckish, bantering replies can easily be imagined. A scramble up the steep rock-steps of the Western Terrace led to the "Green Pillar" which marked the starting point of the Great Slab. There they roped up and set off. AB takes up the story:

> Menlove made no bones at all about that slippery little slab and the long green caterpillar, but it was when I joined him at the top of it that I first saw an exhibition of his enormous strength. Our third man, weighing fully fifteen stone, just made a dash at the slippery slab and shot off into space on the end of 150ft. of line. This antic not only fused my hands, but locked me to the belay and I was helpless except to hold on. Menlove came down to me and without even shouldering the rope, lifted that chap with his hands until he was able to get hold of something and be pulled back on to the climb by the fourth man (Menlove's brother Hewlett) whom it was fortunate we had with us. We then sacked number three and proceeded. But here Menlove's very strong pioneering instinct came into play. He was not going to go across the grass ledges to the corner as per instructions; he was going to go straight up (what is now Bow-shaped Slab, I think). Hewlett and myself had great difficulty in making him come down 30 or 40 ft. and continue with the second ascent which was our objective. And again, when we got to the grassy corner, we had trouble with him. He wanted to go straight on up (Carsten's later route) and only submitted grumblingly to do the original finish.

AB's overall impression of the route was that "the first ascent must have been a splendid example of mountaineering courage. No more severe, lengthy, or complicated route upon such an inaccessible face has yet been achieved in England and Wales: and it was quite unexplored—from above." (The last sentence is a reference to activities on the first ascent of Scafell's Central Buttress, where the crux pitch was inspected from above before being climbed. Hargreaves, based in the Lake District, was actively campaigning at this time for an end to what he saw as an unjustifiable attitude of superiority adopted by devotees of that region towards Welsh climbing.) Of Menlove's efforts, AB thought as follows:

> The knowledge that the centre of the face had actually been climbed made the second ascent only a little less remarkable. It was a very bold and steady lead.

His concluding remarks say a great deal about prevalent contemporary attitudes to the men who were actively engaged in establishing the new standards:

It is hoped that these remarks will not be construed into a condemnation of this climb as "dangerous". It is a truly magnificent one, and perfectly justifiable.

Menlove's version of the day's work is naturally in a much lower key:

> It was considered to be a very fine route of great charm. It was not a dangerous climb under the existing conditions. The "20 ft. of vertical grass" for getting up the lower part of the corner can be avoided by a little pleasant rock work on the immediate left. The 50–ft. pitch up the corner itself was wet and the patches of grass very unsteady here; great care was required, but under successive onslaughts the worst one finally parted, leaving a small foothold. The rock is nowhere too good, but nowhere now is it very bad.

AB must sometimes have despaired of his young companion, for before he could tempt him back to Clogwyn Du'r Arddu Menlove slipped off with Bere to Clogwyn y Geifr, and climbed the "dilapidated buttress of very melancholy appearance" which forms a counterpart to Devil's Buttress on the left-hand side of the Kitchen itself: "It has the general shape, appearance, and characteristics of a slag heap." "The steep bit is an interesting study in mosaics, but they did not finish it off very well . . . you get holds on the bits sticking out: it is decidedly decomposing. Herein lies its charm." "Stockings worn but this is more heroic than necessary. Not particularly exposed. Little technique. Much care." AB looked on in amazement before going off to play safe with the gully era classic, Devil's Staircase.

Two subsequent days look as though they were traded one against the other between Menlove and AB. On the first of them AB led Menlove up the third ascent of the Curving Crack: "slight dampness increased by the party's sweat" was AB's comment. Menlove gave a fuller explanation: ". . . a fine climb, but I am not sure if it is worth it. Definitely it is not if there is a terribly energetic little man swearing about above you on the rope and a tremendously heavy tall man swaying about below you on the rope." Poor Bere seems to have performed consistently badly on this cliff. Menlove's share of the bargain was to introduce AB to his "Columnar Cliff", making a first ascent of the Very Severe Pharaoh's Wall: "Standard Severe—possibly—due to steepness, and very bad rock. Like the other routes on the cliff there is no technical difficulty. It should be noted that big boulders dropped from hereabout tend not to make a mess of the rest of the climb."

Thereafter it was back to Liverpool, and cramming for the now-imminent exams. A fortnight elapsed before he stole another day off and walked up to

Menlove, Stephen, Bill Lancaster and Wyatt on summit of Dôme de Polset, 1930

Menlove on Twin Caves Crack, Helsby, 1930

Menlove leading Spiral Stairs, Dinas Cromlech

Hewlett Edwards and Selsby Walmsley. Wales, 1931

Menlove at the time of his graduation, 1933

Devil's Dive   John Beatty

'Of the climbs perhaps the Devil's Dive and the Devil's Buttress are the best and hardest. The Devil's Dump is nice: the steep bit is an interesting study in mosaics, but they did not finish it off very well. Alternatively it may be regarded as an excavation in the Dump, and you get hold on the bits sticking out: it is decidedly decomposing. Herein lies its charm.'   Menlove

Clogwyn D'ur Arddu once more, this time with T. E. Davies of the LURCC:

> Looked at the cliff and found it suitably moist for nails; looked at the Great Slab Route and decided it might be better in stockings after all. Got up first pitch but No. 2, when he felt the rope pulling gently over to the left, remained at the belay on the right. So in the course of time No. 1 rejoined him. First impressions of this pitch were confirmed, but when wet it is very considerably harder and the grass begins to spread its wings for flight. Luckily there are lots of belays and things. No. 2, of course, was quite right.

The same pair took a full weekend in Wales in mid-May, climbing Dives on the Columnar Cliff on the Saturday, "so called because of the many crumbs that dropped—also because it had intended better things above, from which it was debarred by the hostile elements". Sunday's programme involved a new area of the Kitchen Cliffs. This resulted in two routes, one of them very poor—Cellar Buttress; the other was more idiosyncratically appealing, and is called the Coal Shute Exit to the Devil's Cellar. The first ascent description gives the flavour. The route has moved left out of its parent climb into a steep corner:

> Continue up this steeply and probably awkwardly on rather inferior material. Soon there is good standing place in the gully, another short spasm and even better standing place with some coroner's belays.
>   Last pitch either straight up the gully very rottenly or out on the right wall, airily, pleasantly, fairly difficultly, but unfortunately still definitely rottenly.

(A "coroner's belay" is one of no real value and taken for no other reason than that in the event of an accident the climber, if he survived, could say to the coroner, "Well, we did have a belay.")

Down to the right of the band of rock on which these two routes were climbed is the most impressive section of Clogwyn y Geifr. A smooth expanse of steep rock tilted over to the right, stippled with overhangs, and 300 feet high, it is known as the North Cliff. A week after the Cellar climbs Menlove returned here armed with a new companion, C. H. French, and discovered his two best routes on the cliff thus far. The first of them, North Slabs, although quite short, is an enjoyable Very Severe, delicate, open, and on clean rock with sparse, indefinite holds. The second, Devil's Dive, a Hard Severe is still one of the most frighteningly undergraded and exposed climbs on Welsh rock. It takes a long, narrowing gangway between bands of great overhangs and "probably uses more rock than grass, but neither is of a reliable nature. It is only thanks to the plethora of holds available and the exercise of care that this route can be ascended safely ... one could dive straight into deep water from any part of [it] without any obstacle intervening." An ascent of it gives a very clear insight into the absurdities in the usage of the present-day grading systems, and it is the best possible choice for those who wish to savour the essential character of Menlove's explorations on these cliffs.

Menlove's pioneering tailed off over the next few weeks. Days in Wales at long intervals were interspersed with his finals in Liverpool. His old campaigning friend W. R. Reade coaxed him up to Clogwyn y Garnedd at the end of May. They climbed what is referred to as Glaslyn Gully, which Reade humorously notes was probably its first unaided ascent. (On the only other known ascent the Swiss guide Alexander Burgener was pushed up on an ice-axe by R. L. G. Irving.) This cliff is an awful place, a formless mouldering pile of scree and rotten, mossy rock serving as repository for all the rubbish from the Snowdon summit hotel which lies immediately above. Under winter conditions it is transformed, but in summer Menlove's judgement that "the route is rather pleasant and very worthy" was incredible: he seems not to have been going through one of his discerning phases. The last point is borne out by his record for June and early July: two routes in the South Bay of the Kitchen Cliffs: "... definitely not an attractive area. It is composed of a series of depressingly rotten ribs separating channels which are constantly awash." And one route on the same section of the Columnar Cliff as Neb's Crawl:

No. 3, before setting out from Helyg for the climb in question, discovered that it was cold and put an extra coat in his sack. It started hailing during the first pitch, and No. 3, finding that his several waistcoats, coat, and cut-down mackintoshes afforded insufficient protection, took the coat out from the sack and by a skilled acrobatic manoeuvre added this garment deftly to the pile upon his shoulders. It was a black tail-coat, and would probably have fitted him very well if it had not been made on far too small a scale; unhappily the sleeves, for their part, did not extend far beyond the elbows. It got on much better when the pressure of circumstance discovered extensive outlets down the seams. The route was called Sexton's Route.

Menlove did well in his finals, passing with credit. The Dean of the Medical Faculty, in his report on him, wrote that "throughout his student period he was a conscientious student, and has shown by his examination results that he has gained a thorough acquaintance with the various subjects in the curriculum. I am confident that he will prove a very reliable physician and surgeon." He was to graduate as MB, ChB, on 8 July 1933. Stephen came over from St Helens, where he was a curate, to watch him take his degree, and to take him out afterwards to a celebration lunch. Hewlett was by this time at Cambridge preparing to take Holy Orders. There was some talk of his attending, but he did not arrive. He had gone down to Wales and on 7 July walked over Glyder Fach and Glyder Fawr before slinging his boots round his neck and, in his socks, soloing down Reade's original climb out of the Devil's Kitchen—a feat which bespeaks a high level of climbing competence.

Menlove's degree ceremony went off well, and the lunch afterwards was an enjoyable occasion for both brothers. They parted, Menlove to go back to Formby and Stephen to St Helens. When Stephen arrived home he found a telegram asking him to go urgently to Liverpool Royal Infirmary, where Hewlett was lying unconscious after an accident. Riding back from Wales on his 500cc Dunelt motorbike, he had just come out of the Mersey Tunnel when a man ran into his path from behind a parked car. Hewlett swerved to avoid him and went straight into an oncoming tram. Only hours after their parting Menlove met Stephen again at Hewlett's bedside—the one brother beyond medical aid on the very day the other had qualified as a doctor.

The effect of Hewlett's death on George Edwards, the father, was immediate and devastating; he had set all his hopes on Hewlett, and his attitude now changed almost overnight from a brave resolution and fortitude in the face of his illness to despair. Nowell and Helen, on holiday in Assisi, were not at hand to afford him any solace. The effect of the death on Menlove was no less profound, but he bore it inwardly, giving his support to Helen Edwards, the mother. He made two attempts to reconcile himself to the loss through poetry. The first of these is written in the character of the bereaved mother. Entitled "Receive his Soul", it is not a good poem. Its two recurrent images of valleys and fir trees are so repetitively used and overloaded with significance that they do not convey any great depth of meaning or emotion. Much more telling are some poetic fragments on various scraps of paper. Any order into which these may be put is purely conjectural. They do not constitute a finished poem, but they are important enough to give here:

Come softly lest he hear.
You were ashamed of me.

Lay your hand over me and look us grow, up from the land.
Let not who I am my dear . . .

Yes you were beautiful and strong
And I'd not ask that you should know me.
Lean your head back and I'll
Speak softly lest you hear.

I feel more than he does and may not forget.

Then he flickered and died, wearily torn from that poor carcass.

He was beautiful and so strong,
Drawn by the grey sky, over it a canopy.

Heavy-coloured soil, dead and powerful, the weight of it upon my people.

When they laugh, it is as the earth laughs, when they play it is the earth
playing.

Oh my heavy people, my so huge people, that
Are so kind, so heavy-coloured and so soiled.

There are several false starts and different attempts to work in the same
direction here. What stand out most vividly are the mingling emotions of guilt
and shame combining with an almost sensual adoration of the elder brother.
The fragments tell us more in their directness and honesty—all pretence
momentarily put aside—than anything else we know about the relationship
between Menlove and Hewlett. Defying close analysis, they give us the
clearest sense of Menlove's anguished reaction to the death. Notice especially
"You were ashamed of me", "Let not who I am my dear . . .", and ". . . I'd not
ask that you should know me". Bill Stallybrass remembers that Menlove
found it very hard to accept Hewlett's death, wondering why it had been
Hewlett, who was handsome, popular, normal, and not himself, who might
have welcomed it. His feelings of guilt over Hewlett's death would probably,
given their family background, have been intensified by the fact that Hewlett's
religious convictions were strengthening as he approached his ministry, whilst
his own were fast moving away from the idea of formal worship.

After the funeral Menlove escaped to Wales for a few days, heading for
the solace of his Kitchen cliffs again. He climbed four new routes on them in
the space of three days, covering a great deal of fissile and vertiginous

ground and producing at least one dangerous classic—the Devil's Pipes. The rock feature which this route takes assuredly receives diabolic support to continue defying gravity and the laws of entropy to this day. It may well be the most dangerously loose Welsh rock-climb, and to ascend it involves a massive disregard for consequence or personal safety, as well as strenuous use of perilous material. Rock as loose as this and at this angle was not to be climbed again until Brown and Crew's exploits on South Stack in the mid-1960s. Understandably, Menlove was not feeling sympathetic towards loud spectators. On one of the climbs he did—Hothouse Cracks, which lies directly above the popular path to Llyn y Cwn and Glyder Fawr from Cwm Idwal—he noted that "it is easy to deal with onlooking *Yohos* by a little judicious gardening. The chockstone aforementioned was really quite firm but was round, largeish [*sic*] and trundleable. They had told us to watch what we were doing."

Most of this summer Menlove spent at home in Formby, where his father's condition was slowly worsening. He snatched a few more days in Wales, living on experimental diets of rice and blackberries and climbing the unfortunately-named Grass Route on Glyder Fawr with Roy Beard. The climb is much better than its name implies, and Menlove's assessment of it very entertaining:

Those who do not like grass will probably class it at the end of the Frankly Borings or the beginning of the Definitely Unpleasants. The first pitch is a grassy groove overhanging the old route. I do not know whose fault it is but probably the stuff was badly stuck together in the first instance, and the fact remains interesting for about eighty feet. Above that the right-hand branch of the gully is taken. The second was accorded shelter in a little cave below this, but he still seemed to be deriving discomfort from falling materials, and his agitation appears to have been considerably increased by the sudden loosening of several large blocks in the roof of the cave itself. But beyond getting sympathy, the second did not seem really to mind. He never really minded anything. It is perhaps not generally realised that there are in the climbing world one or two seconds who display more courage and sagacity in the face of emergencies (e.g. the aforesaid cave) than has ever been shown by even the most reckless of leaders. I do not know precisely what these persons are made of, but circumstances (more especially when the stance is small) leave them quite unmoved. They are responsible for many of the best climbs. Their leader dare not do anything else. If, in evil pass, he says, "I think I had better come down", this second says, "Oh", and the leader has to try again. And if a little later he says, "What do you think? Had we better go on?" the second simply replies, "Yes, let's", or "Oh, we might as well", and again what can the leader do but go on if he can and fall off if he cannot? The moral ascendency of the second over the leader is the greatest danger in modern climbing. In point of technique, however, the menace may occasionally be observed to quicken his pace a little, as if not entirely sure of his ground. I have even seen him completely caught up by the turn of events at a moment when he simply had not got a leg to stand on. This is very gratifying to the leader. To return to the second pitch of this right-hand route it has much less loose matter on it than it used to have."

Having expended sufficient energy in the walk up to Glyder Fawr, Menlove refused to travel farther than Gallt yr Ogof and the Kitchen Cliffs on subsequent days. The Gallt yr Ogof climb was fraught with peculiar discomfort in the shape of a swarm of bees. To start off with, Menlove and Bill Stallybrass set off up thick, steep heather: "we progressed largely by plunging our arms in as though we were swimming". When they finally met with rock, Menlove insisted on Stallybrass leading through, as he claimed to have forgotten how to climb, and at the top of the pitch Stallybrass encountered a swarm of bees. They did not much bother him, but when Menlove arrived, they "immediately turned their attention to him. Mr Stallybrass, however, had rebuked them, and they had then seemed equally content with some coils of rope with which they had been presented. They were still routing around when the party had gone; and the party had not fully understood this. It had seemed very queer."

Dump Crack and Piece by Piece Climb were both remarkably messy climbs. A cave on the former drew the remark that it had "obviously not been wiped for many years" and of the latter: "As it has not yet been unearthed this climb should be considered Severe." Dump Crack was almost certainly the climb on which occurred the slight accident to the second recounted below:

I remember on the Kitchen Cliff, it was quite an easy thing and we were at about the last pitch. He looked pathetically up at me and a slight smile broke through. "I think I can do this," he said. "Not so hard as the last pitch, only a question of finding the holds." And he looked down again, concentrated himself on the task in hand, and having found a satisfactory combination of holds he stiffened all his muscles, began to move himself cautiously upward, and slipped off. He grabbed for a huge block with one hand, got it, then the other hand, and the block being a loose block and in no condition to resist the urgency of my friend's appeal, wobbled for a moment and crashed over, hitting him hard on the head as it went.

Poor lad, that was always the way of it. You trust your all to a thing, throw your arms around it, thinking it will keep you up. But it mistakes you, thinks you want it perhaps, and down it comes. And you're not quite ready for that.

A day or two more, a dutiful ascent of Hanging Garden Gully for the Cwm Idwal guidebook he had been commissioned to write—a climb only undertaken because he would not take his friends' word for its difficulty—and then he set off home in the car he now possessed:

It drove us faster and faster through the wilds of Denbigh until, screwing its accelerator to the sticking point, the graceless vehicle turned against the hand that led it, and after a short, decisive battle, pitched us head first out on to the road.

... it was rather a famous car on account of its small size and curious appearance ... in a like mood, the little car charged into the back of a sheep, and, unhappily, with fatal results. The car never regained consciousness.

Shortly after Menlove returned home, his father fell, breaking a hip-bone. He lay in hospital in Southport for six weeks, while Menlove was at home continually in his leisure time to help his sister and mother. He had become house-surgeon at the Northern Hospital, on the Formby road out of Liverpool. The issue of his going to India as a medical missionary was coming to a head. The Church Missionary Society questioned him, but his replies, whilst not evasive and clearly the outcome of his earlier thinking, were very unsatisfactory to them:

God. I think the expression is a crude one. It includes a number of feelings and possible realities, etc, which are (imaginatively) unifiable. I believe one can get beyond the concept of God to a concept of Man.

Whilst Menlove made it quite clear that he was willing to go overseas as a missionary without delay, the CMS thought it advisable that he should firstly serve six months in the Islington Medical Mission, and explained their case in the following very reasonable manner:

In the interests of the work, the Committee has the responsibility of satisfying itself before sending a man out that he has a real experience of the love and power of Christ in his own life and that he has the desire to share that experience with others. The purpose of the blue paper you filled in was to give you an opportunity of expressing what that experience has been in your own case. You will remember that your answers to questions on that paper were so brief as to be almost unintelligible except to the writer, and it was because the answers were brief that your interviewers encouraged you to amplify them—I hardly think the term "probe" can be used in this connection. One thing that did appear in your interview was that you had no evangelistic experience, and it was in order that this lack might be supplied that they were ready to recommend a period of service with some home medical mission.

Those attitudes of Menlove's which can be reconstructed from the above letter—the persecutory anxiety evident in his belief that the CMS were "probing" him, and the giving out of information through statements so personalized as to be incomprehensible to anyone other than the author—are ones which recur as symptoms of his mental illness. In 1933 this was still over a decade away—the signs are already there, but he is still in control, perhaps too firmly in control. Suppression may have been a viable tactic for someone with the moral grandeur and devout religious belief of a Dr Johnson—"To deny early and inflexibly is the only art of checking the importunity of desire"—although even in him it appears to have induced temporary psychoses. For Menlove it was to prove a tragic course, as the pressure of events from this time onwards began to tell against his fiercely and tenuously held stability.

In reply to the CMS letter Menlove insisted that he would go out to an overseas mission at once, but refused to submit to further questioning or serve in the Islington Mission. The CMS wrote back that they had no alternative but to accept his withdrawal. The question of the repayment of the £500 grant was again raised, and Menlove demanded that this debt should fall to him and not upon any other person. The CMS, however, insisted on its rapid repayment, and a few months later received the money from the by-then-widowed Helen. Stephen was furious that a Christian organization could thus demand money from a widow, but the matter was kept from Menlove and Helen perhaps led him to believe that the matter had lapsed. Despite this, the CMS seems otherwise to have acted with a degree of forbearance and understanding towards Menlove in their correspondence. At the age of twenty-three, it was the least he could have expected from a professedly Christian society.

This was the early thirties, then. Menlove's conflicts so far have been chiefly with gentle adversaries or in impersonal arenas—on water, on rock, in the striving for objective control over emotion which is the struggle with self. The direction in which his ambitions were thrusting was not so simple. They were to be judged in a harshly competitive and urgent secular world, from a full engagement with which Menlove had already chosen forms of retreat.

George Edwards died in January 1934, almost 20 years after the accident on the shores of Ullswater which had left him crippled. Shortly afterwards Menlove took his leave of Liverpool and his mother and went to work as a Clinical Assistant in the Isle of Wight County Mental Hospital, and to begin study for his Diploma in Psychological Medicine.

CHAPTER FIVE

"Are those horizons in me?" 1934–1936

ONE GENERATION IS succeeded by another as quickly in climbing as in any other human pursuit. By 1934 the men who had been responsible for the great upsurge in Welsh climbing during the years 1927 to 1933 had all stepped back from the forefront of activity. Jack Longland was in Durham, heavily absorbed in academic work. He had been to Everest in 1933 and the main area of his involvement was now Alpine and greater ranges mountaineering. Colin Kirkus, having survived the accident on Ben Nevis early in 1934 which killed Maurice Linnell and left him seriously injured, although he retained his competence to the end, grew less interested in pioneering routes on difficult rock, had guidebook work to do, had become friendly with a girl at Idwal Cottage youth hostel, and was increasingly concerned in introducing beginners to the sport. And Menlove? There were significant routes to come from him—many of them, in new places—amongst them some of the finest and hardest of his career. There was a strong interest still in climbing for him, but it was a highly critical and dispassionate interest which used the sport as an instrument or regarded it as a disease:

> I, for one, do not wish to take more than the merest tracing-paper outline of these new routes themselves. They are not worth it, especially if there is some day to be a guide. They are not themselves a sport, so much as the brief symptoms of some psycho-neurotic tendency.

It was also very much an original interest. The well-trodden ways, the established routes, were seldom now an end in themselves. True, he would do them now and again, to please a valued friend, encourage a novice, or give himself some exercise when there was no one to climb with or he felt like climbing alone. Unclimbed rock attracted him mostly, though, and he was well aware of the extent to which it existed:

> Of Wales in general, what strikes one most is the large number of unclimbed faces still staring down upon a pretty stiff-necked generation.

What is the fascination to young climbers in the old Slabs and that still older face of Tryfan?

Bertrand Russell, in the prologue to his autobiography, writes of the three passions which governed his life: "The longing for love, the search for knowledge, and unbearable pity for the suffering of mankind." As ruling passions in a man's life they are not unique but they are fine and they were very much at the centre of Menlove's scheme of things. The phase of Menlove's life from 1934 to 1939 was a crucial once, and one in which the pressures built up to a terrible pitch. The longing for love was intense and was temporarily requited, before its object went on his way; the search for knowledge expressed itself not only in the exploration of the detail on given cliffs, but also in his psychiatric studies and practice; and pity for the suffering of mankind found its expression through an obsessive capacity to work on behalf of others, and in the force of his struggle to apprehend both his own and a wider human condition.

Menlove worked at the Isle of Wight County Mental Hospital for six months. His time there in the main was a happy one. His seniors regarded him as a gifted and conscientious clinical worker and thought his researches showed a high degree of promise for one very newly acquainted with his subject. His willingness to put himself out to help others and the natural sympathy he displayed made him well liked with both patients and staff. He played cricket for a local team and on one occasion scored a century. He took only a few breaks away from the Isle of Wight for climbing during this time, his energies being almost wholly directed into his work, and those few breaks were not particularly productive. Early in the year he climbed the Easy Pinnacle Route on Gallt yr Ogof, which is really no more than a pleasant scramble, though Menlove thought it "more interesting than either the Tryfan Gully routes or the Milestone, and it saves the trouble of getting the car out". And also Old Man's Buttress, "The name simply because one felt very aged." (He was 23.) This last comment is to crop up again and again over the next few years. As well as these two routes he attempted the East Gully of Clogwyn Du'r Arddu under heavy snow and ice, but the conditions were so bad that he was forced to retreat. At Easter, Geoffrey Winthrop Young invited him to join his annual party held in the Pen y Pass Hotel, at the top of the Lanberis Pass.

Winthrop Young is a seminal figure in mountaineering history. His own record as an Alpinist was perhaps the most distinguished amongst moun-taineers of the late Victorian and Edwardian era, and included many of the important first ascents of the time—amongst them the Younggrat on the Zermatt Breithorn, the Mer de Glace face of the Grépon, and the south face of the Täschhorn. He had also been involved in the early explorations on Lliwedd, undertaken in the course of the Pen y Pass Easter parties of 20 or 30 years before: Roof Route, Shallow Gully, Solomon, and the Purple Passage were all his discoveries. A pacifist, in the Great War he had served in the Friends' Ambulance Corps. In the battle of Monte San Gabriele (1917) on the Italian Front he had received wounds which resulted in the amputation of one leg above the knee, yet after the war he continued to climb, making ascents of the Matterhorn, Wellenkuppe, Monte Rosa, Grépon, Zinal Rothorn, and many others. Apart from his great courage and indomitability, he was a widely-cultured man, acclaimed as one of the foremost mountain writers of his day, and generally accepted to be the best of mountain poets. Given the standards of an earlier period, the judgement was fair, and his poems are often strongly evocative and direct in their re-creation of mountaineering experience, but to a later reader much of what he writes is sonorous rather than meaningful and rests too heavily on a sub-text of Swinburne, Tennyson or Housman. At the time of the Pen y Pass parties which Menlove attended, GWY was reader in comparative education in the University of London. His Easter gatherings were attended by a very wide range of people—distinguished academic figures, young students, the foremost climbers of the time. Although there was perhaps something of the *poseur* in Winthrop Young—a slightly-too-self-conscious striving after nobility of character and appearance, he nonetheless had a genuine interest in his young contemporaries and held out a warm affection towards them which was quite devoid of snares or demands. He made great efforts to help Menlove in the forties, and we can be quite sure that when the cloaked, stumping figure of Young, his long grey hair and open-necked shirt giving him a Bohemian tinge, met the reserved, powerful, awkward young Dr Edwards, he would have done so with real sympathy and friendly attention as he ushered him into his coterie of privilege, talent and connections.

The routes Menlove did at Easter 1934 were not in the great tradition of Pen y Pass, but he did open up another new area of cliff—the West Wing of Dinas Mot, which had the advantage of being only a short walk from the road down the Llanberis Pass. The easy options on these rambling dolerite buttresses of northerly aspect are not generally very attractive. Two of the three climbs Menlove did here were pure grass, but one was better than that—the intriguing and well-positioned Slow Ledge Route: "The name is due really to not being able to think of another. Also if you did sit simply on the ledge in question you *would* slide off slowly." Another day of the holiday was spent on the Milestone with Sandy Edge. They climbed a pleasantly steep and still unfrequented pitch on the right of the cliff, Little Gully Wall, and afterwards made their way round beneath the shadowy green wall which is the Back of the Milestone, where Menlove commenced work on an odd little route now known as Rope Wall. At a small ledge 80 feet above the ground he was faced with the following problem: ". . . everything ahead is steep and smooth. But across the corner on the right is a large ledge, and a device is used. There is a belay on that ledge so large that it is a simple matter to fling the rope over it and oneself after. The second man comes with a wider latitude of choice." Sandy Edge's choice was to decline to follow Menlove's example and finish in uncharted directions out to the left.

Menlove's only other climb this holiday was Schoolmasters' Gully on Cyrn Las. It had been climbed previously in 1906, but Menlove did not know that, and found a better start than the original one: "The type of interest is that to be found in any grassy, messy gully or on any decaying rock face." The description he gave of the final pitch sums up his response to the route: ". . . dirty work up and out of this unpleasant experience". If Menlove, inspired by the tradition of his surroundings and comrades at Pen y Pass, had been trying to re-live the "Gully epoch", he very definitely did not find it much to his taste and quickly abandoned the experiment.

It amuses me sometimes to ponder on what the conversations between GWY and Menlove must have been like, as the former held his inquests into the activities of each day. Having emerged, say, from the bathhouse, they are sitting on the old stuffed armchairs prior to dinner; the one patrician, elegant almost to the point of affectation, using the full range of his musical voice as he plays over the questions, draws out responses, and reconciles them to his own endless and often very stimulating theorizing on the mountain environment and mountaineering. All this is done with a fluency, charm and grace which is irresistible. The young doctor, on the other hand, twenty-three years old to GWY's fifty-eight, watches and listens intently, his brow wrinkled, his lips slightly pursed. When he speaks it is slowly, in a deep voice which dips, along with his head, at the end of each speech. His vowels are flat and open, the manner of delivery studied and considered, his body tense upon the other man's reactions. And then a laughing release, a quick supple gesture of hand, as GWY takes up the point and with a languid poise describes by tone of voice and the end of his pipe the pictures which those phrases have produced in him, the emotions and memories they have stirred. Even Menlove's anti-authoritarianism, recognizing innate kindliness, concedes respect as it gathers confidence to tease and question the traditions and stances. The vibrancy of mutual affection grows between them as the talk goes along, and onlookers stand by to listen in musingly on this meeting of generations. There are several written pieces about the characters of Young's pioneering hey-day by Menlove, and all show the same affectionate ambivalence as the one given here:

In the good old days climbing was a sport for men of iron and they wore deerstalker caps, were 6′ 3″ in height and broad by comparison. When they climbed a climb they were brave and fine about it and they showed grit and determination of a high order. They took life seriously, these grand old men, and they called a spade a spade even if it was a trowel. When asked if they thought they would succeed in getting up a climb they replied with grave faces that they didn't know but that the odds were about even and anyway, they said, a mountain's a good enough place to die on. But now the boot-nail of the ancients has lost its glory while the rubber shoe stalks abroad through the hills. Now our heroes are no longer men of iron but are made only of sorbo rubber guaranteed to bounce without bursting and there remains only an occasional outsider of stainless steel.

The very gentle parody of GWY's writings is distinctly recognizable and generously counter balanced by a refusal to allow any heroic proportions to Menlove's own climbing era.

Acquaintance with GWY moved Menlove sufficiently to persuade him into a visit to the Alps in 1934. His companion was Graham MacPhee, the man who was Kirkus's second on the ascent of the Great Slab. MacPhee was twelve years older than Menlove, a caustically witty Scotsman and author of the first guidebook to Ben Nevis. He was reputedly the most expensive dentist in the North of England, with surgeries in Shrewsbury and in Liverpool's Rodney Street, where Menlove was later to set up his psychiatric practice. He and Menlove had climbed together the previous year without immediately disliking each other and so, in 1934, an Alpine holiday was mooted. Menlove hated it, MacPhee apparently quickly grew to detest Menlove, and the whole sorry episode ended with Menlove being seen walking down a glacier clutching a small suitcase in his hand, on his way back to England. There is nothing very strange in this – many Alpine holidays have ended thus. Neither Menlove nor MacPhee had a good word to say for the other from that time onwards. (MacPhee died in a fall in 1963, whilst climbing alone on the highest peak in the Canary Islands.)

Menlove returned to Liverpool in the late summer of 1934, having secured a post as Clinical Assistant in the psychiatric department of Liverpool Royal Infirmary. He rented part of a house in Birkenhead, No. 3, King's Mount, Oxton—a grimly respectable suburban villa—and settled down to a serious bout of work for his Diploma in Psychological Medicine, which he gained in December. Now qualified to do so, he took rooms and set up in psychiatric practice in Rodney Street—an elegant row of Georgian houses where the medical consultants of Liverpool gathered together between the town further down the hill and the University at its top. The life he experienced in the city had changed since his undergraduate days. The LURCC, for example, because of its strong bias against women—not all of which can be blamed on Menlove—had rightly been compelled by the University authorities to admit them or close, and had chosen the latter course. An enigmatic letter from Menlove about this event appeared in the 1935 *Wayfarers' Club Journal*, and tells us quite a lot about Liverpool climbing on the way to reaching its point:

Dear Sir,

A year or two ago there was an unfortunate occurrence in the City of Liverpool, and I wish to be allowed to draw your attention to it.

The city has rightly prided itself on being always to the forefront of the world. More particularly to my point, of the climbing world. It is true that in the greater world of mountaineering we have not accepted too prominent a position either of late or previously. Yet just recently one very estimable expedition, even in this domain, not very large perhaps, but surely most efficient, has set out from here to the far off adventure of the Himalayas. All their baggage was collected here, and all their plans radiated from Liverpool as a centre. Of the six protagonists we can honestly state that a large proportion had dwelt within the very walls of Liverpool. Their plans, it is said, were far reaching and slightly revolutionary, as plans from this locality always are. The inhabitants take some pride in this. The measure of success of this expedition was not, of course, absolute, but was undoubtedly great. They enjoyed themselves immensely, and left others a precedent to do so. The inhabitants were rightly proud of such innovations. Liverpool nearly sent her greatest climber to join the recent Everest expedition, but unfortunately was not quite able.

Then our senior Liverpool climbing Club, meanwhile, is advancing by leaps and bounds. Their all night walk—once a year—is a most popular feature. Their activities, they are glad to say, ramify far beyond mere rock climbing. Their hut in Langdale is equal to the very best and the new garage adds immensely to its uses as a centre for walking and climbing. The living room is large, and roomy, and the sleeping quarters comfortable. They claim to have built a bathing pool. If perhaps not a vast deal of actual climbing is done, they can at least boast with some truth that a few of their members, who, when in Wales, alas, do not always fly their particular club colours, are quite prominent climbers in that district. It is probable enough that others do climbs that are more difficult and dangerous, but these must surely be very rash and foolhardy people. In fact no climbers in that district, who are not members of our club, feel that they can blow their trumpet so loudly as can we. This, I repeat, we do with a great show of truth.

All this length of dissertation may seem to be a little beside the point, but I mention these things in an endeavour to show the very important, nay, the definitely central position that our city holds in the climbing world. For, indeed, is it not situated precisely half way between the respective climbing districts of North Wales and the English Lakes? Central position is consequently our due. I have been endeavouring to show you, then, certain commencements from which we hope even further greatnesses may accrue.

Now, what is there more germane to the innate symbolisms of life than this—that a great city should be represented adequately by a great University, each of whose multiple facets shall reflect the larger, but far less exalted and exclusive, corresponding group in the city as a whole?

And this has brought us to a point at which I can no longer hold back from mention of the catastrophe on which I started. The University of Liverpool has lost a Climbing Club. It was admitted to be a most worthy representative of the city, both as regards the speed of its growth and the show it made. The fact that it never totalled more than a very limited number of members shows how exclusive it was, and it always intended to be a very active and fine club. Yet it has gone, the Chairman has gone, the Secretary has gone, and all the club property. What is to be done about this? The University of Liverpool has lost its Climbing Club, and cannot find another.

Being somewhat implicated in this unexpected disappearance, I prefer to remain,

Yours simply,

J.M.E.

(Briefly, the allusions in this letter are to Marco Pallis's 1933 Gangotri Glacier expedition ("one very estimable expedition . . ."), which as well as the named leader included Kirkus, Hicks and Charles Warren, and which climbed two peaks of over 22,000 feet—Satopanth and Liu Purgyal; and to the controversy over Kirkus's not having been invited on the 1933 Everest expedition which is referred to in the sentence "Liverpool nearly sent her greatest climber . . .".)

Most of Menlove's close friends from the university by now had left and were scattered throughout the country. Hewlett and his father were dead, Stephen was married and in Shropshire. Even the visits to Helsby made him feel old:

We found a tiny little boy at Helsby. He was only about twelve years of age and 5 or 6 hands high, but there he was all by himself playing about on the steepest of rocks. He ran up the Grooved Slab: Pigeon Hole Wall, Honeycomb Buttress were nothing to him, nor Marshall's Route where we had had difficulty.

We tried . . .

Jericho Wall we didn't try, being unable to do it ourselves.

Only once in that easiest of all places, Clashooks, he slipped and hurt his nose. Then we thought of Eliminate I . . . he ran up the first part, crawled on to that ledge, lay down on the biggest handholds and yelled for mercy.

We hoiked him out on the rope, pulled him up to the top and sent him away, telling him never to climb alone again, because it was bad for the morale of the other climbers.

There was always Helyg if the need for companionship apart from his work became too great, and throughout the autumn and winter of 1934 and spring of 1935 he fell into the habit of spending every second or third weekend there. On some of these visits, with the few habitués of the place still left in Liverpool and Birkenhead, he went seeking new cliffs. One day he found the Giant's Head Buttress in the Lledr Valley, a very steep little shaley cliff rising out of the woods. He and Brian McKenna climbed two routes on it, which were re-discovered in the 1960s and named Titan and Cyclops: 'One finds a bed in the moss under the shelter of the trees and says what bad rock it was—in the intervals of removing thorn and bramble residues in the fingers." Both routes are about Very Severe, but Menlove had no idea what to grade them. From this time onwards his idea of grades and standards in climbing becomes notably disconnected from popular consensus. He did not, in fact, grade any route of his own more than Severe after 1932 unless strongly persuaded to do so by his second or guidebook co-author. Strangely enough, he was quite prepared to give Very Severe grades to routes which he seconded, or for which others were partly responsible. This gave rise to some remarkable anomalies, and acquired for Menlove a reputation for undergrading of such extent that later editors of his guidebooks felt impelled to include in them cautionary notes and tables comparative with the systems of other areas.

In the January of 1935 Menlove paid one visit to the most popular of modern climbing areas, the dolerite cliffs above the estuary of the Glaslyn at Tremadog. He, Chantrell and McKenna scrambled up to the foot of Craig y Castell: "blackberry bushes lay ahead and the route through them was very trying. B McK, gallantly leading, got scratched and pricked all over and said he was thankful to get through alive." They gazed up at the great overhangs with smooth slabs between, now taken by Tensor and Pellagra, turned to look at the leaning, dripping crack of the Wasp, fronded with ivy, and retreated to Black Rock Sands for bathing in the sea. A week or two later Menlove and McKenna made up for this lack of motivation by climbing the first two routes on another "modern" cliff, Clogwyn y Grochan, near the road low down in the Lanberis Pass.

Stuart Chantrell recorded an incident which took place at Helyg between these two men at about this time:

> The only occasion I saw the least sign of temper was when Brian and Menlove playfully began a wrestling match in the bedroom and each was astonished to find the other equally strong. It seemed for a few minutes that things might become serious and I had to calm them down. Needless to say, both of them were bitterly ashamed of themselves.

(McKenna, a landscape gardener by profession who was responsible for the present-day plantation of trees around Helyg, was killed in a freak accident on Cnicht in 1965, blown off the ridge in winter conditions.)

Menlove's work was progressing well. In the early spring of 1935 he was appointed psychiatrist to the Liverpool Child Guidance Clinic, a post he held until its closure in 1941, and which was to earn him the unanimous good opinion of those with whom he worked. His real strength lay in personal contact with, and treatment of, patients, and there are many testimonies to this. One case was that of a church organist sacked by his vicar because of a growing lack of discipline amongst the choir children. This caused the organist a nervous breakdown, and his wife eventually had to entreat him to go to the psychiatric clinic at the Royal Infirmary, where he was seen by Menlove. It was arranged that he should attend at the latter's rooms in Rodney Street once a week. He did this, complaining all the while that he was getting no treatment, and returned one day to tell his wife that Menlove had told him he needn't come again. "But he's not done anything," complained the organist. To which his wife replied, "Well, everybody says you're all right again now."

Stuart Chantrell, custodian of Helyg, who was becoming a close friend of Menlove's, gives his own summing up of Menlove's practical assistance:

> I had personal knowledge of some of his private cases and of quite remarkable results with several who suffered from asthma. A friend of my

own who stammered very badly was completely cured after weekly treatment for over a year. He, like many others, was given this help without payment.

The fact of Menlove's homosexuality is fundamentally important in any consideration of his life, and by 1935 this matter was in a stage of crisis. We need to go back a little at this point to consider the developing argument in Menlove's mind around the point of whether or not homosexuality and homosexual behaviour was, in Christian terms, immoral. By about 1931 Menlove had firmly concluded that his emotional and physical disposition was homosexual. It was probably in this year that he had, because a situation which had arisen demanded something of the kind from him, made an offer of a platonic marriage to a friend of Nowell's—the one who stayed with the family when Nowell was away at art school, and who had thought Menlove "the best of the lot". It is scarcely worth speculating on what would have happened if his offer had been accepted—whether the girl's comradeship would have given him a strength and a link to humanity which might have sustained him at the cost of a terrible sublimation of her own desires. In terms of humanity rather than saintliness it was not a viable proposition and she wisely turned it down. She was not the last woman to take an interest in Menlove, but she was the last to receive any such offer.

The editors of *Samson* suggest that Menlove "fell in love twice, with the whole strength of his powerful nature". Although the phrase "fell in love" is obviously susceptible to various interpretations, even when allied to the loose qualifier it is here given, their conclusion seems to be contradicted by the evidence of the poetry. It also has to be held in mind continually with regard to *Samson* that the testimony of that book is, on the matter of Menlove's homosexuality, unreliable and possibly even distorting. On a simple basis of the content and chronology of the poetry, he fell in love three or four times. Some connected holograph fragments exist from 1932 which tell of two of these experiences. They are notable for various reasons, and I give them here in full:

> To leave him tore my heart out, and my soul
> And body ache together for this loss.
> Some fragments of my heart have stayed with me,
> For loving other people with, but they
> Are wee, small rags of heart, scarce fit for use,
> For anything, without the greater part
> Which stays with him. I bleed internally
> And cannot staunch my wound. From heaven I

Have gone to hell, and I must live in hell
Where ev'rything I see recalls me to
The thought of him, the joy I've lost, and I
Must make life here. With hope of heaven again?
How scant that hope! . . . the war, the contract time,
And change . . .

Ah, God . . . dear God, I need thee so,
And ne'er have needed more thy guiding hand,
The sureness of thy presence, and thy firm,
Kind touch. For years have I been blessed with these
And knowledge of them. Through the lovely months
With him, still hast thou led me, showing me
Anew in him thy gentleness and strength
And beauty. Oh, Almighty, Merciful,
Please look on me and hold me closer in
Thy tender, loving hand, and let me feel
Its steady pulse until it soothe me. Yet
My grief I cling to, not for grief, but that
It seems to bring me closer to the well
Of joy that I have known. Dear God, I do
Not know what I would pray for, . . . only faith
And patience, . . . trusting, if I only can,
In thy unceasing care and endless love.

I never meant to fall in love again.
I never meant to and I'm scared to death.
Dear God, that this so precious thing, which comes
To me despite myself, will crumble in
My hand just as the other did, or will
Be snatched from me. But, since I did not want
It, will be all right? Is it your work?
It's beautiful enough. I cannot stop
Myself because it is so beautiful.
Dear Lord, have mercy on me. Do not break
My heart again! This man is not like that
Nor any other I have known, but still
I am afraid. But when I am with him,
I'm happy, know that everything is right;
And when we are apart, I only live
That we may be together once again.

It all works out so perfectly, dear God,
I keep my fingers crossed, and pray it may
Be ever so; that this is in your hands.

The poem above, which was later entitled "Postlude" by Menlove, cannot really be judged by any objective critical standards. An extremely literal approach needs to be adopted to it. This is something to be generally cautious of doing with regard to Menlove's writing, for he was well aware of the "innate symbolisms of life" (his own phrase.) At a fundamental level, the poem is interesting. There are two relationships referred to here, both of which have aroused very strong feelings in the poet, who is writing directly and with neither time nor need to adopt a *persona*, as he did in the "Samson" poem quoted in the previous chapter. The startling feature here is the sudden—it occurs mid-line—apostrophizing of God. There can be no doubt whatsoever about the firmness of belief in God, at the time of its composition, which it reveals. Not only that, but the implicit assumption on the part of the writer is that no stigma attaches in the eyes of God to love of a fellow human being who happens to be of the same sex. Indeed, the relationship with a man is a gift of God, and continues under His guidance:

Through the lovely months
With him, still hast thou led me, showing me
Anew in him thy gentleness and strength
And beauty.

None of this is surprising to a reader in the mid-1980s. Over the last 30 years several writers have tackled the question of homosexuality and its religious proscription. Theologians like Oraison, Gottschalk and Sherwin Bailey have all contested the idea that there is definite scriptural authority of such condemnation. But as outlined before, the position in the 1930s was vastly different. What *is* surprising is how little sense of guilt the poem conveys on the part of its writer towards his own homosexuality. And this leads us into a further line of questioning as to what it was that stimulated the later sense of guilt which underlies two important questionings in Menlove's work on the position of the homosexual in society. These are the poem entitled "John", from 1934, and the sermon he delivered in Stokesay Church on 17 March 1935.

"John" is a poem of considerable length, which demonstrates a growing metrical skill and fluency, and which, because of its apparent difficulty, demands a very close reading and some exegesis. It is seemingly written in the persona of St John the Apostle, Christ's beloved disciple, though at times this is ambiguous and the persona may be that of John the Baptist. It takes the form of a vision recounted by him. The vision is one "beginning in the older world" and is of the soul of man, his quest for a meaning, and the forces which act upon him. In the vision he is "in the spirit with the Lord", and sees life—here a feminine agent—unroll across time. The forces and energies at play in life resolve themselves into motion, wind, and fate, whilst man, with a wondering resistance at their use of him, grieves at and questions why he should be the creature of such forces. There follows a passage which inveighs strongly against stasis and thereby calls into question established moral judgement: "Is all of this the grand insistence of a monument . . .?' The poem then moves to an examination of sexuality and isolation in a passage which is powerful despite its conventional language and imagery:

> And as I went it seemed a valley grew about
> Me, with its tall fir trees, so that I saw the thin,
> Long trunks of them rise, straight across the mountains to
> The sky. And there arose a storm of weather from
> Among the mountains, and the great trees called
> And leant to it: but each came not the nearer to
> The next, and none had speech with them. And then I saw
> A scythe was turning it about, among the trees,
> On silent search above the ground of life, and moved
> To cut them as they rose. And when the darkness came
> Again, behold the valley sighed, and drew itself
> together for its leaves.
> For man looked round and recognised his fellow men
> That they were like afflicted with himself. And man
> Began to feel his soul was moved and lifted up
> Towards their sorrowing, so that it went as charged
> With other men, to speak a music mindful of their want.

Menlove's stock symbolism has been brought heavily into play here: the valley can be interpreted as a female symbol, although sometimes in Menlove's poetry it refers to one who takes the passive role in homosexual activity; the tall fir trees are obviously male, whilst the storm may be the arousal of emotion. Its effect on the trees is to make them lean, but curiously they do not approach each other, and certainly do not talk. The scythe is probably the stock symbol of death—the grim reaper—which takes its toll amongst them, leaving the female image to mourn in the approaching darkness—perhaps mortality or lack of understanding. The effect of the presence of mortality is both an access of compassion and a desire to "speak a music mindful of their want". What this encompasses is made obvious in the next few lines:

> Our life is long
> And we too grown to dwell against the load: so that
> We mind us of a putting of ourselves aside,
> And quietly, until we have our licences
> To leave.

The issue raised here is the necessity for repression. Why, he asks, should there have to be "a putting of ourselves aside"? And throughout life? The poem takes up this argument and dramatizes it into an exchange between John and Christ. Christ gives John new hope that his love is valid and can be expressed—indeed, must be expressed. The poem then concludes with the following coda:

Yes, see ye love. The loneliness of love
Is but yourself, that is too little loving, and
Dragged on behind. But love itself is God.
It is not birth is half so beautiful a birth
As death, so see ye love, and I retire in
My Maker. See that ye can bring again to me
The horses of my heart. They swiftly leap
Along the entrance bars of night, so dark against
The last day's gleam: and darkly beautiful.

It is perhaps no little sacrifice that God
Is love. Have we not tried? And felt it so.

The technical skill of the above lines is worthy of comment before discussing the significance of the poem. The alternating lines in hexameter and pentameter are quite regular and yet entirely natural in their movement. Such metrical ingenuity and fluency within a strictly self-imposed scheme is not something that might be anticipated of Menlove, and points up a degree of care in the construction of even quite long poems which is unexpected. It should alert us later on in this book to consider the recurrent self-disparagement to be seen in his comments on his own poetry to Winthrop Young and others. It could also, tenuously, be seen to counterpoint the quest for control over emotion evident in his climbing and water exploits.

The coda is both subtle and resonant. It neatly inverts the idea that "God is love" to validate its final position and bears a dialectical relationship, as does the whole poem, to the first few verses of St John's Gospel. "The horses of my heart" are probably here less apocalyptic, though they carry that possibility, than archetypal—used in much the same way that Lawrence uses the horse-symbol in his novella *St Mawr* or in *The Rainbow*. What the coda finally establishes is Menlove's belief that "All things were made by him; and without him was not any thing made that was made. In him was life; and the life was the light of men. And the light shineth in darkness, and the darkness comprehended it not." But it is very much to be doubted whether he puts an orthodox Anglican gloss on these verses. His attempt, as he put it in his reply to the CMS, to "get beyond the concept of God to a concept of Man" brings him not to a rejection of Christ, for he states clearly that he is "in the spirit with the Lord", but to a belief very similar to that of Blake— that God lives in every human breast. (In corroboration of this, Stephen remembers that when Menlove read the lesson at Stokesay from John I, he left out the words "only begotten" from verse eighteen.) Ethically, this leads Menlove to an intuitivist stance. His actions are morally right if, deity being innate in humanity, he senses them to be so. The difficulty of this line of reasoning lies, of course, in self-reproach, and when that starts to intensify upon the collapse of the relationships into which the intuitivism led him, for a person as finely attuned morally as was Menlove, the backlash is appalling. Once committed to a homosexual relationship, as he is soon to be with Wilfrid Noyce, the complexities attendant upon running counter to public opinion, however discreetly, are such that some feelings of guilt are inevitable and it is very highly unlikely that in the stressful situations which arise as the relationship falls apart, these feelings can be successfully analysed and ascribed their rightful degrees of value. Basically, the moral homosexual who chooses to act authentically within a strictured society is on a hiding to nothing unless he finds a mutually secure and supportive relationship. The best course of action, therefore, is to try to change the society, to try to give it the necessary wisdom and understanding, to try, in the words of St John's Gospel, "to bear witness of the Light". And that, in the Stokesay sermon, is exactly what Menlove set out to do.

Imagine the scene on a Sunday morning in March 1935. The tall, handsome figure of the Vicar in this small parish of South Shropshire comes out of the vicarage. He is accompanied by his wife of less than a year, and by his younger brother, to whom he is pointing out features of this tiny and picturesque village into which he has been newly installed. The younger brother wears polished black shoes and a double-breasted, narrow-striped suit in a sober shade of blue, its shoulders exaggerating his already pronounced stockiness. Short, firm-jawed, brown-eyed with a steady gaze and a head of brown curls, he has about him the slightly nervous reserve of someone with something to say who is shortly to be called up to say it.

Stephen, Ruth and Menlove walk in a leisurely manner towards the church. A few early members of the congregation bid their Vicar good morning—cottagers perhaps, or farm labourers from this predominantly rural parish. As they walk along the lane towards the duck pond and the castle, the slightly incongruous half-timbering of the gate-house raises a smile as it contrasts with the grey stone walls and the squat grey church, which they enter. Stephen goes about his priestly duties as Menlove waits in his assigned place. He looks around admiringly at the old woodwork, the canopied pew, the raised pulpit with its sound-board. In a regressive way, he feels at home, feels a certain sense of peace and belonging, though spiced now by a critical awareness. As the congregation files in he studies them quizzically, wondering as to the effect upon them of what he has to say. Finally the morning service commences, hymns are sung, the lessons read, and then Menlove stands and makes his way to the pulpit, scrutinized by pew upon pew of upturned faces as he opens his sermon with the text, "Sacrifice a meat offering thou wouldest not, but mine ears hast thou opened".*

"First I would like to say that as one who is practising psychology it was a great pleasure to me to be asked to talk about my subject from the pulpit; that is to take it as part of our service to God.

"There was a time when the study of the mind was considered to be simply one side, and a main side of the priest's duties. It was felt that the mind was something to be approached with awe and reverence, and with the aid of God. This was so in the religions of the East, it was so in our Christian religions. The priests educated the young of the whole country, they were responsible for the systems of logic, they even were responsible for the care of the insane. Confucianism, and Buddhism particularly were in some ways less of a religion than a theory about the nature of the mind. The study of religion and the study of the mind were considered to be much the same thing.

"Nowadays we find just the opposite. The study of the mind, education, mental illness, and so on, are treated as lay subjects. They are taken as being outside religion. They are something that one specializes in now, as one might in history or economics. The study of the mind itself, that is, is taken as being different from that of the mind's aims. Yet, obviously it is a study of great importance to us all. One goes through life and the mind is the

---

* This is apparently a misquotation from Hebrews 10:8: "Sacrifice and offering and burnt offerings and offering for sin thou wouldest not, neither hadst pleasure therein; which are offered by the law."

thinking instrument with which one goes. It is a good thing to know something about this instrument, the instrument with which one seeks through life to do better.

"During the last 50 years, then, the study of the mind has progressed enormously, and the result has been to alter slowly the attitude of the world towards a great many problems. It is quite certain, too, to produce more alteration for some time. We definitely know more about the mind than we used to, and we find that many old ideas and customs can no longer stand up to that knowledge.

"The subject is a huge one and one can only pick out one or two points to mention in a morning. But the centre of the whole matter is the practical one—what are our aims to be, and how are we to work towards them in ourselves and help others to do so?

"One of the first things we found out about the mind was that it is a very imperfect instrument, and this is a very important point. We found that it was very difficult for a person to realize what his mind was really doing, it worked to a great extent unconsciously, behind his back, and if he did not know what it was doing, it was obviously rather impossible for him to direct it accurately towards higher things. He might quite honestly think that he was acting out of his desire to please God when really he wanted to do it because of purely his own small, selfish desires. You can see dozens of examples of this in any community daily. Somebody does something that seems to you quite obviously stupid and selfish, and yet he both says and honestly thinks that he is doing it 'for the best'. He really does not understand himself; he does not know his own mind well enough. It is not sinful, it is an unfortunate ignorance, and we are not better ourselves. It is so easy for us to give blame. But what good will that do? We must all the time understand, sympathize and try to make the other person understand. Look at all the persecutions and the burnings that have been done by Christians who gave their whole life to Christ. What a waste of energy. All through lack, not of keenness—they had amazing keenness for good, but through lack of understanding of themselves and others. Be very careful, then, to understand always and never to blame, for in this way is our only chance of helping.

"As for raising our standard of life—Jesus, you will remember, laid down very few rules. No strict rules of conduct. It was the later Christians, from St Paul on, who tried to interpret his teaching into strict moral codes, and a sort of etiquette. I want to say something about such rules and how far they are useful for making us better people. Now, as soon as we start to examine people, we find that they grow up with needs and desires, mentally, that are very far from being all the same. People are different, and as soon as you start to make a definite rule, it may suit most people's mental make up, but there will always be certain types to whose needs the rule is badly fitted. These people will not be helped by the rule, they will be hindered by it. Definite rules are very dangerous things. You can see that those who keep them usually do so not out of the good of their hearts, but because of their self respect and their personal pride. Yet these people will be considered the ideals, the law-keepers. On the other side those to whom the rule is not fitted will have their difficulties despised and looked down on. If they break the rule they will just be punished. There is no help forthcoming from that rule.

"The present criminal laws for instance, they fail to understand that when a man acts wrongly it is the duty of his fellows to help that man to better paths of action; to cure the conditions which led to the wrong-doing, whether it was something in the man's mind or whether it was something outside, like poverty. To lock that man up in prison is simply to avoid the whole difficulty and the whole responsibility. When we examine the so-called criminal we find that in his place we would probably have done the same ourselves, yet we treat him like that.

"Then take sex. At present the institution of marriage is supposed to do for all cases. It can, we all know, be a very fine institution, but is it fair to apply it to all cases? We all know too that it can make things so difficult for people as to ruin the mental and moral tone of their lives, also perhaps their children's. Worse than that, we find that certain people, through no fault of their own have their feelings of love towards people of their own sex. Are we going to use our little rules and despise and punish these people, or are we to let the rule look out for itself and try to understand and help these people? It is no use shutting our eyes to these things. If people are in difficulties we must understand and try to help. If a rule does not fit a case, the rule must go in that case.

"What did Jesus do when he came up against rules? He said, 'The Sabbath is made for man, not man for the Sabbath.' To the woman who had committed adultery, the chief offence against the marriage rules, he said, 'Neither do I condemn thee, go and sin no more.' He did not condemn her, and we take it then that he wished to understand and help her. You can't do that if you condemn or despise.

"One would be wrong to preach disobedience to the laws, that again does nobody any good and is quite a different matter, but moral rules and codes are no substitute for understanding and sympathy. What then are to be our principles? We are here alive on the earth and we are faced with certain needs and desires that are born in us. There is the need for food, the desire to raise one's position, the desire for friends, love and so on. These primary and quite selfish desires are the only things that urge us through our lives and out of them, if, out of anything, we have to forge our desires for higher things. None of these desires are wrong in themselves. Bad may come of them and good may come of them. The stronger a feeling is the more difficult and painful it is to direct into only those paths that one sees to be good, but also the stronger it is the greater its possible power for good, once it is controlled. Never try to get rid of a feeling. It is there in you just as certainly as the apple tree bears apples in her season and not other fruit. What can be done is to direct and control it by bringing other feelings up also and seeing which is to be the best use in each case.

"How are we to know what is best? We must have first some knowledge of the task before us. Take the illustration of sex again, the feeling is there for good or bad and the task is to make the highest use of it. Is it fair to send youth out into the world without any knowledge of the problem? There is a great wealth of knowledge and honest thought available on the subject today, and yet most of our boys and girls come up against it with their eyes practically blindfolded. A certain amount of odd stuff picked up somehow, and a vague idea that the whole thing is unclean. Is that fair to him? Is it going to put him in the way of making the best and the highest that can be made out of that feeling of physical and mental attraction towards other people? It obviously is not. And this at a time when we are just beginning to realize how much of the progress of man has been due to this feeling.

"We must understand, then: we must educate ourselves and others, and beyond that we need principles to aim at. We find that definite rules are no good for this. What then remains? Why should we do this rather than that act? Because our personal interests and desires are always in conflict with the desires of others. We are not alone in the world, and we must mould our desires to bring good and not bad to those around us.

"First then, we must not hurt others. But that is only a negative aim—a must-not. That is not enough. We must achieve out of our feelings something positive, some feeling that makes us actively want the good of others.

"This is what we want, an understanding backed by feeling. Love your neighbour as yourself. No man has seen God at any time, but if we love one another God dwelleth in us, and His love is perfected in us—God is love. Here are none of the rules and regulations, such as we use now and the Pharisees used to use. It goes straight to the heart of any matter. We must do the same. To put it in the poetry of the Testament: 'Sacrifices and meat-offering thou would'st not, but mine ears hast thou opened. Burnt offering and sacrifice for sin hast thou not required, then said I "Lo, I come".

To deliver this sermon to a deeply conservative rural population in the mid-1930s was an act of considerable moral courage—not only on Menlove's part, but also on Stephen's as the new incumbent, for he would have had a good idea of its content. It is, I think, a remarkably good first sermon, with a clear progression from generalized discussion, through particular areas of difficulty, to a personal view supported by Christ's teachings of individual conduct within society. Menlove has obviously brought in an element of special pleading on his own behalf, which is why the sermon is included here and why it retains an interest for us. But his message must have been quite accessible to the congregation, though whether or not it was acceptable to them is less assured. "The subject," as he says, "is a huge one and one can only pick out one or two points to mention." The one or two points he chooses are basically concerned with the conflict between Pauline ethical codes and the Christian tolerance of Jesus. At the centre of his argument he places a plea not only for recognition and understanding to be accorded to the homosexual, but also for allowance to be made for the authentic expression of the individual's emotions. Again, the concluding paragraphs adopt an intuitivist position, with the dangers that entails. What is clear is that by 1935 Menlove held to the belief that Christianity and homosexuality were not irreconcilable and that no guilt attaches if the motives are sufficiently sound—if the partners are, in effect, loving. But what is also apparent is that, whilst guilt does not intrude upon these two important discussions, it effectively forms, by the need for their existence, an alternative discourse to them. Menlove has explored in them his own anxieties but he has not won through to a security of belief because the mode and area of discussion are theoretical and personal, and do not meet the social prejudices against his appetencies on open ground.

To turn once again from abstract discussion of Menlove's concerns to their more concrete expressions, at about the time of the Stokesay sermon, his interest in adventures on the water had revived. The *Liverpool Daily Post* reported one of them in the following manner.

A Liverpool doctor has performed a considerable canoeing feat by crossing from the Isle of Man to the Cumberland coast alone in a collapsible canoe during the night.

He is Dr J. Menlove Edwards of Rodney Street, Honorary Assistant Psychiatrist to Liverpool Child Guidance Clinic and Honorary Clinical Assistant at the Royal Infirmary, and he set out from the Isle of Man at 11 o'clock on Friday night. Dr Edwards was at sea sixteen hours, and landed at Millom after a passage of forty-five miles.

In conversation with the *Daily Post* he made light of the matter, though he said the sea was choppy, and he saw only one fishing boat during his crossing. His friends knew he was to make the venture, but neither they nor he had any fears, for two-seater collapsible canoes of the kind he used were reliable craft, even in quite big seas, if properly handled.

This is a sea-crossing which even the expert modern canoeist, practised at the eskimo roll, with his fibreglass craft of sophisticated design, insulating clothing and close-fitting spraydeck, would think very carefully about and probably not attempt without companions. I wonder how many of them would undertake it in a two-seater open canvas-and-plywood craft, alone, in March? A few weeks later, just before Easter 1935, Menlove and Colin Kirkus set out to row across the Irish Sea. They had borrowed a small boat, and set off from Conway on the evening tide, intending to go with it through the Menai Straits. Unfortunately, a gale blew up and they spent the night in an exhausting struggle to keep the boat head on to it off Traeth Lafan. When the morning came they went back into Conwy harbour on the wind and tide and spent the day sleeping off the adventure, glad to be alive. Then Kirkus left for Idwal Cottage, whilst Menlove rowed the boat the 50 miles back to Liverpool by himself. On his arrival there a wave sucked him under the landing stage as he was being questioned by the harbourmaster, but he escaped injury.

He had not climbed very much in the early part of 1935. The output for January, February and March had been one new route a month, two of them being on Clogwyn y Grochan and once on Carreg Wastad. Indeed, his most notable contribution to climbing in these months was the amusing "Guide to the Helyg Boulder":

This boulder is one to which every Helygian owes special honour. It has excited the admiration and envy of all who have seen it and bids fair to outdo the cottage itself both in longevity and in glory. It is true that by now almost every member of the club takes it as a practice spring before commencing the day's work, but even so our prophet is not dishonoured nor despised by even its own countrymen.

There are by now then such a number of routes up the boulder that a catalogue of sorts seems necessary. By this means members not hitherto aware of the multiple chances offered will be able to take them all in rotation—and so avoid the repetition that attends the unvaried single route, be it never so good.

What follows is a diagram with all hand holds numbered and foot holds lettered, and a list of nineteen possible routes; a sample description is:

"Route B, Hands 5 → 5 = 11 → 9. Feet G & H → F & E." The guide is slightly more than the very elaborate joke which is undoubtedly intended. The "boulder" is only a short wall of rock, twelve feet high, above a very soft and grassy landing, but one or two of the moves which these combinations describe, on full-length routes in more serious situations, would undoubtedly merit a technical grade of 6a—or harder: "All routes are suitable for ascent, descent, rubbers, nails, good or bad weather, etc. etc."

Easter of 1935 found Menlove at Helyg. He and Sandy Edge spent the first day of the holiday in Cwm Silyn, Menlove once more focusing on the Western Cliffs. He climbed a filthy gully, the Little Kitchen: "The view is good, and the rock is not so good. There was also water in the place and mosses. ARE [Sandy Edge] saw all this and remained where the little avalanches would not reach." Edge was understandably unimpressed, and left Menlove to his own devices for the rest of the weekend.

Also staying at Helyg was a seventeen-year-old Charterhouse schoolboy, Wilfrid Noyce. He had already been in Wales for a fortnight, putting up at the Bryn Tyrch hotel in Capel Curig and climbing from there with Major Bradley, who owned it, for a week, and with David Murray-Rust, a master at his school, for another week. He and Murray-Rust had managed some respectably difficult routes together; the Holly Tree Wall Original Route, Long Chimney on the Terrace Wall. But now Murray-Rust had gone back home and Noyce had been turned out of the Bryn Tyrch to make way for the Easter guests. As a prospective member of the Climbers' Club (he was to go up to Cambridge the following year and as a member of its university mountaineering club his election to the Climbers' Club would have been expected or, if he became its President or Secretary, automatic) he was allowed to stay as a guest at Helyg. On his first day there, to his extreme disappointment he was taken up nothing more difficult than Ivy Chimney on the Milestone Buttress. To a talented and advantaged public schoolboy it was something of an affront to spend a Good Friday in such a mundane fashion. After all, in the previous year he had already had two climbing holidays in Wales, had been taken up the Direct Route on Glyder Fach, and the Holly Tree Wall by his cousin Colin Kirkus, and now he had led the latter. He was the proud possessor of a pair of boots nailed with the new tricouni plates. Surely something better than Ivy Chimney was to be expected? And now, here was Menlove Edwards staying in the hut:

> The majority decided to go down to Capel in the evening, for beer at the hotel. They changed to sports coat and flannels and asked if I would care to come. But I would stay, in hope of talk with Menlove Edwards, who had come up; the best rock climber of all, Guy [Kirkus] had said, with Colin

Kirkus and Longland. I watched him as they were eating: a tattered coat over broad shoulders, woolly hair curled back from a face rounded and firm, childlike but for eyes that were old and the jutting chin that forced a fold before the lower lip. They had gone now.

"Tea?" The talk had started.

We went on, about climbing. What of the cliff of D'ur Arddu, photographed on the kitchen wall? And the face of Scafell there, with central Buttress, where you need the rope slings? Of course, the upper part of the Pinnacle face would go some day, said Menlove. No one had dared it yet. At present we were frightened of an exposure of more than a few feet; needed a jug handle every so often, and then were frightened of having nothing to come back to. Standard of nerves would go up, so that we could go on much longer.

This is an intriguing scene to attempt to envisage: the young doctor, with his "eyes that were old", listening amusedly and very knowingly to the ploys and gaucheries of this embodiment of gilded youth, this charming, unknowing boy in the full flush of his first enthusiasm for the sport. And the boy takes the doctor's profound and radical knowledge of the sport to himself and flatters his own ambitions with it. Menlove left a version in writing of the conversation sketched out here.

Good climbing comes from dreams, not from strength or agility. While the person goes stupidly and uneasily and cowardly up that huge line of weakness with its continuous big four finger holds, the mind of the dreamer is not content, it traces other and better lines up the cliff, places where a real confidence and a more real accuracy of judgement would be advisable. True, he does not personally take that better line but it points out to him quite clearly how safe and easy his present line would be—if he were being less of a fool on it. It seems to be the first duty of a climber to be discontent with his climbing, both the detail of it and the fact that he is so keen on it, picked out as against the business of living.

In both passages Menlove's idea of progress rests on control and nerve—on psychological habituation rather than the technical advances in protection and equipment—nylon ropes and slings, karabiners, peg runners, and so on—which were to underpin the next real advance in climbing standards, the major one achieved by Joe Brown and others in the early 1950s.

To come back to Easter Saturday 1935, Menlove invited Noyce to join him for a climb the following day. They begged a lift round to Pen y Pass from Charles Robb, who was setting off to climb on Lliwedd. Noyce again:

At Pen y Pass we met Geoffrey Winthrop Young, driving forth the legions of the Easter party to the rocks . . . I had not dared to hope for this, the first of many meetings. Words were exchanged, a promise given to come in for tea.

"I always go to a cliff where there's a downhill path if possible," said Menlove. We started down the Llanberis valley. The cliffs were small, bushy. We swarmed up, in and out of hollies, rowans, yews.

Noyce has actually got his dates confused here and is referring to the first ascent of Dead Entrance on Carreg Wastad which took place on Easter Sunday: "a continuous line of trees comes to spoil the sport, no sport. Handholds, no handholds, scour the rock, no rock," was Menlove's impression. On Easter Saturday they climbed on Clogwyn y Grochan, making the first ascent of Long Tree Gate:

The opening pitch does not look difficult, and I lay on the grass at the bottom and shouted encouragement, wondering why he took so long. He worked upward very slowly, clumsily almost, and I can see now that it was strength of arm alone that kept him to the rock. At the time he seemed to be making a mess of it. Sometimes he stopped, put a foot up, and withdrew it.

He pulled out, crossed over to the tree, tied on and drew in the rope. The pitch was beyond my technique: holds that had seemed large disappeared, or hung somewhere at my hip. The rope held me, I could take the weight off my arms and ask to be let down. I went at it again savagely, blood gushing from a desperately taken handhold. And again. It was no good.

"All right, you climb and I'll pull, both together," said Menlove. That went quickly. I landed at the tree in some humility. Boys of seventeen, however, are not naturally modest, and I did not appreciate the difference between his way of climbing the pitch and mine. It was an unspectacular technique, a technique that reminded one of wrestling, with every appearance that the battle was a losing one. Then, suddenly, he was on top. That day, as often, he was climbing in clinker-nailed boots which made the struggle more audible. Moreover, with what seemed a pointless and exasperating patience, he would hang on, scrabbling, and peer round for any rock projection that would take a hitched rope. Sometimes the result did not look secure, but it had a way of working . . .

Menlove's comments on the route are rather more terse:

The party mucked about a lot on this route. Apart from the first pitch and the second pitch, there was difficulty with the thread at the end of the third pitch. The fourth pitch then appeared hard to start and No. 1's fingers got spasms of being unable to unbend. No. 2 therefore stood on his head and led this pitch.

The first pitch of the route is still considered a hard proposition at Very Severe. Its awkwardly placed holds and steepness demand a dynamic technique and the use of friction holds for the feet. In clinker-nailed boots it must have been exceedingly hard—perhaps two grades above the modern technical one of 4c. Menlove graded it Severe. Afterwards, they went round the corner and climbed another new route, originally called Coed Trwsgl— Welsh for Rough Wood—but the name was later changed to Scrambler's Gate. The drawback of the downhill approach then made itself felt as they trudged back up to Pen y Pass for tea with Geoffrey Winthrop Young: "It was a striking contrast: Geoffrey Young's superb head in the aristocratic style ... Menlove rough by contrast, a northerner, as he used to say, who disliked southern speech and ways, but who came under the spell. 'Geoffrey's a decent old thing,' he said, and went on to tell how he disagreed with him on almost everything."

On Easter Sunday Chantrell gave them a lift to Pen y Gwryd and they walked down to climb Dead Entrance on Carreg Wastad, as noted above. Easter Monday found them without any transport, so they strolled along the road to the Milestone Buttress:

... it was generally thought that all the good lines had been taken already. The main "trade routes", whitened with many scratches, could be seen from miles away. But that was because, Menlove said, everybody herded up like sheep; nobody had the energy to look round the corner, where the steeper ground of the west flank held moisture and vegetation, both unpopular. He had his eye on a grass-filled crack vertically splitting the whole face, just left of the main buttress nose and the most obvious feature of all if you stood on the road looking up. A direct attack seemed difficult, something for later perhaps. For the moment we contented ourselves with a corner on the left, leading to a large ledge which should take us back to a big grass patch half way up the main crack.

I was perched safely behind a big block on this ledge, while Menlove worked across, out of sight.

"I'm going to jump into the crack. Hold the rope." He did jump: at least I think he did. It was a justifiable gamble, since the worst that could happen was an uncomfortable pendulum swing below. This in fact did happen, as I know from the sudden jerk on my shoulders, then "let out more rope" from below. I had been pulled forward, jammed against my boulder, but the voice that rose was almost unruffled. Excavations before the jump had revealed a hold that made it unnecessary to jump at all. He tried again, and this time landed safely. The rest was a struggle, muddy in socks, up the greasy narrows of the main crack, but this went quickly. Soon we were lying on heather couches, at ease, munching the bread and chocolate that became our usual lunch.

The fall described here was a very minor one, and Noyce later said that, but for his inexperience in rope-handling, it would have been no more than a slither. One of Menlove's Rodney Street fragments deals with falling off: "6–10 times; depending whether one counts. The longest time about 40 ft. Others have bettered that by a long way. 80 ft. CFK . . ." The assessment which A. B. Hargreaves gives of Menlove's safety as a climber runs thus:

> . . . there is one thing no one could say about him—and this is quite extraordinary considering the enormous amount of climbing he did and the exceptional difficulty of it—that he was prone to fall off whilst leading. I do know that he once came off that notoriously holdless place in the Cioch Gully, but I never heard of him making a really serious mistake which could have endangered his party.
>
> My recollection of Menlove is that it never occurred to him that he might fall off. He was just accustomed to sticking on despite holds breaking, points of attachment slipping, and so forth. This was all the more extraordinary because it never seemed to matter to him what he had got on his feet. He must have done many very hard climbs in battered old boots with a sprinkling of wobbly nails.

To come back to the Milestone Buttress, and the first ascent of Soap Corner (the name was changed during the writing of the 1937 Tryfan guide to Soap Gut), Menlove's and Noyce's attitudes were somewhat at variance on the gardening of the climb: "Route is pleasant; of very doubtful standard owing to No. 2's unhappy ideas about the use of grass. CWFN did his best to spring-clean the place, and little of the original climb now remains. The point marked X is where the leader dangled on the rope, and just above there No. 2 set about to rub the rocks down." Noyce's attitude at the top was "no more grass and grease. I must be taken to something clean, like Belle Vue Bastion . . ." Menlove wryly agreed, completing the bargain with the proposition that Noyce should lead it. Which is what, under Menlove's guidance and watchful eye, he did.

There is perhaps something of a Pygmalion-like character about Noyce as a climber. Given that he was exceptionally keen and determined and possessed of a natural physical aptitude and considerable courage, the quality of his tutors is noteworthy. Colin Kirkus and Menlove taught him his rock-climbing, Armand Charlet and Hans Brantschen his Alpinism. His parents were both willing and able to provide funds for long climbing holidays in Britain and a friendship he contracted at Cambridge paid for his seasons with the two very best Alpine guides of the time. Looking back on his mountaineering career, it does give cause to wonder whether the fact that everything came so very easily to him, and with such brilliant assistance and support, made him perhaps less aware of the dangers inherent in the sport, with which other less gifted and privileged climbers would have become acquainted in their slower efforts to reach the heights. The serious accidents he suffered in 1937, 1939 and 1946, and the fatal one of 1962, tend to confirm this point of view; Jack Longland vouchsafes that his contemporaries "thought him accident-prone".

However that may be, this Easter Monday was the last day of Menlove's holiday. He went back to Liverpool to work, Noyce went back to Major Bradley and the Bryn Tyrch, but not before making an arrangement to climb together on Clogwyn Du'r Arddu the coming Sunday. In clinkers, and without using the shoulder of the first ascent, Menlove led Noyce and Bradley up Chimney Route: "the climb is a pleasant one and probably not particularly harder in boots. Would also be good probably for wet weather."

Menlove paid several visits to Wales in May. On Jubilee Day he led Major Bradley and two of his young lady guests at the Bryn Tyrch up Longland's Climb on Clogwyn Du'r Arddu. It was the first time it had been done in clinker nails, and the Misses Corrie and Lowe were the first women to climb it: "It seems time to review this climb, which incidentally none of us had done before. It is quite amazingly well enclosed, and if one avoids using the inserted piton all the stances are very good. It is very reasonable in nails and would probably be suitable too for wet conditions." To the reverential world of climbing, which revels in myth and mental barriers, this was virtually iconoclasm. But its intention was no more than to get down to the practical truth of the matter, to hold a thing at its true value, irrespective of reputation, the ignorant esteem of those who had not done it, or the playful egos of those who had.

Several times during this summer Menlove belied his supposed misogyny and climbed severally with the Misses Glynn, Corrie and Lowe. Of one of these occasions he left a pleasing little record. It takes place on the first ascent of the Bluebell Traverse on Clogwyn y Grochan:

"Well," I said, "you're not likely to find me boring climbing. I shall be almost always round the corner wondering what to do about the next pitch." "That's fine," she said, "it's nice to have a man like that about and

M and I have lots to talk about." Yes. True enough, though I had not quite considered it like that before. The young Lord of the Universe: he is a nice addition, if he cares to bring himself along, and if not, they two will be able to talk sense. The young Lord certainly takes a long time over these apparently trivial pitches of his climb, but no harm in that, they did not come for that: besides, he has the most amusing clothes on, patched all over and terribly tough: good.

Fascinating comedy, but look carefully at the stance of the writer towards his portrayed self—at the facility with which he puts himself into the minds of his watchers.

The rest of Menlove's pioneering for 1935 is very quick to tell. There were a few routes on Drws Nodded, a steep little cliff in Cwm Tryfan, done with Evelyn Lowe: "The place has character and has not yet been 'mopped up' by the fingers of people prying for hold. A good cliff, though only a little one . . . it looks as if it would not hesitate to be difficult." In June he climbed Sabre Cut, the left hand of the three great corners on the Columnar Cliffs, in the belief that it was new, and the esoteric Flat Chimney of Drws Clyd. July produced two routes of great latter-day popularity on Carreg Wastad—Shadow Wall and Crackstone Rib, both climbed with Jim Joyce, a student at Bart's Hospital medical school. Crackstone Rib was thought harder than Shadow Wall, and both routes were graded Severe. The latter route is still an intimidating lead at Very Severe, and one where the sight of a kneeling leader, his groping hands well short of their objective, is still frequently to be seen.

1935 was a crucial year in Menlove's life, for during this time one love-affair ran its course and the foundations for another, which was to prove the most serious and ultimately devastating of his life, were laid down. This last was with Wilfrid Noyce. Their climbing together at Easter brought about no immediate emotional commitment, but there is evidence to suggest that initially Noyce was rather infatuated with Menlove—as would have been entirely natural on the part of a schoolboy being shown favour by the best climber of the time. A sonnet of Menlove's written the following year is teasingly addressed to Noyce:

> In the past, you see, your adoration
> Was far too unilaterally prone
> And—please don't argue, dearest—love is known
> For Nature's chief bilateral invention.

Another poem, written in May 1935, whilst describing an attraction to Noyce, also points to the main object of his affection at this time:

> Your skin is warm and lightly glows
> That lips may meet more easily
> That blush for me, and easily,
> For prettily we are together.
>
> Your face lay calm and so embracing,
> And yet, I wish it had been you, Jim,
> Indeed I love you well, my Jimmy,
> And prettily would we together.

The identity of the "Jimmy" of this and others in a related group of poems is neither known nor important. Everything that matters on the subject is in the poems and in one or two brief jottings. If we take these poems as biographical data—accepting the risks attendant on so doing, which in the case of Menlove's writings are justifiable—then we can hazard a relationship which begins early in the year, reaches a climax in June, and thereafter ends amidst some bitterness and reproach, both of which are temporarily abated by an attempted boat-trip, and a climbing holiday with Noyce. The relationship is probably based on a *one-sided* need to express, both physically and emotionally, affection on Menlove's part. The case seems to have been that Menlove's overtures, once his feelings were made known, were rejected. The first poem in the series dates from March, and gives a good idea of his emotions at the outset:

> The sky is hard above the land,
> Deep blue: the empty shell of it
> And even that, so far beyond the grasp,
> Warns me to keep my glances down
> To where the sunlight cuts the land
> Among the barren detail of the hills.
>
> My love is wandered in the mountains
> Somewhere to climb. He's gone alone
> To gather berries on the heights
> And gaze away to where the sea . . .
> His coat is there between the tufts
> And I can carry it with me.
>
> The waters of the mountain tarn
> Stand idle in the heart, and yet
> The shallow stream careers and chafes

Against the shifting. All the heights
Like knocking on her flank, and so
The shallow stream proceeds, proceeds and chafes.

This is a fairly simple poem and does not required detailed discussion. The sky, deep blue in colour, is an established and conventionalized symbol of romantic longing. (Menlove was reading a good deal of German literature, including 'Rilke's *Duino Elegies* and Novalis's *Heinrich von Ofterdingen*, at about this time.) The sky here, however, is "hard above the land", an "empty shell", and "Warns me to keep my glances down". The loved one gazes out "to where the sea . . .—always a potent symbol with Menlove, and here left deliberately vague (but see the poem "How can we glean", below), whilst the lover's emotional state is that portrayed in the last stanza—one of contained emotional depth which suffers the irritant of a shallow permissible outlet. The typical use of landscape-symbolism in the third stanza is particularly noteworthy. Less good as poetry, but more explicit in its argument, is a poem from June 1935:

How can we glean but from
The corn? Or can one eat
But food? And waves are water if
Their heart's the sea.
Soft is the grip of bed
And soft my eyes,
"Jimmy," I said, "dear Jim,"
That felt affection so.

I stopped. "Jim," his was but
The name returning; yet
How should it be no longer love
That all my love
Had been? Or should the lips
Think whom? It was
"Jim" to myself, "Dear Jimmy,"
When he had answered "No".

Youth is at haste to care
That youth when 'twas
"Jim" to myself, "Dear Jimmy,"
Or let affection go.
Which wave but breaks upon

> Itself? Or which breaks not
> Alone? And food is eaten if
> The man be grown.
>
> Each wave is water if
> Its heart's the sea.

This is all rather metrically inept and derivative. Donne's lines, "Who ever loves, if he do not propose/ The right true end of love, he's one that goes/ To sea for nothing but to make him sick:" lie somewhere at the back of it and the third stanza echoes Shelley's "Love's Philosophy". The physical aspect of the poem is clear; it is an attempt to establish with a seemingly unwilling partner the morality of homosexual acts. (Geoff Sutton, whilst working on *Samson* with Noyce, recalls seeing "at least one reassuring letter from Menlove to Wilf discussing the morality of the physical act, obviously a reply to something said or written to him". This must have been to the same point, although not with the same partner, as the poem, but is now untraceable.) The concluding lines are a firm statement of the intuitivist stance. They present the problem frequently encountered in Menlove's poetry of an overloaded symbolic system, but can be freely paraphrased as meaning that the individual ("each wave") acts authentically ("is water") by ensuring that his impulses are instinctual in origin ("Its heart's the sea")—and therefore sound, because deriving from the innate deity.

The rest of the "Jimmy" poems are perhaps less interesting and need not be dealt with here, but before passing on to events of the late summer, it is worth bringing in another of the Rodney Street jottings. It gives a good idea of the intensity of effort involved for Menlove in repressing in himself in social situations instincts and emotions which he knew were valid and yet could not freely express. The first part is set at Helyg, the second in Liverpool:

Llandudno Junction, Llandudno Junction. Always you settle down, you're mellow and he's mellow too in front of the fire after a long day out, you start wanting to talk and then along comes 6.30 p.m. and off you go to Llandundno Junction. Or else you are walking happily, lazily along staring at the shop windows. You are feeling that you need not even keep in step, then along comes a tram. You are too late to stop it. "Oh damn!" you say, "Have to get that tram!" So you gather a few of your wits together and jump for it. No time to say goodbye. All that existence wiped clean away by a tram. Bound now for perhaps Central Station or afternoon tea, perhaps an interview with Mr Anderson. No time to think, sum up a little, to let the tear gather up quietly and without strain, not even time to say goodbye. No, bundle it all back. Tread it down to swell the rubbish heap and meanwhile must drag away a bit of it, a bit of your mind, for tea, for an interview with Mr Anderson, enough to crease the eye a little, make it mild.

The end of the relationship with Jimmy came about in late June or early July of 1935. In July Menlove wrote to his old friend Alec Keith, whom he had not seen since the holiday at Inverey two years previously. He suggested sailing across to Norway from the East Coast of Scotland, and asked if Alec knew of any boat they might hire. Alec had just started his first house job at Aberdeen Royal Infirmary and even if he had wanted to, which he assuredly did not, could not have taken up Menlove's offer to accompany him. But he did know of a boat. The previous summer he had spent a couple of weeks at Fraserburgh with Stewart Slessor and Monty McConnachie—two of the friends who had been at Inverey in 1933. They owned a boat, and Alec wrote back to Menlove to tell him that since one had just qualified as a doctor and the other was about to do so, they might have lost interest in it and be prepared to sell. Alec approached them on Menlove's behalf and told them of the project. Despite the Linn of Dee episode they did not take the suggestion that he would be sailing to Norway seriously, and agreed to let him buy the boat.

It was an old fishing boat of the kind used by the local fishermen for tending lobster pots, setting down lines, and the like. It was fourteen feet long, decked in for a couple of feet at either end but otherwise open. For ballast a load of small boulders lay in the bottom. The rig was a dipping lug sail on a raked mast well forward, with a slanted yard and a loose lower edge with the sheet, which was never fixed but was held by the steersman. The front end of the sail was fixed by a large hook to a ring in the bowpost, which made the boat exceedingly awkward to manage single-handed, as this had to be unfixed and brought round the mast every time tack was changed. Unwieldiness aside, there was some rot in the bows and the tiller assembly had a habit of finding its way overboard. It was far from an ideal vessel for North Sea voyaging.

Menlove ordered stores from Cooper's, the Liverpool chandlers, and had them sent to the house of Monty's father, Dr McConnachie, in Fraserburgh. He arrived at Alec's rooms in the residents' quarters of Aberdeen Royal Infirmary one Saturday night in August, and the next day Alec drove him up to Fraserburgh and the McConnachies'. Over lunch, as it became evident that Menlove was serious in his plans, Dr McConnachie made known his thorough disapproval, and the meal ended uneasily. Menlove was not to be dissuaded and, when Alec had driven back to Aberdeen, set about loading the boat. He had provisions for six weeks, but intended to complete the voyage in less than that time. At eight o'clock in the evening he set sail, and was spotted next morning by the Peterhead steam drifter *Golden Dawn* twelve miles off Rattray Head.

The boat came up with him and offered to take him in tow. Menlove refused any assistance, tempers rose, and after circling round him for some time the drifter eventually hit him about the stern and damaged the rudder, pre-empting further argument. Menlove was then towed into port, took off his stores, and the boat sank. He phoned Alec Keith and Dr McConnachie to insist furiously on finding out who was responsible for what he assumed to be deliberate scheming to prevent him in his plans. Alec Keith, who had definitely not inspired the "rescue"—despite thinking that perhaps he should have done—thought that "it might have been organized by Dr McConnachie. Or it might have been a quite spontaneous effort by the fishermen, who spot a badly-sailed boat a mile off. If they had considered he was heading for danger, they might have easily considered it their duty to interfere." Menlove's anger cooled, although he remained convinced that someone had plotted against him. He took a room in a house in Findon, a tiny fishing village south of Aberdeen, and spent a week climbing on the small red granite sea-cliffs and bathing, joined by Alec whenever he could get away from the hospital.

Noyce, meanwhile, fresh from Grindelwald and an ascent of the Mönch, was enjoying a family holiday at the Scale Hill Hotel by Crummock Water in the Lake District. Late in August Menlove went down to the Lakes and the two of them met, apparently coincidentally, as Menlove was eating an orange on top of the Honister Pass. Noyce later wrote a brief account of the climbing holiday which thus came about:

Scafell and Pillar Rock became our focus, could their climbing be fitted in with family car movements. And so it was, climbers being perhaps extra-ordinarily selfish and unperceptive, and our family at least extraordinarily unselfish. Menlove climbed mostly in the boots of his choice, myself following in rubbers: Routes 1 and 11 on Pillar, Eagle's Nest Ridges, Sepulchre and Innominate Crack, and then the Central Buttress. This was the climax. It took four hours' hard labour, and then we must run all the way back, not to be over-late for the patient car. But I had never been more impressed by the fly-on-the-wall ecstasy of verticality. The side wall of the Flake Crack seemed to lean more and more above us, as though it were moving against the sky; while Menlove struggled in boots to climb the top flake direct, and, failing, to fix stirrups so that I could climb over and past him.

Alec Keith in Cornwall   *Alec Keith on the Aberdeen sea-cliffs*

The boat in which Menlove attempted to sail to Norway

Menlove on the first ascent of Procrastination Cracks, 1932

Noyce on Pillar, 1935

The Flake Crack, Helsby

Jim Perrin

The weather broke, Lakeland fashion. A. B. Hargreaves had said that
the North-west on Pillar was a wet-weather boot-climb. It must be done
therefore. First up in rain, I thanked God for the squared holds. We
descended the North Climb, by repute easier, for the North-west winds
its way up the harshest angle of the rock. Perhaps it was reaction from the
ascent; I failed feebly at the North Climb hand traverse, descending, wet
and dirty; struggled twice and sat at the bottom looking dully at the rain
and unfriendly grey grass. Three days later, again, I watched through dull
eyes Menlove's boots against the sky, couched myself coldly in mud. It was
on Botterill's Slab, Scafell. His hands gave out three-quarters of the way
up, groping on slimy holds. He was safe to stop. I raced round, dropped a
rope, and he came on.

This holiday provided the inspiration for the most finely-worked of all
Menlove's short lyrics, the poem entitled "You Rock, You Heaviness".

> You rock, you heaviness a man can clasp,
> You steady buttress-block for hold,
> You, frozen roughly to the touch:
> Yet what can you?
>
> Can you stand over me, suffused
> And treading lightly for my love?
> Or when I yearn for you, can you
> Recover? Or, can you seem best?
>
> Oh, you can be for praises for my grasp:
> If thin's the heart you can be cold,
> Or if resolved, you too can such.
> Can'st add to me?
>
> Look how the wind is treading, fleet
> Along the lake. She ripples down
> The mountain waters of the heart,
> Crossing, re-crossing on the breast.

Noyce dismissed it rather briefly in *Snowdon Biography* with the comment
that "the verse is not easy and the metre uneven at times, in a way however
nowise marring the total effect". It deserves more consideration than that.

The poem opens strongly, ringing out a question which is also a statement
about the nature of the medium of rock. Its heaviness and steadiness are

tangible, can be clasped, held, touched, but what is there beyond the challenge and consequent balance—the rock, the man; the inanimate, the sentient? In itself, the rock is an absolute, fixed, immutable. It cannot respond, but can only remain "frozen roughly to the touch". So what, questions the poet, is its power? In the second stanza, where the tetrameter lines are less heavily end-stopped and the hard consonants of the first stanza give way to more assonant sounds, the poet's rhetorical queries as to whether there can be reciprocity of warm feeling and mutual longing between himself and the rock re-emphasize its insentience. It can never be his preferred medium—"Or, can you seem best?"—and if it can never be that, then what can it be? This is the question he attempts to answer directly in the third stanza. His actions upon the rock can adduce such externals as praise; the rock can, given preconditions within the poet, ensure defeat, or it can be an opposition. In all this it is completely unreciprocating—all must come from within the poet. It can take away, but as the sharp, though stilted, dimeter line quizzes, "Can'st add to me? The answer, as to all the other questions posed, is a resounding negative. The poet has fixed his argument and posed problems which, without descending to bathos, can only elicit one response to their rhetoric.

But the poem concludes—and it is here that the tragic resonance lies—by identifying the poet with the landscape of which the rock and the "steady buttress-block" apostrophized at the outset are a part. The final stanza is much lighter than the others, the tetrameter lines flowing into each other to create a sense of movement and interreaction. The mountain scene is delicately and economically evoked. The poet's emotions are symbolized, as in "The sky is hard above the land", by the lake, over the waters of which treads—the word is repeated from the second stanza and its secondary meaning of "copulates" should be borne distantly in mind—the feminine force of the wind, which is instinct, appetency, desire—disturbing, coming and going across his heart and breast. So that although he is a part of the landscape, just as is the rock, he is unlike the rock in that he is receptive, sentient, susceptible. The light "treading" of the wind does prove upon him a response. The bleakness and power of the poem derive from this contrast finally resolved into an irredeemably ambivalent identification. Absorbed into the heaviness of the landscape, what is the possibility that he can tear himself from it to respond freely with the wind? The metaphor established, the landscape upon which the forces of nature act but whose component parts are either feelingless or capable of feeling but not of action, need no longer be seen as simply a mountain scene but can be read as an analogue for Menlove's situation in relation to society. From that situation the very solidity and fixed feelinglessness of the rock become desirable, and so answers the poet's questions.

The date of composition for "You Rock, You Heaviness" is September 1935. Menlove undertook the most serious of all his marine adventures at the end of this year. A few days after Christmas he travelled by night train to Achnasheen and caught the bus to Gairloch, having previously arranged to hire a boat from Urquhart of Portnahaile, on the south side of Loch Gairloch. He rowed the boat across to the Island of Harris in the Outer Hebrides, landing on a deserted beach where he made camp and spent three days before re-crossing to the mainland. Swept off course on the way back he was forced to put into Gruinard Bay (Gruinard Island, in this bay, is the one which was used for anthrax research and which, still contaminated, is forbidden of access by the MoD*. The thinking behind the research was that anthrax spores could be dropped by bomb on German civilian populations in the last war.) This crossing of the Minch, the 40-mile-wide channel between Wester Ross and the Outer Hebrides, took him 28 hours to Lewis, and 24 coming back. It was a preposterous adventure. The Minch is much wider than the English Channel. On very clear days, the Hebrides can just be seen as a faint line on the horizon. To set out from the mainland is to row out into the Atlantic; making land on the rocky coasts of Harris or Lewis is fraught with difficulty; the currents are immensely powerful—all this undertaken in a small, open boat in midwinter, and alone. Menlove described the setting out in a fragment which is moving in its frank recognition of motive and mental state.

"I don't know whether this chronicle will amuse you or not. Very little happened when all told, but here it is for what it's worth.

"There was just the right sort of chap sitting there, in the bus, right by me. He was for Gairloch, I heard him say, and by the way he looked at his map and kept on looking round and talked to the older man, it was clear that he was on holiday and meant to make the most of it. He'd have loved the expedition: I'd swear to that. But years of repression had done their work and all the way from Achnasheen I sat there in a big ugly oilskin and said nothing, stepped out at the end into the pouring rain without a word said and resigned myself to going alone. One is not at one's best either way after a night in the train, and anyhow I had come for a silence, for a rest, not for a party.

"If I wanted company, why hadn't I seen to it months back? Well, I'm as much at sea there as you are, and anyhow, as I've said before, I did not want company.

"I had to walk quite a bit, which was annoying with all the weight of the stuff I had in the rucksacks. I had asked in a loud voice where Portnahaile might be; he had scanned his map, all eagerness, but there was nothing

---

* Footnote 1993 – This is no longer the case.

doing (I might have known it: I'd tried the same map on my own account) and meanwhile several others had got busy with theories of their own about the place. So, as I say, I had got carried past it, and by the time I had talked to old Urquhart, opened my stores, and arranged my rubber mattress on a space on the floor, I can assure you my head was about reeling. It paid no attention to the vagaries of the air mattress and I went straight to sleep.

"Next day was Sunday and in his letter he had said: 'Sunday I do not allow my boat to be put to sea.' So I was in no hurry, made a breakfast of ship's biscuits and butter, and saw the boy of the house. He took me down to look at the boat, and very nice it was, twelve foot long. No spare rowlock and no spare oar, but I said nothing about that. It was clear enough I might as well call the trip off at once as try to explain to old U. what I might want them for, and the boy looked too innocent to start stealing. So I left that, got a petrol tin from the garage, and spent the rest of the day strolling up and down watching the people in their Sunday clothes and letting my mind stray over a number of wild and sensual thoughts that, however, never came to anything.

"You see what I mean? I'm not frightened of being alone, but I do not like not being anything else ever.

"More ship's biscuits, another night floating about just above the floor. And curiously enough, I dreamt I was in heaven, with fairies.

"Breakfast felt a bit dry, so I didn't open another tin of corned beef, just swallowed a biscuit and then the boy and I carried everything down to the boat. 10 a.m. I powdered my hands liberally, drew on a pair of chamois leather gloves, I sat down the wrong way in the boat, sat down the right way, and rowed off. The boy waved. Old Urquhart didn't. We'd had a bit of a dispute. Only that morning I'd mentioned we might be going outside the loch, the boat and I, and he had argued. I waved back and then settled to it steadily. The water was calm and the sky blue but cold. The boat pulling easily.

"11 a.m. Nearing the loch entrance and feeling fine. Broke open a tin of corned beef; chewed half of it, a mouthful of water from the petrol can to wash that down, a mouthful of water to wash that down, then lay on the oars for a bit and went on.

"But I haven't mentioned yet why I was doing all this. The fact is—I can do with very little appreciation as for affection, and I had long since realized that if one cannot do without what one wants of that sort, one had better go hang: but somehow all that year, I don't know, one thing had come on top of another, and now there was nothing for it, one must clear out, get right away somewhere, under the stars, and have another look at oneself from the angle.

"12 noon. Rather a long hour, but definitely out of the loch at last. Having a short rest I decided best to take it standing up. Slight breeze freshening

against me. Skye was well in sight and I set course to beyond North of it.
Feeling not quite so fine.

"1 p.m. Yes, but it was the next 6–8 hours that got a bit boring. I don't know
whether you like rowing, but I don't. My fingers got raw first then they sort of
seized up—couldn't bend properly, and when that area gets numbed you
notice that the wrists are not much better except they can still feel it; and if it
comes to that the rest of the arms are a bit tired, too. And as for the other
things, I'd realized fairly soon that it would be wise to pad the seat with my
coat, but that didn't make as much difference as I'd hoped, and the tide was
going the wrong way, too. As a matter of fact I'd asked a friend of mine
specially which way the tide went, but he must have been wrong. So you can
imagine, when the sun went down and the flood of her reds flaming low down
on the west horizon and staining the dark hills of the coast whence I had come,
the beauty of the evening was of great assistance to me. Time and again I stood
up, and staring fixedly at it here or there, was able to forget all else.

"Food was not important now. I remembered yesterday's food. Nothing
particularly attractive on board. I threw the last bit of corned beef overboard,
gnawed a biscuit, drank a little water and to my surprise found that instead of
disliking the petrol in it I had developed a craving for its lubrication.

"I have no love for staying up doing things at night, never had, and when I
am not comfortable the feeling is intensified. The tide ran the boat swiftly to
the North, six hours, then swiftly to the South.

"My own efforts to pull the boat, creaking, dragged it slowly through the
water foot by foot to the West. And though I pulled for hours through the
water to the West we appeared to get no further in that direction and we
continued moving swiftly up and down the Minch. Then it started raining.
The tent was small and though I put it in the middle of the boat. . . ."

The piece breaks off at this point. Even in its unfinished state it is almost
unbearable to read; probably Menlove realized that, and realized that too
much was being given away, so let the "years of repression" do their work
again by seeing to it that the project was abandoned. The intensity of
unhappiness, and self-consciousness conveyed in the second and third
paragraphs is harrowing enough, but there are two points further on in the
narrative which go beyond even these in their portrayal of near-despair and
the desperate remedies taken to relieve it. The first of these has already been
quoted in a previous chapter, but is worth bringing back for attention here.
"I'm not frightened of being alone, but I do not like not being anything else
ever." The second occurs a few lines on, and expands upon it. "The fact is—I
can do with very little appreciation as for affection, and I had long since
realized that if one cannot do without what one wants of that sort, one had

better go hang: but somehow all that year, I don't know, one thing had come on top of another, and now there was nothing else for it, one must clear out, get right away somewhere, under the stars, and have another look at oneself from the angle." Nowell, his sister, wrote of Menlove after his death that "he was gradually broken by the hopelessness of attaining any integration, and by the depth of endless loneliness involved in his life, aching for some lasting touch with humanity". Her observations are fully borne out by this anguished piece of writing from New Year 1936.

The *Liverpool Daily Post* provided a different perspective on the voyage—slightly at odds in one or two points—in the short report which is printed, entitled "Liverpool Doctor's seven-day venture in rowing boat".

Adventure on water seems to be the spice of life for Dr J. M. Edwards of Rodney Street, Liverpool.

The doctor has just been on holiday at Gairloch, Ross-shire. He took out a small 12-ft. rowing-boat and accomplished the feat of rowing across the Minch from Gairloch to the island of Lewis and back—a distance of 100 miles. The doctor was carried off his course and it was seven days before he was able to return to the mainland.

Attired in a lounge suit, he hired the rowing-boat and gave the owner a cheque with the remark, "This is just in case I don't come back." When experienced boatmen learned of his proposed expedition they advised him to abandon it because no one else had ever accomplished the hazardous crossing.

The doctor, however, was determined to succeed, and stocked his boat with a good supply of food and water. He had neither sail nor auxiliary motor.

Nothing was heard of him for two-days and seafaring folk became anxious. A postcard was received at Gairloch the following day saying he had arrived safely. Several times the small craft narrowly escaped foundering, and he was carried off his course on the return journey, and it was exactly seven days from the start that he landed at Gruinard Bay on the mainland. Owing to a violent gale springing up he had to send the boat back to its owner by motor-lorry.

There were to be no more marine adventures for several years after this, but one of the Rodney Street jottings survives. It is probably a second version or recollection of the "Little Fishes" trip of 1932. The style and play of imagination is closer to Menlove's earlier prose writings than the essays of the late thirties and early forties, and the inclusion of a companion points to its being the crossing to Skye with John Sheridan:

Out beyond the flatlands on the sea coast the swell of the tide crept up higher against the shingle as it swept heavily from South to North, pulled by the cold sphere of the moon. The sun set down upon an empty horizon and laughed at us. Then she went, and the boat shivered and settled down deeper in the cold water. The stores had got too heavy for her, and she was nervous of the dark, of the wind overhead, and of the soft, sweeping waves.

We had our nightly mental exercises to do to pour vicarious balm upon our sore souls: "Pity the poor cattle," it began, "who get linseed cake stuck between their teeth and cannot remove it. Pity the blighted Eskimo who first ate Pemmican—he must have starved for many moons."

The food question is too much with us. Not only does it constantly occur at odd moments through the day, but at night it also causes a feeling of vague unhappiness. We had a prolonged discussion on the ethics of the last item of food in the boat. Ought it to be the captain or the mate who should make the sacrifice of friendship, and anyway, which was which? Each in turn demanded the glorious privilege of providing in person first drink then fresh meat and then a fresh supply of Pemmican for, say, twelve days. Among the angels you could say with pardonable pride, "I made it myself." But it might be simpler to amputate an arm each and then you would still be able to have your turn for a rest. It may be stated that a good ten per cent of this chronicle, and that includes all the boniest of it, is authentically and positively true.

And then the sun got up and looked at us, over an empty sea. The stars, the clouds, they rain and rain on us suspended between. How can they distinguish which drift is the wanderer and which is the wave?

The last paragraph suggests as well as anything we have the attraction Menlove found in this sphere of action, where the forces are natural, recognizable, hugely unconcerned about individual destiny. Perhaps his feelings of isolation were such that only by placing himself in these situations could be gain any sense of integration into the natural world. The last sentence is particularly significant. It clearly echoes the last line of Yeats's "Among School Children" ("How can we know the dancer from the dance?"—Nowell remembered the poem as a favourite of Menlove's), which is the culminating image in a stanza dealing with the idea of perfect integration. Menlove's adaptation is true to its sub-text in this; but rather than the image of joy, as in Yeats, it is one of vast indifference to humanity, pointing up the individual response as being one of dissociation and retreat.

CHAPTER SIX

"Lines for Harmony"? 1936–1939

HAD EVERYTHING GONE along in a stable, unthreatening and fulfilling manner from New Year 1936 onwards, not only in his personal life but also in the broader context of society, Menlove might well have retained what already seemed at times to be a precarious grip on sanity, continued to work for many years through a useful psychiatric career, become an admired and respected figure in his profession and in his recreation activities, perhaps even survived through to a time when his particular sexual orientation was no longer proscribed. Given one wisely-chosen friend in whom to invest his confidences and affections with some possible return upon them, and a sane and tolerant society in which to operate, it could have happened. And for a time it almost appeared that it might do so, for during the early months of 1936 the affection between Menlove and Wilfrid Noyce grew rapidly.

The infatuation—for it was apparently initially one-sided—probably began as that which a boy who had come through the English public school system could easily have conceived for a gifted and original figure from a world to which he ached to belong. Noyce would have been put at a disadvantage by it, and perhaps rendered more susceptible to Menlove's advances, but nonetheless, adolescent homosexual conduct or fixation is not something to wonder at in any way. It is a standard phase in many an individual's development, whether suppressed or expressed. The single-sex public school system tends to retard development out of the phase (if in the individual case it is just a phase), so that the recipient of such an education may take part in homosexual practice throughout school and university (in the thirties the latter were still predominantly male institutions) and still make a heterosexual adjustment in later life. The public school could also be seen as giving opportunities to *eroticize* the perfectly normal unconsummatedly erotic friendships between adolescent boys, or between boys and adults who seek to capitalize on the boy who is either in this phase of development or by inclination homosexual.

In the case of Wilfrid Noyce, we have Menlove's poetic testimony that there was an initial imbalance of affection, but whatever degree of truth there is in this, it would certainly have been inextricably bound up with Wilfrid's view of Menlove's status as a climber. Those who knew Wilfrid Noyce well maintained that he was a sympathetic and kindly character, and the likelihood is that once he got to know Menlove and had been received into his confidences, he would have begun to feel sorry for him and, after some soul-searching (which would quickly have been dispelled or even ridiculed after he arrived, later in 1936, at King's College, Cambridge), would have been prepared to show Menlove the desired physical favours.

Menlove's conduct during the spring of 1936 was as "unstaid and skittish" as at any time in his life. This description of a day's activity on the Milestone Buttress makes that clear:

Poking hither and thither. At one point the leader shouted loudly for a rescue and refused to budge until a rope was given him from above. At another point a ruse was discovered for circumventing the crying curse of the Milestone—its incredibly large population of other bourgeois on holidays. One found a deep crack and settled down therein, unnoticed except by the very few who had seen one enter. At certain yet other points one got up so far and said one would return another day, but, as regards most points, one said one would never return. One also decided during these thus periods that, whatever the meaning of the phrase, it is certain that to travel alone is better than to travel naked. But not for that reason.

There were compensations, for the state of loneliness and misanthropy revealed here, in an occasional few days on the rock with Noyce. In one such break Menlove and Noyce went to climb the Direct Route on the Nose of Dinas Mot, which Menlove wanted Noyce to lead. David Murray-Rust, a master at Charterhouse and willing accomplice to Noyce in mountain escapades, gives this version of events in the midst of a general recollection of Menlove as a climber.

Menlove was a climber without especial grace (quite different in this to Wilfrid) but he was immensely strong and confidence-giving. He was also utterly patient, either in the lead or on those occasions when he was encouraging Wilfrid to attempt a lead. I only once remember him as being near to irritation. Wilfrid was to lead a hard-ish climb—it was the Nose of Dinas Mot. The weather was not awfully good and a third person, a friend of Wilfrid's, wanted to join on the rope. Menlove thought a third man would slow the party, so as to cause Wilfrid to wait about and get cold. The chap did join and all was well, but he was unwelcome. The thought of Menlove was all for Wilfrid's safety.

Murray-Rust is possibly being rather naïve here. It was surely more likely that Menlove wanted Wilfrid's company to himself, and his motive in not welcoming the third person was possessiveness rather than concern for Wilfrid's safety, which sounds like a rationalization. Murray-Rust's account continues:

> I had great confidence in his judgement, not only of his own capacity, but also of others—including myself. Once he and Wilfrid were to climb a Severe on Glyder Fach—the Direct Route. I was to lead Ronald Noyce, Wilfrid's brother, up a milder Severe, the Oblique Buttress. I asked Menlove whether I *could* lead it (I had never led a climb before which I hadn't seen); he gave obvious thought to the matter, then said, "Yes, you can do it all right; there is one difficult bit, near Severe, but you'll do it." He was quite right, and because he had judged my capacity correctly, he helped me, vicariously, to climb at my best. There was nothing dare-devil or irresponsible about him—certainly not when the safety of others was in question.

The events referred to in this passage occurred at Easter 1936, when Noyce had been invited, along with Menlove, to attend one of Geoffrey Young's Pen y Pass Easter gatherings. Wilfrid Noyce was regarded very quickly as one of the brightest emergent talents of the mid-thirties. Along with the leaders of a brilliant generation of Oxford climbers of the period 1934–1937—John Hoyland, David Cox, Robin Hodgkin—he was responsible for the shift away from the hegemony of Helsby-trained Liverpool climbers of the early thirties. He was, as Murray-Rust demonstrates, held to be one of the most graceful of climbers. To fly a kite a little at this point, it is interesting to consider why the mountaineering establishment of the day thrilled to this young and excitingly talented prodigy as they did. His background was impeccable—major public school (he was by now Head Boy of Charterhouse), father knighted for colonial service. He was enthusiastic, artistic, loose-limbed, good-looking, respectful towards elders and their traditions—at times almost to the point of toadyism. (In a review of *The Night Climbers of Cambridge* he virtuously protests that "it is one thing to admire the adventures recorded in *The Night Climbers*, quite another to agree with its theses. These are, first, that it be ..." etc, etc. There is something strangely conformist about this from a nineteen-year-old schoolboy.) He was professedly and traditionally a mountaineer, and therefore susceptible to the afflatus of that creed. And he was a climber of "grace", which latter is the most interesting item in this catalogue. For to be possessed of natural grace argues innate gifts—a natural aristocracy, if you like. Noyce, from his situation in society, being possessed of such was thus an affirmation, unspoken but the more potent for being so, of the rightness of the social ordering of things.

Grace and effectiveness are two ends of a socio-sporting spectrum still operative to a degree in England today (consider the selection of many England cricket teams)*. In mountaineering, here lies the reason for Kirkus's exclusion from the 1933 Ruttledge expedition to Everest. Kirkus desperately wanted to go, and, although relatively inexperienced, was keenly interested in Alpine and greater-ranges mountaineering. His record in the Alps was not by any means so poor as was suggested at the time. On his first Alpine season he had, admittedly, only done "a few undistinguished climbs with Marco Pallis, carried out at Marco's usual snail-like pace", but on later trips with speedier partners he had performed well, and his single trip to the Himalayas proved extremely successful. But, despite Jack Longland's counsel that he should have been included, he was excluded on the grounds of his inexperience. Yet in 1924 the Oxford rowing blue Sandy Irvine had been chosen for Everest, despite his Alpine experience encompassing no more than a few very easy peaks in the Bernese Oberland.

That a class-bias existed in the mountaineering establishment is unarguable. Its distinctions were fine-drawn: the northern office-worker Kirkus was beyond the pale; the Charterhouse and Cambridge colonial who was his cousin perfectly acceptable. This is not, and I cannot overstress this point, to mount a personal attack on Wilfrid Noyce; it is merely an attempt to sketch out the social pressures operative upon him and of which he, as much as anyone, was a victim.

In Menlove's case the same pressures do not work to anything like the same extent. North of England Christian Socialism, an impoverished family background, Scottish public school and provincial university were a recipe for exclusion. Rock-climbing, however great his gift for it, however difficult his routes, merely re-emphasized the gap. Neither Kirkus nor Menlove would ever have been credited with grace. That was a class prerogative, and its presence in Wilfrid Noyce, as representative of that class, an occasion for rejoicing and an entry to all doors. I wonder if there was, in the initial attraction Menlove felt for Noyce, a faintly Tocquevillean envy of the one who embodied all that he could never be and everything he had set his heart against? But even if it was so, it was no more than a small ingredient in the desperately brave experiment of his life.

* Footnote 1993: Thatcherism and the hold of Essex Man over England selection has changed all this, of course, though the southern bias remains.

Guidebooks were firmly in focus in 1936. Menlove's Cwm Idwal guide had just been published, the first of a new series for the Climbers' Club and the result of several years' sporadic effort on Menlove's part. To my mind, it is the finest rock-climbing guide which has been written, the product of scrupulous labour and a thoughtfully imaginative approach. Since its publication there has been a good deal of discussion about the contrast between Menlove's Cwm Idwal guide and Colin Kirkus's slightly later volume on Glyder Fach. Both are exemplary pieces of work and much of the discussion centred upon them has been sparked off by one or two prefatory remarks in each rather than an examination and comparison of both texts. There are differences of style and intent, but the net result is not vastly dissimilar. The main innovation in Menlove's guide is a greater attention to topography and a desire to give a sense of where each route fits into the overall plan of a cliff. His guides are contextualizing masterpieces which demand the reader's full attention. Most guides need the addition of guesswork or supplementary information. Menlove's do not, and given an intelligent user completely fulfil their purpose of introducing a total stranger to the scene they describe. Also, the climber using Menlove's guide will have a fuller idea of the character of a given route or cliff, and some of the phrasing will certainly have stimulated his interest, and offered choice to mood or preference.

> . . . a weakness in the rib on the right can be taken so as to finish up Faith. There is a weight of precedent in favour of the occasional use of this trespass. Indeed on all these routes there is a tendency to go and see what is happening up on the right.

or again:

> The angle of the face keeps a high average. This is emphasized by a surface that is tentative and undulating rather than clear-cut or heavily marked. The detail of the rock, in contrast, is as articulate as can be. Every foot of the surface shows pockets of rock, good, though often small. These tend to surmount bubbles rather than flakes of rock and being carved out, are reliable. Belays in such rock are naturally neither large nor conspicuous, but they are reliable, and are at least not built for deception.

Because of the success of the Cwm Idwal guide, Menlove was commissioned to prepare the second guidebook in the new series—that to Tryfan, and he chose to ask Noyce to collaborate on it with him. By June of 1936 Menlove was already at work:

Considering West Face of Tryfan. There were others there also, but we found that amusement could be provided, even with the rock. One cleared the whole upper face from people, and left it full of those white marks that are caused when large blocks are allowed to career down the surface. Good.

The request to Noyce to collaborate was probably motivated by a desire to have his company at least for part of the summer, for Menlove's affection had certainly deepened into love by June of 1936. Apart from wanting Noyce's company, Menlove also felt a need to impress his young protégé in the areas in which he knew he was most interested. One scheme which he talked of continually in the early summer of 1936 was to solo one of the routes on the South Face of Mont Blanc, which were the ultimate Alpine ambition for the British mountaineers of the time. John Hoyland, the Oxford climber who promised most of his generation, had been killed there two years previously. David Murray-Rust remembers talking with Noyce about Menlove's plans for the climb and feeling very unhappy about the project. But nothing came of it. Another of Murray-Rust's recollections shows something of the strain which the friendship with Noyce was generating in Menlove. It is given here in full because the early part of it reveals what was possibly a typical reaction to Menlove on the part of one who came from a particular background and social class. It should be borne in mind that he is trying to re-create his impressions as a young man of Menlove. David Murray-Rust in his old age was a most sensitive, kindly and liberal man with far deeper sympathies than are displayed here:

Much as I admired Menlove's climbing and his judgement there, I did not find him an attractive personality. This was largely because of my then inexperience and fairly restricted background. I was a bit repelled by his sensual large lips and general un-polishedness. I found it hard to accept that—or rather, I hardly realized that—he was someone of considerable mental capacity and sensitivy of thought and expression. But we accepted each other; he accepted me because of my friendship with Wilfrid. At that time, I had no understanding of homosexuality—my knowledge was limited to the "problems" met with in a boys' boarding school. I knew Menlove was very fond of Wilfrid, but it was a shock for me when Menlove broke down one evening and told me he was "in love" with Wilfrid.

Menlove made the same confession to Stuart Chantrell at about this time, and the intensity of his feeling for Noyce is very plain in the following letter, dated 8 June 1936.

Dear Wilf,

You are nice: and thanks awfully for what you say. But it would be horrid if you looked at me as a sort of poetry machine. Of course I'll go on writing and make it as good as I can, and it *is* nice to hear things like that about it. (But *don't* expect too much.) Remember that where there is an excess cynicism in a person—GWY—by so much there will also be an excess enthusiasm in other directions. Please don't get a false view of me. One of the nice things about you (for me) is that you've got it firmly fixed in the back of the head that I'm really rather an ass and need a bit of looking after. Which others forget. You've gone and put yourself in brackets at the end of the letter. But I *don't want* you in brackets, it's *you*, the person, I want, who touches me sometimes, gets annoyed with me sometimes. Darling. Please—you're far too nice for brackets.

About Wales. If you're going to be in Wales for more than a fortnight with the guide (it's likely) couldn't you *possibly* be there when I can be? Go to Switzerland a *bit* earlier. It'd be grand if you could. I'll do just as I'm told and we'd descend for a bit of company whenever you or I wanted, together or singly or anyhow.

I'm not going to *stay* with Bartrum anyhow. For heaven's sake don't tell him! (I like him much, but I'd get bored to tears I think, or at any rate I'd feel I was!) If I go up to Scotland (quite likely) I'll arrange a trip of sorts and come back via him. He's so very decent.

Dear. I'm not feeling at all bad now. With any luck I'll not feel neurotic enough to turn out any good poetry for ages. But I *want you*. And you can *always* kick me if I get stupid. But you mustn't get downhearted either, Wilfkin. And *don't* listen to the nonsense that people talk about me; that's only one of the more out-sides. They probably won't tell you but you're the one that people really *like*, just you for yourself. And, please, I'm one of your suitors. I want as much as I can get, of you.

There must be an awful lot for you to do. One *can't* do everything: though I don't know about you. You're so good at things and get things done more than I do, and without so much fuss. I expect they all think a lot of you: damn them.

I don't think there's much else to say. It's so nice having you; to know. Nicer still when I can really be with you. And you're so good to me; much nicer than ever you ought to be. I've said all that before, but it's true again each time and, anyhow, it's nice to be able to tell you. And when you write like that one can't help it.

Here's a bit of the accursed poetry—not much good, I think; lacks something. I expect there won't be any more now except perhaps some bits about how nice you are which would turn GWY's hair grey and will never be shown to anybody—not even you—because it will be partly about how beautiful you are.

Wilf, darling, this is a perfectly idiotic letter in a way. But you know what I mean. And I hadn't expected to hear from you for a bit. And I *must* feel pleased about you sometimes.

But don't get disheartened. At least not for long. It must be rotten having so much work, in the summer. Carry on. One knows how you'll do. And you are a worker.

—I'll have to stop imagining now—Go to my clinic.

Love,
Menlove.

Think about Wales, but not to worry.

Noyce must have written back fairly quickly to tell Menlove about his planned holiday in Saas Fee and Zermatt, for three weeks later Menlove sent him the following letter:

2.7.36

Dear Wilf,

You'd be *perfectly* easily able to do the final chimney. Probably you tried to *force* it by some special way instead of relying on cunning. Your damnable courage coming in: which I hate much.

My No 2 said "Ready?" I said "Yes" (quite without thinking). I had the rope over one hand, loosely. A bit ran out. "Ho," I thought "Back, to start again." Realised he was falling and hung on. Couldn't get my other hand to the moving coils quick enough. But he landed very gently, at the bottom of all things. My hand's recovering rapidly. Deserved all I got. Just through carelessness. You mustn't be sorry for an ass like that. It was nothing else. It was nice to see David. But about your Swiss expedition. *Don't* rush back if you want to stay out. I'm a selfish sort of idiot, and don't worry to give way to that.

There are two incidents referred to in this letter and they both occurred on the imposing but not particularly difficult pitch now known as Thomson's Chimney, on the final wall of the Central Buttress on the East Face of Tryfan, directly below the summit blocks of Eve and Adam. Noyce later described his mishap on this problem as "a shameful but luckily safe and salutary fall from the very difficult start of Tryfan's last Central Chimney". In Menlove's case, he was climbing the same route with a good friend and fellow-doctor, Archie Leggate, for whom within a very few years he was to write a memorable obituary.

Noyce duly went off to Saas Fee in company with Richard Hope and David Murray-Rust, and soon felt his allegiance to Welsh climbing severely strained:

> I was bound to the programme of helping with the new Climbers' Club guidebook to Tryfan. The Alps in their hugeness, however, very soon made a Rabelaisian joke of such snippeting. It was impossible, in their long days, to keep up the pretence. Comparisons with our homeland became lost in their immense variety.

Menlove meanwhile was taking what opportunities he could for guidebook work. On the date of his second letter to Noyce, an interesting event had taken place on Tryfan, in his guidebook area. An arrangement between the Workers' Travel Association and the *Deutscher und Oesterreichisch Alpen Verein* had brought about an exchange visit, with expenses to be paid by the host country because of political and currency difficulties, of German and British climbers. The sixteen-strong German party arrived in Britain at the end of June, were shown round London for two days, ushered through the august portals of the Alpine Club to be introduced to its President, the redoubtable Colonel Strutt (the warmth of whose welcome to them is open to question—quite likely they would have received a roasting for their recent Alpine antics—Strutt was highly critical of new-wave German Alpinists), and finally were spirited away to The Llugwy Guest House in Capel Curig. Priestly Phillips and John Jenkins of the Rucksack Club were put in charge of directing them to appropriate climbing venues. On one day, under the guidance of the latter, Teufel and Sedlmayer (who was to die on the North Face of the Eiger) went to Tryfan. Jenkins takes up the story:

> On July 2nd my party insisted on going to Tryfan, the sight of which had attracted their fancy. I had Belle Vue Bastion in mind, but on reaching the Heather Terrace I remembered an old project of mine to force a route up the wall bounded by the Gashed Crag climb and South Gully. There was a chance that no continuous climb would be found, but I egged on Teufel to try something. A rain-shower delayed operations, but he soon warmed up to it and worked out a route which far exceeded my expectations. It was a very fine lead under the conditions, and provided six excellent pitches, all of consistently high standard. Three pitons were used.

A week later, on a wet and windy day, Menlove was taken up to Tryfan by Jenkins and shown the line of the route, named the Munich Climb in honour of the Germans. Also in the party were Jim Joyce and Sandy Edge. They climbed the First Pinnacle Rib of the Central Buttress, from which they could look across and plainly see a piton and bronze karabiner gleaming against the rock on the nose of pitch three. A sense of outrage was generated and the vow taken to remove the offending object. A fortnight later the same party returned, strengthened by the inclusion of Dick Barry. (Noyce was to be impressed by the latter's climbing ability: "I envied his long looseness and the ease with which he seemed to caterpillar up the Terrace Wall's Central Route. I wondered if all climbers I did not know climbed as well as he. For he seemed of another and more aggressively proficient school." Dick Barry died in a climbing accident a year or two after this date.) The climb takes a system of steep grooves and offset facet slabs up to and round a nose overhanging the South Gully, and remains an impressive and serious climb. Menlove managed to protect himself on the difficult slab pitch up to the nose—where there have since been two fatal accidents—by lassoing a loose block on the ledge above (a manoeuvre which would have given him no more than token security). He then led round the nose where Teufel had used two pitons for protection without making any use of the one left in place, and Barry removed the bronze karabiner before knocking out the piton with the Helyg poker. The serious part of the climb now over, Menlove ascended the *Teufelkamin*, a steep and exposed crack with good, sharp holds, to a grass rake, whence Barry took over the lead and climbed two new and more difficult pitches up a steep crack and wall to the right of the line taken by the Germans. John Jenkins and Sandy Edge had to be pulled up these. British honour duly vindicated, Menlove whimsically noted that his party's mode of ascent "has the advantage that the leader can really climb with a rope above him all the way. I do not know why leaders do not make their rope precede them more frequently in this way. Saves a *lot* of trouble." Within the month he had returned to lead the climb without lassoing or any other form of aid.

Towards the end of August Noyce was back from his Alpine season, Menlove took some holiday, and the two of them struggled up through the heather of Cwm Tryfan, the wide flat basin below the East Face of the mountain, and pitched their tent near its head. A concerted attempt was to be made at finishing the guidebook. Noyce recalled that they "wrote the book squatting over mugs of cocoa in the evening light. I would write up a climb, then pass the description back to Menlove. It would come back with almost every phrase rejected or corrected. For measuring the pitches we climbed on 100 ft. of rope and took the average of our two estimates. Despite this apparently reasonable method there were days when every pitch turned out to be sixty feet, or others seventy feet, and so on." One of Menlove's Rodney Street jottings describes another oddity about this holiday:

Tryfan. The bilberry pickers—Came up of a morning—but never went back. It was rather mysterious. Of course it's fairly simple for a person to disappear, but we could not think what on earth happened to the milk cans—couldn't even find the milk cans.

I don't know what happened; they never came back. Yet next morning there they were again on the stroke of eight.

They found a considerable number of new climbs during this fortnight: the Scars Climb on Terrace Wall—"What was wanted on this place was Another Route. Belle Vue Bastion's only two moves (or one), Central Route is a specialist business, and only goes half-way. So, the Scars Climb. It strikes a happy medium and steepens up now and then delightfully"; Yew Buttress—"Severe and worthy"; North Side Route—"the rather aged No 2 would have been able to find an easier route up these rocks, but was by then wedged firmly in a crack miles from such things. So sighed and trusted to the protections of heaven"; Belle Vue Traverse—"Why stop at the Grove of Bollards when going round this face? Continuation is neces- sary, for the Grove is practically speaking in mid-air. Besides, the route is clear ... Good views. The rock is not bubbly, but one mentions it since the moss does well in place of that"; the direct pitch to Soap Gut—"One never knows what a little hot water and washing soda would do, but it seems to me it would still remain a nasty business"; and Hangman's Gut—"Having been up this climb we feel we are now safe in recommending it to others".

One sunlit evening, as Noyce and Menlove were lounging outside their tent, Colin Kirkus joined them. He had soloed up one of the Tryfan buttresses and down another, and sat in his shorts at their campsite for a while, smoking, before loping away to Idwal Cottage. Noyce remembers him offering Menlove a cigarette, and Menlove's reply:

"You're the only person I take a cigarette off, Colin."

"But the habit grew on him later," continues Noyce. "After Colin had left Menlove remarked that Colin had been 'very decent' to him at a time when others were stand-offish. They were an interesting contrast. Colin slim to the point of slightness, standing by a few principles in which he believed with all the strength of his modest, essentially straight-seeing character; Menlove rugged and burly, warm-hearted and lovable but also with the black well of loneliness inside him so that already the puckish laughter was growing less frequent ..."

(The "well of loneliness" is perhaps a coded reference to Menlove's homosexuality, the image possibly deriving from Radclyffe Hall's novel of that name, which treats of lesbianism.)

Two other men who climbed with both Colin Kirkus and Menlove offer interesting comments on their respective characters and climbing styles. Bill Stallybrass, whom we have met before, has this to say:

> The names of Colin Kirkus and Menlove Edwards are so often mentioned together in connection with Welsh exploration that it is hard to realise that [Chimney Route] was one of the very rare occasions when they climbed together. It was not that they did not get on together, but rather that, though they both lived in Liverpool, they had different sets of friends and their work on the guidebooks naturally took them to different cliffs.
>
> In character they were very different. Colin was a cheerful, straight-forward soul, with a keen sense of humour, devoid of intellectual pre-tensions and utterly free from the affections to which the "tiger", like the prima donna, is sometimes prone. He experienced to the full the joy of lesser mortals in simple things and was as happy walking over compara-tively low hills or leading a beginner up an easy climb as tackling a new route. This is reflected in his book, *Let's Go Climbing*. Days spent with Colin were light-hearted, free of tension. One in particular stands out in my mind when we meticulously measured some of the standard climbs on the Gribin Facet for the Glyder Fach guidebook. Such a day would have been inconceivable with Menlove. Though he was an equally lovable climbing companion, days spent with him were often tense, dramatic. He hated walking, was at first a rock-climber pure and simple, and never developed into an all-round mountaineer.

Paul Orkney Work, who arrived on the scene in the mid-thirties, has an equally interesting impression:

> Although I climbed with [Menlove] on Lliwedd, at Harrison's and in the Beddgelert area, I did not enjoy doing so. Probably this was solely due to our being entirely different types, to my abilities as a cragsman being so far below his, but perhaps I had been spoiled by having Kirkus as my instructor previously. Colin had told me in 1936 that he felt Menlove was a much better climber than himself and was very safe. Menlove felt his way up, Colin thought his way up. This being so, Colin could vocalise his technique the better of the two, which to me made a climb with him not only more instructive but more interesting. Both, however, were fas-cinating to watch, Menlove because I could never see how he did it, Colin because I could and so could he.

Kirkus's character comes over supremely well in his instructional book for boys, *Let's Go Climbing*. (It was a copy of this book in the library of my school in Manchester which first enthused me about the sport. Its lyrical freshness, the generous enthusiasms of its author and the sharp, deft, uncluttered pictures he evokes make his book, for all its great simplicity, one of the very best about the climbing experience. The man who wrote it cannot have been other than an utterly likeable, honest and brotherly soul, and one whose friendship and company Menlove must have held very dear.)

To come back to the camp in Cwm Tryfan, Noyce fretted a little at the task and insisted from time to time on taking a holiday from Tryfan. On one occasion they climbed Lot's Groove.

> For me it was something of a snob climb, desired, and greatly, for its name and repute. Steep quick upward moves I found, the fingers gripping tightly on tiny edges; the body braced and taut, the breath almost still, as if afraid. There is, when you come to three-quarter height, a big rock spike which would make it possible for the children of Lot, if they so desired, to look back. "You could easily get out on the right, actually," said Menlove.

On another day they went to Clogwyn Du'r Arddu and climbed the Great Slab route, which, in the three years since Menlove made the second ascent, had started to achieve some popularity, lost much of its grass, sprouted a few pitons, become much cleaner and sounder and had its aura of seriousness and difficulty almost completely dissipated, particularly after Linnell's ascent of the much harder Narrow Slab in August 1933 had opened up a more forbidding section of the West Buttress. Noyce was still very pleased to do the climb, and settled quietly back into the guidebook work thereafter. One of Menlove's jottings imparts the flavour of their activity:

> . . . the Grooved Arete—lot of stuff round here! Leader for instance took No 2 to a belay (discarded its partner: threw it away), then, a little higher, took him to a belay (I mention the belay because though you would not pick it out as anything on rough rock this rock was rather smooth), then telling him to hang on stood upon him. The pile creaked and groaned but by the Grace of God got down again, for instance, and No 2 was hung out and left to dry for a bit.
> Other such things.

With the beginning of September came the rain. The tent, in its high, exposed site, flapped and bellied in the wind, its confines shrinking to a few clammy feet between slapping canvas walls. Noyce and Menlove retreated to

Helyg, and then on Menlove's motorbike over the moors to his home in
Birkenhead. The holiday was over. As Noyce puts it, "the tidying of [the
guide] was left to Menlove, as usual the worker, who added patiently to his
other burdens. The guide completed itself over the end of the year." Anyone
who has worked on the production of any book will know that they do not
simply complete themselves, and that the first draft of a manuscript is almost
the simplest task to achieve. Yet surely enough, in 1937 the Tryfan guide
appeared, Noyce's name preceding Menlove's on the title-page, and in the
first ascents of each of the routes they had done together. On Menlove's part
it was both an act of self-effacement and one of tribute to the boy he loved,
but it was far from an accurate indication of the respective contributions.
Although this was Menlove's intention, there were one or two other things in
the published version which rankled with him. It seems best to quote:

> ... the Cwm Idwal guide ... was complex often in its terminology, trying
> to do more than it did, trying indeed to do a great deal, and using various
> alterations in methods. The sections are not all of equal merit. It was a
> slow business. Then a burst of activity, a stage of elation in the Climbers'
> Club, and out pops the Tryfan guide quite suddenly, with Glyder Fach to
> follow almost at once. And the method used for Tryfan is altered still
> further. But there are traces of struggle in this guide, for the committee
> notes that they cut out parts of the authors' history and introduction: the
> present scrap form of the history reads stupidly in parts, and in the
> introduction the attempt to give atmosphere that had been kept up
> through the Idwal group is now not there.

Anyone who feels inclined to blame Wilfrid Noyce's collaboration for the
diminution in quality of the Tryfan guide compared to the Idwal volume
would do well to heed these words. The late G. R. Speaker and the
committee on which he served seemed to have kept a tight rein on Menlove
after the Cwm Idwal guide, and it must have been a very fraught situation on
both sides. Work as carefully produced and considered as was Menlove's
does not readily submit itself to editorial interference, and to force it to do so
is to produce bitter grievances. It is cause for lamentation that we cannot
now read Menlove's original copy.

Noyce went up to Cambridge in October of 1936, and Menlove settled
back into his psychiatric and guidebook work, his only outings on rock that
autumn being a couple of forays onto Gallt yr Ogof, where he climbed Stack
Wall—a repulsive little route on the right-hand end of the cliff—with Alec
Keith: "Not a bad little route ... Bad rock, grass, etc. If one had pulled out
the big loose thing on the important part one would have pulled oneself with

it, so it is still so"; and Chalkren Stairs, an entertaining climb, Very Severe in standard, "Vicissitudes, but does go all right . . . lots of grass, peeling grass, lots of it, all peeling", done with Archie Leggate. Menlove graded it "Very Difficult in nails".

Menlove's poetry continued, and continued to be an earnest topic of discussion between him and Noyce:

> Yes. I keep all my poems. But indeed you've seen them all, except one or two very early things which I daren't show you. I've written almost *nothing*, you see. But it's awfully nice of you to be like that about it. Awfully nice. But you *must not* expect me suddenly to turn up with screeds of good stuff. I can't do it, my Wilf. I've really very little "feeling" for poetry in most ways. Here's another bit: a "fable" supposed to be going to be part of a longer thing. But I can't keep it up. And it's very "laboured". Don't answer that because there *is* truth in it, and I do want you to see it *more* than at present. I want you to be *well* aware of my *very* great limitations all round.

The degree to which Menlove is prostrating himself here is noteworthy. If we consider, for example, the metrical ingenuity of the love poem to Noyce composed shortly after this letter was written the revealed disparity between Menlove's self-opinion and his actual achievement is significant. The poem itself is striking, not least for its sensual imagery and the frankness of its sexual invitation:

> No, but come to me
>   come quite.
> So, even darkly,
>   we could share the night.

Not only his own poetry came under discussion between them, but also that of others—Geoffrey Winthrop Young's, for example. In one rather tart letter to the editor of the *Mountaineering Journal*, he took issue with a friendly, if simplistic, reviewer of GWY's *Collected Poems*:

> . . . he felt that the importance of the poems was in Mr Young's unique mountaineering experience. I disagreed. He referred to their philosophy. The use of the singular number surprised me. He quoted to show what he meant, and then it didn't surprise me, but I was quite certain I disagreed. And talking it over with a friend afterwards, we said "take 'Wind Harp' for instance—the whole body of it."

Noyce was reading Shelley at the time, and the subject crops up in their correspondence. Menlove comments:

I think *Prometheus Unbound* is "fine". I *don't* think it's deeply true any-where in detail, just in general feeling. He seems to me to have no *deep perception* of the nature of the difficulty (or the type of solution) and the nature of man's mind. Just a vague, fine feeling, beautifully expressed. To say it is of adolescence is to my mind no dispraise. One usually has a clearer perception of the necessity of aiming at ideals when young, but *less* knowledge and experience and insight and actual perseverence in actual, more accurately (in its complexity) seen difficulties. Shelley *is* young and, in some ways, more fine for it. If he'd grown it would have intercom-plicated itself and perhaps lost itself a bit. That's the tendency. I'm glad you like him: don't feel it bad or wrong in yourself, ever, to be apprecia-tive. It doesn't need to mean that one doesn't see faults.

Comments which deserve to be warmly endorsed.

In another letter there occurs a passage on the early Norse Sagas which gives a good indication of some of Menlove's early reading, and reflects back well upon his own poetry, and feelings about life and literature:

I did read bits of the Icelandic things and loved them at the time. Bits of the *Song of Roland* too but couldn't abide it! A different type of tradition in so many directions. I liked the rough heroics and the sea and storms; the Rolandic additions to heroics didn't appeal, except the title and the end! Poetry is queer stuff, relying on the many emotions aroused and associa-tions all round. Those older civilisations, especially those that happened to have been early editions of all our own directions, are crammed full of associations and feelings for us to start with: the whole thing is there in a nutshell so that a simple passage from their life recalls innumerable facets of our own, long since split up into more complex factors: not foreign to us.

Surely the *Iliad* is greater to modern youth than it can ever have been in its own day: even the rhythm somehow must have gained?

It is easy to understand how the elemental conflicts, the sense of vagrant fortunes and a ruthless destiny, which underpin Njal's, Eirik's, or the Greenland Sagas, would have appealed to Menlove more than the decorous affectation of the *Song of Roland*, the basic ethos of which had descended unchanged and ever-bloodier from the eighth-century court of Charle-magne to the inter-war clubs of the Establishment and their nurseries on the playing fields of Charterhouse or Eton. A last point to be made here is that both the above extracts show Menlove to have been a serious and intelligent reader of literature. This is worth bearing in mind for the frequent occasions on which he disparages his own poetic talent. For he is judging himself in these, by the very highest standards—by comparisons with great literature. Inevitably in the comparison he will be worsted, for in literary terms he is a very minor figure, but that should not blind anyone else to the individual qualities of his work. It should rather alert us to the extremely rigorous standards he held out for it.

Noyce came to Helyg for a fortnight before Christmas with the Cambridge University Mountaineering Club, but he was preoccupied with teaching a new friend to climb and Menlove did not join him there. Immediately after Christmas, however, Noyce and Menlove met up together in Buttermere, at Lower Gatesgarth, the holiday home of Arthur Cecil Pigou, Professor of Political Economy at Cambridge.

> It had been a casual meeting at first, at King's. It seemed a casual invitation to collect a party for the Lakes. But after that, each endeavour was undertaken under a critical, fairy-godfatherly eye.

Pigou was a fellow of King's—Noyce's college at Cambridge and the acknowledged centre of English homosexual sub-culture. Noyce quickly came to look upon him, as mentioned above, as his "fairy-godfather". It was Pigou who picked up the bills for Noyce's Alpine seasons with Brantschen and Charlet, tagging along himself merely as a spectator. He was, like that other celebrated Fellow of King's, E. M. Forster, a homosexual*, (or, as the coded language of the DNB puts it, "Into [his] private world few women were admitted") and he appears to have been rather besotted by Noyce. One highly embarrassing incident on the holiday came about because of this. Noyce's birthday was on New Year's Eve, and after dinner, a lavish meal prepared by Gatesgarth's resident housekeeper, presents were given to him. Professor Pigou, as host, gave his first. It was a Leica camera, the best of the range, complete in a box with various filters, a set of lenses of differing focal lengths, cleaning materials, a case, and film. When it came to Menlove's turn to offer up his gift, rather hesitantly, a little hurt perhaps, he handed over a smaller package. Noyce opened it. It was a Leica camera—the basic model—just that.

How Menlove felt about the square stone mansion amongst the woods we

---

* See also Andrew Hodges, *Alan Turing: The Enigma of Intelligence*: (Burnett Books, 1983)

do not know. Certainly it was redolent of many of the great names of mountaineering history. Winthrop Young, Harold Porter, Harold Raeburn had all stayed here. It was ideally equipped for the climber. A stone-flagged hall received his wet clothes, and they were whisked away to be dried as he stepped into the huge hot bath which awaited him. There were billiards before dinner and a private beach for bathing:

> ... we raced round the lake in rain and refused to race up Fleetwith Pike, even to compare ourselves with the amateur record; first ascended in wet socks the frowning Birkness Front of Eagle Crag under the critical professorial eye—fled the Grooved Wall of Pillar under a mixed coating of snow and ice; shivered in a January bathe and warmed up on the front door slab. It was a new, less desperate angle on the Lakes; one from which pure fun could be seen mingling with every form of activity. The house graded effort and merit after the Army system, with more wit ...

To Noyce, it was the type of world for which he had yearned, and into which he was perfectly equipped to enter. Not so for Menlove. Already, by the New Year of 1937, because of their vastly different backgrounds and circumstances and Noyce's having moved into the glitter and excitement of a different social sphere, because of that great divider geography, because of parental disapproval, because of the differences of ambition, outlook, inclination and age, Noyce and Menlove were beginning to drift apart. It was natural, inevitable, and in no way can be held against Noyce. His early emotional response to Menlove was predictable under the circumstances, and a man of greater emotional experience and less urgent emotional need would have seen it as such and placed no great reliance upon it. A part of Menlove's tragedy is that he did not have the worldly wisdom to see that—the house of his hopes was built on a sandy-haired boy.

Nevertheless, though Menlove must have sensed that the relationship was beginning to recede amongst Noyce's priorities, he made the attempt to keep them together. The Lliwedd guide of Archer Thomson was out of print and out of date. It had to be re-written and so Noyce was again invited to collaborate. At the end of July they spent a few days on the cliff, exploring the Far East Buttress and making an attempt on the outstanding problem of the Central Gully direct. It had already been attempted by Stoeppler of the visiting German party, in the previous year, but he had given up quite low down. Noyce was now thrust into the lead. "We had circumvented a slightly greased first overhang; the swoop of the slabs, seeming to run briquette fashion (like books in a shelf, and easier to take out near the centre) scared me. I knew I must fall." He drove in a peg and retreated—from the climb, the cliff and indeed from Wales, for he had an assignation in the Oberland with Professor Pigou and the guide Hans Brantschen. Menlove continued about his work for a little time, with such companions as he could find. There is a poem from slightly after this period which states the situation most movingly:

> Pause, stand on the scree edge and look back,
> You who too hastily—watch carefully again,
> There is the cliff; its Eastern incline steep
> With furrows there and there: How well I
> Know them. When we were climbing there,
> Do you remember, how from that tiny earthwork,
> You remember, stretching; then upon the slab:
> How powerful the fingers . . .
> And then that other day, rocks wet, wet everything,
> How on that bare wall on the right,
> Where from the stance a craftsman riskily . . .
> And there again, still on that Eastern slope,
> Day after day repeats, day after day
> The clouds pass over, or the wind occurs,
> Or snow. Sparse growth on it, on this
> Dull cliff, dead or asleep or living.
> But the thoughts return.
>
> Or am I mourning for the dead?
> And is it You? You, where
> That stream of sunlight shows
> The texture. You. Watch
> Carefully again: there it is
> Steep and solid there, broken more
> Here over on the left. Yes
> It is you, you only.
> And on our form the dusts will come,
> Thy walls do lichen grow.
>
> On with your coat: walk jauntily
> And turn your back: be gone
> Over the springy turf: so
> Should we celebrate departure.

Noyce's explanatory note in *Samson* tells us about this poem that "He is remembering his second passion. The cliff is Lliwedd." The relationship between it and the story "Scenery for a Murder" will be mentioned below.

During the spring and summer of 1937 Menlove had been seeing a good deal of Alec Keith, who was working at the time in Birmingham. They decided on a summer holiday together. Menlove quickly squashed the idea of an Alpine holiday and suggested one in Norway. Alec had been to the Lofotens in September 1935—the year of Menlove's abortive attempt to sail across—had liked the country, and was keen to go back. He went up to Liverpool for a weekend with Menlove in the early summer so that they could decide where to go, and took with him a map. He was hoping they would decide to go to one of the well-known mountain areas to make some ascents. They spread the map out on the floor of Menlove's sitting-room, pored over it, and before long Menlove pointed to an area in the far north marked Bindal, where there was a fjord, no large mountains, and no towns. Alec was disappointed and blurted out that there was nothing there, to which Menlove replied that that was exactly the reason why he wished to go. Eventually, Alec was brought round by Menlove telling him that they would traverse the side of the fjord from end to end, keeping at a constant height above the water and never going to the top of a hill, and it would therefore be just like Shipton and Tilman's exploration of the Rishi Gorge into the Nanda Devi Sanctuary. Dates were arranged and responsibilities divided up. Alec was to book the passage to Oslo, leaving Newcastle on 7 August. Menlove had charge of the food. At Inverey in 1933, he had complained that the diet was sub-standard. At Helyg, apart from odd eccentricities, such as rice and blackberries eaten together, he always seemed to dine well, so Alec was quite confident that his choice would be acceptable. In the event, it turned out that he brought only three types of food: corned beef, Mapleton's Fruit Slab in lemon and raspberry flavour, and chocolate, and justified the monotony on the grounds that it was nutritious and would need no cooking. There was enough for ten days, they had no eating utensils, and despite its weight Menlove carried it throughout. Apart from food they took a spare shirt and stockings, a sleeping bag each with waterproof covers from Robert Lawrie's, and a Zdarsky bivouac sack. Climbing equipment was limited to an ice-axe, 100 feet of rope, some spare loops and a few pitons. They had no stove, waterproofs, or compass, but did manage to purchase a map in Trondheim.

They duly met in Newcastle and on the ship three English girls travelling to Oslo took them under their wings. Alec remembers that although he quite enjoyed this attention Menlove remained his usual reserved and withdrawn self, not bothering to speak to anyone unless he had to, but urging Alec on to make friends in the hope that it would increase his enjoyment of the journey.

By train, bus and car they reached a point 25 kilometres past Majastina on 11 August, whence a path ran down towards the Tosenfjord, their objective, and Bindal. After paying the driver, they ate a lunch of sardines and bananas and set off along the path. The topography of the area into which they had ventured was extremely confused and by the time they made camp, at about 8.30, they had only the vaguest notion of their whereabouts. On 13 August they reached the head of the fjord at Tostbotnet, bought bread, eggs and milk, were invited into a family's house for bread and cheese and blackberry jam, and started along the shore of the fjord, carrying their eggs in a paper bag. There was a precipitous spur almost immediately, and Alec recalls that "Menlove was being very careful and where I would have been inclined to take a chance and maybe rope down he wouldn't move unless he saw a safe way down. This accounts for the amount of upping and downing we did, and the time we spent on it. All the time we did what Menlove said, and all the time he tried to save me trouble and fatigue." On this spur they encountered for the first time the thick scrub and dwarf birch which covers the lower part of all slopes rising from the sea in Norway. It was difficult, unpleasant ground, swarming with insects, and extremely uncomfortable on a hot day and carrying bulky and heavy rucksacks. By the time they reached the shore of the fjord again at five p.m., having climbed a thousand feet and descended a wooden gully, they were exhausted and spent the rest of the evening basking in the sun, bathing, and eating their eggs, which had miraculously survived unbroken and were cooked over a birchwood fire. The midges were terrible, and they were frustrated at not having brought a line to attempt to catch the fish rising in their hundreds in the fjord.

They were up by six the next morning and moved off at 7.15 after a breakfast of what Alec was beginning to refer to as "that fruit stuff". A path led easily along the shore as far as Kjelvik, beyond which boiler-plate slabs and cliffs dropped into deep water all along beneath the summit of a mountain called Kalklavtind and they were forced to gain height. One problem they encountered was an immense basin of slabs, steep at the sides and top and lipping over at its foot into a vertical wall above the sea. Its angle in the middle, where it was seamed with watercourses, was quite easy, except that, like the Etive Slabs, there were vertical steps running across its surface here and there. It was about 1500 feet high and 900 feet across; the traverse of it took most of the afternoon. From its far side, a connecting series of rakes and steep gullies eventually led them to a bivouac site on the steep Kalklavodden ridge, leading back down to the fjord. The summit dome of Kalklavtind, above them, was steep, and composed of sound-looking granite. It looked as though it might give good rock-climbing and Alec nearly broke

Menlove's resolve not to go to the top of a mountain, but eventually inertia or the accepted plan prevailed, and they clung to the idea of a traverse of the fjord side.

Dawn on the 15th brought a high wind and unsettled weather, so they descended the ridge, which consisted of a series of 30-foot rock-steps separated by steep grass and tree-covered slopes. Alec recalls that "Menlove was still being very careful and I must have been narking him a lot before he consented to use one of our pitons and rope down". Once they had reached Kalklavodden, at the fjord side, after a gruelling descent, they had virtually given up the idea of a fjord traverse, and the vegetated and steep aspect of the next section decided the issue. They struck inland, found a path running parallel to the fjord on the plateau above, which led them back down to the fjord at Kolsvik. One more day, which was virtually a double march, took them to Helstad, only a few kilometres from Bindal at the foot of the fjord. According to Alec, Menlove was in a hurry and wanted to make sure of catching the boat at Bindal, as he had an engagement to climb with Noyce for which he did not want to be late. He was also complaining now of sore feet, and asked if Alec would mind taking a bit of his load, which he did. They caught the boat on 17 August. Alec's recollections of the rest of their holiday are amusing:

> From now on there was a constant struggle between Menlove and me about food. His view was that we had food of our own so why spend money? He was continuing his holiday after we got home and was reserving funds for this. My holiday ended when we got back to England and I could spend my money and was all for wallowing (mildly) in the fleshpots. I horrified Menlove's thrifty soul by throwing a tin of bully beef overboard on the journey back to Trondheim. You'd have thought he was the Scotchman in the party.
>
> Occasionally he relented and we had a meal in a café or on board ship. In Trondheim he bought about a kilo of goat's milk cheese—the brown, sweetish, gritty stuff which, to me, is pretty sickly even in small quantities. He thought we should live on this—with bread—and we had quite frequent meals of it, the last one on the train from Harwich to Liverpool Street. We didn't manage to finish it, but I was surprised when it turned up again at Helyg a few months later. It didn't taste any better to me, but it was quite popular with a party from Bart's Hospital who were in the hut, and we got some of their delicacies in return.

They arrived back in Oslo on 20 August, spent a day there, and then crossed over to Copenhagen to catch the Harwich boat from Esbjerg. In

Copenhagen, Menlove bought a copy of Joyce's *Ulysses* in two volumes, one of which he gave to Alec to carry in his rucksack through customs for him. But before they landed he took it back and carried it through himself.

What chance, really, for the openness and tolerance which Menlove needed in a society which could ban *Ulysses* as obscene?

On his return from the expedition to Norway Menlove went back up to North Wales, where Noyce and his family were staying at the Royal Hotel in Capel Curig. Noyce had had a fine third season in the Alps with Hans Brantschen. They had made ascents of the Younggrat on the Breithorn, the South Face of the Weisshorn, the Zmutt Ridge of the Matterhorn and the Viereselgrat of the Dent Blanche, rounding off the holiday with a traverse of the Matterhorn and Dent d'Hérens. After this, Wales and more especially guidebook work on Lliwedd was an anti-climax, and not only that, but the weather was bad and Menlove's holiday was coming to an end.

Noyce had arranged to go up to stay with Professor Pigou at Lower Gatesgarth for a few days' walking at the end of September, and Menlove was invited to join him there a few weeks after the August holiday. On 21 September a fine day broke a sequence of rainy ones; a party of five set off towards Styehead. At the pass Ronald Noyce and two friends branched down to climb on the Napes whilst Noyce and Menlove struck on for Scafell. Before parting company with the others they examined the first aid equipment on the pass, Noyce wondering if they should ever need it, thinking how seldom people fell. Then away to Scafell, to lunch on Mickledore and gaze over to the cliffs.

The Central Buttress, over to the right, looked clean and dry, with only a little streak of moisture here and there. On the left was the East Buttress, 250 feet of rock which bulged and dripped, shadowy and threatening. There were only five routes and a couple of variations on this steepest of Lakeland crags at the time. They thought to try Mickledore Grooves, Colin Kirkus's great climb of 1931 which had opened a new phase in Lake District climbing history. "It should be dry," they said to each other, "and anyway, Colin did it in socks." They walked over to its foot, changed into rubbers, and roped up. Noyce led the first pitch, needing a shoulder from Menlove to start the little overhanging wall, and Menlove led through up the twin grooves to the grass ledge and poor belay below the tilted slab of the main pitch. The run-out on this was supposed to be 140 feet. They had two ropes, one of them a khaki-coloured synthetic fibre balloon-cable 100 feet in length, the other of 70 feet. So they tied them together. Noyce changed to socks and set off. He climbed steadily up: "It was still a little wet, and the socks' edges crinkled at times over the holds. The moves were to be done quickly, catlike. At each I wondered whether it would be easy to get down, if I wanted to." At the top of the difficult groove, 90 feet above Menlove on the belay, he made the awkward step to a great sod of turf on the right. Standing there, he struggled to ease some rope round a frail spike of rock, hoping that it would protect the last few feet across the awkward traverse and up the mossy wall to the top, hoping that his socks would not slip. A party on the easy ground above called down to ask if all was well, and the answer came back that of course it was. Hardly daring to congratulate himself yet, Noyce added that he would need a lot of beer that night. And then the turf moved, slid, accelerated, hurled into space and Noyce with it, the earth wheeling, smacking him into ledges, Menlove struggling to take in the vital few feet of rope which would keep him from the ground, bracing himself; a savage jolt, flesh ripped from his palms as the rope ran, then silence, Noyce swinging limply below, only feet above the scree, his face shattered, bleeding. Two strands of the balloon-cable had parted—perhaps nicked as they pulled from the spike—but the knot and the third strand held. Menlove roped down, cradled the injured boy's head, expertly stopped the bleeding. Help came, the body was carried down. There was difficulty about transport in the valley, but they got to Whitehaven Hospital, an emergency operation was carried out on the head, and after being unconscious for three days, Noyce opened his eyes and pulled through. Had he been climbing with anyone else but Menlove, he would have died. He fell 180 feet and was desperately injured, but he was climbing with a man of enormous physical strength who was also a doctor. He saved him in the fall and sustained him after it. David Murray-Rust had a most interesting view of Menlove's role in the aftermath of the accident:

> There was something immensely powerful about Menlove (a conventional observer, brought up conventionally, might have called him a "weak character" because of his abnormalities, but they would have been wrong); and this power was not just physical. The extreme instance was at the time of Wilfrid's near-fatal accident on Scafell. First, Menlove by his competence and strength probably saved Wilfrid's life on the mountain. But later the real test came. Wilfrid was lying unconscious and very near to death in hospital. Menlove refused to leave his bedside during all this time; and I am quite sure that in some way Menlove's support – his *willing*, as it were, for Wilfrid to live— was the critical factor in that coming about. I am certain that both Wilfrid's father and mother recognised this and, through their gratitude, accepted Menlove's friendship for Wilfrid, for I am sure that Frank Noyce would have felt in ordinary circumstances that it was a friendship he wouldn't approve of.

So Noyce survived the accident, and began to mend, convalescing at Gatesgarth until his facial bones had knitted well enough for him to undergo plastic surgery, which left him with the tight-skinned and slightly mis-shapen appearance he kept through middle age to his death.

In many directions the pressures were beginning to mount on Menlove. In his voluntary work for climbing he had not only taken on the job of preparing the Lliwedd guide, on which he would now have to work alone, but also the editorship of the quarterly *Mountaineering Journal*, of which he prepared three issues before it folded in the spring of 1938. He brought a distinctly new editorial policy to what was the only commercial publication in its field at that time: "We, therefore, the commercial one, will be a collector afterwards of the things of others, will take news for our mainstay and plagiarism for motto."

Apart from the policy of producing a wide-ranging mountaineering news magazine, he also decided to make some changes to its graphic design. Running heads and a serif typeface were introduced and the layout generally tidied up and put into a logical order. He did virtually all the reviewing and wrote a considerable amount of editorial matter. He included only a little of his original work, and even that little was not as well received as were the changes he made to the *Journal*:

> Regarding your short story in this quarter's Journal "A letter from a man." It seems to be the unanimous decision of my friends that the man in question didn't receive his cards soon enough. What he should have received was a strait-jacket and a shaded room. The only way we can account for his outburst in the hotel is that the solitude had been too much for him, or that he had a touch of the sun.
>
> We all seem to be of a fair average intelligence, but cannot understand why you print two pages of such unadulterated tripe in such a fine issue—the best since we started reading the MJ.
>
> Perhaps you will give the solution in next quarter's publication so that just an ordinary climber can have his money's worth. After all we all don't make a study of warped minds.
>
> Congratulations on your new Journal. It's a fine effort.
>
> Yours, etc.
>
> C. Robinson Wilson

The robust philistinism of this response is no more than the climbing writer's common lot since the 1930s, but this particular example is terribly ironic in view of what was to come. (For "Letter from a Man" see

Appendix.) Menlove's professional career was not going as well as he would have wished. Although he had become Honorary Physician to Liverpool Psychiatric Clinic and in 1939, Consultant Psychiatrist to Birkenhead Corporation, there were disappointments as well. He applied for a medical post at Birmingham United Hospital, to be near Alec Keith, was interviewed, but did not get the job.

He placed a great premium upon his research generally, and thought more highly of it than his clinical work, at which latter he was extremely good. He wrote to Noyce that "there was a grand psychiatric research job going in Cambridge that I'd have given anything for but I'd not have had any chance at all for it: nothing to be done but just plod with this accursed everlasting clinical work". A colleague in Liverpool, Dr Barton Hall, glowingly referred to his practical work amongst other points in this brief memoir:

> In the domain of medical psychology he entertained strong original views, particularly relating to the treatment of patients, a field in which he was conspicuously successful. He possessed the quality of being able to influence profoundly other young people. I know that he published one paper, but, speaking generally, he experienced much difficulty in committing his psychiatric ideas to conventional prose. I know how hard he tried to conform to the view of others, and to tolerate orthodoxy, but where his principles were concerned he was quite incapable of insincerity or compromise, and at no matter what cost to himself.

In his clinical work it was re-stimulation of the will to fight in a patient—even if against his physician—which was his chief aim. For all the respect it gained him from others, his practical psychiatric work he looked on as nothing more than preparation for the great effort of research which lay ahead. In this, his scheme was both simple and grandiose. He rejected out-of-hand the work of Freud and Adler, founding fathers of the science, and held to the view that a comprehensive theory of mental action could be arrived at which would not only help in human relationships and individual psychoses but would also have its wider application in world affairs. His quest was for a single natural law to which all mental phenomena conformed, and which once discovered would enable the reactions of people to given situations to be predicted. He believed that the will could be trained to control the nervous and muscular systems of the body, and also the subconscious and instinctual parts of the mind. Chantrell remembers him discussing his research programme seriously in cafés and as they walked along crowded Liverpool streets, counting on his fingers the numbers of decades it would take him to prepare. "And if he could not get it across and died first?" He shrugged. "Well, anyway, you'll have left us a few climbs to keep us busy." He replied that his climbing was of no importance at all.

His preparation for the task was meticulous and massive at the same time and, in terms of contemporary psychology, probably quite bizzare. On the one hand, minute jottings about his own memories, aspirations, states of consciousness; on the other a systematic programme of reading in history and historical biography. He experimented on himself with drugs, with journeys to the limits of fatigue and beyond. Chantrell gives a good physical description of him from this time:

Height about 5 ft 9 ins. Not large skull. Short, curly, very dark brown hair. Slightly sallow complexion in town, soon tanned on hills. Eyes light hazel rather wide apart. Normally slow and dreamy usage of them. Mouth a weak one, lips curled. Chin very small with deep indentation. Neck thick and normally rather contracted. Shoulders broad and very powerful, likewise arms and chest. Hands and fingers also muscular. Wrists strong but very supple. Legs proportional, rather small feet for height of him. Voice deep-toned and he pulled back his chin towards termination of sentence to make it even deeper over tensing neck muscles. Wrinkled brow. Always practised a direct conscious control in gestures rather slow, self-conscious, and usually evidencing his great strength and determination. But frequent punctuations in form of muscle release gestures evidencing supple swiftness. Linked muscle power gestures with deep, serious and sympathetic conversation; confidence-inspiring understanding attitude to listener. Himself a very patient listener with a knack of disinterested interest in other person; very much in tradition of sympathetic doctor to patient, with the usual effect that he very soon had his companion talking of himself. Menlove finished by knowing his companion's affairs, and the latter knowing nothing about Menlove's. Very reticent about himself, and convinced you that the feats that made him outstanding were really of little importance, not especially exacting or beyond the average man. This he did by relating the ordinary details at random rather than the feat as a whole.

His letters from patients he kept, and many of them were still in Nowell's possession after his death. Some address him by christian name, others in terms such as "Dear Aggravator . . .". There is one from Compton Mackenzie asking for his assistance with a young man who besieged him with odd letters and telegrams:"If not cream bedadery Sunday afternoon paganism prommed." Others bear witness to the confidence he inspired in his patients: "I feel safe when I have written to you," and again, "Your time has yet to come—perhaps your work is more widely known than you realise. Even the nurse at the faculty knew you . . . and the way she spoke of you made me glow with pride." Yet others give insights into the problems with which he dealt and his methods of treating them:

Dear Sir,

I have got myself into one of my usual messes, and once again I appeal to you for help. I have already written two letters to you which I never posted, and I wish to God I had, as I am sure this would never have happened.

Now that I have created all sorts of trouble by getting run down and hysterical, I am calm, frightened, and sorry; and I wished I could undo everything.

I went to the doctor a little over a week ago for a tonic. I have been depressed off and on for a long time, but believe me, ever in my mind has been acceptance, no self pity, and discipline.

I feel dreadful writing to you, as I feel you cured me and it was up to me to conquer. Don't be too hard please. You will hate me for saying that, as I always want kindness instead of truth, but we do fall by the roadside sometimes. That is no excuse, I suppose, but I have nothing else to say.

I am writing this because I fear they are going to ask you about me. I hardly mind anything, but the caring as I do for another woman, that is too private, and only you and I can know that. I cannot ask you to do anything wrong, but I would like to be spared this.

Dear Sir, also I want to stay in this life. I have found it lonely and dull, but I do not wish to go home a failure again.

I will rally soon, with fresh strength to try again. I do hope you will forgive me, but I am desperate. Don't let the world know. I have grown, Sir, in my seven months here, and I *will* go from strength to strength, in mind, it is only time. How I wish I could undo this. Some day I will learn my lesson, and never give in, but lock everything in my heart.

Ada.

The advice and treatment which Menlove gave to "Ada" came from a man who knew very well the problems she faced.

Menlove's mother had left the house in Formby by this time to live with Nowell in London, but Nowell was to be married in 1938 to her father's cousin Hewlett Johnson, whose first wife had died in 1931. Menlove, therefore, invited his mother to live with him and found for them a flat at 24 Devonshire Road, Liverpool. It was near to his consulting rooms in Rodney

Street. Opposite were the grassy spaces of Sefton Park. An avenue of lime trees ran down the road in front of the scrolled and corniced three-storey houses of soot-encrusted sandstone. They had a Welsh maid in to help Mrs Edwards. Her other two surviving children now settled, the mother fell happily into the routine of looking after her youngest son, spoiling him with his favourite chocolate, having his meals ready for him and washing his clothes. There was a large room at the front of the flat with a bay window looking out on to the park. One of Menlove's letters gives an impression of the routine of their lives:

> Now I have just been working, sitting in this big room. But there is a concert at 8.00 and I have turned on the wireless for it. Mother likes something doing in the evenings so we compromise: it goes on for concerts and I start to write.

After the accident to Noyce, Menlove did very little climbing for several months, but he did meet Alec Keith at Helyg for a day's climbing in December. Alec's journal gives a good account of a typical winter weekend in the hut:

> Helyg was badly crowded by a party of Bart's Hospital chaps, including Jim Joyce, and odd stragglers. I'd eaten by the time Menlove arrived and after some tea and much talk we got to bed about 11.30. It was good to see Menlove again, and he seemed well and not so tired as usual. We managed to get the upstairs to ourselves and lay and talked for a long time before going to sleep. It was blowing hard by then, raining and the night was very dark.
>
> We got up about 8 a.m. with some difficulty, for it was very cold, and had our breakfast before the crowds, but it was still nearly 10 a.m. before we were ready. At the garage we found Bill Stallybrass in difficulties with his car. He had left the ignition on overnight and the battery was run down, but it started with a tow. He seemed stranded so we suggested he come with us to do something short on Lliwedd.
>
> We were at the bottom of the West Peak by noon, there was some discussion about what to do, but we opted for Primitive Route.

Although quite easy, this 1,000-foot climb scarcely qualifies as "something short on Lliwedd". Menlove's guide to the cliff describes it as "two mildly steep pitches of which the first is the harder; the rest comprises about 700 feet of height so we have to make a virtue of this fact and use it for non-climbers, ice and snow conditions or an easy way off". Alec now relates the ascent:

There was a lot of snow on the mountain and the face was quite white, and we had some difficulty in getting to the bottom of our climb through the loose, deep, powdery snow. The first few pitches went well enough but felt rather precarious and it was bitterly cold. Eventually we reached a ledge below the crux—50-foot pitch with a small overhang halfway up. Menlove did this very slowly and we down below were covered with the snow which he swept off ledges and holds, and soon became extremely cold. At last he was up, and we followed only slightly more quickly, both of us coming on the rope to a greater or lesser extent without actually leaving our holds. The next two pitches were simple and led to the foot of a long groove, rather holdless in its middle part. This took a very long time, as every hold had to be cleared by hand of six inches of snow, cleaned and tested before use. And the footholds soon iced up so there was a general feeling of insecurity, added to considerable exposure. Menlove was taking no chances and climbed very carefully, bombarding us with chunks of ice and quantities of loose snow. It was much easier for us when we came up because all the holds had been discovered.

Above there was one nasty step on a very small hold which was completely iced up, but after that the angle eased, though without an ice-axe between us we kept the rope on right to the summit, which we reached as the light was failing having been five hours on the climb.

The snow gave us some light on the way down and we got back to the cars about 6.30. Back at Helyg we found tea waiting for us, which was more welcome than the jokes about search parties which followed.

Woollen jumpers and gloves, balaclavas, old jackets held together with blanket pins or in Menlove's case the patched and tattered old Fettes blazer which was still doing good service for his climbing. No ice-axes, clinker-nailed boots. No slings. How many climbers nowadays would go on Lliwedd clad and equipped thus in these conditions?

To take up the theme of search parties, David Cox by a curious coincidence found himself involved in the late thirties with two accidents on Ysgolion Duon—the Black Ladders cliff at the head of Cwm Llafar, above Bethesda. On both occasions he went back to Helyg for help, and on both occasions found Menlove there alone. He now takes up the story:

The first of these accidents involved an unconscious man* halfway up Western Gully. In those days there was no rescue organisation and someone had alerted the police in Bethesda. They called out about a

* The Birmingham University climber Bob Beaumont, who was in fact fatally injured.

hundred Bethesda quarrymen, and by the time Menlove and I got back the lower part of the cliff was covered with quarrymen, all unroped and many of them stuck and in considerable danger of getting killed. We couldn't start to lower the actual casualty until all the quarrymen had been got off the cliff. The way in which Menlove managed this was quite astonishing; he took complete charge, and somehow produced order out of chaos in a relatively short time. I particularly remember him standing on quite a wide ledge, but without any belay, holding a rope while two or three men at a time slid down it. It was impressive the way they all took orders from him. Similarly, it was Menlove who took charge of lowering the stretcher down the cliff. This also was an impressive performance; his strength was enormous and he seemed to do the work of four men.

The second accident only involved a broken ankle incurred right at the start of a climb, so there was no difficulty in getting the man off the cliff. On this occasion, Menlove insisted on carrying him pig-a-back the whole way down Cwm Llafar to Bethesda.

It makes an interesting contrast to turn from David Cox's gentle adulation to Menlove's own persistent anti-heroics and self-denigration. The latter has given rise to a good deal of theorizing along the lines: "Was he a classic case of a man who climbed to prove himself to himself, and then refused to accept the proof?" Perhaps Menlove's own words, from the Idwal Guide introduction, are preferable:

> . . . as one who has been shown by Idwal the feelings of the hills, their waters, the sky, and the grey spread of rock that gathers them, he would wish no more than to have place and memory as they have been, and to leave the details of action as futile among them as in fact they are.

Should the actions need to be recounted, then let them be made to seem somehow absurd. The account given below is of an ascent of Shallow Gully by Menlove and Alec Keith at Easter 1938:

> See all my climbing career: reputations, boots, purity, no pitons. Old age: Alec and the Rocker Route, carrying pitons. This Easter holiday great crowds, more than once recognised and accosted—the appalling publicity that can be achieved in a small world like the climbing world, number of people limited, number of cliffs to which they go also limited.
>
> Shallow Gully: a standard climb, cliff dry as a cat, not too cold.
>
> Roped up passing the time of day with some distant acquaintances who were hanging around. On to the rocks. Though always a determined boot

climber I put on a pair of rubbers ... hours ... now in climbing it is neither wise nor prudent to push things beyond a certain limit. I therefore called to my trusty second, hauled up a piton, small hammer, and was soon in a position to get up that bad piece. Further ... chimney ... but surely in climbing as in other things when one has made an honest effort and put out one's very best forces without effect, then one should be content and call in that help from other people that they may be only too willing to give. I therefore looked carefully around, shouted to No 2, pulled up a small hammer, a piton, long before I had put the worst of it below me, and the crack being a deep crack and fairly well out of sight of the public it wasn't ... but perhaps nothing in this world goes right through without a hitch. So far we had, I think, not been seen. I settled myself, called to No 2 to come up, but first he must remove the piton. He hammered away at it carefully, not too much noise, lest those around should know what had happened. Good, he had got it out, and then—the karabiner ring slipped and fell. No 2 made a wild effort to catch it but it eluded him. It ricocheted, tinkled, gathered speed, shot ringing like a bell past the astonished heads of a couple of parties on Route Two, bounced, narrowly missing some other parties near the foot, sprang, leapt clattering down ... and buried itself in among the screes at the foot of Lliwedd. And there it still lies in the company of my own reputation in that romantic spot, in the company also of a pair of light-blue socks I once saw there, the end of the blade of Mr George Abraham's pen-knife, the blood of at least three martyrs, one small stone cross, the juice products of very many too-much-leant-against oranges, also of sardines, sweat, pennies, who knows, pieces of eight and many other such things, things all discarded in the struggle unwillingly by their owners.

Now all this had taken time. The climbing had taken time, more than we cared to think: even the descent of the karabiner ring had taken time; so too had the shouts of ribaldry, and the remorse in our hearts.

But we pulled ourselves together, a bit of chocolate, half an apple, we didn't carry much, and went on with renewed confidence: we weren't halfway up yet. We scrambled quickly up 150 feet of easy loose muck, showed dexterity and speed on the little cave pitch, climbed carefully but well up the short confusing terrain west of the Great Terrace, and then to our disgust found ourselves up against another pitch clearly quite beyond our powers, so as the first half of the gully had taken five hours and the second half threatened to put an end to our time on earth entirely, we fetched a short circuit, the sun now going down, to make any last watchers think we were perhaps exploring and then escaped up the easy Terminal Arete; thence with no strength into the night.

All that really happened here was that, Menlove having used one peg for protection and another to safe guard a stance, Alec dropped the first peg and its attached karabiner. By 1938 pegs were being quite widely used by leading Welsh climbers, to an extent that Kirkus was asked to put the matter into perspective through an article in the 1939 *Wayfarers' Club Journal* entitled "The Ethics of Ironmongery".

Paul Work recounts an impression of Menlove gained at this same period:

> . . . at Easter 1938 he joined my camp below Lliwedd. I noticed that Menlove preferred to sleep out than share our ample tentage. What I did not suspect at the time was that he was homosexually inclined, although I made two observations that Easter from which a more subtle psychologist than I might have concluded something. First, after he and I had met and entrained at Rock Ferry we took our seats. A few stations later the compartment got crowded and a young man was left standing for a moment, whereupon Menlove rose and insisted on surrendering his seat in the young fellow's favour. Second, our companion Gerald Bryan was exceedingly good-looking and Menlove went some distance out of his way to climb with him then and in the following August and to correspond with him.

As the last few pages have shown, this narrative is now beginning to focus on Lliwedd as Menlove engages with the work necessary for the guidebook. The events of the rest of the summer, with a little explanation here and there, can be told in Menlove's own words, with occasional interjections from one or two others. The best preliminary to this is a review, from the 1937 *Climbers' Club Journal*, of A. T. Hargreaves' guidebook to Scafell, published by the Fell & Rock Climbing Club. It is the most succinct and witty statement of Menlove's guidebook theory:

> This guide is an honest piece of work. There are between 80 and 90 climbs in it, with some very exact details about each. The descriptions are concise, neatly tabulated, clean and accurate, pitch by pitch. It is No 2 of the Lakes series—there are going to be five—and, they tell me, they are all going to be exactly alike, these guides, as like as pins.
>
> And it is very difficult to think of things to say about it, for the sight of it does not stir me that way, but only to memories. How I hadn't climbed on the cliff at the time: was a beginner, not allowed out on such things; but I read it, read it again, poured myself over it, and photos and diagrams; later on used to get lost on the cliffs, among its buttresses.
>
> There is not much to be said about detail. I have only been to Scafell

half a dozen times, but I am sure of that, that everything is as right as makes no matter. And apart from detail there is nothing in the guide: even the historical note is stuffy with detail. So I may as well say straight off that I think it is excellent, a very great improvement on the previous edition, and on Kelly's Pillar guide too; that it gives me a headache to have to read it; and that I wish to attack it.

First, on the score of use. It seems to me to be wrong in plan. The description is a tiny, narrow spotlight moving in a single line, "a chimney", "a little slab", then it travels on, "a crack", "20'", "a grass ledge"; and that is all; the rocks might be any rocks, and the conformation of cliff and climb might be any conformation, might be in mid-air, for the spotlight sheds no rays aside, and gives no light on such matters. So, strictly speaking, you do not know where you are. If, for instance, you once lost the track, it would be no good looking round at how the rocks stood, you would have to go down and start again. But for the diagram the method would again and again be useless. The diagrams are luckily fairly adequate and do give quite a good idea of the main areas. I have heard others praise them more highly. There is also an excellent frontispiece drawing much better than the Pillar one, but there are no photographs, no relief. I admired the terse engineering touch that made the best of a bad method; it gives more grip than there is in the Pillar guide. But, even so, the network on these cliffs is not portrayed by it.

Then the headache. Just as there is not a scrap of visual power in the guide, so, among these 80 to 90 individual tracks, there is not one type brought out, and not one character. The history is prep. school history, epics, crowns, best days still to come, just as much as the classificatory scheme is a stupid, prep. school, straight up and down scheme, with the old kings treated in charity. You can see nothing, and you can feel nothing. You can read it, the dry print, but only with a headache.

I do not know. To write a guide like this takes a great amount of trouble, and to write one as well on the larger scale would take more. It may not be worth while for a man to spend so much effort on a climbing guide. But at present we are considering only the point, how good is this one? And for that I have laboured these as my opinions and can stop there: that progress is a thing of ups and downs, but mostly also of desire; that this guide is the best yet of its kind; that there is danger of standardisation at this low level: and that, as for stultification, the method has gone far enough, being sufficient already to cause pain.

The "standardisation at this low level" has been without exception the rule for the last 30 years, and Menlove's review poses with great precision and sardonic humour the question of what use a guide is if it imparts no sense of character or place; if, by using it, "strictly speaking you do not know where you are". The working premise here is the need for a broad view, and for a wider *human* perspective on the cliffs, so that some idea can be given of response, texture, and feel. Also that the actions of the men upon the rocks—the history—be seen for what it is; an amalgam of desire, accretion, knowledge, the development of technique and confidence. What Menlove is again seeking to undermine and discard are the overblown heroics, the awful bourgeois at their trumpets again, the proclamations of vanity and the presumptions of superiority which Menlove would never allow himself: "The history is prep. school history, epics, crowns, best days still to come . . ." Why climbing should be stimulus to these attitudes is an intriguing question, with the simple physical image of height and detachment too facile an answer. But that so many *good* writers on climbing have the capacity to deflate and prick pretension is cause for gratitude.

Having let Menlove state his method, let him now describe his efforts to unravel the mysteries of Lliwedd for the guidebook. The first extract is his initial version of the fortnight in which the work began:

It is not often that man gets a chance of four consecutive weeks in the hills, for man is a busy animal. What then on this occasion was lacking, for here we were, and here we would stay all that time. Not only that but where as a rule there is great difficulty each day in picking the venue and the scene for the exploits, on this occasion the whole four weeks every day was ready mapped out for us. What more could a man desire? And then that grand old pile Lliwedd: there is probably no more grand, certainly no older, no more piley pile in the whole of Wales. What then was lacking to make a man full?

The first we did was the Rocker Route: fear and trembling, yes, but we did it. What more could one wish for? You know the Rocker Route? It is an epitome of the whole mountain, and we had picked it out this one from all the others only by its outstanding ease.

Then the rains came, not the cold, hard rains of winter but the sweet warm rain of July. It seeped into our sleeping bags, laid our tent flat upon its face on the grass of Cwm Dyli, filled our cliff, but it did not defeat us. It was however impossible to maintain our previous average of one climb per day, and it was very difficult to maintain the previous standard of difficulty. Yet the work went on, we used Helyg, waterproof, as our camping ground, and we had as much corned beef as we could possibly wish for; and Lliwedd is as memorable when it is wreathed in mists, its rocks streaming with water and its turf sodden, as in the hot days when the rock is perfect, indeed more memorable. Could any man ask for more?

Then fine weather came. The sun streamed out, the sweat poured from us and the rocks day by day became drier. The standard of our climbing leapt up beyond its past record, we drove a piton into Solomon, skidded on the Child's Face, and in three consecutive days we achieved the summit of the East Peak about an hour before nightfall. We became bolder. We brought a novice to the hills, desiring both company and admiration, we were pulled bodily up the last overhang of the crack of the Central Gully, we followed the description of the Great Chute climb pitch by pitch up the wrong side of the East Gully, we cut the young man's rope with a falling boulder of terrific dimensions and the next day dropped a large brick sixty feet direct onto his novice's head. Could anything be wanting? We had accomplished little it is true in a direct sense, but we had had an eventful week, then with the heat and the moisture the weather broke, the thunder and lightning and a deluge of rain, and our climbing was for a momentary lull cut short. Again we could wish for no more, and laying our heads dirty upon our pillows, thankful we slept. AMK retired to Birmingham. Gerald Bryan retired to hospital, RWB and JME extant . . .

Menlove had curiously missed F. J. Dodd out of this reckoning. Fortunately Dodd left an account of the first ascent of Central Gully Direct which fills out and corrects the impression which Menlove gives both here and in his article "Up Against It". The report is, slightly confusingly, written in the third person:

Party traversed to above Central Gully Direct and FJD was lowered to a well-marked spot below the final overhang. This went with sufficient ease to confirm his growing suspicions that an assault on the whole repulsive crack was to be made.

After lunch, JME led up over the first overhang in most heartening fashion, and belayed ten feet higher on a piton which had resisted his efforts to dislodge it. FJD, under the transparent pretext of preserving his energy, was hauled up, and continued, Agag-like, to below the final overhang. Here, with much knitting and profanity, a system of belays was fashioned. JME came up. FJD then unsnarled himself and, spurred on by his loathing for the place, escaped as rapidly as possible over the overhang and onto a belay fifteen feet higher, where JME joined him, having made light of the *mauvais pas*.

This route is singled out for attention not only because it is still graded Hard Very Severe and held to be a serious climb at that standard, but also for the fact that over the next quarter century it was to see only two repeat ascents. It was in fact subjected to the sort of inflation of which Menlove thoroughly disapproved and in his own hey-day sought to discredit. Menlove's guidebook assessment of the route was modestly precise: "A fissile rock structure, the angle and an absence of large ledges all go to make it one of the most attractive routes on the mountain. There is also a spice of technical problem in the two overhangs."

Before we turn to Menlove's fullest account of the month's work, it is helpful in setting the scene to bring in a page from Alec Keith's journal. He and Menlove have met at Helyg, packed food enough for several days, and carried it along with camping and climbing gear up to a suitable spot beneath Llydaw, where they made camp but didn't pitch the tent before ascending Rocker Route, "slowly and with groans":

July 25th. Wakened early in morning by fine rain; still dark. Rain got worse and beds got wet until about 5 a.m. we could stick it no longer and got up. Back to Helyg, set the stuff drying, had some porridge, then bed for two hours. Up again and found weather still bad. Got stuff dry, re-packed, and went off to Pen y Gwryd. Stopped here for most of forenoon and lunchtime, looking at the locked book [in which the early pioneers recorded their activities], talking, and eating two pleasant strangers' sandwiches. Met Lockwood and talked with him, hearing about the Giveen accident. Then to Pen y Pass where we had tea and looked at the Book. Still pouring rain. Ran down to Llanberis, ate some chocolate: then back to Pen y Pass where we spent the night.

In the morning Alec and Menlove walked back up to the campsite, erected the tent, and went off to climb, doing three new pitches to the right of Craig yr Aderyn, and descending back down Primitive Route, which Alec found markedly easier than on their last experience of it. Menlove opted to sleep in the open that night, but the rain came on again and he crawled into the tent. A wet day dawned, they climbed Bracket Gully, fusillades of loose rock thoroughly frightening Alec, and then decamped once more to Helyg. This was the desultory start to the holiday described most completely in "Up Against It", which appeared in the 1940 *Wayfarers' Club Journal*:

"We all like to gloat over a thing and as the year goes by we think of summer and what to do in the holidays, whether some great feat, but this year, age creeping on, no, I said, this year a rest. It was not to be. Won't tell you why, take too long, but here I was at the beginning of August, four weeks to go, and the four of them booked for Lliwedd, the guide.

"We had meant to camp but what can you do, the rain pouring, the tent blown down, sleeping sacks drowned, and not wanting a repetition who but a fool would do anything else. We shifted back down the valley. We had a car just then. And the climbing? It's no good telling chaps like you trash about all we did. You wouldn't be interested. It's new stuff you want, and we weren't really on for that, we had work to do. We had meant to do some, but once we started, you can't give up climbing, go soft, without an insidious weakening coming on and so it was with us we found. We had to do the ordinary climbs first.

"We started off on the Rocker Route first day, early start, photograph of cliff in sunshine, last chance for two weeks but we didn't know that, strode over the grass, up the screes and stood panting a little but full of hope at the foot of the Rocker Route. Nice easy climb, but it was on the second pitch I began to wobble, being some way off the ground by then and very nervy if you don't trust your footing, then on the fourth pitch I couldn't do it at all but could take a shoulder, and after that, you know what it is, you've got to do it somehow but how, you may come adrift any minute and go for six, but we went on, grim as death we went on, a little light refreshment half way didn't we need it, 3.00 p.m., and the worst is yet to come, but we went on knuckles scraped knees bleeding, 5 p.m., 6 p.m., 6.30 p.m., the summit: what a victory: what a life: but if every climb was going to be like that what about the guide, we'd never do it, not in four weeks, not in four years. So Alec and I, stout friends, we drew in our belts, shook each other by the hand, swore faith to the end, and that we must be very careful, that we had bargained to be bad, but not quite as bad as this, no, but we have four good pitons and we will keep them ever round our belts. So we couldn't come to too much harm we felt whatever happened. Then as I said the rain came and we got wet, wet through, and then the tent blew down, and there was nothing for it after three nights like that only to go down and cart all the food away again, though we left a little just in case, and bread is such a bulk to carry, though when it's wet it very soon gets mouldy, but the birds might have it. You may think we laughed but we did not, it was too much for us, and over the next two weeks I draw a veil. It shall cover also the climbing, our cheeks, pale then though now burning, and that we did not quite do one climb per day.'

'But you say then, how is it, how can it be? It came thus. It was I started it, I said we will do the Great Chute, two Rucksackers did it, it can't be too bad—I hope not. Then we got there. '. . . the mouth of the East Gully . . .' Yes. '. . . band of quartz . . .' Yes. So up we went, slow of course, and getting higher we said these Rucksackers they lie and it was all loose, and we were not at all safe, but we went on, not without doubts and followed it up foot by foot reading what was said about it, and only not doing what we should when it was certainly impossible. Near the top it got harder as it said it would and we stepped with difficulty into the unsuspected crack on the right, as it said we would, then we stepped with difficulty up it as also told, and dropped a very big block which cut the rope and knocked away the ledge No 2 was standing on, the rock was not good, so that he hung by his hands, and he shouted and I hauled in the rope though in no position to do so greatly to my credit, but as I say the rope was cut, after which we were very careful and we went on and reached the summit. But when we got down again we found the Great Chute went up from near the same start indeed but not up that side of the East Gully at all, the other side, so that what we climbed was not a climb at all. So we wrote it up new, and said how funny, we would never have done it otherwise, and it has been a great day for us, but hush, not a word about that in the guide. We only did one climb that day too because we were quite tired out and you know what a strain it is always to be climbing, and if you are frightened, and if you are on one cliff day after day, there is no variety. We gave it a name, the Runnel, to sound aristocratic we thought and au fait.

"Then another week went by bad as before but not so atrocious. One climb after another we did, one day after another, nearly even, but not quite for on one day or more we were too exhausted, so that we could not rise up in the morning but lay there stuporous until the day after. Nothing new except a variation here and there, especially I must say the Birch Tree Terrace Route, which wandered heaven knows where all over the place before we did it, but that was a flash in the pan, no true harbinger. Things were altering though yes, looking back you could say that, it was D's before and no harder but now it was VD's too and VD goes a long way on Liwedd, there's nothing much on that cliff. And the party changed. One went. Then we tried to find the Great Chute again and it was even harder to see where the words went on this side of the cliff where it did go, than on the other the Runnel side, where it didn't. We got tied up a bit and when I was off the route on one side I got stuck, and I got off the route on the other side next and dropped a very big stone again which landed 80 feet below on the side of No 3's head so he fainted a bit, and when we got down to look at him we had to abandon that climb and get him down, take him to hospital. So another went. Next time we tried that climb too the last chap nearly went, but we digress, we go too far. It happened like this. We got so far, then the steep bit goes up a crack 30 feet which then opens into a great V chute suddenly, a very great one but no stance, not till 40 feet up the great V chute, and I got there, the top of the crack, and feeling giddy with the air and on a good foothold, for twenty minutes I rummaged and got a first class thread at the back of the crack, got No 2 up there and tied him on and a thunderstorm started, a real cloud-burst, the sky dark, the birds stilled, there were six that week and very heavy ones. Very soon there was a big stream down the great V-chute getting bigger, so I stayed to see what would happen for I felt a little giddy still, and No 2 with the water breaking over him couldn't move, not more than six inches at all and that didn't take him anywhere, being tied on, but I stood on one side, and the storm was over in two hours, praise be, and then I got up, I was soaked right through; so as I say he nearly went, but he was tied on, but we digress. Then when three weeks were up he did go and Dodd came. Dodd was good, too good, better than I but less pushing. He had a little MG too which he took along every day to the causeway, we two in it, and that was balm indeed, with the long walk otherwise, it put new life into the party. And it is funny isn't it how when you can do a thing the whole cliff is different from when you can't, but we still had a lot to do and no time to do it, but what's the use when all's said, and there's more fish in the sea than ever yet came out, and there was one thing that really must be looked at, Central Gully, next on the list, hadn't been done, and he said you do the first bit then I'll do the rest, which he knew, and I said, well, on a rope I had looked, because of its reputation, and on the rope never had I been in such a filthy place, and it with water down it, and at the first overhang I didn't fall but before it started I had said pull now, pull please, and you will have to pull very hard I am finished, but I said, I think I am better now and we will see. So we did a new bit first on the left and called it the Squiggle, his name, to warm up, and because there was another party looking on applauding. Then we did the Central Gully as he had said and there was a piton halfway up because a lot have nibbled at it, Central Gully, but we couldn't get it out, tried we never so hard, and the blood streamed from our fingers where we hammered it, so we left it in but we didn't rely on it, it being battered too, so we said Wales forgive us and we went on.

"Then we said now we have that behind us, and it has been a great day, what ought we to do else now, but I said I am tired, and I have got to keep fit, and I have come here for a rest; so we did nothing else that day. But the next day we went to and worked again, and there was the East Gully the right hand branch which had not been done, the next thing. So we did that, I must admit below the hard part I stuck a piton in to stick my rope through it for you never know and the piton was loose in anyhow. Then there was Purgatory that day too wanted an end, and we did that though such a stretch is needed and my legs so parted got jerks and let me down had I not acted, but I will not describe those climbs, you would be bored, you can see for yourself, and I have left some out. But we still could not do more than two that day because of the slowness, and because I was bad, my nerves out of order. We really were going splendidly considering though, and then a man fell off a cliff in some other part of Wales and we had to help, so we stayed in bed next day, tired out we were, and the day after that we did climb again but very badly, something had put a stop it seemed such as it was to our jollity, and we did only one new climb, very easy, and called it, his name not mine, the String Climb, and it was a lovely little climb we thought, and such as in the evenings we had longed for, and we said how strange, and life, and so the next day we had a whole day off, we thought better, and we went to see little Miss Temple in Rebecca of Sunnybrook Farm at Bangor, then the next day we felt much better and went up from Birch Tree Terrace to Avalanche, which was needed, then we did a new Anklet on which very nearly I came off exploring, then we had to go to the Central Gully again because it was challenging and we looked at one bit on a rope because I was afraid, and then we did it, right up, across, left up, on the walls of the direct part, the first part I hadn't looked at because it was known to me before when the writer of the guide took me up but he had had an accident, so we were finishing off now though it took us a month because we were slow, and if you multiply even 28 by 1 or less you don't get many. We did this climb though and we called it Swastika, I did not think of that name he did. Now we must hurry on, two days left, but boredom came over us even greater, that come on also over our reader, days such as the toughest only could stand; no I have got it wrong, I forget, we did this the last day, it was the two days before, we went to the West Peak and we did this and that, tidied up the cliff a bit for it needed it, climbed a nasty little brute the Clam, not my word, he said it that damned Clam, and then on we went, finished off Three Pinnacle Gully, the Slabby Patch, three other parties, pioneers avoided it, oh yes and I forgot we had had great trouble there ourselves when wet a few days before, or I had, but been rescued thank heaven not able to stick on, off the side of it. And that was all but unexpectedly we had another day, extra, with another party, and that day we did the Quartz Babe direct and called it The Sword and that was my name. But this is ridiculous, a mere catalogue, what on earth do you imagine you get from this. Then we failed on another thing and another thing. I don't know why, then we had to go to that Central Gully again, because it exerted a pull, I say it yes we had to, and we did another route on it on its walls, left up, right up, right, crossing the other one and we called it Swastika 2, and that was my name also. That was all we did that day, then we came down and for an hour or so we felt joyful, I can remember that, I can look back upon it and testify, and I think I have not felt so conceited in my life, before or since; and numbers two and three I do not say what happened to them on these two things, they were out of practice rather and I wasn't.

"We ran out of petrol late going home that night, but August was up now praise be to God, and I was happy I just sat in the car, and I would not ever need go near the place again, I thought, and petrol or no petrol, I don't care."

The Lliwedd guide appeared the following year (1939). Although he had taken virtually no part in its writing or research, Noyce's name preceded that of Menlove on the title page. Winthrop Young contributed a broadly-based, stately and stylized historical essay. The guide met with a mixed reception. Some extolled it as the very model of a climbing guide, whilst others who found their favourite climbs and the great achievements of their youth demoted to the lowlier grades were peevish and demanded restitution. (This was actually given in subsequent editions by the inclusion of a list of comparative grades between the Lliwedd and Glyder Fach guides.) Nully Kretschmer, in his preface to the second edition, provides a correct defence: ". . . it is for this quality of understatement that the guide has been criticised by some as misleading. However, as long as it is remembered that the authors mean what they say when they use words such as steep, fissile, difficult, etc, the user of the book will not go wrong."

The most interesting aspect of the guide for the purposes of this biography (and the authorial credits are symptomatic of this) is the degree to which Menlove has attempted to write himself out of climbing history on the cliff. The prose of "Up Against It" (Joycean influence on which is quite pronounced—the reading of *Ulysses* had left its mark) gives little clue as to the amount, difficulty, or quality of Menlove's pioneering work and the guide itself continues this policy of concealment. The size of his contribution was minimized in appearance by a division of the first ascents into three sections. On the same subject, important and difficult pitches which he added to climbs—and Lliwedd is of such a nature that pitches on most lines can usually be avoided by easier variations—were either uncredited, or noted in small print under the credit to those who climbed the easier lines. In many cases, these pitches constitute the sole value of the climbs under whose headings they were described. He was also quite prepared to credit routes to previous parties on the strength of little more than rumour. And the under-grading for which he was castigated by so many was nowhere more marked than with his own discoveries. Here are a few comparisons between the 1939 guidebook's assessment of routes, and those of its 1972 successor:

The Squiggle . . . ". . . one or two very short delicate passages, making a pretty pitch . . . Mild Severe probably, but a little gardening may make it more easy." (1939) "Very Severe . . . An excellent little climb, involved and intriguing. Graded for dry conditions at the crux." (1972)

The Clam . . . "The sticky bit is unfortunately short. Very Difficult; or it is perhaps more true to say very annoying." (1939) "Just Severe . . . A good climb. The crucial moves can be made absurdly strenuous or unnervingly insecure if the proper skills are lacking." (1972):

Elliptical Face, Flame Route . . . ". . . a bright finish . . . Mild severe by the Flame itself." (1939) "Very Severe . . . Good climbing on sound rock with a choice of difficult finishes." (1972)

One of Menlove's own jottings gives a spirited response to his critics on the subject of standards:

The word Severe has long since become a mere label. It is not the warning of great hardship that it was. The whole standard of climbing has run up a little; its labels alone remaining steady at the old points. The standard is still running up and is likely to continue to do so indefinitely, but if we liked to transfix these labels at this moment and write down roughly what they seem now to signify to the average climber's feeling, we could arrive at something to make the words a little more real. Easy and Moderate means not a climb at all. Difficult means here we start. These are the novice's first steps. His nerve may for instance be bad. He may be slow or retain the carefulness of a generation more heavily loaded. Otherwise he commences at the Very Difficults: he takes his lesson in technique for a few hours before launching out on to rock climbing and finding his devious way up grade upon grade of Severes. There he has glimpses of infinity. He postulates a human limit and even if he takes that as fixed he knows that each succeeding rise will only add its fraction of the unfulfilled remainder. Never the whole: never a finish.

   Footwear used to be changed according to the climb in question. Quaint notion. Now we change it according to weather, except only in that place where a precarious few climb up balancing on their latest route the bubble of reputation.

   I met a man who did Paradise and Route II on Lliwedd. What did you think of them, Oh, nice enough, standard, Oh both about the same. Now this impressed me a lot and I saw that it contained truth. Not on my own feelings. My own feelings whilst doing the climbs have been very variable and would not be suitable for a guide. I have never had the slightest idea what was the standard of any climb I have ever done. All the standards are taken on the opinion preferably of the less troubled, for it is troubledness that seems to depart most quickly from its old occasions as time goes on. I ask my second, who can judge best of all, being objective and not biased by the great dangers of leading, and sometimes I am very annoyed with my second secretly in my heart but I take what he says. Or if there is a leader he can be asked. It is good also and my habit to listen to the people talking about the climbs, and to pick out, both from the rabbit and the tiger-talk, what everybody thinks.

I asked then, is it Severe? No. But it is more surely than Difficult. Yes. Difficult, no. By God, he says, if I have nearly fallen off it once I have nearly fallen off it 50 times.

Very Difficult. It is a very wide standard including many things, a safe standard. Sometimes it seems to me and I think to others after talking all night that all the climbs I have ever done are of Very Difficult standard. Why quarrel with it? One thing is clear in a very different subject and that that standards are usually Very Difficult, especially Lliwedd standards. Besides I think the old guard are wrong and that five or ten years hence the conservative party will agree with us about the standards of these routes.

What are you doing on the cliffs at all say I if you cannot find your way about on them, and when it is all set down in black and white for you to look at—and in any case if you come and stand here for a minute it is easy to see it, what I was talking about, just round the corner. Is that what you mean? But of course it is, can you not see?

It has to be said that the Lliwedd guide over the 30 years it remained in print did acquire a reputation for impenetrability and difficulty of interpretation equalled by no other guidebook. Its charm of expression was admitted, but its closeness of definition often denied.* Perhaps Lliwedd, like life itself, was too big, too repetitive and homogeneous in feature to lend itself to Menlove's guidebook theory. Perhaps here was a mirror-image, in his attempt at writing the Lliwedd guide, to his psychiatric research in quest of a single natural law to which all mental phenomena conformed. But if the Lliwedd guide was in a sense a defeat, its being so was the type of cosmic joke in which Menlove at one time would have delighted. Natural circumstance and contingency were not things he could ever hold as personally antipathetic. Society and work were the centres for those forces, and by 1939 they were gathering in earnest.

This concentrated spell of climbing activity has taken our attention away from Menlove's emotional life, and we must come back to that now to study

---

* J.L.L. "Menlove's Lliwedd guide was *admirable* for habitués and old hands—you could recognize where you and the book were at. But it must have been awkward for novices, and for those climbers who expected the narrow moving spotlight."

the most considered single statement he made upon it, the short story from the 1939 *Climbers' Club Journal* entitled "Scenery for a Murder". It is significant with Menlove that the bouts of intensive and assertive rather than subsidiary-role climbing serve the purpose of holding his emotional life and its continuing crises in abeyance. The rebound effect, though, is all the more powerful because encountered in weak and fatigued periods consequent on these strenuous efforts at self-mastery. Although Menlove was attracted, in the spring and summer of 1938, to Gerald Bryan (the man upon whose head a rock was dropped during the guidebook work), his affections still lay with Noyce, who had made an excellent recovery from the Scafell accident, and who, in the company of his "fairy godfather" Pigou, had enjoyed a prolonged Alpine season in 1938, guided firstly by Hans Brantschen and later by Armand Charlet.

The attraction to Gerald Bryan, following the disastrous affair with Noyce, led Menlove into a musing on the ending of relationships, and the lack of reciprocal feeling he had met with:

> Even now my arm goes round youth's well-shaped shoulder and it gives a rapter thrill than it receives. The young head pressing back with devotion that myself was used to feel. Yes, pretty one, there's that in you that surpasses any sorrow, and yet—forgive. I cannot look all happiness, there's that will soon be sorrow in you too.

As with his psychiatric research, he made the attempt to schematize his experience in order to render it comprehensible:

> You get attracted. An essence of perfection appears visible in human form. Acquaintance is made. There is love and spring passes into summer. Ecstasy seems no longer adequate and you wake up. You are two people each with a room of your own. You have been holding another person, and in the long run you do not very well know what to do with a person. Back then. There's nothing more to say for that, you're back in separate rooms holding out a hand perhaps to each other and fumbling. It turns out your room is still empty. No one had come.

This refers obliquely to the events which took place between Easter 1936 and New Year 1937. The "essence of perfection" as seen at the time was Noyce and the progression of spring into summer in the course of their relationship was actual as well as symbolic. Then came distance—separate rooms—and the accident. Menlove buried his emotions beneath his guidebook and other work, and they do not surface again for serious consideration until the composition of "Scenery for a Murder". This is a piece of some length and in order not to interrupt the narrative again—for it does not in itself help that forwards—it has been reprinted in the appendix. In this reading a close knowledge of its text is assumed. The opening paragraph is crucial, and sets out the unequivocal reference points for the succeeding allegory. (The term allegory is used here simply as denoting an extended narrative which carries a second meaning along with its surface story. "Scenery for a Murder" differs from conventional allegory in that its two characters are not personifications of abstract types, but are closely modelled on actual people.)

What the first paragraph states is that a murder has been done, unbeknown to anybody, and that the narrator intends to tell us all about it, but must be careful what he says because "the murderer is a gentleman and very well connected", and must be spoken of as if he wasn't there or didn't do anything. From that factual basis we move on to the allegorical part, and immediately learn that a well-known climber and friend of the narrator has been frozen to death. The freezing here—like the snow in the poem "now here we are, my sister", which "grew about my thighs"—is figurative and refers to an emotional state (it is the same image as that used by Lawrence for the death of Gerald Crich in *Women in Love*), and the narrator knows about the death of his friend because he was there.

How the narrator meets the boy who is his companion in the story is enigmatic. He picks him out from amongst others "over the wireless"—at a remove—by the quality of his singing, his "head thrown back a little". The singing may well signify enthusiasm, youthful energy, a sort of spiritedness which the narrator sees in the boy, and sees even then as a tragedy—because it must inevitably give way to those pressures which keep him "in line with the others". A long span of time passes before one day the narrator, talking to someone idly in Berne, sees the boy passing by. The precise location here is important. It is one of only two in the piece. The other, the Albert Hall, has an obvious symbolic role, but Berne is the single teasing specific Menlove is prepared to give us in the whole narrative, and it makes most sense when we consider that this was the city from which Noyce set forth for his Oberland seasons of 1937 and 1938 with Hans Brantschen. The equation starts to make sense as Menlove describes the boy walking past: ". . . you couldn't miss it, the same look, the same attitude: . . . it stood out all over him: power, courage, love, honour, the heroes . . ." and it recalls Menlove's deeply ambivalent response to Noyce: ". . . your damnable courage which I hate so much".

However, the narrator and "Toni" set out for the mountains and in doing so pass through one of Menlove's standard sexually symbolic landscapes,

"leaving the fir trees one by one, along the scorched dry bed of the valley
. . ." The narrator is both critical and appreciative of his companion, records
that he doesn't seem to notice much but also that he "seemed to transform
the land, he gave it an atmosphere, a scenery, an *hauteur* that made the bare
places and the vivid sky seem beautiful". It is Toni's presence, his aura,
rather than his apparent personality, which is powerful: "He spoke a fair
amount, but that was nothing. It was his atmosphere, in which the features of
the country became more beautiful than I had known them." This is much
the same as the implicit suggestion in the poem "Pause" that the companion
can imbue the landscape with a quality beyond its effect on the single
individual, particularly when viewed retrospectively. The next paragraph
closely parallels reports of the frequent conversational topic between Noyce
and Menlove in 1936. Noyce synthesizes Menlove's ideas in the following
passage from *Samson*:

> What Menlove disapproved was the mystique, as he would have called it,
> of the mountains. The North, he claimed, has at the back of its mind the
> idea that mountains are lumps of rock or grass or snow. It is what we do on
> them, not what they are, that matters. The Southerner, more steeped in
> the Victorian tradition, speaks of the "Queenly Weisshorn", of Mont
> Blanc or Snowdon "lording it" over surrounding peaks . . . The sight of a
> lonely snow peak by moonlight reminds us of medieval ladies; or a tower
> like the Muztagh epitomises brutal masculinity. It was no mere pose that
> made Menlove forbear ever to use such expressions. He simply did not
> feel that way. "Good old Tryfan" might slip out, or "Idwal's a nice spot",
> but he would have called that his irrational self in an unguarded moment.
> His real self knew them for what they were.

If we accept the evidence of the imagery, what the "Southerner" actually
betrays here is an obsession with rank, power and privilege.

Menlove proves Noyce's memory, if not his interpretation, to have been
accurate in the direct statement: "I think there's nothing I've hated so much
in my time and so reasonably as the love of mountains," from which he
carries on to expound the chestnut theory, testing the response of "Toni" at
the end of this by asking, "We are right?" The response dutifully and
uncomprehendingly comes back: "Yes, he said. So I went on talking; for he
did not understand: he had less experience of having other people's feelings
himself than a child of ten."

What we have so far, then, is a narrator whose attitudes are very close to
those of Menlove, and a well-known climber who is youthful, saturated in
Establishment values, possessed of a certain charisma, and tenuously

associated with Noyce. And the narrator/Menlove's summing up on him is that "he did not understand: he had less experience of having other people's feelings himself than a child of ten". Furthermore, the journey the two undertake together is through a landscape rich in Menlove's stock sexual symbolism, and the *cabane* they reach, where for a time they are alone together, is in a small steep armchair valley whose structure has about it echoes of their campsite high in Cwm Tryfan, with the "great ridge opposite" and the shape of the mountain up on the right. All this has been general evocation in allegorical terms of Noyce's and Menlove's relationship. When they set off on the climb, the judgement comes in that "He has a heart of stone, this boy, he cannot respond. All my kindness, my special treatment is to no purpose." Essentially the boy—Toni or Noyce—is not there out of an especial affection for the narrator—Menlove—but out of an overriding obsession to climb, to which end he will use what means he may:

Ah, now my friend, let me not be angry. In the cold morning air I can forget. Well? You take no notice? You do not understand? My hatred and my forgiveness have nowhere to go? You have come here welded, set into something, I believe, and your weldedness, your one object is to climb, apparently, this mountain.

They set off to climb. The route is undifferentiated, and for the first day uneventful. It is merely the setting, the upward endeavour which they share. On the ledge where they spend the first night the narrator finds that, although he can suppress his thoughts during action, in repose they come back to him: "he could drag those same thoughts out of me still". These are much the same as the "wild and sensual thoughts" of "Rowing across the Minch", or of the last line of the second stanza in "Pause".

The details of the second day's climb are reminiscent in several phrases of Menlove's accounts of climbing with Noyce in 1936, and the complaint at the end of this day is explicitly that "he was thinking already more of the cliff again than of me". Then the snow comes, used as an image of the death or suppression of feeling in the same way as it is in the poem "Now here we are, my sister" of 1937. It brings to Menlove the revelation that "I am the barometer of this party; I go up and down. Oh no, I had forgotten. As regards pressure that boy doesn't oscillate; if you put him in space he wouldn't alter to speak of; he doesn't know how. Screwed up to a certain pitch throughout his conscious existence, for the last ten years or so, he has had no experience of any variation. If he had a barometer it would not move, unless it had burst perhaps, or unless, protesting, it had begun to vary like me on its own account."

The realization here is that the *potentiality* of feeling and fullness of outlook which Menlove recognized in the boy—the "young voice, one in a million, high, sung full out"—is condemned to defeat because the boy has been "screwed up to a certain pitch throughout his conscious existence" and "has had no experience of any variation". His class and educational background have affected him to such an extent that they would inevitably weigh against any authentic response or personal fulfilment. ("The murderer is a gentleman, and very well connected.") The barometer of his feelings is utterly fixed and rigidified. (There is not the space here to seek corroboration for Menlove's judgement in Noyce's own writing, and it is anyhow incidental to our purposes, but my instinct is that it is a fair one.) They carry on into the storm—again the stock image—and Toni's face now "was rigid and he did not look quite full at me". The wind sets round to the north; they climb on as far as they can go. Menlove asks, "Toni, why did you listen always to the sounds of the mountains and to those things; and if you had listened some time to me also, and to my voice." And then the boy dies, and Menlove turns on his audience to tease at their response:

> But murder, you say. There was no one else present, you say, no murderer. So? Nobody else? Have you forgotten the singing, have you forgotten the scenery, the wild scenery? And how are you here to tell the tale, you ask? How! Do you not understand?

He finally rounds on the reader and asks who was killed, himself or the boy? The answers lie back in the allegory. The boy's potentiality to feeling was killed off by his education and background, against which he could not rebel, so his natural inspiration was sublimated into a fixed barren obsession acceptable to his social code. And his siren singing having drawn a response from the narrator, his inability to come across has killed off the narrator's capacity for feeling, frozen him by a lack of reciprocity in response. Both the scenery *and* the murder are the society in which Noyce and Menlove must live.

One final gloss on the allegory is provided by the very last letter Menlove wrote to Noyce, after the latter had sent him a copy of *Snowdon Biography* (a collaboration between Noyce, Geoff Sutton and Geoffrey Winthrop Young). "You, for instance, write nicely, intending what? It is what a man would do to help through a murder and give himself a bit of apparent cover . . ."

Noyce's comments on Menlove's work in *Snowdon Biography* must have brought bitterly back to mind the insight at which Menlove had arrived nearly 20 years previously: ". . . he did not understand: he had less experience of having other people's feelings himself than a child of ten".

It remains one of the most grimly sardonic jokes in climbing literature that what has been regarded for over 40 years as one of its central texts was written only peripherally *about* the sport, and is a personal and social allegory which offers up a scathing, angry, yet still humane critique of the effect on the individual of the society in which Menlove lived and in which we, to a lesser extent, still live.

CHAPTER SEVEN

"And you, my greatest hopes, my flown away ones"
1939–1944

THE LATE THIRTIES was not a time for intelligent opinion to remain politically uncommitted. Menlove's natural allegiance was to the political Left, as was the case with many intellectuals of the era. His childhood background inevitably led him in that direction, and his homosexuality would have reinforced the drift, for the man who feels himself alienated from a society and forced into a radical questioning of it is perhaps more likely to align himself with the compassionate and ameliorative stance of Socialism than with the victimizing, amoral, and devil-take-the-hindmost attitudes implicit in other political stances.

Menlove did not become actively involved in political agitation, but he did seriously consider joining the Communist Party and attended meetings in Liverpool during this time. He read the basic texts of Marx and Lenin, and their influence carries over into some of his writing. He did not eventually join, perhaps sensing the onset of a Stalinist opportunist and reformist line which became predominant in the late forties but which was already being espoused by some party members in the last years before the war. Perhaps again certain aspects of the totalitarianism of the USSR, and its unquestioning acceptance by the Communist Party of Great Britain, disturbed him. (In his work for the Socialist Medical Organization his chief line of argument was against over-centralization, and the dangers of rigidity which it entailed.) Whatever the reason for his refusal to join the Party his dalliance with it had a clarifying effect upon his political thinking from 1939 onwards, and in itself this can only have exacerbated the terrible effect which the Second World War had upon him. He had been aware of its likelihood since the mid-decade. Noyce remembers him in 1936 "balancing a tea-cup in somebody's sitting-room and explaining why he would not fight". An address which he gave in 1939 states very clearly what his attitudes were to the use of war as a means of solving international problems. Delivered on a Hospital Sunday to a Liverpool working men's institute, its stated theme was the role psychiatry had to play within society. The style is very straight-forward and simple, and gives a good impression of the Menlove his patients must have known—a man with a profound gift for presenting complex problems in simple terms and with real sympathy.

The opening paragraph of the address shows that although Menlove had by this time ceased conventional worship he still considered himself to be a Christian. Warming to his subject, he takes up the argument:

> Now at present the energies at man's disposal have increased very greatly, but they are not well directed. The individual life is badly directed. So is the corporate life—the life of industry, of politics, of society. Why is this? There are innumerable reasons, but the central one is the nature of man's mind, for the mind is an imperfect instrument, very complicated, with which it is difficult to see facts plainly, and with which it is easy to make mistakes.

Having stated his initial premise he follows it through in these terms:

> Man does not know clearly what to do for the best and has no sure way of knowing. He can only get towards the truth by continual self-criticism, comparison, qualification, continual doubt. And even so the whole process is very slow and laboured. Indeed it is difficult to get the brain to criticise itself really at all. Man's brain is a clumsy instrument. If we study the history of civilisation we can see how slowly man realises things and how often he makes a complete mistake—mistakes which may persist, take thousands of years to rectify, lead to endless trouble, wars, violence.

He proceeds to give a few examples of men using their mind to improve their lot or to seek truth:

> Some have marched thousands of miles through the Andes, killing the inhabitants and seeking gold; some have made themselves so sensitive that they cannot bear the thought of eating flesh; some have lived as hermits, have mutilated themselves. St Simeon Stylites lived on top of a pillar three feet in diameter to be nearer heaven.

Questioning wryly which of these directions is most worthwhile he passes into an examination of the role of the Church, which "thought for a long time that it was of primary importance to banish all sex thoughts". (Another example of Menlove taking issue with St Paul.) His analysis continues with an interesting progression from historical contexts to contemporary facts:

> There was a period too when they thought it best to be ruthlessly cruel to the body to drive the soul to God. There was a period when war against the

unbelievers was a Christian duty; a period when brotherly love was considered quite consistent with slavery; a period only just ending when it was considered right to be horrified at anybody who committed a crime or did anything bad, instead of trying to help him; a period still present when brotherly love is considered consistent with remaining rich at the expense of poverty and distress among others.

If we accept that Menlove's voicing these sentiments is not mere tokenism, their massive, simple good faith is very moving—all the more so when the realization comes that to believe steadfastly in those ideals is to run entirely counter to the thrust of Western "civilized" society, where the basic ethos both in individual and political terms lies in the accumulation of wealth and defence of property. The statement thus becomes a riddle: can the man who holds to these beliefs, in a society whose recognition of them is merely gestural or notional, manage also to hold on to his sanity, especially in time of a war with which he does not and cannot agree?

Menlove turns next to examine some popular heuristic notions of psychology:

> . . as a man looks at himself, he sees certain feelings he would like to lessen or avoid, feelings of depression, anxiety, self-consciousness, anger, desire—all sorts of feelings that are troublesome or that may become troublesome. He tries to make himself more balanced and happy, and there again he has only the very vaguest ideas about how to do this. There is a great wave of people nowadays trying to get confidence. The advertisements say "get rid of those doubts and fears, regain your old confidence", and so on. I mention that particular instance because it is a fine example of stupidity and of whole masses of people trying to do with themselves a thing that it is not possible to do, struggling for the impossible, and even if they were able to achieve it at all (this self-confidence) it would do them more harm than good, for a man looking into the future necessarily sees the snags in it, that is what his intelligence is for, and the greatest power towards accuracy in a man is precisely that self-criticism—doubts and fears about himself: you cannot have those things without the corresponding feelings. Rather the same way with depression; there is literally nothing more depressing than trying to get rid of depression. *And in other ways, more complicated often, a man in his honest efforts to improve his lot, may simply end up in a thorough pitched battle against a perfectly useful and inevitable part of himself.*

The italics for the last sentence are mine. There is something plangently self-revelatory about this statement of Menlove's. It should be read alongside the Stokesay sermon of four years earlier. Menlove had been forced into the situation outlined here not by "honest efforts to improve his lot", but by social pressures. He understood very well the pain of acting, either willingly or through societal coercion, in bad faith:

> It wastes a dreadful lot of energy and may cause great distress: distress again not due to lack of goodwill or lack of effort, but due to plain ignorance. Left to itself the mind is stupid, it simply doesn't see what it is doing, it doesn't see. It doesn't see the nature of its own feelings, it doesn't see their side effects. . . The amount of gross mental disorder and indeed bodily disorder arising from these misuses and mistakes is appallingly great. The average mind at thirty years now is in a much worse mess than the average body was five or six hundred years ago. The level of mental health is very low. The mental death rate . .

His words tail off here, the question left to hang in silence before his audience. Falteringly he picks up again:

> The mind is a very alterable thing, very alterable, malleable, especially in children, but in my experience it is equally true of the mind at any age. It can turn right round at any time, but it also is extremely complicated, and nowadays it is almost usual to turn it not into a more useful, more accurate, more healthy thing as one grows, but simply into a mess.

How much this bore upon Menlove's own experience is made clear in the following detail supplied by Paul Work:

> In 1940 he told me he realised that he had "made a hopeless mess of his mind" and I could see that although only thirty years of age he had many of the characteristics of a very old man. The bloom of youth was something he could now admire in others, even others much older than himself, but could never share.

Work—an early devotee of the Alexander technique—goes on to offer an analysis of Menlove's physical and emotional state which, despite the dated technical language in which it is written, is the most piercing diagnostic insight we have into Menlove's demeanour and perhaps his mental state:

> He had over-used his muscular system, which, he remarked in a letter about Alexander's work, "is always the easiest system to bring under conscious control", and I am sure that had another friend of mine (also a

brilliant Liverpool-trained physician) been allowed to take electro-myograph recordings of Menlove's muscles *when no drug was operative*, the graph would have read excessive amplitudes, denoting cumulative tension which the subject cannot feel on account of its numbing effect on the general proprioceptive sensitivity . . it is no great step from muscle tension to emotional and mental tension and even Menlove could not escape the final breakdowns which always ensue . .

To come back to Menlove's lecture, he develops this through some general comments about education and understanding and works up to "a few words about the even more complicated question of the relation of groups of people to one another, so-called mass psychology, national psychology". (Although it would be very illuminating to the argument of this book, there is no evidence, even though he read German, that Menlove was acquainted with Wilhelm Reich's *Die Massenpsychologie des Faschismus*, which did not appear in English translation until 1946. He may well, however, have read abstracts of Reich's papers, or references to his work, in some of the psychological journals of the time.) The closing passages of the address are particularly important for the insight they give us into Menlove's attitude to the imminent outbreak of war:

> For a long time the one method of competition held sway, and for three or four thousand years actual war has become a standard, time-honoured method of trying to get one group to give another group what it wants, and of settling any dispute that may arise.
>
> Then again people try to deal with criminals, that is with people who have stolen, forged or whatever it may be. Our methods are pure childishness there again, for we try only the one method of punishment, and of social opposition to the person, as if that were likely really to reform him. The mind is moving very slowly towards these things, very slowly indeed. We still, when we dislike another country's methods, hardly stop to think what might really be most likely to alter the mind of each of the people in that country. We still simply spend our time in feeling virtuous and saying how wrong this or that is. We still, for instance, treat all the totalitarian countries as if they were the same, yet even on the most surface analysis they are diametrically different. Japan's has arisen on a wave of over-confidence, Germany's arose on a knowledge of their own power combined with bitter disappointment and disillusionment and a long period of frustration. Russia's arose out of feelings of brotherhood of the proletarian masses, and a determination to stand together. In the light of the slightest examination of those things our old methods of dealing with them have been crude and stupid for lack of knowledge.

Now I have talked about these things to try to put before you the task that lies before us, that lies before the mind, the situation we are in, and have tried to make it clear that we are now only beginning the attempt to get the knowledge that must be got if we are to deal with our own life situation. These questions are of central importance all round, some of them are now most urgent, especially the international questions. What are we going to do about it? We can go on trying to oppose each other and put our efforts into that opposition or we can try to understand, to understand what we are trying to do, to understand what they are trying to do. And it is time too that we realised that in this world nothing comes without effort. We need not wait for knowledge to fall from heaven. If we put our effort into better armaments and better cars and wireless then we will probably get the better armaments, cars and wireless and we will get the consequences of that way of thinking. If we put our efforts out to increase our knowledge of ourselves and of our fellows then we will in time get knowledge, and we will get those consequences. The world must choose what it wants and then not sit and wait, but let each man direct his resources and his efforts towards that end.

With so large a subject before us, research, knowledge require a longer arm, more people set aside for it, more money to allow them to study. We want actual material effort from you. You can set the people to study the mind or you can make them make arms and explosives. If they study the mind they will bring us and the mind nearer to health and sanity.

Menlove ended with two verses from Isaiah (58:5–6):

Is it such a fast that I have chosen? A day for a man to afflict his soul? Is it to bow down his head as a bulrush and to spread sackcloth and ashes under him? Wilt thou call this a fast and acceptable day to the Lord?

Is not this the fast that I have chosen. To loose the bands of wickedness, to undo the heavy burdens, and that ye break every yoke.

Again, the relationship of this passage to that from Hebrews with which he began the Stokesay sermon is very close and its reiterated import is that sterile religiosity is meretricious whilst true godliness lies in realization of the innate good. Although he is now applying it to the need for understanding between nations it is essentially the same message as when he proselytized for homosexual tolerance in Stokesay Church. And in 1939, preaching pacifism, the net result would have been about the same— suspicion at best, and possibly scorn and despite. Menlove's stance was fully compatible with Christ's teaching in the Gospels, yet its reception by those to whom he later had to explain it was, as we shall see, both unchristian and inhumane.

Menlove's work in Liverpool was progressing steadily. With encouragement from some of his senior colleages he was preparing a thesis on pain, and a scheme he put to Birkenhead Corporation for the further development of facilities for mentally defective persons was accepted. He felt unsettled, however, anxious to move on in his career, and was applying for suitable jobs whenever and wherever they came up. One such in London is referred to in the following letter to Alec Keith, dated 23 August 1939, less than a fortnight before the war broke out:

Dear Alec,

Congrats about the Glasgow job: really an excellent show. Must have lifted a weight from the mind rather. I hope it's something that pays you reasonably well, or with reasonable chances of money of some sort. You'll be well off in a war, incidentally.

Pity we missed, over the hols. I had a day in London when you were away, for my interview. Failed to get it though I thought I had a fairly good chance. No influence at all! I never have. But maybe I'd not have it anyhow. They were all Freudian on the selection committee and made a big point of it. I would have given up consultant work for it. Being keen on that side.

I did *nothing* when away. Lazed for a bit in Canterbury till London interview then Brittany, lazing, then, a bit of lazing and reading in North Devon for the last few days. Decided to do nothing for the simple reason that if I don't get on with work I'll be sunk for anything that I want. Felt fairly weary too. Funnily enough I caught a bug too, though no ill effects other than a heightening of even my usual degree of irritability. Got it at about the dirtiest place I'd seen: a farm: had to stay there because it was Bank Holiday week and everywhere else booked up: a lot of people unable to find anywhere at all.

Must see you soon. I've no chance for Helyg. May have to go down to London but that would be a Saturday if at all and anyhow you're not likely to be there. Not that I'm likely to go but am trying to see about any possible kind of research. I'm getting stuck in work at present. Will be in Rodney Street for the rest of my life if I'm not careful.

Congrats on the job. It *is* good.

Ever yours,

Menlove.

For the holiday in Brittany, Menlove had intended to hire a boat and sail across, but this proved to be unavailable so he had to use the normal ferry. Noyce provides a recollection in *Samson* that "there were no cliffs in the part he visited, only one rounded, impossible-looking great boulder in the middle of a fashionable beach. One morning the fashionable bathers rubbed their eyes to see a cairn on top of it." (Whether or not this is a first-hand memory is unclear. Noyce was convalescing with a leg badly broken on Ben Nevis at Easter at about this time.) The holiday in North Devon was not a wholly new direction of interest; in the autumn of 1938, as a rest after the guidebook work on Lliwedd, Menlove had spent several days' gentle walking on Dartmoor and along the North Cornish coast.

The force of feeling behind the wistfully repeated congratulation at the end of this letter was made more apparent the next time Menlove wrote to Alec, six weeks after the declaration of war:

17.10.1939

Dear Alec,

What is happening to you these days? I very much hope nothing interfered with the new job. Perhaps just meant a not too busy time at the start of it. You'll be a grand old man of Glasgow now. With what sounds to be a better job than any of mine. I've failed to get so many jobs during the last year whereas you, blighter, get them all. But I do hope the war didn't make a muck of things in any way.

Things here are going on about the same as ever—pending air raids. Rather slacker all round except for a considerably greater number of breakdowns coming in to Birkenhead Hospital and little or no room in the mental hospital that serves us.

Wilfrid is at Manor Farm, Birmingham, immediately opposite your hospital there. He's learning to be a Friends' Ambulance Unit, being a pacifist. (So am I a pacifist.)

May be moving house. I'm not quite sure.

Yours ever,
Menlove.

Alec wrote back immediately to tell Menlove firstly that he had got married, and secondly that he had been conscripted into the army. (Janet Keith, Alec's wife, has one of several recollections of Menlove by women at this time. He seemed to her, beyond his very likeable and warm demeanour, to "have something mysterious about him". Paul Work also recalls an initially similar reaction to him by a young woman whom he met at Liverpool School of Art: "Without immediately disclosing that I knew him pretty well I asked her what she thought of him. She said that for a while he had made her feel curious, then rather annoyed." And Charles Marriott's sister Winifred was, in Nea Morin's words, "rather taken with Menlove before the war".)

Menlove's response to Alec's news was very prompt:

26.10.1939

Dear Alec,

Rotten luck about the army: but surely it would be illegal to keep you in: reserved occupation and so on. You should run away and then find sanctuary in BMA House . .

I'm *very* glad you've got married: a really excellent thing. I feared you might have gone along without. Janet seemed a very satisfactory person to have around. Before I forget it—what do you want for a wedding present: give me some idea: I've been trying to think since I got your letter and have only decided that I've not got the vaguest idea what you would like and what not, nor what you have already got and what you haven't; and it is necessary that the man should have something, especially if he is in the accursed army.

Wilfrid might like to go over the Cripples [The Royal Cripples Hospital in Birmingham, where Alec was working at the time.] Anyhow he has now got your message and can do as he likes. He is very keen and is likely to use it if he can get a bit of time . . They seem to get no contact with the practical at all at present: just learn the stuff off without seeing a single injury: not the brightest method. On the whole I think I'd sooner be an army officer than an ambulance unit.

The next section of the letter is particularly telling in relation to the direction and degree of acceptance of his work:

Life here is not amusing. My own psychological reading and research goes forward slowly, much too slowly. Official research has stopped. I'm getting out my scheme for psychopathology in general but the odds are that even when I do get it into shape, and even if nobody else has by then brought out the same things, it will never be looked at. One has to have a pretty big starting point before one has anything glanced at unless it is along very straight lines or unless one's chief sees to it (which mine would *not* care to do). However, that is only the situation that is steady for the next ten–fifteen years I suppose, or for life.

I often regret or am inclined to regret not having chosen more orthodox approach jobs into actual research. It is getting harder to get accepted into such a job from my present sphere even now, I think. But we're all in the same boat for the war anyhow. Everything stops. Though I've not at any rate been kicked out so to speak: luckier than the Alec.

The final paragraph of the letter changes the subject completely and refers to the abortive attempt on a climb which gave the inspiration for the last of Menlove's important essays on climbing, "A Great Effort", which appeared in the *Climbers' Club Journal* for 1941. Here is the conclusion to the letter:

Was down at Helyg yesterday and didn't get up a climb: not able: got 20 feet or so in four different directions but was beaten beyond that: no good! Will try to get down again later: at Christmas or New Year: see if we can't do it properly then.

"A Great Effort", which is included in the appendix, gives the clearest possible statement of Menlove's enervated condition. It is less the description of an abortive attempt upon a climb than a generalized meditation upon failure. To read it closely, with an awareness of Menlove's state of mind at the time, is, despite the pawkiness of its ending, a harrowing experience. What needs to be borne in mind is Menlove's constant sense of the "innate symbolisms of life". The climb—unspecified, location unknown, though it undoubtedly existed and was probably somewhere in Ogwen, perhaps on the Milestone Buttress—is less a climb than a condition of existence. Throughout the essay there are pointers which open it out into a much richer and more resonantly allusive piece of work than the simple mock-heroic for which it is sometimes taken. (Noyce saw it as an "amusing and penetrating satire on climbing states of mind".) Having said that, it must also be said that it works extremely well on a literal level—that whilst it undoubtedly contains reflections upon contingency and choice which are of some philosophical depth, and whilst it is a desperately sad indication of Menlove's emotional life at the time, it is perfectly possible to read it just as a wry treatment of failure to climb a particular, if rather vaguely realized, rock face. The amount which the essay manages to express, the sheer density of possible meanings, is impressive, and it is this vibrancy of allusion which has made it one of the most frequently reprinted of all climbing texts. A couple of quotations should serve to illustrate the complexity it conceals behind apparent simplicity:

Do not mistake me, the choice of cliff and pastime had been free, it was unhampered by any conditions either of expediency or friendship, there was no particular unhappiness on me at this time beyond the normal. Yet I sat down. And as I lifted my head, stones, blocks of rock, sky, cliff faces lay round the field of vision arranged in various ways.

And again:

> The view had changed. There was heather now in front of my eyes, and some of the thin dust that goes with it. I took a handful of heather in my right hand. It seemed firm but when bent back it snapped and broke off. A bad material. I made a final effort. Look at yourself I said, and do you know what this is, that it is schizophrenia, the split mind . .

As with the extraordinary series of climbs on the Devil's Kitchen cliffs in 1933, the failure on this piece of rock provides Menlove with an objective correlative to his mental situation, and it is from this that much of the force and significance of the essay derives.

The hopelessness of Menlove's professional situation during the war is conveyed in a very matter-of-fact manner in the following letter to Alec Keith dated 15.11.39:

> No, the war's no good to me. Will keep out of any Government work. Two or three of my jobs will go Government if air raids get going. If they don't—just hack work for the duration and no chance of either the help required to do the jobs decently or of getting out into a job where I could do work I'd like better! But why after all should one expect to get what one wants? An acquired habit and a bad one. I don't know that there's much real honest work about me, though I'd like to think it.

He continues the letter by relaying some information about a companion who had been with them during the guidebook work on Lliwedd in the previous year:

> Young Gerald Bryan is training for the Royal Engineers. Sent him a Lliwedd guide on demand. I gather it's his main non-technical literature, poor man. The old guide will be out of date after the war: and then a new crop of climbs from somebody. Puts a period to one's life more definitely. Damn life—not very suitable to think about: not too good to get on with either: but nothing better offering. I quite like it really though. What a letter to write!

He concludes with some suggestions to Alec on what to purchase with the book tokens ("you'll be amused at the confession of failure") which he had sent as a wedding present: "Marco Pallis's *Peaks and Lamas* has next to no climbing in it but makes quite interesting general reading, and it is an excellent study of Buddhism .. Irving's Anthology, *The Mountain Way*, sounds good."

Menlove's next letter to Alec (17.12.39) reveals a continuing sense of malaise and encroaching despair: "Life's a competitive and treacherous sort of business, as ever it was." As an antidote, he was looking for company:

I'm going to Welsh Wales for Christmas, rather for company than to climb, though I think I'll perhaps try to get on to a rock at the same time. G. W. Young is up at Pen y Pass and I'll probably go round there one day to climb with his son—who is about to be a naval officer.

I'm afraid a large part of me would like to be in on this war. Though not any part that one would care to back up.

The added pressure which the feeling voiced in the last two sentences must have put upon Menlove's pacifism is obvious. The Christmas excursion did not produce much climbing. John Barford and Nully Kretschmer were staying at Helyg and on Christmas Day Menlove teamed up with them and went down the Llanberis Pass to Clogwyn y Grochan. Menlove sat at the foot of the cliff and watched whilst Kretschmer and then Barford attempted the first pitch of Long Tree Gate—the climb Menlove had discovered with Noyce at Easter 1935. Both Kretschmer and Barford were unable to get much beyond fifteen feet up, even after several hours' struggle and the fixing of a sling and insertion of a piton. Menlove declined to attempt the pitch, but advised them to try reaching the Long Tree by climbing up Ledge Way and traversing out to the right at a higher level, which they did. "An elegant ascent to the foot of the Long Tree was then made by HEK by the simple expedient of climbing the rope, held firmly from above. He then continued his simian progress by climbing the Long Tree in the position usually adopted by sloths in search of honey. The rest followed, but after further investigation the climb was finally abandoned, and the Long Tree descended, again." Menlove and Kretschmer duly went round the corner and climbed Scramblers' Gate, apparently the only route Menlove did that year.

He seems, however, to have enjoyed the company, and began to renew his climbing acquaintance in 1940. He attended the London dinner of the Climbers' Club in February, and at Easter planned to go to Helyg: "There will be quite a big crowd there I think with so many holiday places gone out of the running." He had also been asked to revise his Cwm Idwal guide for a second edition, which appeared in the summer of 1940, and wanted to refresh his memory of one or two of its climbs.

The 1940 Easter meet at Helyg gathered together many of the most active climbers of the previous decade. Jack Longland, A. B. Hargreaves, Colin Kirkus, Bill Stallybrass, Stuart Chantrell, Nully Kretschmer, David Cox, all attended. The Saturday was wet and few ventured out. Menlove, AB and Jack Longland went up to Lliwedd and climbed the Rocker Route. On the Sunday, Menlove was claimed by the younger generation. Sandwiched between Nully Kretschmer and David Cox he climbed his own Girdle of the East Wall of the Idwal Slabs, before crossing over into Javelin Gully, where they attempted the direct finish for some time before a top rope was let down and the climb completed. David Cox's account is a good one:

> The normal finish to Javelin Gully escapes out to the left by a mantelshelf move, and we thought, wrongly as it turned out, that the gully bed itself had not been climbed to the top. It proved to be a short VS pitch, which characteristically Menlove professed to be too hard for him to lead. He of course came up it very much more easily than Nully or I, and it surprised us that Menlove, whom we still regarded as a bit of a legend, turned out to be such an unassuming and easy person to climb with.

On the final day, the Easter Monday, fittingly Menlove and Colin Kirkus climbed together for the last time. There is something immensely poignant about these two men, the great rock-climbers of their time, being ushered into each other's company on a fine spring morning, setting out for Cwm Idwal, making their way up Hope on the Slabs, then the Holly Tree Wall and afterwards traversing across to scramble up the Cneifion Arete and walk across the summits of the Glyders—the two men who had set the tone and the standards for an era coming together for a last day of simple pleasure at its very close.

Most of Menlove's friends by 1940 were in one or other of the armed forces. Noyce had given up the Friends' Ambulance Corps and joined the army; Colin Kirkus was in the RAF; Alec Keith in the Royal Army Medical Corps. An already lonely and alienated man by reason of his homosexuality, Menlove's pacifism and high idealism directed against the war was now increasing his isolation. The idea of the comradeship and the excitement of an army at war held out a considerable attraction for him: ".. wish very much too that I could be in on things. Damn it. It would be grand to try and do some tough and cunning stuff in Norway: for which there must be lots of need!

"But one has chosen the other side of life .. "

In May of 1940 he wrote to Alec Keith in a more positive vein than his letters of the previous autumn:

4.5.1940

Have been trying to think of something to do in the summer. Something mildly worth doing, or something like harvesting preferably of some hard variety. Damn. In the hills or on the sea.

Last year in the hols I did next to nothing at all and it didn't seem to go down very well really. I feel rather like the wandering Jew. Though really I'm pleased enough just to go on.

Work's going on: all long-term plans but fairly important I think, in their way. Later on this year sometime I suppose I'll be registering as a pacifist!

He registered as a conscientious objector in June: "I do not see how to do otherwise." In July he went to stay for a short holiday in Harlech with Nowell, and spent his time hay-harvesting. On the subject of holidays, he commiserated with Alec:

26.9.1940

Poor, not getting a holiday. I've never tried doing without one myself but can imagine it must be pretty foul: the working world is so very full of troubles and frictions and inadequacies, and escape for patches is good.

In the same letter he noted that he had "got two days' climbing in August—the farming arrangements turning out to be moderately slack at times". The two climbs which he did on those days stand as markers to the next phase of climbing's development. Menlove's relation of them to Alec is distinctly low-key:

Did two new climbs I'd had my eye on, on the Llanberis Pass cliffs: not bad ones: I wasn't as bad as usual thanks to the tone-up of general condition at the farm. It was good to get to it again.

The climbs were Brant and Slape, the first significant routes on the steep and complex central buttress of Clogwyn y Grochan. How understated Menlove's above comment was is revealed by his second John Barford's account of the ascent of Brant, the easier of the two climbs:

JME after farming at Harlech for some days was in extremely good form and produced a climb considerably harder than any of the others which have so far been done on these cliffs with the possible exception of Long Tree Gate.
    Name: The Brant   395 feet
    Standard: Very Severe, strong arms required and a just appreciation of the value of loose holds.

After the very detailed description of the route Barford adds a comment about Menlove's climbing of it:

> This was a fine lead, entirely unseen, and certainly the best I have ever seen done in Wales or anywhere else. It was done in rubbers in an intermittent fine drizzle, which kept all the grass wet, although the rock was only slightly moist.

Menlove wrote the description for Slape, the more difficult companion climb to Brant which still ranks in the modern guidebook's graded list as the hardest Very Severe in the Llanberis Pass.

> A companion climb to The Brant on Clogwyn y Grochan, named *The Slape*. It keeps fairly close right of The Brant all the way, using some of the same stances.
> Standard: Severe: possibly VS but I don't think it's possible to say what it will become. Difficult to compare with The Brant; a more uniform standard and with a greater number of steep pitches but probably no pitch as "strong" as No 1 of The Brant. Fair lot of loose rock.

Menlove's description of the infamous crux pitch, the short wall which is still graded 5a, is well worth bringing in:

> 3.   20 ft. Go straight up the wall about two-thirds of the way to the left edge. It goes surprisingly easily once launched but is fairly energetic.

The next time Menlove climbed was in October, when he again teamed up with John Barford to ascend Horseman's Route on the Columnar Cliffs. The intention was to attempt Ivy Sepulchre, the right-hand of the cliff's three great corners, but they had trouble even reaching its foot and so took a long traverse line across to the right to reach an imposing little corner high up on the cliff. Although Menlove led this—the only real pitch on the climb—in his description he characteristically plays down his own role and passes all the credit on to Barford: "The middle pitch [to the foot of the main corner of Ivy Sepulchre] was so hard that JME turned back. JEQB however drove on without effort." It was the last climb Menlove was to do until the following Whit, and by that time his situation was changing radically.

In the autumn of 1940 Menlove had been appointed Chief Psychiatrist at the Liverpool Child Guidance Clinic. His work-load was thus considerably

The first pitch of Brant   John Beatty

Western Slabs, Dinas Mot

John Beatty

increased, but that was balanced out by a falling-off in his consultant work from Rodney Street. The research by which he set so much store had become virtually impossible. German air-raids on Liverpool were taking place almost every night, and even daytime raids were by no means infrequent. One bomb landed near the house in Devonshire Road and lay unexploded for days until defused. He moved from Devonshire Road to the Childwall Road, farther out to the east of the city. At the end of November a bomb exploded near that house, blowing out all the doors and windows whilst Menlove lay asleep in bed. Glass from the bedroom window fell all over him but he escaped without a scratch. He was forced to move into his consulting rooms at 11 Rodney Street for a time and his mother went to stay with Stephen and Ruth, who by now were at the vicarage of Bullinghope, south of Hereford.

In April of 1941, nine months after he had first registered as a conscientious objector, Menlove was called to appear before a tribunal which adjudicated on such cases. It was held in Liverpool and consisted of A. A. Kerr, Sir William Hart, and His Honour Judge Burgis. The reasoning behind Menlove's pacifist stance is best expressed in a letter written to Geoffrey Winthrop Young. Dated 23 March 1944, it is worth bringing in prematurely at this point:

About being a C O: Taking two aims as being desirable under the terms 1) maintenance of the structure of justice; 2) the refusal of means so wholly wrong as those involved in war, I regard both as necessary. I regard 2) as the one that may have to go if it comes to a genuine choice necessity between the two. I regard it, however, as an extremely high priority to advance 2) at all times, even the worst, and when the general organism turns over to 1) at a point demanding dominance effectively over 2) then that 2) should even so keep a hard core of lastingness and of refusal to co-operate in war by some individuals wholly standing out, and bearers of their flag in their own eye and that of the public.

This may and often will endanger the whole?

Yes: it's probably not the most immediately safe policy.

What Menlove is acceding to here is a Christian—for by his own lights he still professed that religion, though in no conventional form—compulsion to bear witness against falsehood and evil in the world. His notions verge on the simplistic (as indeed do those of Christ) but the deep ethical conviction which supports them is of primary importance. He continues his argument:

Then who, and why me? It's in the line of my job, I think. Those who look to me, took it for granted I would do so: so did I. Temperament? Yes, that plays its part. I've no objection, as a matter of *feeling*, to killing people: but a considerable objection to doing psychology under army conditions . . .

The point which emerges in his refusal to do army psychiatric work is very acute. In treating soldiers under these conditions he would have been placed in the compromising and invidious position of having to sustain patients whose psychoses were probably chiefly induced by reactions identical with his own to wartime situations.

His application to the tribunal read as follows:

I have been convinced for many years of the necessity for maintaining and working towards the pacifist ideal, indeed ever since I began to think seriously as to ideals of conduct of life at all.

By pacifism I mean the refusal of violent means, particularly means so violent and destructive as war, even for the attaining of good ends.

This, for any reasons but also because the strength and the high elaboration of violent means and of violence in almost every department of human life, has shown itself liable easily to submerge all other directions of effort, including any good that may be aimed at.

Standing by my ideal, as I must do, it has not been easy to decide what practical position to take up as a medical man, and as in this modern war itself I have decided to accept no position set up for the armed forces, and that in respect of any chance service cases that come into my hands in the ordinary course of my work I can accept no pay.

It needs to be said that had Menlove claimed exemption on the grounds of war being against his religious conscience, and supported this with evidence of belonging to an established church, he would have gained it pretty easily. His refusal to do that, and his attempt to defend his stance on intellectual grounds by use of the ethical sense which he held to be the portion of divinity encompassed in man, is a proof of the degree of his moral integrity. It was treated with scant courtesy by the tribunal. The comparatively trivial cast of their minds is revealed by the question they asked which rankled most with Menlove from this bruising contact with authority. "What," they quizzed, "would you do if an enemy soldier attempted to ravish your sister?" (Woman assimilated as the symbol of property which the capitalist enterprise of war must defend!) Rightly, Menlove refused the metaphor and answered literally that he would protect her. The tribunal's notes on his application and evidence run thus: "He now belonged to no religious body but took up an agnostic stand."

Apparently Menlove's refusal of formal worship and belief in the innate deiform potential of man rendered him an agnostic in their eyes: "He was a qualified medical man and was partly in private practice and was doing all the medical psychology at the Children's Clinic and the Infirmary."

Again, their understanding of his purely factual evidence was faulty: he was doing all the psychology at the Children's Clinic, but not at the Infirmary.

> In answer to questions he said he had turned down an offer of service in the Armed Forces which would have benefited him financially.
>
> At present he was devoting twelve to fourteen hours per week to humanitarian work, some of which only he was paid for; he was also undertaking fire-watching in his neighbourhood for one night in nine, and on call every third night; he was also doing fire-watching at Rodney Street.
>
> He believed he was devoting as large an amount of his time to hospital work as he possibly could. The only reason he could not devote his whole time to hospital service was the necessity for continued study in his profession.
>
> He was a member of the Medical Peace Committee until it disbanded in 1938. He believed it would be better not to use war as a means of settling international disputes.

The cold doubt and distance of the last sentence is astounding. As if there could ever be any doubt that war *is* an inherently wrong and evil method of solving the problem which arise between nations, and seldom anything other than the manipulation of peoples and arousal of populist fervour by politicians to further their own ends. (Although it needs to be said that on the Allied side the Second World War was a probable exception to this rule.)

The notes continue thus:

> He was not sure that his attitude would help to free Europe, but he believed it was better than war. He believed it would be wrong to take life even to save his own.
>
> He believed one should still not take up arms even though the outcome of such an outlook might be impossible.
>
> His conscience was guided by reason from reading and conversation.

After a wait of several weeks, the tribunal committed their findings to paper. His application was rejected unanimously. Their reasons:

The applicant has unfavourably impressed the tribunal; his views are hazy and he is groping and has not yet arrived at a conviction. He has had difficulty in saying what conscience is to him and he says that his conscience is trying to do the best under all circumstances. He has said in terms that he finds it difficult to say what guides his conscience and after many halting efforts he says that it is guided by reason.

We cannot believe that because he says that in the case of individual violence he would restrain it by force, but in the case of international violence he would leave it unrestrained; we think this is to exalt the affairs of the body above the affairs of the Spirit.

He says that he has no feasible suggestion to make to stop the present state of things. We do not think he is allowing reason full play. We think that his aim in life is to be left alone and to be undisturbed. We think that he is lacking in any depth of conviction and therefore he is lacking in that element which distinguishes views from conscience.

How many of the readers of this book would be thus adjudged at the promptings of Mr A. A. Kerr, Sir William Hart and His Honour the Judge Burgis? Menlove immediately registered his appeal and took himself off to Wales for Whit weekend to recover from this damaging encounter with officialdom.

His companion was Jim Joyce, who was attending a course at the School of Tropical Medicine in Liverpool. As if to increase Menlove's developing paranoia, on the Whit Saturday night at 1.30 a.m. planes passed overhead. Half an hour later their engines were heard again, followed by the whistling of bombs and four explosions just across the River Llugwy, between Gallt yr Ogof and Gwern y Gof farm. "Please," pleaded the custodian, "pay particular attention to the black-out."

On Whit Sunday Menlove and Joyce went round to Clogwyn Du'r Arddu, where they set off by the start of Linnell's 1933 route, the Narrow Slab (though they may well not have known what they were on). Having climbed so little in the last three years, and attempting what was then probably the hardest route on the cliff, Menlove understandably found it hard going, and attempted to push Joyce into the lead. He made a couple of half-hearted attempts on the intricate, thin traverse known as Linnell's Leap before handing back over to Menlove, who managed to make the crossing. They then traversed to the base of the 40-foot corner of Great Slab, where Menlove tried to cross the rib round to the right, for his designs had not been on making a repeat ascent of Narrow Slab, but on a girdle traverse of the West Buttress. Perhaps fortunately, in view of what lies beyond, he failed to get round the rib, and they were forced to finish up Great Slab: "Had meant to go right but were not able. Whole party was on this climb utterly rotten: took eight hours and that only by hurrying."

On the Monday, ambitions equally high, they went to look at Suicide Wall in Idwal, the then-unclimbed face at the top left-hand end of the East Wall scarp. Menlove climbed to the grass patch on the route later taken by Chris Preston, and had to be hauled out on a rope. Not noticing the scoop round to the right now taken by Suicide Wall Route One and Mur y Meirwon, he looked at the still-unclimbed wall above the ledge and concluded that it would be impossible without the use of pitons. They retreated from the cliff and spent the rest of the day sunbathing and resting.

Alec Keith by this time had been posted to Moston Hall Hospital near Chester, and the Friday after Whit Menlove motored over there to take him out to Helsby for an evening. After doing a few climbs together they drove back towards Chester. Menlove seemed uneasy:

> On the way to Chester again he stopped the car so that we could talk, and he told me he was a homosexual, which I had not guessed. Looking back on it, though, I remember that when we camped under Lliwedd he insisted that I should have the tent and he would sleep out . . . he did not want to share a tent, which would have been the natural thing to do.

On the last weekend in June the two friends went to Wales for a weekend, Menlove picking up Alec on the Saturday lunchtime and driving down to have tea with his mother, who was holidaying with Nowell in Harlech, before going on to Helyg. The Sunday found them walking up to Clogwyn Du'r Arddu, to try the start of what is now Bow-Shaped Slab:

> We were a poor combination—he never seemed to climb well with me and the lack of confidence flowing up the rope met the apparent lack of confidence flowing down and the sum was hopeless. Why I should have had so little confidence I don't know, for he held me once when I came off, and several times pulled me up over bits I couldn't do.
>
> We looked at the climb from the bottom and Menlove got about fifteen feet up and then down. Then a different start—no good. Then the first way again—still no good. Then round and up to the top to look at it from above. No good: and so on and so on. Eventually we went and lay by the Llyn, but he was so discouraged he didn't even bathe.
>
> We then went back to Helyg, where we found Stuart Chantrell in a state of excitement because there had been an accident on Holly Tree Wall and a rescue was on. He suggested that we—particularly

Menlove—should go and help, but Menlove pleaded hunger and fatigue and that he had to get back to Liverpool.

Stuart kept on persuading, and I also helped, and eventually when Stuart said he would have food ready for us when we came back we went. Menlove grumbled along to the Slabs and then up the Ordinary where he really went at a fantastic speed. We found a party on the Terrace; big strong chaps with a Neil Robertson stretcher, standing about doing nothing effective. Menlove at once took charge and no one argued. A naval doctor had come off the Holly Tree and thought he had broken his hip. I made what I now think was a wrong diagnosis and told him he hadn't, but he didn't agree and it was decided to take him down the slabs in the stretcher. Menlove organised it, supervised all the tricky bits, and gave a hand whenever strength and steadiness were needed. We got him down to the ambulance waiting on the road and then hurried back without ceremony to Helyg.

There was a magnificent meal waiting for us—in spite of rationing—and Menlove finished the lot after I had had my share.

Menlove's car began to behave very oddly as they drove back to Chester: "I got back again in the car okay with one more stop—and at terrific speed, for she started going okay at 40–45 mph only. Birkenhead and the tunnel probably didn't know what to think. They cleaned it up after at the garage without committing themselves to any definite statement, except the new idea that I might need a new engine. But it seems okay now."

The following Thursday Menlove attended the appeal tribunal in Chester. Within a week he heard that he had been unconditionally exempted: "A wholly different atmosphere from the first tribunal." He was now registered as a conscientious objector.

His clinical work, meanwhile, was collapsing beneath him: "At Liverpool things are pretty muddy. Difficult to know what's happening. Will be glad to get out." In July the priorities of war asserted themselves and the Child Guidance Clinic was closed down. Its chairman wrote of Menlove in a testimonial that "we have greatly valued his help in a field as yet comparatively unexplored, and appreciated the immense amount of trouble he has taken in individual cases and the success which has attended his work". With not enough alternative consultant or clinical work to sustain him, Menlove decided to pursue his research in earnest. He came to an agreement with Colin Kirkus to rent, for the sum of five shillings a week, an isolated cottage in Wales which the latter had bought before the war:

> . . . will try to get some work done there, in the interval between jobs. The first few weeks will *have* to be holiday anyhow because the cottage will take a

good deal of settling into. It's fairly out-of-the-way and unkempt. If I can get some work done, then jobs can go hang for the time being. For money there's a life insurance I've been paying almost since qualifying, which ought to sell out at a fair price; also the car. Had been growing quite a hump in those ways without realising it.

On Saturday 2 August 1941 he left Liverpool and travelled down to Hafod Owen, in the shaggy ridges between Nant Gwynant and Cnicht.

Hafod Owen nestles into a thicket of rhododendron on top of the hillside above Llyn Dinas. The nearest road is half a mile away and the village of Beddgelert three miles distant. From the knoll above the house you look straight up the winding valley of Cwm y Llan to Snowdon, at its head. The cottage is whitewashed and small, out of sight from most angles until you are almost upon it. Its lop-sided arrangement of three windows at the front faces to the south-east. Huge boulders give foundations to the whitewashed walls; the roof-slates are as irregular as if wind-rippled, and the tumbledown dry-stone walling round about is mottled with pale green and grey lichens. There are few more lovely places in the whole of Wales.

For his first two weeks there, Menlove was preoccupied with getting books and furniture across the half-mile of rough, boggy track to the house, and with putting it into watertight and habitable condition against the coming of winter. A month to the day after his arrival he sallied forth to climb, from Helyg, in the company of his old friends Bartrum and Reade. A day on the Idwal Slabs was followed by another on the Milestone Buttress, at the end of which the two old schemers he was with set him to work on the Central Block. This is the great wedge of rock standing out from the top of the cliff between Soap Gut and the final chimney of the Direct Route. A great V, which had recently been painted on the rock from an abseil by soldiers in training and is still faintly visible, probably drew their attention to the feature. Longland and Noyce had previously top-roped a pitch upon it, but had not returned to make the lead. Menlove, too, accepted the offer of a top-rope and then went back down to the foot of the pitch and led it. Although quite short, it is a very impressive piece of climbing. A line of thin and fragile flakes leads out to the left into an unseen grove beyond. The wall is very steep and to start the traverse across it demands a step from a large ledge on to an exposed, committing and strenuous series of moves. Before the advent of modern protection techniques, the pitch gained a considerable reputation. It was seldom led, and held to be "exceptionally severe", although it looks far more imposing than proves to be the case. Menlove's grade for it, inevitably, was "probably Severe". Perhaps he really did think or find it easier than Longland's Route on Clogwyn Du'r Arddu, even by

ABH's Cannon Hole approach to the Crevassed Stance, which he climbed next day?

On his return to Hafod Owen John Barford and Nea Morin called on him. Barford was limping as the result of a fall from the first pitch of Curving Crack, so Menlove agreed to join their party for some climbing. They went to Clogwyn y Grochan, from which Barford retained "a very pleasant memory of JME writhing slowly in one of the slimiest places in Wales—the great overhang of Goat's Gully—for upwards of an hour". Giving up the idea of this repulsive cleft's being fit to climb, Nea and Menlove crossed round to the left and took the curving line of weakness up the front of Goats' Buttress to which Menlove gave the name *Nea*, as it was she who led it.

After another couple of days Barford had more or less recovered and the party walked up to Clogwyn Du'r Arddu, where they spent a curious day's activity prospecting amongst the lower pitches of the West Buttress slab routes. Barford begins the story:

> An attempt was made to get on to the buttress over the initial overhang at a point below the foot of the Concrete Slab. This failed, although the possibility remains and should be tried again in really dry conditions. We retired to the Terrace and walked down it to the beginning of Narrow Slab. Then we went round and up past the foot of a small ash tree and started to traverse to the right. We were stopped by a smooth, untraversable groove-wall with a rib surmounted by some large blocks on its far side.

Nea now takes up the account:

> I suggested we should lasso one of these blocks and swing across. At first this unconventional method was not accepted and we lost a lot of time before finally resorting to it. We joined the Narrow Slab again just above Linnell's Leap. Here Menlove pointed up to the White Slab and asked me if I thought it would ever be climbed . . . We continued round past the foot of the Narrow Slab itself and along to the top of the first section of Great Slab. Bow Shaped was now directly above us and Great Slab above and to our right. By this time it was late and to me with my odd continental habits the obvious thing to do was to bivouac. But I was told this was "not done" in Wales and so it was decided to go down. . . . We returned via Linnell's Leap in reverse, then on to the top of the first pitch of Narrow Slab, round to the foot of the slab on Longland's, and so to the foot of the cliff.

Menlove returned the next weekend with two members of the Rucksack Club and climbed the feature for which he had been aiming on the attempt with Nea

Morin and John Barford, and the earlier one with Alec Keith. (Nea's account was, of course, written with hindsight.) He named it the Dark Slab, because it "goes straight up the face of the dark, rather uniform slab left of and overhung by the left wall of the whole Great Slab and bow-shaped slab massif". This was done on 19 September. On 20 September, with the same companions, he worked out an elegant and difficult line up the last-mentioned feature, the Bow-Shaped Slab. His route up the Bow-Shaped Slab was not the one normally taken these days by climbing up above the stance and traversing back down to the left. Instead he made a much harder sequence of moves across horizontally from the stance and then up towards a diagonal break using poor, indefinite holds. John Barford later prevailed on him to give it a slightly higher grade than its original one of Severe. The Dark Slab, which he also graded Severe, proved to be something of a disappointment, for it was found to be not a new route but Linnell's *Narrow Slab*, once the first ascent description had been checked. After this relatively intense bout of activity, Menlove did not climb again for a year.

He began to settle into the business of living in a remote and isolated situation. All water had to be brought from a nearby stream and fuel gathered from the woods below. Supplies had to be bought in weekly. Stephen came up from Bullinghope for a few days in the autumn and donated ten gallons of paraffin—a great bonus in days of rationing. He also caught a sea-trout in Llyn Dinas and this augmented Menlove's meagre diet. Menlove deliberately practised an ascetic way of life. Believing that pacifists should, as far as possible, be self-supporting rather than dependent on the society the values of which they had rejected, he passed on his clothing and sweet ration coupons, lived on an absolute minimum, gave away butter and sugar to those who visited him, and tried to settle down into the rigorous self-discipline of academic work.

Anyone who has not lived year-round this sort of life in out-of-the-way places might easily equate it with the dreamy romanticism of sitting out the days on a high perch above the autumn glory of the Gwynant Valley. True, there are those consolations, but the whole truth is more exigent. There is the rain of the Welsh uplands, which can persist for weeks. There is the sheer physical effort involved in providing the necessities of life—heat, water, food—and planning for them with none conveniently to hand. There is the cold of winter, the wet clothes and the grey days, and above all the aching loneliness of mid-winter afternoons spent in knowledge as certain as the fading of the light that no one will call—not today, nor tomorrow, nor perhaps even for the next several weeks. And man, at root, is gregarious and needs the sometime society of his fellows. Isolation can cripple the emotions and leave them halting and craving, distort perspectives, emphasize fears.

Christ's 40 days in the wilderness would destroy most men. It is a profound irony that many patients and friends wrote to Menlove during his time at Hafod Owen, expressing envy at his peace and certainty of purpose, perhaps taking their cue from Cowper's lines:

> Oh for a lodge in some vast wilderness,
> Some boundless contiguity of shade,
> Where rumour of oppression and deceit,
> Of unsuccessful or successful war,
> Might never reach me more.

They would not themselves have desired such a retreat for more than a few days at a time.

There were, however, those who sympathized with the reasons for, and the difficulty of, the course of action he had chosen. His brother-in-law, Hewlett Johnson, wrote to him:

> I am sorry to hear you have been unwell. I am not surprised. You have undertaken one of the most arduous of all tasks in war: that is—opposition to it. However much I may disagree with the particular application of the principle I admire immensely the stand you have made and I know how supremely valuable and indispensable such stands for conscience' sake are to the real spiritual health of a country. They always meet their rewards, though they may not be obvious yet—none of the really big things are. But I also know how exhausting these single-handed contests are, physically and psychologically. You must expect it.

The final comment of this kindly and understanding note is important. Menlove doubtless did "expect it", but it is only a small step from the expectation of animosity and opposition to the suspicion of persecution, conspiracy, and exclusion.

This apart, at a distance of months Menlove could look back on the situation in Liverpool with some equanimity:

13.2.42

At Liverpool all my suspicions seem to have been wrong I think: the clinic closed, but there were lots of minor, summating reasons why the committee should feel that the only thing to do. The chap who *does* dislike me a lot there was quite clearly getting laughed at by the committee.

   Everything had been hellish muddled and hectic at Liverpool and I fancy I'd been trying to fit in a bit *too* much work. It would have been *possible* to stay there, but only by getting other bits of jobs not quite in my line, and going on rather uselessly. So I decided to cut right out and get a cheap cottage . . .

I'm getting on, quietly, with my research stuff. And incidentally feeling about thrice as fit as I did before. Seems a poor thing to do in war time: but I think it may be my best contribution in the end. A psychologist at Liverpool University advised me in that direction; he knows *something* of my work, though not really enough to judge on.

Anyhow here I am and here I stay for some time yet. It was an *immense* relief getting rid of all the masses of patients! This is a fine place . . . an old four-roomed cottage with a fine outlook and no immediate neighbours. Had a very leaky roof, but that's pretty well okay now.

Noyce came to visit Menlove at Hafod Owen on two occasions. The first was in February of 1942, during an army sick leave. It was a bitterly cold month, snow thick on the ground, the streams frozen into silence, dark, brittle crowns of rushes standing out amongst the icy marshes to give poor sustenance to the hill-sheep. Noyce went out each day for long bouts of step-cutting up the Snowdon gullies, returning at night to Menlove's food and fire. After a week he left for Helyg and some climbing with a Cambridge acquaintance on leave. Noyce wrote to thank him for the holiday and tell of his climbs from Helyg. In his reply, Menlove explained amongst other things why he would not accompany Noyce on the hills in the week they were together at Hafod Owen:

I am not one who can do something (excitingly) different from work and then come straight back to it efficiently: at least not this work: sort of slow, pondering stuff. I find it beastly difficult to concentrate anyhow on any work, too: mind always wandering vaguely around and just day-dreaming, very easily: partly due to my very slow tempo, and other habits of thought according. You mentioned your mind going over and over the motions of climbing, etc, after your big day. Mine does that (not so much the last two years: but would if I started "driving" as much again) regularly after climbing, at the Lakes, Tryfan; used to be regularly every other visit or so at Helyg, and at one time took (sample) sedatives to get a bit more sleep when I went there.

The letter goes on to make some observations on his social relationships and reactions to people which throws a clear light on to aspects of his work and character:

A bit the same with people; and always in my dreams every other night still climbing—always falling off—or trying to persuade a patient, or feeling a fool back in school days, or a real blood and thunder nightmare for a change.

My over-great intensity with people is not very good for them either (except that it is necessary with patients to be absolutely following every least mental shift [not that one succeeds of course] and that has kept the habit very high: it was getting too high at Liverpool): gets too hectic too easily for friendship purposes . . .

You're always very decent about my work, which is very trusting of you. But it does not matter, for I feel happy about any sort of life that may come, not just as a matter of forcing myself to like it, now, but actually sort of feeling that. Many of us seem to get that feeling more after thirty or thereabouts.

The conjunction of Noyce's visit and the snow-covered landscape gave rise to a memorable poem:

> Cover them over, tenderly,
> And with a white cloth overspread.
> Cover them? No. Nor tenderly. Shall
> A man hide so great a riches? Strip back the cloth
> Look, look again where the whitenesses were; beautiful,
> Red with an earth-drenched sheen, purple, colours
> As of the spring, as of the autumn air,
> Colours of winter, hill upon hill, brilliant,
> Sky upon sky, banked,
> Stretching away and away.

Writing to Geoffrey Winthrop Young in 1944, Menlove offered a detailed interpretation of this poem. It is one of the best entries we have into a close reading of his work. The poem is naturally inspired by more specific feelings than are admitted to here, but the generalized account is still of immense value:

The scene and the white may be any scene covered and uncovered, one way or another, preferably by white. Yes, snow in my Welsh cottage started that in my mind. But it is also the total scene of a man's mind, in its feelings, the whole of his past, that is, the wounds that it contains and the pleasures also, that by being past are felt as easily as pain now. Looking at these, the man starts by rejecting them—no—cover it over, tenderly, let us look no more. Then he says "To Hell, no—the pain is nothing, look again. Yes, life—that was my life and it's been worthwhile, it's been a beautiful thing." Only he says it not quite like that because he's really just looking at it.

Although the poem does not really carry the poignancy of the personal significance, it is at last much more an individual and personal voice, free from the Tennysonian or Wordsworthian echoes of his earlier verse. Its line of thought was logically developed into another poem, in which the existential affirmative of "Cover them over" is replaced by a negative, phantasmal quality. It is of particular interest because, as far as can be ascertained, it was the last-but-one poem which Menlove wrote and it contains not a ruined scrap of optimistic belief. Even the form is hollow-centred, a near-reversal of the poem above:

> And you my greatest hopes, my flown away ones,
> Where are you? With these wood valleys where we wandered,
> Should I not follow you? Does not the oak tree
> Bow before the wind? Does not the eagle?
> And you were stronger, stronger than the wind,
> And more beloved. Ah,
> Could you but carry me—but no,
> Carried I am and swift; and where we go
> There is no other world. You precious leaves,
> You buds, how should you flower? You seedlings
> Borne ahead, whence might you spring? For we
> Are gone, the soil, the fragrances, into the air
> Ascended, gone, trinkets and baubles, flown away.

The imagery here is very accessible, with its suggested relationship to the David and Jonathan story in Samuel I:23, but it is still not superfluous to give Menlove's own gloss, from the same letter of 1944:

These hopes are the highest flights of this man's longings and desires, for love, for affection, for excellence: all those that went, the finest of them, when his youth and idealism went. Should he not still follow them, still so desirable and so strong? Yes, but wait, all that was best in him *did* follow them, and in doing so the organism was carried to a state and to circumstances where the realities of life—and feeling for that matter—could not be, or where thus—things were not real, and thus for all practical purposes trinkets and baubles, but NB they *did* promise great beauty.

Winter wore on. The snow melted, bud and blossom flecked the black-thorns by his window, the whole landscape of fawns and greys became shot through with an emergent green. Noyce visited him, loping over Snowdon having struggled alone up Curving Crack in the grip of a "fascination, overmastering and fatal as was ever the blindness that took Pentheus to his doom among the Bacchae", and stayed for a night in early May before bounding off again across Bwlch y Saethau and the Glyders to Helyg. Nea Morin brought her children to see him, and they were amused by the great sacks of nettle shoots he had gathered to eat. She took away some of his psychological writings to be typed by a friend of hers in Cricieth. He was vacillating between courses of action. On the one hand there was the resumption of his professional career:

> Am very glad to be away from Liverpool, in all sorts of ways: will try hard to get elsewhere for my next job. Am just showing some of my work to a psychologist I've mentioned from Liverpool. He may probably help to the sort of job and place, *if* he thinks it's any good (which after all is very unlikely).

And on the other the attraction of the life he was leading:

> My part of Wales is very nice just now; rhododendra flowering all over the place like weeds. I like this being on my own much better than I've ever liked anything else I'm afraid: seeing nobody all day just suits me: though a few years ago I'd have been dashed lonely—but having got over that. Could stay in this sort of life very happily the rest of my days, only for wanting to play a rather bigger part in things, and money of course. And some notion of duty. But it could be *such* a pleasant life, taking a bit of a job, enough money to get away some place on the cheap, then a bit of work again.

John Barford visited him on a few occasions, and together they wrote the 1942 interim guide to Clogwyn Du'r Arddu. Menlove's old mastery of topographical description is evident in this, and a light humour plays around some of the writing still:

> . . . the early climbers noted that the Clogwyn was peculiarly fertile of its grass and that wherever a blade was able to rest its foot it grew and flourished extraordinarily: in most of the early accounts it is put down variously as the situation dictates for admiration or horror; for praise, amusement, contempt; for cursing or blessing, or a careful silence; for

agonished efforts at its detention where it was already not firm. The disparity arises however not in paradox but because both grass and climbers so far have tackled only the easiest and thus the same places. Viewing the future, the relation of the two is competitive and man's force seems overpoweringly the greater.

The introduction, which conveys a good deal of the character of climbing on the cliff at the time, continues with the often-repeated quip:

> One would not advise a beginner to lead on them too immediately. Pitches are apt to seem long and belays not numerous, though a careful eye largely denies both points. Some degree of experience is needed to protect the rest of the party on the West Buttress, where a man is liable in falling to fall over the edge of the route on to a different and less easily negotiable aspect of the cliff; and experience of the use of thread belays (spare loops and a snap ring are useful) is valuable on the East Buttress for with these almost anywhere on the present climbs one may be safe though frightened. But with some experience one may have here for a short time something of that much-desired feeling of being on ground not broken in to man's foot, and have it still almost actually in truth.
>
> When one is not immediately climbing, there is the magnificent beauty of these crags and of the Llyn, unvarying, never the same, at all times, and in any weather.

During the summer of 1942 he began to apply for jobs and fellowships. Despite his experience and the excellence of his references, none of these came to anything but rejection. He worked away doggedly at his psychiatric research. Most of this was in the form of extremely condensed notes and data upon his case work. Some he showed to Nully Kretschmer and drew a comment from him that they seemed a little difficult to understand, which Menlove parried by telling him that they were not for purposes of communication but laid up against the time when he could write for exposition. "Were they wellings-up from the subconscious taken down for later?" The question drew a blank, although in view of the nature of the very few which survive it was a fair one.

Kretschmer managed to tempt Menlove from his work for two days' climbing in September. Javelin Buttress and Grey Wall by Procrastination Cracks were the itinerary for the first of these, and on the second a day's exploration in the Carneddau, a route being found on the obscure and vegetated Craig y Tri Marchog. News of the death of his old friend Archie Leggate reached Menlove at about this time. Archie had known Hewlett at

Cambridge and was a link with better days. In the *Climbers' Club Journal* Menlove gave him an honest and affectionate obituary:

Archie was a bad climber. He had no knack for finding holds on rocks or for using them when found. This may have been accountable by his loose build perhaps: he was long and thin; or by his lack of strength, or by other such things, but the immediate and outward result was that under the suggested physical danger that climbing entails, he fell into a state of paralysing fear and profound mental demoralisation. This greatly annoyed him. Going, therefore, to some standard Difficult climb, perhaps, he would confront his condition with an even more profound determination to become, by hook or by crook, as other men are, in respect of climbing. Then jackets ripped, trousers were torn, his knees knocked, blood like water, desperation was arrived at, was passed, to where effort ceases to last, success, perhaps, a tense interval on a stance, then another pitch. Then, the day far spent, at the top, flinging time away, we would eat and, as mortals should who have stormed Olympus, we laughed and laughed until we could not laugh. A magnificent fellow to climb with; he could see a joke; he could make me see one; and he could talk on and on, carefully, wittily, with truth; argue happily all night; or with seriousness honestly into his problems. An education for us. He never really climbed very much; efforts at the full stretch of our capacity cannot be every day; also he had work to do; and with others he did other things. But he very much desired climbing and physical command, and he hoped much from it, and, of course, he loved the country, the hills, Scotland and any adventure.

He took a theological course at Cambridge, but found himself doubting and changed over to medicine. He graduated. His work was in every way excellent, and in the tradition of his family, every action was examined and weighed against the ethical criterion of the good of others.

The war came soon after he had qualified, and he joined the Naval Medical Corps without hesitation. He was kept on shore work for a long time. On his first sea voyage he wrote home happily and then bombers caught the ship off the coast of Cornwall. He was last seen working at the operating table with the ship going down.

He leaves wife and friends.

There was worse news to come. Later in September Colin Kirkus, who was serving as a navigator in one of the pathfinder units of Bomber Command, was shot down over Hamburg. Although never very close friends in the way of spending much time together and making a show of their mutual affection, Menlove and Kirkus held out great respect for each other, mingled in Menlove's case with gratitude for the regard Colin had shown him throughout their acquaintance, and the encouragement he had given in the early climbing days. When such a friend dies, it puts an era to one's life. It also cancelled out yet another link with Noyce and the consummate brief happiness of 1936. Apart from his tenure on it having become uncertain, Hafod Owen must have seemed a haunted place now. In the second week of October, before the onset of another winter to be spent in its small-windowed, dark and cramping rooms, he left:

14.10.42

I've decided to move down to London and try to get in on some voluntary work and thence hopefully perhaps to something paid. All this damned mucking about with no money doing all one's own fetching and carrying, cooking, cleaning, etc. is good as an education but is beginning to waste an increasingly large amount of time, damn it.

Not anything one can seriously grumble at, though, for I've got enough, and if and when I do run right out of money I could still pretty certainly drop straight into a luxurious Mental hospital job. Meanwhile, however, in combination with a particularly dirty day and the prospect of carrying my damned furniture to the nearest farm, to be removed in a day or two, I'm indulging in a bit of swearing . . .

Expanding on his reasons for leaving, he observed that:

I've done quite a bit since coming here, but nothing compared with what would be necessary to make any success of it. Now I need a shaking up, and more material, and I *must* get a foot somehow into some position of *some* medical standing, if I can. If not, of course, like most things, one could do within it . . .

And finally, he summed up on his year at Hafod Owen:

. . . it's been a very perfect year. I could in fact live very pleasantly in this sort of way: some local job: ambition, the trouble-bearer, put on one side.

The present depression really *is* a very localised phenomenon. I like being alone, but I like company too.

Hewlett Johnson, Nowell's husband, let a flat to Menlove at 8 Meadow Road, South Lambeth, on the south side of the river near Vauxhall Bridge. Menlove wrote to Alec Keith from there at the end of October:

... the flat here has needed a lot of doing up, being in a fairly foul mess.

Have approached one or two people re. work: so far without luck, but with lots of possibles still outstanding. Saw Crichton Miller,* father of the Fettes person; not very helpful though extremely well meaning; a pretty pompous old blighter, feeling rather hardly the decline of his reputation and perhaps of his powers.

London is looking fairly all right. A bit dingy and lacking in paint and polish. A considerable amount of open scars still more or less untidied—much more so in the poorer parts, as one might expect. ... People seem much more inclined to be helpful than I would have imagined, to a total stranger.

He busied himself about getting work, calling on acquaintances and contacts, visiting clinics and hospitals to explain his situation and get his face known. Towards the end of November he recieved his first two offers of employment, both of which were to start on 1 January. One was in the Child Guidance Department of the Great Ormond Street Hospital for Sick Children, the other was work with adults at the Tavistock Clinic. After a certain amount of hesitation and doubts, they each decided that he would be paid £100 per annum—£200 a year was enough to live on reasonably comfortably even in London at that time. He did not seek to set up in consulting rooms or take on private work, preferring instead to persevere with his research. His situation was thus still by no means secure, for there was no guarantee that the jobs would last, and they were anyway unusual, the standard procedure at both places being for staff to work unpaid for the prestige and contacts they brought, and to gain their income from private consultations.

After three months in this routine, he wrote to Alec Keith to tell what was happening, Alec having obviously expressed concern:

24.3.43

My status is unnamed at each place, but by implication about as low as possible. But I'm glad I came here and the people seem pretty decent. I fancy that Liverpool must have given me fairly decent (private) references actually—which rather pleased me—although the results in terms of jobs are so unimposing. Am all the time half-hoping for a research job but it seems pretty impossible—absolutely not a sign of a chance so far—I mean even so far as "if it were peacetime ..." or as to prospects when peace comes.

However all's well for the time being, and meanwhile I must try to show

* At the time Head of the Tavistock Clinic.

up reasonable actual results on cases; they take some time and I don't know yet how they'll go. London standard is very "safe" so that a failure always ends up able to be put down entirely as the patient's fault. But we'll see what happens.

London as a place to live in is certainly not much use. I've got a bit of a flat at £1 per week, with plenty of room in it, and do for myself entirely. Quite amusing, though I'd rather be done *for*. Pleasant enough to do my own cooking, and allows of a simple and healthy diet without being constantly pestered with food you don't want or rather do want but are better without. Not that I cut down the amount really.

Furniture was no bother. I have a basic amount that I've been carting around with me since the beginning of the blitzes . . . fits comfortably into any room I've yet had.

On Saturday I take four hours or so on the bike and can just get to fresh air and sun, between South Croydon and the area south-east of that. You may know those lanes from Orpington days. Warlingham, Sanderstead, and just east of both of those.

Now and then I go to a baths instead, if it's wet: but most often it has actually been fine. I miss the country, and the beauty of Wales very much when I think of it, which is moderately often. Yes, it would have been bad to stay there much longer. But I feel a devil of a lot fitter for having had that period, and I'll always remember it.

> Yours ever, being very sensible now,
> Menlove.

The craving for fresh air grew more intense as 1943 drew on. In June he took two weeks' holiday and travelled south-west to the Climbers' Club property known as the Count House—an old mine office built above the cliffs between Zennor and St Just, on the north coast of West Penwith. The climbing on the rough and often sea-washed faces of Cornwall's granite was still in its infancy, but the area held out obvious attractions. The power of the Atlantic waves against the cliffs, the intricacies of feature where the two met, provided a sphere of recreation and discovery which must have been redolent of the holidays at Port St Mary as a child. A. W. Andrews (who had, to quote Winthrop Young, "rubber-roamed, goat-like, up ribs-–solitary and sturdy wanderings in rubbers and audacity, high among the Lliwedd cracks and juts", in the first decade of the century), who had co-written the first Lliwedd guidebook of 1909, and who had espoused the cause of rock-climbing and revealed it to the massed worthies of the Alpine Club, was living in Cornwall, and gladly took his weary successor as rock-climbing radical into his charge for some of the time. The hut-book's record is terse:

A fortnight overlapping with two other parties at the end, but mostly in the company and under guidance of AWA.

A lot of scrambling, of very good quality: such a very large amount of fine climbing faces. In particular a traverse of Carnelloe Zawn; a traverse out of Porthmoina Cove to the west on excellent rock at a bit above high-tide level; on East face of Porthmoina Island a route—starting third way along foot, low tide, up on a slung rope and then fifteen feet steeply to the easy ground and then on up some yards right of the flake crack, up a nice corner and then traverse right and up. The first of these, the zawn, was done on a rope, but with proper route is only about 3B or 4A standard, and needs no rope.

(The Climbers' Club was experimenting at the time with numbered grades similar to the continental/Vallot system; these should not be confused with the modern technical grading of climbs.) Menlove concludes his note with the following comment: "Even better than the rocks, the waves gave good sport; also a large baulk of timber from Porthmeor Cove."

In a letter, Menlove wrote that he had "marvellous bathing in bits of waves mostly; best I've had for years and years . . . I joined in a bit with other parties most of the time". For sport, Menlove would allow himself to be carried in against a cliff by the waves and let them wash him high up on to the rocks, where he would seize hold and scramble out of reach. Those who have experienced the shock and surge of water around sea-cliffs, and the lacerating nature of sea-washed rock, will realize that to anyone other than the most powerful of climbers and swimmers such recreation is suicidal. Three Royal Marine commandos who were watching, and who later tried to copy him, were drowned in so doing.

Back in London once more, and briefly refreshed, Menlove struggled on to gain preferment, or even just recognition for his work. Alec Keith had written to him offering to introduce him to his uncle Sir Arthur Keith, the anatomist and former Conservator of the Hunterian Museum of the Royal College of Surgeons, if the contact would be of any use. Menlove quickly replied:

12.7.43

The offer of going to see Sir Arthur is very good. I may take it. Will see how things go. I like the idea of him. Within the next year or so I may begin to think about starting to write a small article or two and it's hopeless doing anything of that sort from *no* official background. *Any* covering letter or anything seems to do the trick. But he might be interested in part of my stuff anyhow and it would be a nice contact. But don't *you* do anything about it because (a) I won't go unless I need to—I'm no good at being just pleasant,

etc. and (b) that way I can just turn up on him, and he can more easily
more or less say so if he's not interested and doesn't think the stuff
worth while.

He went on to outline his hopes for the work through the channels which
were already open to him:

> ... it's not beyond the bounds of possibility that one or two of the
> Tavistock or Great Ormond Street people might be sufficiently
> interested to read through an article for me—I don't know—I've simply
> not tried.
>
> I wanted to get the psychologist from Liverpool (who was encouraging
> before, once) to look through some of my pure psych. stuff for me, but
> he's too busy. (He *is* really busy but of course it also means not
> interested *enough*, doesn't think it worth while.) But it would be decent to
> have the chance of your uncle—he seems directly on the look-out for
> anything always in his whole nature: not that I really know much about
> him. My work itself just wanders on ...

His persistent self-denigration seemed to be deepening into self-
disillusionment. He was having to fight off self-pity:

> I'm so damned slow and inadequate and not even very persevering.
> Don't get the idea I'm in a bad way though: very much the opposite. I
> feel rather happy about life and don't—in a way—care much what hap-
> pens to these particular ambitions, as ambitions. Actually the other med.
> psych's at the clinics seem to be increasingly decent (I don't mean a
> propos my work but just in general, pleasant) though they take me to be
> pretty odd—but they seem to have more or less stopped minding about
> that!

Menlove was putting a brave face on it: "Life's too short when it isn't
too long." The news from the war was good. Old friends passing through
London looked him up. Bill Stallybrass "spent at least one happy evening
with him in his South London flat, and on another occasion he came to
supper and a West End theatre with my stepfather and me, and we greatly
enjoyed each other's company". But with regard to his work, from which
he seemed already to be trying to convince himself at some level into a
retraction of hope, there was a bitter blow in store: "A chap J T McCurdy
(*sic*) has just come out with some stuff that's been part of what I've been
working on for the last seven or eight years."

MacCurdy's book, *The Structure of Morale*, ranged widely over preoccupations which are echoed in what little we know* of Menlove's research interests: fear, morale, the effect of bomb-explosions, the over-rigidity of centralized social systems, the public schools, the rise of socialism and pacifism, the opinions of the British working class on the value of an aristocratic class, are all covered in greater or lesser degree by MacCurdy, starting from a left-wing political standpoint and published with the full support of the Syndics of the Cambridge University Press. The professional ground had again been cut from under Menlove's feet. He was forced to look back into his work to seek for new directions:

> Have just been looking over some of my theoretical stuff again, a particular bit I had put aside six months ago as pretty complete in itself, but now found it full of important gaps. This is of course, and to some extent was, to be expected, and has happened a lot of times before, but it's always rather a curse naturally.

He had moved at New Year 1944 from Lambeth to Pattison Road in Child's Hill, which runs up from the Finchley Road towards the Leg of Mutton Pond on Hampstead Heath: "On a bit of a hill and has a view and fresher air and is nicer altogether." It was also nearer to his work. Perhaps anxious that some part at least of his writing should gain recognition, in February 1944 he sent a few poems to Geoffrey Winthrop Young: "I'd rather have liked your opinion on them . . . they are just odd bits, left over from a period that is gone." The poems started a correspondence between the two men which is crucial to an understanding of Menlove's mind at this time. The first letter, dated 2 February, continues:

> The CUMC people wanted me, very kindly, to give a lecture up there but I've only got about two-thirds of my slides left—not enough for a lecture—also my mind just doesn't run on the themes now and I couldn't do it. The sort of thing that I would be able to make up now would be dead dull . . .
>   Have in fact dried up pretty considerably, as always felt likely. Perhaps it's partly with being too much always on my own all these years; but enough of all that; dried up or not I feel pretty contented and my way of life at present seems rather to suit me. Anyway one goes on and sees what happens. The Welsh year, in the cottage, was most pleasant.
>   Wilfrid writes pretty often: you will know, though, of all his doings. He

---

* All Menlove's psychological writings were destroyed after his death.

seems to be putting in a great deal of work at his languages: he must be pretty *considerably* good at them I should think.

Winthrop Young was very active at this time in trying to bring about the use of what came to be termed "outdoor activities" as an educational medium—a project in which Jack Longland was also closely involved and which was to bring about the opening of the country's first outdoor pursuits centre for schools at White Hall in Derbyshire. It is the formative phase of this movement to which Menlove refers in the next paragraph of his letter:

It will be interesting indeed to me to watch your wide "education" schemes going forward. There must be a lot of the right sort of talent for it too in the climbing world? A man like JLL [Jack Longland] obviously of the right personality and training for every aspect of it, (experience of course!) Big movements seem so much closer to one, when people one actually knows personally are doing them: an odd experience for me.

Sending these poems reminds me of those others I used to send, and how much your letters meant to me, so that I read them again and again. It seems a terrible long time ago . . .

One of the poems which Menlove sent to Winthrop Young for his opinion is, to the best of our knowledge, the final one he wrote. It was written in January or February of 1943, and could be taken as a classic statement of schizophrenia. (The best commentary upon it is to be had from the doctor's report dated 25 April 1945 and quoted in chapter eight.) Menlove gives a brief preface to the poem for GWY's benefit:

Sentinel. Is the person's grammar clear? The whole speaks in each first line; the sentinel part in all of the rest and is addressing the whole which is thus "master" or "you", "him" being a different person. The cliché is supposed to add to the atmosphere.

Here is the poem:

Ho sentinel! What of the night?
Master, I look at the night, gazing out far away into her. Sometime soon
When the day comes I will report to you waves,
Other waves, too, coming after, to us as we go over the water,
A dolphin passes, a bird, or the spar of a schooner;
But, Master, here I see nothing, only the night.

Ho, sentinel! What of the night?
Master, I look at the night, as my eyes have been always accustomed.
Time was, a long time ago, when figures of men were seen passing: some
Floated by, and were bloated, some dead, some were comely.
And some were seen live and stepped across out of the water towards us
But here, Master, now I see nothing, only the night.

Sentinel! Sentinel! Tell me, what of the night?
Master, sleep, sleep softly I pray you. I look out into the West, now over into
    the East,
And there far away, yes, there is a lighting, as of a dream that is bright.
Yes, Master, the news is good. They are fingers, I see them, large
Lifting over the dark horizon, golden, fairshaped, out of the blackness come,
And they bear him swiftly, bringing you happiness.

Menlove's full exegesis of the poem to GWY runs as follows:

> The ship and crew is passing through the night; these are the total sum of
> man. The main part are asleep now but have left a sentinel on the lookout.
> But not wholly asleep being restless and ill at ease and calling out now and
> then, or muttering if you like in the sleep. The sentinel is less touched by
> the feelings of the whole and is the observing aspect rather than the
> feeling; yet anxious to serve the whole and for its welfare. The whole man
> has been long-isolated and is desirous of company but has come not really
> to expect or *in a sense* to desire anything better ("when the day comes, I
> will report to you waves"). Then unexpectedly in a vision (of the boat) or
> in a dream (of the man) there is a brighter thing and his loved one is
> brought by it, by the dream. This taken automatically by both aspects of
> the whole man to be the greatest good possible in their life in which night
> or no night the heart lives in darkness.

Poem and exegesis together obviate the need for much further comment.
The section, "The main part are asleep now but have left a sentinel on the
lookout. But not wholly asleep being restless and ill at ease and calling out
now and then, or muttering if you like in the sleep", has a frighteningly
ingenuous aspect to it. What, we are led to question, will happen when those
feelings—The "Master"—shrug off enforced sleep and wake to confront
finally the surrounding night? For the hope and vision are certainly an
illusion, depending on something—the "loved one"—from the past. It is the
last piece of Menlove's creative work we shall have to consider, and there is a
gravity of implication about it which is ominous.

Winthrop Young had obviously experienced difficulty with the meaning of some of the poems Menlove had sent him, which gives the reason for the fullness of explanation Menlove thought necessary. There are a few comments at the opening of a letter of 23 March 1944 which give an idea of GWY's reaction to them:

> Yes, they are primitive, and creaking, and I think that's true of me all round. I agree my little bits would not generally be understood. Obviously as a matter of intelligence if anyone would get them it would be you. Though as a minor point, I have noticed that the previous ones some saw bits though they were not of special intelligence, but had a similar mood in dominance recently . . .
>
> They are very personal of course—and very few.

Reassured by GWY's interest, and the intelligence of his response, Menlove seems to have felt free to unburden himself in a very long letter which examines his professional interests and prospects, and of which the above is the start:

> Then me and what to do with me. For this I'll give the estimate of my work which I'm implicitly working on in general plan as to possibility, but that may be mistrusted wholly always for many reasons, and that must not be mentioned except to one who knows one well enough to recognise it as recognised possible foolishness, and not to be led either into too seriously expecting anything in the way of real results.

The extent to which Menlove was beginning to lose his intellectual control is obvious here. He is tying himself in knots in the effort to excuse the possibility of not living up to the expectations which may be placed upon him. (One of his ex-patients wrote to him at about this time in the terms: "Go bury yourself and moulder—stupid! I begin to think that the doctor should take the man in hand: the latter is just wrapping himself round with stupidity. And I hope I infuriate you.")

The letter to GWY fortunately gains cogency as it goes along, and launches into a professional self-assessment which attempts to rationalize the obsessive approach he had adopted to his work:

> In my own opinion I'm better at theoretical psychology than at these other things: than practical psychotherapy certainly: than with words—perhaps not as regards that half-hour in five years or so when my feelings are

strongly roused that way—but for the majority of the time and for my main working span. Taking it that this is correct—what dispositions to make? To make a job (or to try to—for at any point with science if it's wrong it's wrong however well one tried, though in descriptive work that's less wholly the case, less wholly right or wrong) of the theoretical requires a very high allocation of time and energy and an equally high absence of distractions: a high degree of isolation is necessary actually (in my opinion—and I've watched the matter in myself pretty closely) to my purpose, and its advantages outweigh the also considerable disadvantages, for that purpose, the theoretical work. So that choosing that aim, to push it to any conclusion worth while at all, means cutting out other aims if they make any demands on one's time during that period of life.

There is something about the self-duplicity of this passage strangely reminiscent of the little extract beginning "Have you ever watched a beginner on the Slabs? A most instructive little psychological study." quoted in chapter three. What Menlove is asserting is the basic necessity to believe that he is acting in good faith, the result of which is that he can ascribe the personal cost and the psychological consequences of his actions to that. He carried on:

The degree of grind required has cut out those moods very largely that I need for writing: though personally I sometimes hope I may live to retire in older age and then that rummaging in the drawers one may write perhaps a bit: as well as occasional bits if they come to mind in the interval.

In response to a suggestion of GWY's, he adds:

The other sphere I've wanted to try at *is* that of "leadership": most forms, however, demand full time allowance. I do not prefer it to the theory aims because I consider this latter the more important—the advance in knowledge in the form of science, especially that *re* the mind: and I fancy my chances in it.

Yet the possibility of, if ever possible, combining or running concurrently these two aims has always been strongly in mind. There seem a few possibilities that might or might not turn out in practice. Leadership needs a position to work from: any success in the theoretical would help this. The demands of the theoretical for exclusive time might possibly relax—I would perhaps know that in a year or two from now. Or of course if it failed.

But you see I rate my chances in the theoretical as worth going on with; and as more than my chances in the other.

This section of the letter ends, prophetically, with the thought that it "is full of hubris. If the gods are alive surely they will let it rise further perhaps a little and then strike it down." He fends off a suggestion of GWY's politely: "Yes, I agree it's good to mix psychology with lots of practice. But it's difficult to explain how extremely demanding the theory is of time." The end of the letter is obsessive and pathetic: "Unfortunately I've had no adequate outside opinion on whether my theory efforts are worth going on with, as relative to other possibilities."

Apart, of course, from the psychologist in Liverpool he does not seem to have shown his material to any of his professional colleagues for opinion or comment: ". . . must use my own judgement. Have been at it since '35 and would be a fool to give it up with failure unproved."

In absolute terms the failure was to remain unproved, for the material was never presented in full and in a coherent and systematic form to anyone who could properly judge it, and it has all since been destroyed. Finally, he gives a promise:

I'll try to help if I've time, after the war; and will think myself very honoured, too, to be allowed any part, if it so happens. That's all too short. It omits, eg, that I long very much often to be free of my damned work and to be off on just such a scheme as yours: that I will never forgive it what it has demanded—the constant disappointing of friends also. And perhaps all for nothing: but that's my own look out of course.

At the end of April, the pressure of disappointment increasing, he went to Helyg.

Arrived for a holiday of indefinite duration. Mucking about plus a tiny bit of climbing with B L B [athurst] . . . Found Helyg excellently cleaned up, but why should the mattresses be using the one bath in the place when I want it, even if they have got fleas in them.

During the fortnight he was at Helyg he climbed only twice, spending one day on Lliwedd where he found his Elliptical Face routes easier than the grades he had given them in the guidebook, "due perhaps to gardening?" And another day on Craig yr Ysfa, which he decided was a good cliff after all, having repeated Cox's route of Sodom* (an ironic name considering the

* Curiously, G. R. Speaker also prevailed on Cox to change the name of his route, which he did, from Sodom to Spiral Route. The climb is VS, and its solo ascent by Cox was an outstanding achievement in the pre-war era.

Climbers Club had persuaded Menlove in 1931 against its application to the route now known as Spiral Stairs) and Kirkus's Pinnacle Wall. David Murray-Rust, the former Charterhouse schoolmaster who had been Noyce's friend and climbing companion in 1935 and 1936, met him at Helyg on this visit:

> ... one evening he walked me up and down between Helyg and Ogwen—talking, talking wildly. It was confused stuff which I barely understood—but it was all involved with his work and the way in which "they" in the medical profession were ganging together to frustrate him and do him down.

On his return to London, he became increasingly estranged from his fellow-workers at the two clinics. He harboured the delusion that he was being sent young male patients by his superiors in order that they might find out about his sexual leanings. He was probably also being offered guidance as to where his theories, or what his seniors knew of them, seemed errant or ignorant of previous work in the field, and was reacting violently against any such implied criticism. And he seems also to have been clinging desperately to his own approach to clinical work regardless of how incongruent it was with that adopted by Great Ormond Street or the Tavistock. His attitude towards the air-raids was becoming more frightened and intense. In March he had been able to shrug them off:

> The raids: only bits of things and the rumours all seem extremely exaggerated—those I've heard: keep one awake for a time and as the evenings get lighter they come later and definitely interfere with sleep. But they've all been short: ever since I got to London ...

By July 1944, with the new and frightening threat of "doodlebugs"—the V1's—he was beginning to feel personally threatened and left London again in August for a holiday on Skye. He had not been there since a visit with A. B. Hargreaves in the early 1930s, but despite his very slight acquaintance with the region he made the first solo traverse of the Cuillin Ridge, including Blaven and Clach Glas, the two outliers above Loch na Creitheach, in the rapid time of twelve and a half hours. The only food he carried was a packed lunch of sandwiches supplied by the landlady of his lodgings in Glen Brittle, from whence he set off at eight a.m. and to which returned from Gars-bheinn in the dark. Robin Hodgkin and Nully Kretschmer were on the island at the same time, and Hodgkin remembers the embarrassed mumblings about Menlove: "Poor chap, he's having rather a bad time of it!" At the end of the holiday he hired a rowing boat and—always a sign of great trouble with Menlove—took to the water, rowing across to Rhum and Canna, the two islands to the west. In squally weather, he was eighteen hours at sea on the crossing to Rhum.

His mental deterioration in the autumn became very pronounced. There were no friends at hand who could help him. His mother, who was in Harlech with Nowell, received odd and disturbing letters from him in October and asked Stephen to see him. (Stephen was by now living in Staindrop, near Barnard Castle in County Durham.) Stephen sent a telegram to Menlove saying that he had business in London—a pretext—and would stay with him for a night. When he alighted from the train a day or so later, not having mentioned any time of arrival, Menlove was waiting for him at the barrier. They went back to Child's Hill, packed a few of Menlove's belongings, and the next morning took the London and North Eastern express from King's Cross to Darlington. Menlove's professional career was over.

CHAPTER EIGHT

"Years of tragic waste" 1944–1958

STAINDROP, THEN A village of 1,500 inhabitants, lies amongst meadows twelve miles west of Darlington on the main road from Durham to Barnard Castle. To the south and west the land drops suddenly to the deeply incised valley of the Upper Tees. It grew up as the estate village for Raby Castle, the parkland of which lies to the north, behind the yellow-ashlar houses which line the wide village street. The vicarage is one of these, a double-fronted house whose bow windows look out on to the village green. Its front doorstep of yellow sandstone is worn by the feet which have trodden it since late Georgian or early Victorian times, and at the rear only a wall separates the garden from the estate, where each evening in early summer the woodcock could be seen roding over the plantations of beech and larch. The Parish Church lies a little to the east, where the road turns up the hill towards Bishop Auckland. Saxon in foundation and a former collegiate church, it has about it that aspiring and organic feel of the very finest English churches: triple lancet windows in the Early English and Transitional styles let light in upon Romanesque arches in the nave; the lines of the Saxon roof and windows can be seen in the walls; the interior is rich in features: sedilia, rood screen, memorials and misericordia. And on the outer wall of the squat tower at the west end of the church the following text from St Matthew is inscribed: "Watch therefore: for ye know not what hour your Lord doth come."

This, then, was the peaceful, archaic place to which Stephen brought back his younger brother from the terror he had found in London. And there was a terror upon Menlove. Ruth, Stephen's wife, remembers one night when he was so afraid, so shaking with fear, that she had to give up her bed to let him be near the calming presence of his brother. Stephen, too, remembers walking in Raby Park, hearing a 'plane, and Menlove's panic-stricken utterance as he looked up: "They're watching me!" Helen Edwards, the mother, came to stay, anxious about her youngest son, and the vicarage was large enough to give them rooms and a kitchen to themselves where she could look after Menlove's needs. Ruth recalls an occasion in this kitchen when she came in to see Menlove's hand clasped trembling over his mother's arm, pleading with her, "You won't leave me, will you?"

Being back amongst his family did have some quietening effect. There were Stephen and Ruth's two daughters, but very young, with whom he could build bonfires and for whom he could make swings in the trees. The pattern of family life asserted itself around him. All gathered together for the midday meal, whilst in the evening Menlove and his mother ate in their own kitchen. But conversation was never easy. His irritability was well to the fore, and any chance remark might annoy him. Also, he talked as he wrote—in dense, allusive, gnomic phrases, which made continuity difficult and casual speech impossible. The year, however, progressed peacefully enough. After doing nothing for a few weeks Menlove found a job in the forestry planta- tions of the Raby Estate. "He became very much liked by the villagers with whom he worked. Long after he had gone they used to ask after him most affectionately," Stephen tells.

November was wet, trees dripping, paths deep in mire, mist seeping up from the valley, the river swollen, dead leaves circling aimlessly in its eddies. Then the weather became cold, frost breaking up the brown earth, ploughed over after the effort of its fruitfulness. Menlove kept more and more indoors, more composed now but brooding deeply. Sometimes he could be heard muttering violently to himself. The Christmas festivities of a country vicar's household came to lighten the gloom, but Menlove stood apart. With the New Year of 1945 came snow and a bitterly cold north wind. One Saturday afternoon early in January Stephen asked Menlove if he would care to come for a walk with him, but received the by-now-usual rebuff. Ten minutes later the front door slammed, boots rasped quickly across the front step and crunched away through the snow.

Stephen waited anxiously, sensing there was something wrong as the hours dragged by. Finally he went over to the police station to talk with Sergeant Topham, who suggested that they go out to find him. They hurried down to the Tees at Winston Bridge—a favourite place for walks—and found nailed boot marks leading along the bank, which they followed in the wind and approaching darkness for over a mile. Finally they decided the prints could not be Menlove's, for the nails were ordinary hobs and not the clinkers with which Stephen thought his boots would be nailed. They turned back.

Half a mile farther on, Menlove was lying unconscious beneath a hedge, his face burned by the chloroform-soaked pad he had bound across his nose and mouth.

Stephen went home to bed: "That night was one of the longest and coldest I ever remember, and I kept waking from a dream of seeing the river running between rocks and stones covered with ice to wonder what had happened and where he was." Meanwhile, Menlove revived, and with his senses drugged and reeling threw himself into a deep pool of the river, but landed in its one shallow part. Brought to by the shock of the freezing water, he struggled out and knocked up a nearby farmhouse to ask for help. They took him to the hospital in Darlington and the next morning, a Sunday, the police rang from there to tell Stephen, who had just returned from taking the eight a.m. service, what had happened. On condition that he was kept under close observation and later taken to a mental institution for further care, they agreed to take no further action. (Attempted suicide, it should be remembered, was still a crime in Britain until 1961.)

Two days later the hospital phoned Stephen to tell him that Menlove had caught his watcher off guard and hurled himself through an upper-storey window. He was badly cut by glass but the snow cushioned his fall. The hospital understandably refused to keep him any longer. Stephen contacted the resident physician, Dr Archdale, at Middleton Hall Mental Hospital in the village of Middleton St George, just east of Darlington, and Menlove was taken there for treatment.

Middleton Hall is an extensive two-storeyed redbrick Georgian manor-house set amidst lawned gardens, pleasant enough in the summer but now gaunt and sparse—bare rosebeds and winter trees. Like every other mental hospital in the country, the shocks of war had crowded it with suffering. Menlove was to spend a little under three months here.

The response of his circle of acquaintance to the news of his breakdown was immediate and generous. Few of his friends had seen him during the war years and were genuinely distressed at the state to which he had been reduced. Chantrell and Bartrum organized a fund which collected several hundred pounds together for his use.* He received letters offering help and advice, quickly became submissive to the treatment he was receiving and started to feel anxiety about the future. He wrote to Winthrop Young in February 1945:

I want to withdraw the exaggerated statements I made in letters last year about myself, also about my pacifism and about being alone. And wish you could help me in any way to get out of this mess I am in, and with any influence you have.

---

* Menlove's mother refused to accept this, and it was subsequently returned to the contributors.

The admission here is how dearly the effort of sticking to his ideals had cost him. But what lay ahead for him? What possible new direction could there be?

> I want primarily to get my life on to an easier footing now and not so isolated. Am giving up psychology—have sent my theoretical work up to London. Now want to get out of the mental hospital and settled somewhere—out of any "leadership" or scientific experimental situation. Am very doubtful if anything would come into mind in the writing way but would encourage it if so, unless people objected, if I had leisure over and money enough. This looks unlikely as at present I have virtually no money.

At about the time this letter was written Menlove also had his name taken off the roll of conscientious objectors. The editors of *Samson* suggest that this "was not probably of any moral significance". They were, I think, wrong in that assumption. The attempted suicide, so desperate and so extraordinarily thwarted and bungled, was surely an attempt to break not only an obsession but also an inherited and developed moral imperative with which he no longer had the emotional strength to cope.

The desire for death, which culminated in this by no means half-hearted series of attempts to attain it must in part have been a desire to be relieved of the responsibility of being one of the "individuals wholly standing out and bearers of their flag", and the removal of his name from the roll of conscientious objectors a continuing recognition that he no longer possessed the resources to contend on the part of those causes for which he had felt the necessity to fight. The admission—for which he had been tacitly preparing himself for perhaps two or three years—was one of defeat, but it was not devoid of moral significance. Menlove survived this suicide attempt, but he survived into a changed world, haunted by the memory of values once held very dearly, peopled by those who, in Menlove's mind, had traduced those values. What hope was there in it for him after so comprehensively devastating a defeat, and one which had done irreparable damage to any regenerative capacity? For the defeat was so overwhelming that Menlove could only respond to it by retreating into a delusional system of which there had been occasional signs even before the war (his reactions to the CMS questions; the grandiose scheme for discovering the "single natural law"—the latter quite probably a strong contributory factor in the non-acceptance of his theoretical work).

As the letter to Geoffrey Young briefly recognized, the only hope for Menlove lay in a fresh start and a different direction, but so complete a confession of failure was impossible for him to make, and there was no sufficient attraction in any other direction to tempt him to do so. His ideological effort and his professional work* had been the centre of his life and focus of his energies. Their defeat, his alienation, the lack of (or inability to receive) objective guidance, led to the explosion of character which was the attempted suicide. It was a gesture of impotence which compares curiously with the self-immolation, in Prague in 1969, of the Czech student Jan Palach. I say compares, but Menlove's attempt was more nearly a reverse image of Palach's gesture. In the case of the Czech, the enemy was real, obvious and deadly, and Palach's suicide was immediately comprehensible as an act of hopeless opposition. Menlove's attempt made no such common cause, though his inwardly-identified but only obliquely and infrequently outwardly-condemned enemy—the intolerant, insane society which persecuted, cast out, judged and warred—was as deadly in its way, as productive of oppression and human unhappiness, as were the invaders of Palach's formerly free state.

Menlove left Middleton Hall on 17 March, against the advice of his doctors. They had also advised Stephen that it would be most unwise for him to go back for any length of time to Staindrop, as its associations with the attempt to kill himself might bring about a recurrence of his illness. It was arranged that he should go to stay with Stuart Chantrell on the Wirral, and perhaps seek work on a farm or market-garden. Stephen drove him over to Chantrell's, and the party stopped at an hotel in Kirkby Stephen for lunch. Menlove had a drink—a gin and orange—before this, and it reacted with the drugs he was taking to reduce him to a state of helpless giggles. They met Chantrell in Liverpool and Menlove went home over the river with him, Stephen having conveyed to him the following report from Dr Armitage:

He has shown slight shut in and paranoid tendencies from time to time for a year or two, which culminated in an attack of depression and suicidal impulses when staying at his brother's house. When admitted he had obstinate constipation, numerous cuts about his left buttock, thigh and leg from broken glass after an attempt to jump through a window, parasthesiae or hallucinatory sensations in certain parts of his body and fears of organic disease.

He soon became co-operative, showed much understanding of his condition, and accepted the idea that for a few years he must enjoy some

---

* It is unfortunate we know so little about his theoretical work. From the little we do know a sense comes over of interplay between the moral compulsion and the direction of his psychological writings. If this was so, it is quite possible that the intuitivism of the one would adversely have affected the scientific method required of the other; but this is extremely hypothetical.

occupation other than his professional work, and that he can only undertake responsibilities and stresses very gradually.

The arrangement with Stuart Chantrell went well for a brief time, but
Menlove's condition was still deeply unstable. Any serious topic of conversation he managed to lead back round into vitriolic denunciations of his former
colleagues in London, or of anyone who did not wholly agree with his ideas.
The old ideological apartness had now become a terrible refusal of connection. And soon Chantrell too, for all his kindness, was included in that
refusal and his charity received as gall. Menlove packed his bag and went to
stay with Wilfrid Noyce in Cambridge.

Noyce's years in the army and at the Aircrew Mountain Centre in Kash-
mir, and the pain and frustration of his accidents had probably all conspired
to broaden his understanding, but nonetheless it must have been the worst
possible place for Menlove to be at this time. He didn't stay long. A friend of
Noyce's who called during the visit describes a scene: the two men listening
to music, Noyce and the visitor afterwards exchanging idle remarks on it and
Menlove coming in with a question to the visitor: "But did you *really* like the
music?" The following conversation was halting, each man feeling the need
to consider his responses very carefully before committing himself to them in
front of the silent figure in the corner.

When Menlove left, he travelled down through London to Nowell and
Hewlett Johnson's house at Charing, near Ashford in Kent, where the
Johnsons were living whilst the bomb-damaged Deanery at Canterbury was
being repaired.

The Towers at Charing is a large house, built between the wars, of ungainly
design and set on top of the downs. Beyond the two large bay windows which
Hewlett added to the front of the house, the view spreads out across the
Weald of Kent with a feeling of great width and distance. All along the chalk
scarps on both sides are woods and fields, bright with the wildflowers of
chalk regions in the spring. This was to be Menlove's home for the rest of his
life.

His friends had meanwhile been busying themselves on his behalf.
Stephen had made an appointment to see Maberley, Head of the Tavistock,
to try to find out what was causing Menlove's illness: "It was a wasted
journey. I could find no common idiom with him, and his explanations were
cold, involved, and quite outside my understanding. I did feel a certain lack
of sympathy and concern also."

Samples of his psychological writing along with a summary of the direction in which he was working were sent to leading authorities in the field at

the time by other friends. Jack Longland arranged to have them vetted by Maberley at the Tavistock. The response was not encouraging. It conceded that the work was by a man of great intelligence, but went on to add:

> It is impossible to tell whether Menlove has got hold of something unless he works out stuff in detail with evidence and authorities. The problems set out in the summary being mainly concerned with the psychology of thinking and learning are *prima facie* best approached by way of laboratory experiments (e.g. rats in mazes). It doesn't seem *prima facie* that clinical experience, which presumably has to do chiefly with the psychology of emotion, is likely to throw much light on these problems . . .
>
> Has he worked at all, for instance, at the behaviour stuff of the Americans, and does he know straight (academic) psychology? . . .
>
> This summary gives an impression of an amateur coming into the subject.

From an academic point of view this is entirely reasonable, but it doesn't tell us very much about the work and its criticism is entirely methodological. If Menlove's extant writings provide any basis for judgement, then it can be assumed that his summary would have been intuitive rather than scientific and deductive. When we consider that academic discipline in all spheres is firmly founded on the rigorous application of method, and when we remember that Menlove at no time had any formal academic training, then the reaction is not surprising. It is still very sad and leaves a mystery around the real quality of his work. The response does also have a slightly uneasy air about it of rejecting the outside *per se*, the offhand usage of "amateur" as a pejorative perhaps implying a certain disdain and refusal of dialogue?

Those doubts aside, it has to be maintained that Menlove's rejection of authority in his professional field seems to have been done as lightly and summarily as it was when he rejected preconceptions in the early days of his climbing, and this time in a domain where the substantive evidence of his gifts was much more difficult to show. Had a figure of stature comparable in the world of theoretical psychology to that of Winthrop Young in mountaineering taken a personal interest in Menlove and pointed out to him that in academic work the quality of mind is always subservient to the demands of form, perhaps the final result *would* have been different—but that begs the question of Menlove's likely response to such pressure, and is anyhow purely conjectural.

Not long after his arrival in Charing Menlove consulted a psychiatrist* as

* Probably Crichton-Miller.

to his fitness to continue practising medicine. The latter's reply, dated 28 April 1945, is of great interest:

> I am sorry to hear you are feeling tied-up. What you say about yourself is a common finding in many people. I suppose it is due to the fact that activity engendered by a focused plan such as you had on coming to London hides underlying tensions and so the individual is not "ripe" if he happens to start an analytical process synchronously. One might even say that if an analytical process were posited as part of the plan being posited by other, it would be resisted (unconsciously) by the individual. Subsequently, as you say, frustrations from within and without bring about a recrudescence of anxiety through the slowing down of the activity.
>
> I think that any "basic" anxiety is not a barrier to psychotherapy being practised by that individual for cases that do not need a deep analysis. But I think that it causes a mounting up of the basic anxiety, because one is a kind of "stooge" to get out the anxiety in one's patients.
>
> The homosexual content is a nuisance if it is coming out *unconsciously*, because it is allowing deep self-preservative aggressive impulses to canalise. If one is aware of the H S content and *suppresses* it, the aggressive-self-preservative impulses are not canalising unless one's plan is going well. And no plan goes well unless the feeling and emotional life are getting a sufficiently good expression.
>
> Here we come to the crux of the matter. It is not enough to get an activity that satisfies *only* in one's worklife; one wants the capacity to *enjoy* life in one's non-working life as a counter-balance. And this means object-relationships that include both emotional feeling and the sexual urges; this combination either as heterosexual relationships or as H S relationships in which the feeling and the sex act together for an object. But you are not an invert so you cannot do this in an H S manner satisfactorily. On the other hand you cannot do it satisfactorily in a heterosexual manner because of some inhibition of your emotional life.
>
> As a result you have the kind of ruminating, fretting anxiety in the mental realm. I think there are a lot of reaction traits which are always a difficulty because they cover the *wanting* tiny self by a *non-wanting* attitude to life.
>
> If you are feeling anxious it is quite likely that you might get something now from a spell of analysis that you could not get before. What you have to focus is: Am I getting enough out of my non-working life?

Jack Longland's comment on this is apposite: "I think he is covering up essential puzzlement by imprecise assertion." There is certainly little of any substance or integrity in it other than the sub-text of what Menlove chose to tell, and its blend of pomposity, cliché and outdated technical language is quite remarkable. It cannot, however, be completely dismissed for it gives some idea of the masked bewilderment of a traditional psychiatrist when faced with Menlove. It also created a degree of confusion in the mind of the most intelligent reviewer—Francis Keenlyside in the *Alpine Journal*—of *Samson*, in which it was quoted, and this needs to be cleared up. The key line is: "But you are not an invert so you cannot do this in an HS manner satisfactorily." (It is faintly amusing that the psychiatrist cannot bring himself to spell out the unspeakable.)

This is in fact crucial to Menlove's case and its subsequent treatment, and to understand the point we need to consider some erroneous beliefs from early psychiatric theory about homosexuality. This took as its working premise the idea that, by nature, men want sex with women (female homosexuality at this time was barely considered by the presiding patriarchy). In order to explain deviation from this norm, the theory embraced two categories of deviant. One was the invert—the man who was really a woman in a man's body, and who therefore desired the love of, and sexual penetration by, a "real" man. There was also, of course, the pervert—the man who was a man inside a man's body, but who was excited by the dirty, perverse thrill of defying his proper nature, and who desired to do those things by which any decent, sane man would be revolted. (I am grossly simplifying matters here in order to bring out the underlying fact that we are not dealing with objective analysis but with traditional moral value-judgements.)

The theory continues by colluding with the gender-stereotypes in order to further define its categories. Women (or inverts) are coy, subservient, compassionate, diffident, whereas men are adventurous, decisive, dominant. It doesn't take much imagination to see why Menlove, therefore, could not possibly have been an invert, and the extensions from this are quite appalling. Everything inside Menlove told him that he wanted the love of men; all the expertise of psychiatry, which he knew in detail, insisted that it could not be so. The theory to which his profession subscribed asserted that sexual satisfaction was not possible for him, since it could only be achieved between partners of opposite *inherent* gender, and the moral judgement discounted the logical pairing of invert and pervert.

Once Menlove was subjected to psychiatric care, which was obviously at his point of absolute low resistance, the distress he felt in a loveless world would have been exacerbated by his being belaboured with the powerful argument that if the cause of all his sufferings was a useless clinging to perversion, then locating the root of the perversion and exorcizing it should cure not just the homosexuality, but the mental distress and instability too.

The cure was simply the destruction of the homosexual urges, upon which any mental disturbance present in the patient would have been blamed, and every form of coercion, insult and seduction would have been used to achieve it and suppress his homosexual desires. His fight for tolerance was lost. Menlove would have emerged from his treatment as the broken man portrayed between the lines of this psychiatrist's report.

Quite clearly Menlove was not fit to practise medicine or psychiatry, and so he settled into a routine of life at Charing. The summer of 1945 was a fine one. Menlove was given an allotment behind the house, and worked hard to establish a small market garden on it. He was paid a weekly allowance by Hewlett Johnson, which was to be the only regular income for the rest of his life, for this and for general gardening work.

But his work soon became sporadic. Nowell's two young daughters were there as playmates and increasingly he was to be found back with his books and notes. At the beginning of November he wrote to re-establish contact with Alec Keith, and to ask whether he could take up Alec's old offer of seeing his uncle, Sir Arthur Keith. At the end of November he wrote to Alec again:

> 30.11.1945
> Many thanks. Sir Arthur wrote kindly, and I got his letter this morning. Will arrange to go along next week or sometime I hope.
>
> Yes, the work has gone badly. No jobs and my theoretical stuff getting no further. I do not know why: but a long story.
>
> Am now here at my sister's and doing odd spots of gardening . . . am getting paid . . . but want a reasonable job in my own line—naturally. And from other people one reasonably wants open justice and so on—you should know . . .?

Menlove did go to see Alec's uncle, at this time Master of the Buckston Brown Research Institute at Downe, near Bromley in Kent, and gave Alec the following account of the meeting:

> [no date, but before Christmas 1945]
> I saw Sir Arthur yesterday. He seemed to approve of the work well, but offered no actual help; but that one might use his name as having seen and thought good in applications for job or etc. Said he was out of touch but gave no reason. A very nice tea though . . .
>
> I was quite glad to have had the chance of going over the rough outline of the work; and to have seen him, a name only to me before.
>
> Found the way all right and got there much too early, having reckoned

on a much less frequent and short bus drive from Bromley.

Then back here to my sister's. The two children are very attractive: they are both quite young, 3 + and 5 + . . .

Alec supplies the additional information on this meeting, so tenuous in its grasping after any connection which might help, that "Menlove's stuff was not in my uncle's line and he was baffled by it. He was also out of touch with anyone at the Atheneum who might have helped, and was unable to do anything for him." So it went on throughout the winter of 1945/1946: ". . . still no job in my own line. Am gardening and other oddments here rather pleasurably, plus a bit of quiet company. But I suppose I'm not properly a gardener by profession and have not fully got the dodges of it yet." And again: "Am wanting to get my psych. stuff published . . . that of it that is advisable." Mention of climbing could arouse a flicker of interest: ". . . no climbing for a long time now and no visible chance of any. Would like to, though, in various ways."

Noyce wrote to him in the spring of 1946 and a brief correspondence ensued. The first letter from Menlove is dated 2 April:

You say you are anxious to help, and I am very glad of that. One thing you could I know help by telling. Why has your attitude to myself changed in the last two years odd, and what is your present aim, what do you want different in our relationship or in anything else to do with me: that you should act so. It seems to me that these things are best done with fullest explanation, done openly.

Then too a little before (after?) Easter two years ago your father (you would know of him) wrote that I would find myself in deep water for various reasons. (Not all he said, nor he alone changed attitude.) Various other things happened, very numerous, but I am very unsure of their significance. You would clearly have known of some at least of these things. Anything of the truth about them would be very good, so that something of the rottenness would fall off from myself, and my work, from you and any others that have, intending right or wrong, blackened themselves in the situation that was made about me. The good could be retained and bettered.

If you will help so you could then surely help more also.

Again some seemed to know something perhaps of my psychiatric work, but I do not know who or to what extent.

So if you wish to help you certainly can. You yourself are normally so much *not* regardless of honesty, *not* gym-crack etc., in your ways, not second-rate in preference: as that situation has been. For myself I'm glad I kept in a sense a diary of the years before '44 in writings. By far the bulk of it in my day to day "psychology". Tendencies of those years are I think fairly largely verifiable: the things one meant more deeply and the things more conversationally etc.

Will try to give my side of anything if you wish to know any points concerned.

If you're acting as part voluntary devil's advocate I could wish you better employment, and with honesty. A rotten situation again.

The loss of the "diary of the years before '44" is lamentable—almost certainly its "writings" would have been amongst those destroyed after Menlove's death and the Rodney Street jottings were probably surviving fragments of it. The other interesting detail in this letter is the question of what passed between Frank Noyce (Wilfrid's father) and Menlove at Easter 1944. Why would Menlove have found himself "in deep water for various reasons"? (The question can only be answered by surmise, and the mental state revealed in this letter should be held in view.)

In a letter to another friend, written at the same period, Menlove is calmer but reveals similar preoccupations and suspicions:

There; that's about the first letter I've written on the subject for a long time that wasn't to the background of a furiously bad temper at the unfortunate turn events had taken and at the continuous pinpricks received without having any idea why or for what. What I really want is a research job, to try to work out my stuff. As regards fitness for work, it seems to me analogous to being fit for fresh air if one is suffering from carbon monoxide fumes . . . some previous attempts to get work all came to nothing. Deliberate lies told I think. I don't know why . . .

Has my homosexuality anything to do with it . . .? or politics . . .? The most people around are just very nice as always, but presumably have little knowledge or say in events.

Noyce replied to Menlove's letter of 2 April without any long delay, and Menlove wrote back on 16 April 1946:

Very glad you have a chance for the poems. Would like to know any details.

Sorry though that you did not help in the other way. Dotty, yes, but that leaves the ethical and other aspects insufficiently characterised. But many other things too were said. I do not know the significances.

Going to Harrison's Rocks tomorrow. All week I have been hoping for a spot of rain for the garden, but now am praying for fine again, that the rocks of Harrison be not wet. Will go by bus, and am hoping that the journey proves an easy one, not too awkward connections and easy for repeat visits.

GWY? As concerned in the poems' chance? Many thanks to him if so.

Would like to have the chance of talking these things over in an honest situation. So much more use all round.

Paul Work went with him from Charing to Harrison's and, to contradict the psychiatrist's report of the previous April, recounts that he was "not at all surprised . . . when in 1946 on the way from Charing to Harrison's Rocks he mentioned casually that he was homosexual. To my earlier question, had he ever thought of getting married, his only reply was: 'I couldn't I'm impotent!'"

The opportunity for the poems mentioned in the letter to Noyce was created by Winthrop Young, and also by Jack Longland. The latter had sent copies to Michael Roberts, the mountaineer, poet, anthologist and critic, to ask his opinion on whether or not they would interest a publisher. Roberts' comments were cautiously favourable:

> I like the rhythms, and in the best of them (which seem to me those dealing most closely with climbing, or making most choice of climbing imagery) there is a memorable choice of words. Half a dozen of them I would like to have by me to re-read when I feel inclined, and that's a good ration for any book . . . a publisher isn't concerned with kindness to an individual, and he knows that a genuine poet will go on stumbling along his rocky road however barefoot he may be. I'm not a publisher's reader, and so my word is nothing more than a personal impression. I can only repeat that I've been glad to read the poems, that I feel there's a good quality of mind behind them, and that I hope one day to get to know that mind better.

Winthrop Young had sent his copies to Hugh Kingsmill Lunn, the rather old-fashioned editor at the *New English Review*, and his opinion was terse, but also favourable:

> I agree with you that the poems are very interesting. I don't think they are sufficiently clarified, but that is natural in the circumstances, and after all it is very rare to meet with poetry that is both clear and intense.

Lunn accepted three of the most Tennysonian poems, and Menlove duly received a cheque to eke out his slender income from gardening.

The Deanery in Canterbury was repaired and ready to live in again by June 1946, and Nowell, Hewlett, and their daughters moved back in. The question of where Menlove should live arose. It was impracticable, because of his gardening, for him to go to Canterbury, but the house at Charing was too large, too expensive to heat and too lonely for him to occupy alone. Nowell thus invited Menlove's mother and his father's sister, Aunt Lornie, to live with him there. So Menlove and the two old ladies continued in residence, Nowell visiting them weekly and Menlove busying himself about his gardening. His psychological work continued to obsess him: "I've tried a number of avenues to research work but they too have failed without giving reason and whilst urging that it was worth continuing. So a foolish situation has been contributed to by many very honourable hands." He applied for work lecturing on psychology to the local WEA, but nothing came of it. And so it went on. A fretful resignation started to come over him:

A very comfortable home here with my mother. Working in the garden quite a bit of the time. I had been doing a little psychological work of a mild sort, in respect of getting out older stuff into rather better shape.

Then lately was getting to another part of the work and found it becoming more complex than I think I should wisely tackle; so I've dropped it.

. . . one cannot do more than one can, likewise one thinks more or less what one thinks till one thinks otherwise and on the data available to one: even though very unsatisfactorily.

In the spring of 1947 he went again to Harrison's Rocks, to meet John Barford and Nea Morin there. Harrison's at that time, in contrast to the present day, was an idyllic place. Unmarked and largely unexplored buttresses of warm red rock rose from the green turf of a bluebell wood. A small, friendly group of habitués were the only persons to be seen.

Nea's impression of Menlove's climbing was one of dominant strength— an ability to grapple, seemingly for hours, with problems, trying every conceivable method of ascent and combination of holds until finally, almost inevitably, he would arrive at the top. On this day at Harrison's Nea remembers him wearing an old open-necked rugby shirt (many climbers then still wore a tie) which revealed a pronounced goitre he had developed since they last met. A photograph shows him wrestling with Slim Finger Crack—still quite a hard and strenuous climb. The crown of his head is bald now, but the muscles of his shoulders stand out powerfully as he forces his way up the awkward, overhanging crack. Another climb he did on the same day was the first ascent of Edwards' Effort on the Isolated Block (now regarded as a classic amongst the older hard routes of the outcrop), which nobody else could manage.

The whole family took a holiday in Harlech at Easter 1947. Nowell remembers walking with Menlove past a group of young climbers in Beddgelert and their ceasing conversation to gaze with evident awe at him, dressed in the immediately recognizable insignia of his old Fettes school blazer, now tattered and patched, faded with age and shapeless from hard treatment.

Menlove was more relaxed than he had been for several years, and in the warm summer of 1947 spent a further holiday with his sister and family in Harlech. It passed in the traditional Edwards family style. They had a boat which they took for little excursions along the coast, landing at places like Shell Island to bathe and then build a fire to warm themselves, boil a kettle, cook sausages and bury potatoes in the embers, before rowing home in the evening, the tired children clutching their booty of many-coloured and grotesquely-shaped shells. On other days the family walked up on to the plateau between the Rhinogs and the sea, or into the valleys of Nantcol or Artro to picnic and idle away the hours amongst the mossy boulders and oakwoods, or by delightful bridges across the streams.

At the end of the holiday Menlove took himself off to Helyg for a week with the possibility of climbing in mind. Michael Ward, a young medical student later to go on the 1953 Everest expedition, gives his account:

I looked into the hut at Helyg and saw a short, thick-set, broad-shouldered and immensely muscular man, with brown curls on a balding head, sitting in the kitchen. He wore an open-necked rugger-shirt, and was finishing his breakfast. It was a warm, sunny day and whilst I cooked myself some food we started talking. He had a hesitant manner and talk did not come easily to him. When he had finished washing up his plates and pans he sat down across the bare wood table writing up the log book. Being British we had naturally not introduced ourselves and had in fact only communicated in a gruff, monosyllabic way.

I glanced at his writing—even upside down I recognised the spidery scrawl of the legendary Menlove Edwards:

"Are you by yourself?" I asked him.

"Yes," he replied, "but I'm only lazing about and letting time go by for a day or two."

"Are you still climbing?" I asked.

"Oh, yes. On and off."

As we had by then introduced ourselves, I asked him if he would climb with me during the next day or so.

"Well, I'll certainly try," he said, "but let's have some more food." By then it was lunchtime . . .

Menlove and Nea Morin attempting what is now Sickle, on Clogwyn y Grochan, 1941

Menlove on Slimfinger Crack, Harrison's rocks, 1947

The last known photo of Menlove. With Nowell and her family on the beach at Harlech, 1947

Little By Little, Helsby   Jim Perrin

Pigeon Hole Wall, Helsby   Jim Perrin

Hafod Owen   Jim Perrin

Ward notes that Menlove "certainly showed no particular evidence of mental illness", before going on to describe the climbs they did together: "For the first two days we climbed in the Idwal Valley where I did an extremely difficult new route on a group of cliffs called Grey Wall."

(This is slightly exaggerated. What he and Menlove did was a new and very much more difficult start to the latter's 1932 route, Procrastination Cracks. It was probably the hardest slab pitch in Wales to that date.) "We then decided to do a new route on Cloggy. The night before I slept only fitfully as I was tightly wound up, thinking of the moves that I would make."

The next day, 9 August, they brisked over to Clogwyn Du'r Arddu and set about the start of what was then known as the Concrete Slab, and is now White Slab. They failed (the first ascent was made by Ron Moseley and Morty Smith nine years later) and a little disheartened sought consolation on Longland's Climb, which Ward had not done before. He takes up the account from their arrival at the Crevassed Stance, 400 feet up the cliff:

"Why don't we continue up the slab proper?" I asked Menlove. The named route went diagonally right, up a steep crack. "Has anyone done that?" He peered round a corner to the left and looked at the final piece of slab. "I don't remember even thinking about it. Why don't you have a look?" I changed places with him. This true continuation of Longland's Slab was narrower, steeper and fiercer than the lower part, and was covered with loose rock. It was also fantastically airy and exposed, even for Cloggy. "I can hold an elephant from here," I heard Menlove say.

Ward made a fine lead of what, although inferior to Longland's original finish, is a difficult and impressively exposed pitch, and Menlove congratulated him on it as he arrived at the top. His old ability to encourage and give confidence to eager young climbers, and his reticence at pushing his own claims to leadership forward were still there, just as they had been ten years before when he had climbed with Noyce.

The family's confidence in, and hopes for, Menlove's recovery was now growing. His work was still tacitly not a subject for conversation, but he would talk freely and easily with Nowell upon a wide range of other subjects. Literature was a frequent topic of discussion between them and Nowell observed that he particularly enjoyed Rilke's "Sonnets to Orpheus" (understandably—Rilke was well-acquainted with alienation and terror, as well as with the "innate symbolisms of life"), and also Pound's "Cantos" (with Pound, too, he could find parallels to his own career). The thirties' poets, Auden, Spender, Day-Lewis and MacNeice, were apt to disturb him into political haranguing and to dwell on social injustice, with the underlying sense of the injustice which had been done to him. But there was refuge in discussion of Old Norse saga-literature, to which he returned with a deeper attention and affection in these years; and in music, where his taste was chiefly Romantic, centring on Beethoven and Brahms.

In the autumn of 1947, with Menlove seemingly in a stable condition, arrangements were made for him to work at an Outward Bound school in the Lake District. He stayed at the Deanery for a night before catching the train for Cumberland. Nowell recalls waving to him as he walked down the drive, and feeling full of hope that at last the balance was changing and fortune's wheel on the up-turn again. The next evening she glanced out of the window to see him shambling back up the drive; after years of isolation, he had been unable to face the proximity of youth and his fellow men.

So the years run on. June 1948 found him writing to Alec Keith:

5.6.1948

Writing to you partly as not having written for very long and partly because I've just been looking at an advert for a psychiatrist at the Victoria Infirmary [Glasgow—where Alec was Registrar and Consultant Orthopaedic Surgeon at the time] and was wondering whether or not it might even be the slightest use applying for it? Not having any idea what's been happening so far as my own status is concerned for four years now and having had no explanation of anything that has happened. I don't know what might or might not be worth doing towards this or that end. Though obviously one wants to get out of the really disgusting situation of these last years! From their attitude one gathers that they have been told a great many lies about me—or at least some important lies; and similarly perhaps I about them. Since I lost the London job I've had no other, despite some efforts to do so and consequently am getting badly out of things. There's no hope of keeping up technical reading under present circumstances, and still less of getting on with what I think is important theoretical work. Seems a pity.

That his condition was outwardly more composed is revealed by comments later in the same letter, although even here there is some confusion of thought:

I went to the doctor I was under at Great Ormond Street Hospital however and she said she would try to get me part time work nearer home. So will see what comes of that, and am not putting in for the Vic. job therefore.

There was a measure of guilt and remorse, too, along with the continuing paranoia.

> ... it may be also that a lot of people may have been trying their best to help me. I've been unable to tell what the background intentions were, not knowing what has happened, so mostly have been simply unable to tell who was trying to help or not, and who rightly or wrongly. So I may have hurt people who were trying to help. In which case a thousand apologies must be due though I dislike the whole thing and it seems to me a dirty business, from what I've seen in all—*many* misunderstandings *maybe* I think? But I do *not* want to wrong people in mere ignorance of what they have done: perhaps greatly helping me: where thanks might be very much due. Work nearer here, if it's forthcoming, would really suit one better. My mother has had a *very* messy time of it these years and I must look after her. She has bad rheumatics, and has always longed for the south.

The summer of 1948 was a poor one. Menlove spent a month in Harlech: "Got over to Helyg for one night but did not climb. It rained solidly the whole of that day! Had hardly intended climbing anyhow." In the October Helen Edwards had a heart attack and was very seriously ill for four months. When she finally returned to Charing she was deeply depressed. The atmosphere of the house—never very good, for relations between Menlove's mother and aunt were not cordial—worsened. Hewlett Johnson, himself tired and overworked, took Nowell away to Italy on holiday in June 1949, the two old ladies went to the Deanery and Menlove, left alone, travelled up to North Wales to stay for a while at Helyg. He made three more new routes to add to his tally on Gallt yr Ogof before moving over to the newly acquired and renovated Climbers' Club property of Ynys Ettws, in the narrower confines of the Llanberis Pass. Roy Beard, custodian of the hut, joined him there and together they climbed Central Gully on Clogwyn y Grochan, one of the least popular routes on what, since Barford's guidebook of that name was published, have come to be known as the "three cliffs of Llanberis". (This despite the fact that even on the most illiberal count there are four of them.)

Their old Liverpool friend Brian McKenna, with whom Menlove had wrestled in the ill-tempered bout of Helyg before the war, joined them after Central Gully and on subsequent days they did little, the most strenuous activity being a walk over to Llechog, the unjustly-neglected cliff high up in Cwm Clogwyn which had hardly been visited since Archer Thomson's exploration in 1910. After a single route, they "indulged in one of Menlove's swimming orgies", of which Menlove had to say, "the lake nearest the cliff is very deep, as good for bathes as any I know round here".

By this time Nowell had returned from Italy and was at Harlech with her children, so Menlove joined her there. On one day, as they were walking up Moelfre, a grassy little outlier of the Rhinogs, Menlove detached himself from the family group and walked ahead. When they came up with him a few minutes later his features were contorted with rage and he mouthed violently against those who had brought him into his predicament. The children were frightened and Nowell tried to reason with him. A trial of will ensued, and she sent Menlove down off the mountain. They continued to the summit, and on their return home found that Menlove had prepared tea and was in a settled, amicable mood, quite oblivious to anything having happened.

The holiday rather soured by the incident and Nowell now less prepared to entrust him with the children, Menlove took himself off to Ynys Ettws again for a few days at the end of July. He did one important new climb— Rift Wall on Craig Ddu, in company with Frank Monkhouse, Geography lecturer at Liverpool University,* and on this he used slings and karabiners as running belays for the first time. The crux of the route is a very strenuous corner crack, which still puts the climb amongst the top dozen of its grade—Very Severe—in the latest Llanberis guidebook's classified list. Menlove thought it "perhaps just into the Severes". (Joe Brown climbed the same line three years later and, thinking it new, called it Anthropology. It rapidly became very popular.)

Apart from a lone venture on to the basaltic sills of Esgair Ffynnon, his climbing on this visit was restricted to Craig Ddu and Clogwyn y Grochan, at the lower end of the Llanberis Pass: "This really dreadful excess of attention ... to the exclusion of other cliffs in the neighbourhood requires some apology. Only excuse is that I was mainly trying to get in some bits of reading."

He was back home in Charing for most of August, and working again at his gardening, but the friction between the two old ladies in the house had grown even more marked, and at the end of October Menlove once more went up to Wales, ostensibly to look for a job. The weather was dismal, rain drifting in grey columns up the Llanberis Pass. He stayed at Cwm Glas Cottage, set in a hollow between ice-scratched bluffs on the marshy hillside opposite Clogwyn y Grochan, and very recently bought by the Climbers' Club as their third property in North Wales. Even today, with electric lighting, the cottage is gloomy, its bare walls and tiled floor making it cold and damp. If houses can be said to have atmospheres, this one's is not of the happiest. I have stayed there alone myself and felt unnerved and depressed

---

* And in my schooldays author of almost every Geography text-book used.

by the place. A group of Sandhurst cadets, arriving a few days after Menlove, found him in the bedroom at the rear of the cottage. He was in a coma, suffering from a drug overdose. The cadets ran to Ynys Ettws, half a mile away, and Roy Beard and Peter Hodgkinson came back with them. Menlove was taken by ambulance to the Caernarfon and Anglesey Hospital in Bangor, where his stomach was pumped and he was given oxygen. He revived, and struggled so powerfully that two men were hardly strong enough to restrain him. Stephen was sent for and came immediately from Staindrop. The police had to be notified too, and questioned him. The young doctor who was looking after his case asked if he would go voluntarily to Gwynfryn, the nearest mental hospital at Denbigh, or whether he would have to be committed, in which case it would be harder for him to get out. He argued and refused and was certified and taken away, to spend the next four months at Gwynfryn:

17.1.1950
I was brought in here while still semi-unconscious from a supposed attempt at suicide, and they unfortunately had me certified on that score, so I've been pretty much under their thumb, and no say at all in the matter of the treatment they wish to apply, which has been a rather vicious and long course of deep Insulin.*

Apart from the insulin, he was given electro-convulsive therapy. He was very sceptical, but resigned to everything the staff at the hospital were trying to do for him. Knowing that he was a doctor, they explained its supposed effects, and he accepted without argument. He was allowed to walk in the wintry lanes outside the hospital grounds, and given as much as he wanted to eat. Roy Beard visited him there, taking his young son along, and Menlove produced a seemingly endless supply of chocolate bars from his pocket. The goitre was by now very pronounced, he put on weight, the edges of his mouth puckered with an incessant bitter smile. He took his being in the hospital as further proof of the conspiracy by his friends or society to do him down.

On his discharge in February, the physician in whose care he had been wrote to tell Nowell that he had suffered irreparable brain damage, and that sooner or later his suicide was inevitable. She had to live with that knowledge for another eight years.

His first six weeks away from Denbigh were spent with Paul Work, who

---

* Insulin was used at this time to put the patient into a deep coma ("Insulin-induced Hypoglycaemia") which was thought to have a beneficial effect in the treatment of schizophrenia.

was farming at Carneddi in Nantmor, close to Hafod Owen where Menlove had lived for his solitary year in the war. Weak after the sessions of "therapy" (the definition of therapy is "curative medical treatment"), he could still move a boulder which weighed half a ton off the drive and up a hillside by himself and with no more assistance than that offered by a crowbar. And they went climbing:

> ... he was still muttering violent denunciations of [his former medical colleagues in London] to himself in between perfectly sane conversation with myself as I was taking in the rope while he came up the last pitch of Christmas Buttress on Moel Dyniewyd.

Drugged into relative stability, he returned to Charing and the frictions of that situation. They were not to continue long. In the early spring of 1951 his aunt had a stroke and died, and his mother once more went to live with Stephen:

> It's really better for mother to be with my brother at the moment I think, and better for me to be on my own: means too that I can get a wee bit of work done besides the gardening, though nothing much nor serious.
> Once a fortnight I go to Ashford Chess Club for a game: am not any good at it but it's good fun and brings one into their company to that extent.

He got away climbing occasionally: to the Lake District for a weekend in 1950, and twice to Wales in 1951. On the second of these latter visits, he climbed with Rudolf Loewy, who gives the following description of what they did, and in doing so gives a glimpse into the feelings of the ordinarily-talented climbers with whom Menlove often chose to keep company:

> I had gone to meet him at Ynys Ettws on the Saturday afternoon, and on the Sunday we strolled casually across the road and down the Pass a little to Clogwyn y Grochan. Menlove picked a crack that led up the cliff and found a way up. I followed but soon found I could not make one move. I tried, came back, rested, tried again and came back again, crestfallen—not so much at my inability to make the move as at the thought that I was spoiling Menlove's climb for him, right at the start. This so spurred me on that I made a third attempt and succeeded ...
> On the second pitch I came off. Menlove held me, but it seemed obviously the end of the climb for me. A pity, I thought, but I had tried. So, with regret, I called up to him to let me down.

"Try and get on again," he called down. That had never occurred to me as possible! So I did try, and after a lot of effort I succeeded in getting on again and we completed that climb also.

Later, in thinking about Menlove and climbing, I saw the incident as an example of how an outstanding climber can inspire others to excel themselves and make moves which they thought were beyond them. It is a grateful memory, supported by a brief correspondence on other things, seeking to encourage him when he was at a low ebb.

(The pitches done by Menlove and Loewy were the Very Severe direct variations on Central Gully.)

Wales was the venue for climbing again in 1952, in which year he had perhaps the best of his later climbing holidays. Roy Beard was his companion:

… my wife and I arranged to go and pick him up somewhere near Penrhyndeudraeth. We started late and just before we got into Penrhyndeudraeth something which appeared to be the biggest rucksack in the whole of North Wales was seen approaching under a body bent almost double: it was Menlove, carrying as usual everything he could lay his hands on, or nothing at all; in this case it was everything. We bundled him into the car.

I had always wanted to climb on the East Buttress of Y Garn, above Rhyd Ddu. I don't think that it really interested Menlove that he should do this, but he came there and we climbed it together. Beautiful sunshine and real old-fashioned mountaineering which appealed to me and still appeals to me if I can ever get the energy to do it. After that we went down to Lockwood's Chimney. To the left of this there is a climb which I have always known as "Kirkus's Climb", but I think that is probably not the correct name for it; [Beard is quite right: the route, climbed by Tilby and Reade in 1934, is called Forest Wall.] It is steep, pleasant and I think, or used to think, quite difficult. Menlove of course had done this, so the inevitable thing was for him to find a direct route and this he did. I tried his route but even with help from him could not do it. We did a lot of other good things in that short time together, all in good weather, all with great fun.

There is an entry in the Ynys Ettws logbook which is, although closely modelled on a famous passage from Joyce's *Ulysses*, redolent of the old Menlove in its humour and some of its style, although it is perhaps unnecessarily unkind to his companion. It describes Beard's attempts to second the Very Severe route Fallen Block Crack, on Clogwyn y Ddisgl:

On the FB Crack the hon. custodian of this hon. hut nobly seconded No 1, wedged massive in crack on slight hold: then following, accosted the steep bit, mounted inch by inch, struggled heroic, horrible to look upon, long time, then movement upward ceased, movement downward inexorable began to supervene, and eventually brought him to the stance again. He took off several layers of clothes and sent them up on the rope: No 1 got to the final ledge and tied by double rope, with legs secure in a place where the greatest possible leverage could be exerted. Hon. Custodian then accosted the steep bit again. He mounted inch by inch, then came struggles, longer, more heroic if possible, more horrible to look upon than the first. No 1 heaved with all the force at his command. Then movement upward ceased, movement downward exorable began to supervene, and some time afterwards brought him to where he stood, dejected, massive, symbolic, with the Fallen Block.

Roy Beard having gone home to Shrewsbury, Menlove teamed up with a London climber, Courtney Bryson, whom he had met at Harrison's on occasions and, in the same week as Beard's valiant efforts on Fallen Block Crack, once more made the long slog up to the foot of Clogwyn y Ddisgl, high above upper Cwm Glas. The route he and Bryson climbed took the rib and wall on the right of Fallen Block Crack. He named it Route of Knobs, and graded it Mild Severe, from a conviction that no one of his age could climb anything beyond that standard. When Joe Brown made what was probably the second ascent, nineteen years later, his impression was: "serious, unprotected, and sustained. The crux is a really unnerving move and the standard is at least Hard Very Severe."

Whilst Menlove had been away Nowell and Hewlett had applied to the Medical Officer of Health in Maidstone for permission to convert a tiny two-roomed farm-labourer's cottage in a field in front of the house at Charing, and on the very top of the downs, into living accommodation for him. Initially they were refused, but after visiting the Mental Health Officer, whom they found sympathetic because of the similar plight of his brother, the request was allowed on the written undertaking that it would never be let or sold for the use of any other person. The house was closed up, the cottage converted, given a name—"The Mead"—and in the autumn Menlove moved into it. Menlove wrote to Alec Keith in December to send him the new address and tell of his activities:

Managed to get two weeks in Wales this August and had great fun. The standard has gone up enormously of course since the war. A most impressive lot of new climbs on Clogwyn Du'r Arddu, as you will probably know.

Have not (done of course or even—) been taken up any of them; hopeful to be so some day on a strong enough rope.

Am settled in to my little "house" now. Two rooms 11 ft by 13 ft each, plus a few inches. Most of my work books and papers have had to be put in store in a deanery attic but just for living purposes it might be a great deal worse. I garden in the morning to add up a living and do what reading is available in the rest of the day. Visit out now and then for a game of chess.

An outing to Eridge Green Rocks near Tunbridge Wells in the spring of 1953, where he met Nea Morin and spent an entertaining day tussling with the problems of Eridge Tower and Amphitheatre Crack, or lying amongst the bluebells at the foot talking with other climbers, brought an invitation to him to accompany Nea to Cornwall at Whit. He seemed disinclined to accept, but Nea applied her arts of persuasion and he finally agreed. They set off for Bosigran from Nea's home in Tunbridge Wells one day late in May. Norman Albon, a lecturer at University College, London, was driving and throughout the journey Menlove was on edge, continually making comments, warning him of the dangers, insisting that he slow down. Others of the party were at the Count House, the Bosigran cottage of the Climbers' Club, by the time they arrived and Nea sensed almost immediately that her gambit to draw Menlove out of his isolation was not to be a success. The place was filled with young, laughing people. Menlove shrank into himself, refused to eat with the party, retreated into a corner with his own food and complained about the people crowding round him.

The first morning's climbing was on Bosigran Face. Menlove led Nea and Albon up a new and quite fierce start to Doorway: "perhaps leftish of correct route . . . How should one know?" Wearing a new pair of *kletterschuhe* he made the pitch, over a square-cut block overhang, look deceptively easy. At the top he was short of rope and used the most inadequate of belays. Nea followed with some difficulty, fearing to fall off lest she should pull him off his stance. She took him on a subsequent day to Chair Ladder, the castle-like cliff on the south coast of West Penwith, and showed him a steep chimney-crack on a facet wall which she had previously climbed on a rope but failed to lead. He led it effortlessly and mischievously suggested for it the name "Nearly".

Charles Marriott, whom Menlove had known before the war, joined him for a day's climbing thereafter, and whilst Nea and Norman Albon climbed on Fox Promontory, they went to Carn Les Boel and climbed a new variation to a route there before going into the back of the cliff-bound Folly Cove just as the tide was turning to come back in. They attempted a line up the back wall, but at rather more than half-height came across "a deployment of falsity in the rock so massive as to be fit almost to prop up a fascist". The tide had cut off their retreat and Nea, watching from the cliff-top, saw them strip, tie their clothes into bundles, and swim for it in a choppy sea. Marriott was amused by the incident: "Getting out of Folly Cove two hours after the turn of the tide emphasizes the reason for its name." But Menlove's reaction was morose.

The wind rose that night, blowing hard around the Count House, rattling windows and gusting smoke down the chimney. The morning dawned grey, squalls of rain driving in off the Atlantic and a heavy sea running. Menlove, Nea, and Albon set off down the path to Porthmoina Cove, but where the paths diverge, one going over the Commando Ridge and the other across to the Main Face of Bosigran, Menlove decided that he wanted to go over to the Rosemergy Ridge area, on the far side of Commando Ridge, to climb the Very Severe Window Buttress. Nea and Albon looked at him askance, knowing that with big seas running the base of the buttress would be washed by great waves. Menlove grew irritable and stormed away from them to do the climb by himself, leaving the others with the enigmatic and evidently annoyed remark that "two climbers are better than one".

The party broke up next day and returned home. At the end of an even more strained journey than the outward one, Menlove was found to have no money to pay a contribution towards the cost of the petrol. Nea paid Albon for him, but it was an embarrassing scene.

He returned for a visit to Wales in August, climbing the Upper Slab in Cwm Silyn with Roy Beard and his son, but his mind was again painfully disturbed. After Beard's departure he stayed on by himself at Ynys Ettws. It rained. He walked over to Helyg to find company, found it, but still it rained. He failed, in the rain, to repeat his own route, Rift Wall, and at the end of the week wrote in the Ynys Ettws hut book:

> . . . a few days here alone. Disastrous to much ambitions for climbing, but otherwise not wholly unwelcome to one whose personal position, despite (?) the efforts of some individuals and despite (?) powerful injections of quite other material, is still in the main, these nine and a half years, dishonourable and dirty.* Not, it seems safe to say, by his own actions. To use mild phrases.

(The very precise time mentioned here is curious, for the only other detail we have which refers to that time—round about February/March 1944—is in the 1946 letter to Noyce, in which he says "a little before Easter two years

---

* The frequency of this adjective's occurrence in the last letters is very notable.

ago your father ... wrote that I would find myself in deep water for various reasons ..." His last letter to Noyce [see below] also hints at an awkward situation having developed at this time.) The present note continues:

> One wonders, sitting in the climbing hut of a climbers' club; is it really necessary for so many climbers and others to tell so many lies; is it necessary indeed in this instance to tell any; is it quite idle in these hills to look for moral courage; or even ordinary moral decency. Even in this.

If the *questions* posed here are essentially "mad", of which I am not convinced, they are of quite a different type of madness to the outpourings and endlessly circular questionings of the years since 1944. Because what they express is not so much the delusional system of paranoia, but rather a moral outrage at people's behaviour, which *stems* from a personal sense of injury but seems to work out from that rather than turning in as previously. (It is a direction and manner of feeling, a savage unfocused indignation reminiscent of Swift, which grows increasingly intense in Menlove's last years, and which has a curiously coherent and logical quality about it, as though the ideals and aspirations for which he struggled before his illness were now, beyond hope, reasserting themselves, shrilling and rattling around in the patched and ruined vessel which had formerly contained them, and which their power had ultimately shattered.)

Sometimes his bitterness and feelings of futility fastened upon specific objects:

> 26.12.1953
>
> Wilfrid Noyce did seem to do very well on Everest—"seems", a poor way to put it but arising from fact that I've not really heard a lot about it and am more vague than should be. Yes, have heard from him—but—present circumstances don't mix much as so far used, with anything like friendship, I fear—too much like trying to house a nest of rats alongside the food in your larder. I gather he suggested the Climbers' Club Hon. Mem. business—very decent.

(Menlove was made an honorary member of the Climbers' Club in 1953.)

He was now beginning more and more frequently to look back to his earlier years. Almost any association would set a train of nostalgia into motion. Mention of Glasgow made him think "how *very* dreadful it is to motor-bike through in the winter". When the subject of Fettes came up in correspondence between himself and Alec, it inspired these thoughts:

10.1.1954

Been thinking quite a lot about old Fettes since you wrote. An odd business always, growing older, and remembering this and that amount of the journey ... Thought it had a good general cast of thought in, particularly, a number of ways. And the "foundation" a very good effort towards equality of opportunity, for its period ... And so on and so on: could run on for almost ever: so had better not.

Another letter, from just after Christmas 1954, takes up from the same theme:

28.12.1954

Wonder if you will send any of yours to Fettes as their time comes? Went back once with Pinkerton—also at Liverpool University—and was glad to have done so. Asher must be getting on in years surely now. Can't imagine Lodge with a beard at all: should have thought quite the wrong figure for such an extra, but you never know ... There would be not many one would recognise straight off.

Down here seems a bit of a distance from all that. I sometimes fear it's just about the furthest place in the country from anywhere.

And Morar: know the bay on the coast, and have had one look up the loch itself ... Hope it may be possible to get up those ways again some day. Though it always did mystify me how on a family holiday up there people managed to survive the cold of bathing.

Also some memories come to think of it of what very long walks.

Nothing much happening here. A bit of gardening, woodcutting, a lot of foolishness. My work nowhere.

Quite a large part of the roof blew off just before Christmas. We got some corrugated iron over it and a tarpaulin, to hold over the holiday, until we can get repair materials. Bit of a nuisance, but the weather has been unusually good since.

Got to Wales for a week: *very* wet. Wee bit of climbing earlier on at practice rocks. Perhaps a bit more chance next year. One can but hope, and of course do what one can. Have heard it said that before now it has happened that this or that tide has turned if the moon continued its pulling. So perhaps one may take it as an omen for other things without being necessarily wrong.

I do *very* seriously think though that the propaganda situation that has put up round me is very filthy: and of course towards myself is that and quite unjust in a great many ways. I keep on saying these things because my opinion has been so much misrepresented. And take the risk of boring you, though not really wanting to do that.

I do very much hope things will go on OK with you and all the family. Rather nice to think of; working steadily and home growing. Hope it goes well—

Best wishes

Menlove.

The qualities of splintered insight and shattered logic which became evident at this time and which suggest, but do not attain, coherence crop up with particular strength in a letter from January 1955. (Why this time of year should have been so productive of trouble in Menlove is another issue which is notable but, as a question, insoluble.)

Have been doing an extra job these last two months, felling trees in a wood for a timber merchant here, and it leaves me considerably extra soggy in mind; as also I've not been doing any (at all worth while) mental work for a long time now—curse it—though my capacities *should* be just at their best for that sort of thing; caught up in this silly piece of dirty idiotics, that this country has put up round me, and which has turned everything it touches round me to so much mere dirty hypocrisy or outright filth.

Though always there are some who manage to find and to show somehow, however ineffectually—in this case—some element of decency; and those further from myself and from immediacy round my situation have been less corrupted by it, in general, I think.

Have been able in it to help quite a few, but they have returned to me only a continuance of evil. Had thought that England could do better than that: indeed it very easily could, very certainly.

Those that have particularly "liberty" on their lips have been foremost to take mine away; and those have particularly the idea of economic fair[ness] have been in the van to leave me without it to the point of wholesale theft.

And so on and so on, through almost any principle of human relations you can mention. The West was anxious perhaps—no great harm in that—and took a dive into a cesspool as part of its response; and a good deal of harm in that, though it has been fairly successful in refusing to talk about the whole incident.

Obviously have not been able to make any useful friendship or co-operation—with groups—in any proper way across a mound of lies like that. Consequently extra glad to keep going anything from former days—if not too corrupted by these things—in the hope it may some day as it so easily could any day, come to ordinary sane usage again.

The habit of wholesale lying and lying implication seems to me a poor thing anyhow, even in the West, and even when it seems not very effective in other ways: even apart from my own situation. It seems to me that democracy shows a very poor face where it dirts itself like this—as soon as the nature of what it is doing becomes at all known. I am not talking of others of the West's actions, but of this.

Seem to find it difficult to say much, across oceans of thick disgust. Have been accustomed to try to speak openly of injustice—or of other events—and that others should do so. What a foul stink the whole thing has.

I would be quite willing to take on trust several of the social criticisms voiced in this letter. "The habit of wholesale lying and lying implication", for example, *does* show a very poor face of democracy and *does* seem to be deeply entrenched, endemic even, in this country's (and America's) process of government. The present Conservative administration is particularly given to the habit and often blatantly so, but I doubt if any government is wholly free from the taint. So how does a man of Menlove's massive integrity respond to such chicanery? In asking this, I am not putting forward the idea that his madness is a form of sanity—the Laingian view—I do not think it is. But in its uncontrolled impotence there is still, in what Menlove writes, an underlying desperate authenticity of response to the conditions imposed by a society which itself is—and I use the word advisedly—psychotic; a society on whose behalf Menlove had attempted to intercede and to the vices of which it is possible to argue that he had become, through their effect on his idealism, a sacrifice—and one made to entirely false gods.

So to the last years. Holidays: in Wales in 1955, where Evelyn Leech (formerly Lowe) met him on top of Tryfan (20 years after the two had climbed together on Drws Nodded). She had just soloed up Grooved Arete and looked down to see Menlove, alone, picking his way up the Very Severe Belle Vue Bastion as if it were the easiest route on the mountain. At the summit they talked. She remembers his conversation as irrational, confused, full of vague, dark references to the way Nea Morin had turned against him and was concerned with *them* in his downfall.

Colin Mortlock remembers a chance meeting with him in the same place at some time in the early to mid-fifties:

One of the earliest recollections of such a lesson [in humility—the passage is from his book *The Adventure Alternative*] was in North Wales as a young climber. I was sitting on the [Belle Vue] Terrace on Tryfan feeling very pleased with myself as I had just led my first Very Severe—Belle Vue Bastion. Climbing in plimsolls, as recommended, I had found the climb somewhat open and exposed but had generally enjoyed it. As we sat enjoying the view what appeared to be a middle-aged, somewhat scruffy figure arrived on the Terrace from the track at the side. Ancient rope draped round his shoulders was matched by an old pair of trousers and an even older pair of ungainly boots. He passed the time of day with us and then, to our utter amazement, he walked to the top of Belle Vue Bastion, and then disappeared down the route. We later discovered that it was J. M. Edwards, who in his prime was one of Britain's finest rock-climbers. His nonchalant performance put our efforts into a more realistic perspective.

Another sketch of him from this period is provided by Liverpool climber Ken Pearson, who was staying by himself at Cwm Glas Cottage when Menlove turned up and suggested a climb. They walked over to Clogwyn y Grochan, opposite, and when they got to the foot of the cliff Menlove, wearing old army ammunition boots without nails, discovered that he had forgotten his rubbers so he asked if Pearson would like to lead. Pearson tied on to Menlove's khaki-coloured old rope and set off up the first pitch. He got to the top, belayed, and took in the rope as Menlove followed. When the latter was nearly at the stance, Pearson came across a great bulge in the rope wrapped about with insulating tape. "What's this?" he asked Menlove. "Well, you remember I was climbing with Noyce on Scafell and he came off?" the reply came back. "This was the rope we were using. A couple of strands broke, but I've spliced them up and I expect it will be all right."

A Cornish holiday in 1957; Peter Biven climbed there with Menlove and describes his "powerful, brooding charisma to match the physique—head hunched into huge shoulders, standing apart from the group. We climbed together on the main face at Bosigran and I've never seen anything to match it for ruthless efficiency: hand on hold, move up." In the Bosigran hut book, after a record of his activities in Porthguarnon Cove ("All about 60 ft. Thought worth recording. For the mild repertory. Rather like Halldrine, but a grade better I think.") he made a comment on the history of the area ("*à propos* a remark by Biven in Journal, CFK was here once seriously, but *not* long. I not at all till in the war, when not intending to climb. District really ninety? Seven percent left out by our lot") and then rounded into an attack probably provoked by Noyce's writing in the book *Snowdon Biography*:

Round me I wish people could recognise dirty prurient sadism, and not call it wine or such. Or pretending that the long, uninterrupted dirty tricks by them to me were really a climb, or such, by me; or that others, not they, were doing them. Or any of the miserable little rabbitries that have served the place of anything else to me.

From Cornwall he drove up on the motorbike he now possessed, paid for by savings from his work for the timber merchant, to North Wales, where he sought out an old friend, Arvon Jones, for a climb. Arvon, a small, voluble Welshman assiduous in manner and with an irrepressible grin, had started life as a cobbler. Climbers who needed their boots nailing took them to his house in Capel Curig (where Ellis Brigham's mountaineering shop now stands) and were entertained to cups of tea and endless anecdotes as Arvon repaired their boots to their individual specifications. He had branched out from that into selling climbing equipment, opened another shop in Bethesda, and in a small way become a successful businessman. He remembers Menlove on this visit sitting by his kitchen fire, talking amicably, then suddenly descending into the muttered denunciations, his whole visage altered by the emotions expressed.

On the day they went out to climb Menlove strode out in front, purposeful and intent, the little cobbler nervously trailing behind, an uneasiness induced in him by the warnings of friends and by Menlove's declared intention of climbing straight up the waterfall in the Devil's Kitchen. It proved quite hard technically at Very Severe; Arvon duly followed and added another story to his string of anecdotes:

We roped up at the bottom. Menlove led off and I belayed beneath a projecting rock, to get away from the spray, but the water still dripped down my neck. He squirmed into the vertical crack down which the stream flows, and fought his way up it, puffing and gasping for breath. I shouted up to him to say I didn't want to do it, but the only reply I got was a bald head and a red face, glowering down from the black, dripping rock, looking like the very devil. Needless to say, he completed the pitch and I too was forced to take the plunge.

This was Menlove's last new climb. He drove home by way of Pembrokeshire, where he spent some days alone climbing and bathing in the St David's area before continuing back to Charing. Near Redhill in Surrey, he suffered an accident. Nowell takes up the story, in a letter to Noyce dated 22 October 1957.

Menlove has had a very bad time since the middle of August when he had the motorcycle smash. He was coming back from Pembrokeshire, and near Redhill came up behind two boys on bikes. One of them suddenly turned in front of the motorbike, Menlove swerved but hit the bike, the little lad of twelve was thrown off his bike and hit his head. He died, soon after. Menlove was unconscious, and came to in the hospital where he was lying next to the dying lad. He says he knew at once that he was dying, and also knew somehow that it was the same accident that had brought him to hospital. But he could remember nothing else, he didn't remember where it was, the road, or the boys; and it is still all a complete blank.

Menlove's arm was badly broken near the shoulder and he had various cuts and grazes. They put him in plaster down to the waist with the arm held out on the level with the shoulder and kept up by a strut. He should have been in hospital some weeks, but persuaded them to let him out after about ten days. Hewlett and I and Keren had been in the Polish Alps, we had come home and gone straight on to Harlech where we heard of the accident on the first day there. I couldn't leave Harlech as my help was ill and I had all the family to feed and look after. However, we arranged various things.

We were all very worried and anxious about this accident, fearing it might be Menlove's fault and wondering what the result would be on him. Mercifully the inquest brought out that it really was the boy's fault—he had seen blackberries he wanted and suddenly turned right across the road.

This was a great relief; we were home by now, and our man took Menlove by car [to the inquest], but I did not go as I feared the possibility of being asked questions abut Menlove in front of him, and having to give answers that would upset him.

Menlove had managed by himself nearly all the time, he wouldn't be helped, not even with meals, but he suffered a lot of pain and discomfort, couldn't sleep with the arm in so difficult a position—it also swelled in the plaster. Then he began to get a bit better, and to potter about the garden. One day he sharpened a sickle somehow and started to trim a hedge; he then had a second horrid accident. He sliced off the back of the hand in plaster, severing the tendons and taking off part of the knuckle bone.

This has caused him very great pain, and he was very poorly with pain and shock. He had to be rushed to hospital. We brought him back here for a day or two, but he wouldn't stay long. Last week he took the plaster off himself—it had cracked, and the support gave way. The arm has healed, but again he had a wretched week; the pain of new positions after two months held rigid, plus the hand which has been slightly septic, swollen, and super-tender. His resistance is low now.

However, over the weekend he was better, and we go over to see him again tomorrow. We still have a tiny flat by his place, and try to go over for a night a week which means I can see him and look after him then. Also Fred Crowe, who's been with my husband since he was a choirboy, is there at week-ends, with his wife who lives at the café, and has been very good to Menlove all this time. Mentally he has been extraordinarily stable this last two months. We have had no trouble, nor has he complained.

Before we have for years had constant mental trouble, and as so often in these cases when things are bad they are worst against those nearest to him. He has often told me, and Hewlett, and Mother, that we are the cause of all his troubles, the loss of his work—and that we all, always, conspire against him. And this, I gather, is what happened in his relations with you, and with Stuart Chantrell?

Noyce had been deeply concerned about Menlove, and had written to Nowell to ask if there was any way in which he could help after the accident. Nowell's advice, such as she was able to give, was this:

I don't know what to advise, I feel myself the only thing is always to go on just being there, someone when he wants someone.

I can't believe that he wouldn't highly value a letter from you now, and if you do get a broadside back again, I think the only thing is not to care about that, but if you can to send another note sometime again.

I am surprised he didn't want his poems published; I will look them out and try to send you copies. I think perhaps to Menlove, the memory of these things brings back too much, all those great hopes and loves that have died so very hard a death all these years. It is better perhaps not to talk to him of them now.

We have all rejoiced in your lovely book *Snowdon Biography*; it brings back a Menlove one had almost forgotten; a precious memory, that photo of him. I should have written to thank you for it.

Noyce did write to Menlove, and did receive a broadside in reply. It is a long letter, and contains some important material:

4.11.1957

Thanks for yours. Nuisancey accident. The chip off the index knuckle has been hanging around for 4½ weeks now, swollen up, and refusing to get any more than *very* slowly better. Not important in a sense of course. May lose most of the use of that finger, and it has held back the case of getting movement and use back into the arm. Have noticed it more in the absence of anything better to do, and in the general atmosphere of fatuous idiocy into which the country has brought my life, and destroyed all my opportunities for work.

Yes, poor young chap. Rather rotten for him and family.*

Did not know Nowell had read Snowdon Biography. You will remember that she and I have not spoken ordinarily of anything actually happening for more than 13 years now, any more than with any of the rest of you.

You write nicely of my stuff. As incidentals—my climbing was not a matter of mood but of (usually very low) amount of recent practice and training and relative to other work done, tiredness etc. (As with many—) *You* might easily have thought it a matter of mood, but not in other company where the feelings were less engaged. Also—the "conclusions", "answers", in my attempts at writing, meant in general little or nothing to me: because I reckoned to be getting much further and in the same subjects in my other work. Attempts at expression, communication, not analysis, as the front edge of their intention. And often rather trivial of course, against any touchstone involving detailed, accurate, understanding. You would not likely be much aware of that as we did not talk of my main work much, or really perhaps at all. And the vicious set-up of the last thirteen + years has made that sort of main work virtually impossible again: though I have done enough of it by then to be aware that it was of very much greater value, effectiveness—as soon as it got going. Especially in my case.

But necessarily the main point is that however much you say it was intended as a tribute to those years—in what it said—it is—your book— and the other contributors in touching on me—at this date in fact, in what it did not say or partly implied, a tribute to or part of, what is probably one of the most disgusting single incidents of sadism in our history. And one of the most dismally fatuous too perhaps. I mean the effective attitudes, modes, actions to myself, of all the people concerned. And more particularly of those people whose opinions agreed in a greater degree with mine. They were presented with the opportunity to get some advantage from my opinions, while in return doing only—over all—a number of very dirty tricks to me. I have had only this miserable, contemptible rats' muck to look at ever since: the natural product of all of you keeping up the main fact of the dirty set up round myself, or of never making any attempt to alter that.

As the years have gone by, I have had quite a good view of what was

---

* There is a curious insensitivity about this if it refers, as I think it does, to the boy cyclist. Menlove is now a very long way from ordinary human concern.

happening round me; and of why. Strengthening as the degree of insanity lessened (an illness induced artificially by your set-up to me, and rendered them so exciting a bit of sadism for the public). And a view too of what was being effective and what not, in this or that direction—of these things round myself, I mean in this round me—not talking of other things—I am reasonably sure they have always taken the wrong choice, elaborating the dirtiness of my situation and their dirtinesses to me, or, at best, carefully avoiding any shift of the set-up round me towards the better. And that done not because of any actual greater effectiveness. Just a bit of dirt: and would have been, would be now, so easily altered, slid over, by anyone. That it had in fact, in itself, done a great deal of damage: in this instance, this activity set round me, relative to other methods.

Things had been better if I had had even one single friend who had not been wholly corrupted by my enemies, or who had understood my methods, or for some other reason had stood by me. Even just one, would probably have been sufficient to alter the whole business. In the number of my enemies one must include all those who agreed with me but were determined to keep to the main dirty tricks alone, as their effective means towards me.

Do not of course know the individual's intention in a given case. You, for instance, write nicely, intending what? It is what a man would do to help through a murder and give himself a bit of apparent cover, or in the present idiocy of thought round it, a man might or might not, think it a means to almost anything, by way of some elaborate idiocy. You do, in fact, keep the dirt in place, the main (vicious in effect) injustices.

I will be resigning my membership of the Climbers' Club in a month or two if I can get no decency or co-operation. Resigned membership of my few political ties quite a long time ago—the political left, UNO,—such few they were. Have not read the papers or etc., for two years. Only things left to do—and to go: in protest against your and their destruction of my effective work and life.

The accidents have made me put things off by a month or two.

Difficult to know what else to say under the circumstances. Your mother must be quite getting on now—Rosemary?—The children coming on?

Yours

Menlove

I could wish those old days back again, in this instance.

The old days, the camp under Tryfan, the New Year at Lower Gatesgarth, the accident on Scafell when he had saved Noyce's life, were 20 years gone.

All his professional work was in ruins. He was quite alone, but for the weekly visit from Nowell, in his little house on top of the downs. And the winter was coming, the colour of the grass grading down to grey, the woods bare and grey, sharp flints sticking up through the sparse growth in the field around. Christmas came and went. The hand refused to heal and he continued in pain. The death of the boy finally registered, and troubled him increasingly. He repeated the threat he had made regularly to Nowell for the past half-year: "I can find a way out."

At the end of January, in reply to a letter from Alec Keith—who had been perhaps his staunchest support apart from his immediate family throughout his life—he wrote back in terms which made it obvious that he was putting his affairs in order and preparing to go. Just as with the letter to Noyce, there is a weight of truth carried along by the paranoia and the wild and stumbling expression. I doubt if there are many who can read this letter closely and with understanding, and not at the end of it feel a little shamed, perhaps even in a sense inculpated, and yet at the same time thankful for the way in which Menlove had stood out for that in which he believed, and at terrible personal cost.

28.1.1958

Glad to hear from you. But sorry that you could not make a step out of the usual cesspool of an attitude towards myself. How can anyone pretend that there is any friendship or indeed any other quality worth having in the dirty, sadistic idiocy that all of you and England in general has put up towards me. I've never met anything so damned disgusting—to one person—even in all of a fairly wide reading. Filthy, slimey idiocy. I have no interest in playing any part with people who are behaving like that. Meeting it all the time, it makes one sick with sheer disgust. A miserable, hystericalised ecstasy of slime production. I'm not talking about back-ground principes of politics and thought, and such more important things, but about this artificial idiot of false propaganda set up, round me. Not a party matter at all, in fact, as each has merely copied each other's dirt—quite artificially—round me. And in the absence of one single friendly voice or anyone with any courage at all in the matter, I have not been able to get it better (by the artifice of the set-up—can't get co-operation if the co-operation of even anyone is refused—).

A pity. It would have been so easy, and at any time by anybody, to have slid out the sadism and in the good work elements; but this situation left to itself of course was likely to work the other way round, leaving the sadism and stopping any good work. As it has in fact done.

Like that *Snowdon Biography*—So many people (relative to the number

I've spoken to! i.e. about half a dozen—a large *proportion*—) have come up oilily to the subject and said how nice and smiled oilily to think how bloody nasty we've been really and what *very* clever dirts we've been—. One instance, out of thousands of the same smell. Evil rat's muck. Wilfrid did my climbing writing justice or rather more: the others a bit way here or there—my climbing, before '44. And all the *lying* about everything else connected with me, and doing me complete *in*justice, very dirtily—with smelly little dirt additions in the corners. Actual theft, induced illness, dirty tricks, insult etc: really in everything: with one smelly little non-excuse or another. I did what I could to help but clearly as year succeeds year; and one is answered by nothing but dirty tricks, on and on, there comes a time when one has to make such protest as it is possible for one to make; especially when one thinks the whole thing an evil business in other ways too. Nobody would put up with being insulted (and injured) as I have been, by you people and by England (and others) without protest. And my chance of making any genuine contribution were, as aforesaid, progressively cut out by the absence of any of the means of study, and by the increasing time of removal from them.

Have often thought of coming North on a visit. Simply no money earlier on. This year past though I've been spending my bits of savings. Got a motor cycle and spent the year holidaying more or less. Broke an arm with it in August; and then cut the knuckle off the index finger of same hand; in a piece of dreadful carelessness. (The break not such—). The latter very slow mending so waited till it was on the mend, in case I made a mess of getting away. Mentally have been more fit than at any time since these attacks on me started. A propos of those holidays incidentally surely one can think nothing at all of those groups that can use a 2nd rate holiday as a better advertisement for themselves than they can use work of a much higher quality. Though each of these sorts of argument are automatically stultified because the other groups have been as bad or worse really, in this highly specialised and unrepresentative situation round me.—But it does again emphasise the prevailing idiocy of the whole affair. Its constant pathological preference for dirt, for sadism, for a poorer quality as such. And it's certainly been highly successful in that—in reducing quality.

I'd be very glad indeed too to help anybody who would help me. My work capacity ought to have been coming to fruit too now. A smelly, dirty little waste.

These views are of course not a product of the season but are of near 14 years steady growing. Made my final plans one year and to two and more years ago, and allowed loads of extra time, in case anyone wanted to put up anything worth while in my direction, or even just help me off with these thumb-screws. But still nobody lifts a dirty finger. Have not, I think it's true to say, regretted the decision for five minutes together, since. Though regretting the situation that made it necessary, always, and the drunken idiocy that England has put up round me, to I think also her own considerable relative hurt.

Made a will a day or so ago. Money—part to my Mother—she has tried to help me with that—Rest half to Communists half to Spanish Falangists.* Am anxious that as little as possible of mine should stay in England while she is still, so long behaving like that to one. And in protest against the whole false vicious rabbitry, in all concerned. *Amount* of money left is of course v. slight in total—just the intention counts: as the wind up of my affairs. As aforesaid, the whole thing seems to me a piece of incredible idiocy all round.

You impute cowardice ("venture to Scotland"—) seriously or not. I think with no justification. Seems to me the word has its area of accuracy in mental affairs, of course, and in thought too. Much more complex than the present hysteria makes it seem, of course. *Important* though to *realise* and to realise more accurately. Processes, like so many other useful processes, hindered very much by the present propaganda set-up. (Am not trying to argue against propaganda as such of course—speaking just of this.) The "moral lead" chaps have done as bad I think in dishonesty *round* me, putting up a sheer filth as such; as the "courage" talkers, *round me*, have put up themselves surely and practically pure rabbitry. Both capable of so much better. And being principles of great force in human life, despite this dirt here. Again am only talking of the events round myself.

Have changed quite a bit since earlier days (not talking of "views"). I daresay that you too. Would have liked to talk of old days often—looking back. A good deal one didn't realise at the time—or this or that other reason. You often rather sensible. I have not wanted any quarrel with you. Am sad about my work. Had I think quite a lot to do. More effective than this sort of stuff. A poor do. And one as easy to put right as pulling up one's sex [*sic*]. But the fact is I cannot accept the sheer dirt England has put up to me in return for quite good services.

In this situation, in me, cowardice or other, has very little influence at all I think. The people I've helped have always been in this at least as disgusting as their opponents: the whole situation being the vicious thing: not the this or that way use of it, so much at all.

Have had a lot of nice smiles from the young chaps.—You know I

---

* Menlove did not in fact leave a will.

like—. The only ones virtually who have shown any desire to speak or so on. Would not have left me so, I think. But their elders always not worthy in that or other parts of this: to me: not talking of other things: motives—and the actions in it. And degree of good will from people not knowing much what was happening. But over-all—England the dirty little stink-rat sadist will be a thing I'll be very glad to leave. And that's really the only part of it I've met since before the end of the Nazi war.

(Never was a Communist—I expect you know well————) (Would have gone there gladly though if they'd helped this.) In case you didn't know.

Sorry to have found too, in the end, not one single friend or relation who was worth having: and not one in England who would bother to lend a hand: against extreme injustice.

Somebody on the wireless putting up smelly little lies about dying for one's country! and for peace! Drunken dirt. Where much better was available. The church—for a year and more half crazed about sacrifices and martyrdom and such, and the left similarly. In other things their distinctive differences. In this—all into the same very filthy cesspool.— Utterly contemptible.

Can't very well send good wishes after these years of dirt sendings towards me always—in fact—by you people.

Ever

MENLOVE

The way out came on 2 February, 1958, by swallowing potassium cyanide: an appalling way to have to die.

There was an inquest. Menlove's body was cremated at Ashford Crematorium. Stephen conducted the service, and remembers feeling thankful that his brother's suffering and torment were finally over. A few weeks later the ashes were taken up to Wales, where Nowell and Hewlett Johnson scattered them from the prominent wooded knoll which looks down on Hafod Owen, and then stood silently in prayer.

Nowell used to tell how, as sometimes happens in the Welsh hills, the clouds parted briefly to allow a single beam of sunlight through, which travelled across the oakwoods and the dark waters of the lake, picked out momentary detail on the shadowy crags opposite, and faded into the drift of cloud round Snowdon's summit. Perhaps, beyond all defeat, anguish and disgust Menlove could have smiled gently again in appreciation of the "innate symbolisms of life", shouldered his rope and sack and clattered away down the track in his old way, in hope of a better world?

And as we went back home that night following the white scratch marks over the rocks and through the heather the evening cleared as it had cleared before and the view was still fair to look upon, golden and with line upon line of hills through the sheen of the air and with the sound of the hills.

The gods having died.

The false gods, that is. . . .

APPENDIX

Menlove's Prose and Poetry

End of a Climb

IT WAS AN easy route, but I made a mess of it. My friend had to rub my middle for me, and that more than once all over, before I could get up the bad pitch. Even so I trembled violently all the way up.

Courage comes and goes so stupidly. I have never been able to discover the way of it myself, nor whether it was a good or a bad thing. Some people seem to get firmly into the habit of it and then it seems usually a bad thing. Perhaps it is that bravery is an accident, something to be explained away, or deprecated, or at the very least something to be kept very secretly to oneself, to use for one's own personal admiration. One can use it too instead of wisdom and so on in one's decisions, and it can then make life much easier, both to live and to take a pride in. As for the question of how to get this courage, I am myself convinced that here again it must almost always be acccidentally come by: either it is put upon one because the world has left one too empty here and too full there, or else one catches it as one might a cold, from some odd circumstance, a friend rubbing one's middle, for instance, in just the correct manner.

Anyhow, be the reason what it may, we did get up the climb, standard probably easy V.D., and at the top I was so exhausted with the conflicting emotions of fear and pride that, instead of thanking my friend for his kindly ministrations, I lay down full length in the heather and fell straight away into a deep sleep. The chief reward of virtue had come to me: but unfortunately my happiness was not complete, for out of the depths of an otherwise princely portion of unconsciousness there came to me a dream, a long and difficult dream.

Perhaps it was due to the inner conflict of feeling I had been through, or perhaps it was that while laying my upper half carefully on the heather I had left the lower half to fend for itself on the rocks: one way or the other I dreamt that I was in two parts, and that each was frankly annoyed with the other. For some time indeed they glared at each other without a word spoken. Then the legs could hold back no further. "Look here," they said, "we've been doing this all up the climb: it's about time we had it all out." And to my alarm and disgust they began to pull yard after yard of the unpleasant-looking material from their insides. It was plain enough that the wretched halves were simply doing this to annoy each other. The atmosphere of hate was in it, and they were showing how rotten the inside of a person can be when brought unexpectedly outside. I could do nothing to prevent it, and the cliff was rapidly getting into very nasty condition. They went on shouting and cursing and throwing out half-digested material on either side until the climbs were no longer worth doing: excellent routes covered with this, as I say, half-digested stuff that one usually prefers to stow away and take for granted.

In sheer disgust at the sight they made I took to flight, and floated off into the fastnesses of the Alps. But alas, speed as I might, they were there before me standing there still, for I might as well be honest, strewing their guts all over the mountains. I rushed rapidly on through the air towards the Himalayas. I never got there. Whether it was my hurry, or perhaps that the lower part of my bed was not only hard but a little slippery, I suddenly felt myself drop. Down I fell into the sea, then a sick, heavy tremor crept along the marrow of my bones and I sank slowly through the dull water. What sea it was I do not know, but it was quite warm and may well have been the Persian Gulf. It must have been deep, too, for I seemed to sink for a long time before subsiding on the bottom. That may have been deceptive though, for I certainly remember that even the last few feet took ages to go by. I hated it, and as I sank, I cried out my fears. "It is no earthly use trying to get to the Himalayas," I cried. "What shall I do now?" Then with a sudden dead calm I stopped breathing.

You may think that was a highly satisfactory ending for a man's more fine desires, but it was never to be consummated, for, soon after I had stopped breathing, I was surprised to find that by far the greater part of me was still perfectly well alive. Either it did not require air at all, or it could get it from some internal source. The apparent necessity of logic was being dispensed with, and as I realized this I began to rouse myself from the mud of the sea-floor in which I was being already systematically fossilized. I struggled hard, but the words were still floating about above me and it required a terrible effort to grasp them. "Er—er—Oxygen's a farce," and as I gasped it out I rose at once to the surface of the water. "I need air?" I went on, "but—dash it I'm full of all sorts of air, and anyhow you know nothing about it." Apparently, for without the slightest sign of breathing or anything that might support its further existence, my love detached itself and sailed strongly down the wind to the cliff where it had started, flicked off the mess and began climbing again without a qualm.

I was pleased at this, and not hesitating to put my mind at rest I seized the chance as it came and rose half a mile into the full heat of the sun. There, from that elevated and pleasant position, I was able to survey the operation below me at a proper distance and with a proper detachment.

It seems wrong to pass straight from dream to reality, yet, as this is what actually happened, I do not wish to falsify the truth in any way and will stick to the facts. I fancy I slept on undisturbed until I finally awoke. Awoke, but it was not a very definite awakening. I became conscious of a calmness in the air, then of faint sounds of the hillside. One might wake up a little more.

It was indeed a warm day and a good spot. The cliff was below us and its height carried us up above the rest of the steep valley side in a little castle of rock. On this was our patch of heather, dry and thick. The other side of the valley stood over against us in a ridge, hard and dark, for beyond and behind it the sun was declining into the faint mists of a still further horizon, somewhere over the flatlands beyond our range. Its rays lit the hillside round us, and down the pass we could see their straight lines slant across with the light in their arms. There was no need to move. The comfortable heather pressed into my back, filling out its angles of restlessness.

The sunset, the grinding of atom against its neighbour atom, force against its neighbour force. Fortuitous, perhaps, but moulded now into this by its necessities and a long chain of use. Moulded now into a colour of paradise, then driven away again along illimitable change. And a little figure looks up out of his own preoccupation and catches perhaps something of the size. He, too, is nature. He knows the change, the decay and long births, the mills grinding, and he, too, standing aside at the end of his climb can see, spread in his eyes, a terror and a glory within him. That his poor feelings are nature, but are no aim for nature. They are incidents, instruments, to be excited in him and caught up in him, dazzled and torn by him and used as goads upon him fully while there is any power left in them and until they are quite done. Use, and not satisfaction with nature, except that we can imagine ourselves dead a little.

Yet my mind would not gather together its profundities in that pause at the end of our climb. There was some tune that turned round and round in front of me, and my mind refused to recognize the silly jazz and put a stop to it. Poor, sleepy mind. the energy in us has always been like that. It kicked on and on inside of us until it was tired, and then only it let us stand aside. For once it gave leisure to look around us at the end of the climb in suitable perspective, but—the mind, too, had finished its climb, and was gone to sleep. When we pause it is because we have truly come to a pause, and that is often a pity.

My mind was in fact vaguely on the subject of climbing. Fancy lying about on the heather like this, after a single short climb halfway up the pass. This was not what they used to do in the old days. The heights for them; and some good solid foot-slogging, to work the city life out of stale muscles. We have it in the matter of standard though, and quality of what we do; and presumably they will get better still later on. The next generation would be quite exciting in the Helyg log, if we could see it now. Think of the efficiency required.

"... From this ledge a small sod is detached ($6'' \times 4''$) and placed on the extreme edge at a point marked by a little scratched arrow. Stand on this and slide over the overhang. 110 feet below there is a small ledge and here, with careful attention to balance, the climber will come to rest. The sod will fit the ledge exactly and is necessary for friction. Those not familiar with the technique may find it wise to fasten the turf to the feet with a loop of rope. Now the route becomes more obvious. A layback leads slightly left for 180 feet to a small nail stance ..."

And:

"... Found some new scrambles on Clogwyn du'r Arddu. The rock is seldom even perpendicular for any distance and is literally covered with small holds. Yet novices may like it."

Then a note by that ambitious young party of rock-gymnasts.

"Repeated Outward Bound Route. Three falls, only two fatal. A.B.C.,* X.Y.Z.,* F.W.B., O.K.

(Signed)

(Signed) Ferdinand Bounce.

*R.I.P."

Yes, but perhaps, one never knows. For oneself it is nice to be a bit old-fashioned. There were those awkward moments one had on Charity. Besides that dry efficiency above one's own level is more depressing to the marrow than the bottom of the sea in the Persian Gulf. Baron Munchausen (*sic*) is more to taste. He would have been a hot lad on the rocks, and he would have told them all about it afterwards.

"Then, judge of my surprise, there I was hanging stuck by my coat collar in a position whence there was no possible means of escape. Neither above me nor below was there anything to which I could hold, and for a moment I was at some loss as to the proper course to pursue. My mind has become accustomed, however, to work at an unusual speed under the stimulus of instant danger, and after casting about a little I hit upon a plan. I rubbed the nail of my forefinger against the rock and pared it carefully down to a fine point. This I was then just able to insert into a small hole high above my head and, thereupon, rotating about this as an axis, I brought my feet close to the summit, and with a last supreme effort leapt up feet first to safety."

That is better, one can afford to laugh at that.

We certainly do crave to excel, however little we may be prepared to give to the more difficult question of putting that into practice. But why should we always think like that about standards? Alternately thinking that the standard of climbing has risen so rapidly that it must necessarily go on rising fast, and then that the standard is already so dangerously near the limit that for sane men it can go no further. And if one turns up the table cloth and looks beneath, behold, both these ideas rest on the delightful notion that we ourselves are such extremely fine climbers and so immeasurably better than those others. No wonder we keep such ideas going. It satisfies our craving for height and with a minimum of effort, so long as we keep our eyes shut. The standard progresses towards the infinite of what is ideally possible to our physique, and we add a little or a lot of nothing to the advance, but concentrating on personal achievement, we credit ourselves with the excellence of the whole attained. A path is being steadily lengthened, but it is something definite in the way of success that we wish to add to ourselves when we climb, and we do it by walking along the path and stamping it in when we get as near as we reasonably can to the end of it, then we credit ourselves with the whole gain. The path has undoubtedly lengthened, but as for whether we, the particular people, are better than those before, it should be judged on quality, intensity or something, rather than on the precise position and amount of the stamping. In any case in climbing the aim and direction must be a thing to consider, and in climbing there is the complication that the aim is, we hope, not climbing.

I remember once, years ago, in Skye, I was talking, happy and excited. "Sir," I said to the weather-beaten old man with his iron-grey hair.* "Sir, we have discovered a New Route. It lies up the Northern Buttress of Sgurr-a-Gumain and starting at a point twelve feet to the left of a little dagger crack it goes up, though both steeply and awkwardly, to a point on the summit ridge just halfway between two very obvious stones. A large one on the right shaped just like a baby, and a small one on the left shaped like nothing on earth. We climbed, sir, in rubbers, but it seemed to each one of us to be very, very severe."

---

* Quite possibly there is the recollection of a meeting with Norman Collie behind this. J.P.

He sipped slowly at his whisky, and the thin runnels of heat swelled out among the vessels of his throat. "Young man," he said, "in the winter of 'eighty-three I remember cutting my way up that very buttress in ice and snow. We experienced considerable difficulty in the ascent and there have been one or two points about it graved on my memory ever since. I can see it now. A yard or two to the right of where we started I stood and put a match to my old pipe in the shelter of a small, dark crack formed like a dagger. It was growing dark when we came out on to the ridge, but looking around me I could discern dimly through the driving snow a large stone, and it looked ugly like a babe new-born. We turned away to the left and as I strode forward my foot caught, I fell full length, and my old briar lay on the ground, smashed to atoms. It was a small stone, young man, and it looked like nothing on earth."

Yes, but perhaps I have stressed it all the wrong way. It seemed to make it nicer for ourselves. We allowed that some of them might perhaps by some accident have been in some ways as good as ourselves, but we did it by way of a joke, and then only as if some of those elders must have been quite incomprehensible supermen.

What twistings we make in our minds: and on these rocks, too; pulling them and pushing them as if we wanted to make some difference to them, as if it had results beyond those of our own manifest contortions. It is just as well we pull and push all the rest of the circumstances in our lives; as if it were they that had to be re-arranged and not ourselves. Yet circumstances would hardly make so bold as to laugh at us, nor would the cliffs, for we are giving ourselves good exercise and giving them little trouble. We are avoiding unpleasantnesses such as getting stiff and dying, and since it is all very real to us there is no harm surely in allowing ourselves the conceit that it is equally real to the rest of the universe. Imagination makes our game of life seem so much more noble and we so important, and that in turn helps us to help ourselves to more of this living. If we had to wait on reality to show us our importance we would never get any thrill at all. Besides we will drop each conceit when it has served its turn. When it no longer directly deceives us enough to help we will keep it near for a time for the odour of its sanctity, and when that is forgotten—well, it was never more than a figment of the brain, so it should go easily.

We draw ourselves out and educate, and climbing has come to be part of our education. We naturally make a mess of the things we educate ourselves on, and that thing is naturally the world. It is not easy for a limited number of people to make a mess of things so comparatively large as cliffs and hills, for instance, but we do our best, and the mountains are likely sooner or later to be placed on the altar of man's education. Meanwhile we had better cling tight to the old that we love, the grandeur, the isolation, the things untouched as yet by this man, aesthete at one end and vulgarian at the other, a species to which we are unpleasantly accustomed. These things, things from outside, help us to keep our little spark glowing. A spark of readiness for something further and different; for one must keep clear of the crowd even to be in touch with it. That little spark will indeed move heaven and earth before it is done, all to keep itself as clear away as possible. To consider it, it is just this struggle for individuality that is the greatest necessity of the greatest affection, as well as perhaps its only prize. It is the necessity of all mountains, whether of the earth or of the mind, if they are to remain mountains. And education? Education in its turn will not worry its head much in practice about the high places of our feelings. The two certainly work to the same end, but they are only powerful while they oppose each other, each wanting the full mastery over us. To be alike and then to be different, and dreams must always be at war with reality. For the time being the mountains are still the mountains, and we can keep our heads well away on their slopes. We will each make a little image from what we like to see of ourselves in the mirror of the hills. One will laugh at the image, so one-sided. One will make it into a grey God and will then fall down and worship himself. Another will set it up for the great spirit of Man, and will lay down his life to his own image.

The eyes could close themselves that night and miss nothing, for there was a mood of waiting in the air; the evening was waiting: the heather still moulded round me, and there was a diffused glow over the whole surface of the sky. The sun's rays fell higher up the hillside now: like narrow arms carrying the weight of the evening warmth across the valley. Above them the air was deep with colours. There were many blues and there was silver down towards the sea. There was gold on the slope above us, and the hillside opposite was sheeted in fold upon fold of the emperor's purple.

We were small to that. So many generations has man been lifting the stones, little stones, big stones, to clear a small pasture: stones of all sizes, lifting, carrying them, pushing them out of the way. Those men who years ago worked and made their walls, and fought and cursed each other down the secrecy of the pass. Then strolled out into the evening and the door banged to behind them for a minute.

Dreams of a little people. I remember a boy we saw climbing two or three times, on the Idwal Slabs. He would stand and gaze at the foot of the rocks, scanning them to right and left for some path in their expanse that the foot of man had not yet utilized. Then he went to the foot of the Ordinary Route. As he ascended, however, it was clear enough that he was no ordinary climber, for every now and then he stood, and looked around him with that air of expectancy that is the true explorer's heritage. We realized that at any moment, maybe without the least warning, he might break out on to fresh ground. Rather to our surprise he did actually continue up the Ordinary Route. Perhaps there was something in store for us now, for there he was, gazing with a wide purview above, below and to either side. The preliminaries were over. Clearly he knew these cliffs well, but was now eager above all things for fresh endeavour, new pasture. Sure enough he made no pause for rest, but turned round and with every appearance of one whose mind is set to conquer or to die, he made his way laboriously down the Ordinary Route. We laughed at him at the time and called him the Idwal Slab. He looked queer too, and just fitted a rhyme we had then in our heads.

> What a wonderful thing your face is
> That its nose can begin without basis.

Yet he was an excellent youth, and we would have been dull indeed not to admire something at least in that devilish abandon with which our slot-machine culminated time and again in that grand finale of liquorice all-sorts. Indeed we had gone through just the same antics ourselves, only a few yards higher up. We both found mirrors in the cliffs like that. Perhaps it is really just that look of his that is the true explorer's heritage: the man lifting stones, little stones and rather larger stones, clearing a small space round him for pasture, and dreaming that they are all very big.

We got up and shook ourselves, for the warmth had left our rock now, and the thin arms of the sun were rising steadily as their burden grew lighter. The colours, however, went still deeper, and then, as if the liquid of the sky became oversaturated with its intensity, it suddenly seemed to sigh and as it did so, it shed a slight greyish precipitate, that gathered and clung nervously together in a thin strip down the centre of the blue. As it formed, the earth seemed to come out a little and its detail began to rise coldly up the sides of the hill. The arms of the sun, as if driven into quick motion, lifted their beams clear of the earth, and the particles of their warmth, despairing, concentrated their last effort in a soft rose light along the western aspect of the strip of cloud. Down on the rocks a squat yew tree, clinging to the face, shivered and drew itself up. The shadows came together and lay cramped stiffly over it.

We turned our backs finally to the hills and began to chatter: setting about to make our minds easy. But behind us, fighting their slow wars, the forces of nature also shifted steadily on.

Published in the Climbers' Club Journal, 1937

Letter from a Man

I AM THE man about town type myself and a chap who can show sympathy into the bargain. I have a huge correspondence and an immense number of friends, and that is not just a form of words: they know they're safe with me. One of them, a nice lad, immature, sent me this the other day. There is no need for me to talk about it, but it does show what there is, in even the dullest of us, when you've got the tact to bring it out.

Of course it doesn't do to encourage this sort of thing too much, so I wrote and told him I thought it was quite good: didn't suit me altogether, brought up in a different tradition, but that I would send it along, see what happened.

This is it.

You may say that the whole fuss is about nothing, but I counter that, for it may be about nothing at one end, but at the other end it is about me. Then if that end is about nothing too you must still admit that I complicate that. So see me through will you, till I get home again?

I will start by telling you how the thing began. My mother was badly off when I was young, but she didn't sit and mopse about it as some would. There I was, young and screaming, needing everything of the best: who was she to have scruples, she says: so she took it, a bit at a time, first from one shop, then from another, and left the scruples to me. So, as you would imagine, I grew up exuberant in body but with a nervy, craving mind. It was wanting something more, something tangible. It sought for reality intensely, always as if it was not there. For the rest, my father was of French extraction and I owe little to him. We have little in common, less now perhaps than ever.

But you see at once what I do. I climb.

I was nineteenth when I started the sport, and just beginning to think things out for myself. I was serious, you see. I was aware it was not one of the most immediately useful pursuits, but it seemed to fill a gap in my life. After a climb my mind would sit still, just sit still for days, quietly enjoying itself. Climbing meant a lot to me.

But just now there've been one or two things which have happened to me. I want to tell you about them. I am not sure what they mean, so I will give the plainest statement I can.

I am rather good at climbing, and I was keen in those days. In season and out of season: if I couldn't get a cliff I got a door or a chimney: if I couldn't get those I wound one finger (I took them in turn) tight as the devil round the grip of my suitcase. I put the very best of my energies into it. I bore weights. My courage and my resistance to fatigue were soon colossal.

So when it was summer, and holidays came round, I felt things had worked up for something big. I went to the Alps. I loaded myself up, scarpetti, zdarsky sac, bacon fat, a few pitons, all the rest of it, and then set out. I was twelve hours out, 24 hours out, 36 hours out; 48 hours, yes, out full 60 hours; and still the giant scarp precipice rose foot by foot about me, the last defences, hung with ice, high up near the summit of the mountain. The sun sank over the shoulder to my right, and as he went low down towards the West horizon the majesty of his reds rose, swept up over the sky, over still, then they lay down, crimson, faint, staining the snows, the mountains in the East, the Weisshorn, the Matterhorn—And the beauty of the evening was of the greatest assistance to me: for shifting a little against the pressure of the rope loops in which I sat I was able to stare fixedly at it, and forget all else.*

So I ascended my cliff, I got down again, was praised as I deserved, and wandering down the valley with the holiday now finished, began to let myself be as was now my habit, and pack up the energies of my mind against such time as I should next be able to use them. The sun shone high in his heaven. The little flowers ran beside the path. The noise of the cicadas rose and fell among the grasses. There was a river running down in the valley which made a sound, a sound like the streams in the hills where there are many streams, by my home.

Perhaps it was stupid of me. I had not felt quite like that for many years.

In the hotel later on it was perhaps understandable that I should burst out. It was evening. They were talking off and on, talking about nothing, and as I say I burst out. Speaking abruptly I gave them a parable. I said, It's the planet Neptune I'm talking about, just plain ordinary Neptune, not Paradise, because I don't happen to know about Paradise. So you see this means you, nothing more, just you. Now there happens to be a big spot of rock I said, up there, and I must warn you that people are pretty stupid up in Neptune, chiefly because they each live all tied up in their own

---

* Cf. passage from "Rowing the Minch" (p. 160).

string. And some of them, whom I had wanted to mention in particular, some of them had got themselves absolutely determined about that mountain. You wouldn't believe it, I said, life or death, use or no use, these people have got the habit, and they now spent their spare time and all their energies in chasing the clouds of their own glory up and down all the steepest faces in the district. And one and all they came back uplifted. And well they might, I said, for it was amusing that even in Neptune most of them made shift to chase themselves pretty safely up the easier faces. But anyhow there was uplift, and indeed it was observable, both in the resolute set of their faces and in the gratification that shone in their eyes. And as I had pointed out, this was in Neptune not Paradise, where it may be there perhaps is nothing else to be done.

It made a man laugh, I said.

The people in the hotel said all sorts of things: said I was tired. One chap said I'd seen light. But as to them I had to say that I certainly was tired, and that I had seen the light often, seen it on the Weisshorn, on the Matterhorn—seen it admittedly after certain emotional crises also, glowing on the inside wall of my heart. But that meanwhile if that was all they had to say, then I was not concerned to wait to hear the rest of their pronouncements. I was going off, and they might go too, but for God's sake let them be frank, I said. Let them go to sleep.

And I took my baggage in hand as a climber can, and walked away out of the tobacco smoke, followed the road up the valley, up the pass, with the white dust on my shoes, walked over the frontier, France, and back home.

When I got back I found a book waiting for me, from the shop, a guide I'd ordered. There was a good deal else too, nothing special, but there was this too, the little packet laid out flat on the table awaiting me. I opened it up and found just a slip of cardboard. I turned it over and over but there was nothing else to it. Just a thin slip of cardboard. But why I mention it is because I saw at once that really there hadn't been any guide in the packet at all, all the time. Just a slip of cardboard.

And because nothing much else happened.

I settled down and did some work; and still, after a time you remember, I had still had my father and my mother.

But I thought I would let you know.

Published in the *Mountaineering Journal*, June 1937

Scenery for a Murder

I DID START by trying to write an essay, but it was soon clear that it was not an essay I wanted to write but the facts; the plain facts as they happened. What do I mean? You will see what I mean. The fact is, there has been murder done, done under their noses, and the fools can't spot the murderer. So I will set it all out: but I will have to be a litle careful, for the murderer is a gentleman and very well connected; one is supposed to talk of him carefully, so to speak, as if he wasn't there, or didn't do anything.

But the story.

This is what happened. I opened the paper one morning at home and saw that an accident had happened; a well-known climber killed in the Alps, one of the most notorious slices of cliff in the world; frozen to death on it; three nights out; now trying to get the body; and it was he, my friend. But that is the barest summary. I can tell you more than that. For I was there when it was done.

The first time I saw him was nothing to do with climbing. It was in the Albert Hall. In fact, strictly, I didn't see him; heard him over the wireless. Eight of them; they walked down the centre of the hall on to the platform, and I didn't notice him, naturally, during that part of the business; but then, what they had come for, they sang, a dozen or so of the folk-songs of their country; and then I couldn't help it, for a really fine voice does not need careful comparison or notice to pick it out: it stands out of itself, and this was a young voice, one in a million, high, sung full out, accurate, but a wild voice. What a voice! The Albert Hall faded out in two seconds: he stood still, head thrown back a little; you could see that, though he stood in line among the others.

And even then you could see it was tragedy.

Of course that was years ago. Then one of those strange things happened. I met him. Got talking with a German boy in Berne: was leaning up against the railings watching the sky over the roof-tops and I saw him, quite suddenly, walking past, and you couldn't miss it, the same look, the same attitude: didn't even have to ask his name: it stood out all over him: power, courage, love, honour, the heroes, fame, God, the Devil; no, I can't phrase it, but you can take it from me it was not the boy so much as the scenery. I've never seen such wild scenery; it stood out a mile. So I got in tow. He was a tall young fellow, and could obviously climb as well as any man, but, as I say, I was in luck that day, and I got in tow.

Skip a few days, and the two of us, Toni and I, enormous rucksacks on our backs, walked slowly out of an hotel, together, sweating we were, brown, in the heat of the sun, out of the village, past the few last houses, beside the hay plots, and up, leaving the fir trees one by one, along the scorched dry bed of the valley, the hills sloping high on either side, up the track towards the thin, far-away line of the mountains. I think I have never known a hut walk go so well. Toni looked around contentedly enough, but he seemed not to notice much; yet he seemed to transform the land, he gave it an atmosphere, a scenery, a hauteur, that made the bare places and the vivid sky seem beautiful. Noticeable with me, for in myself I am dull. Like most people, perhaps, the things that happen to me come, pass over me, then they travel on; but as they go I go also, with them, into the past; and if I walk out, for instance, I am often behind-hand and cannot catch up, cannot produce in time the right attitude with which to appreciate a scenery. So to me the effect on the valley was remarkable. He spoke a fair amount, but that was nothing. It was his atmosphere, in which the features of the country became more beautiful than I had known them.

We got to the hut in good time, had a meal and sat over it, and my mind was still running over the same subject so, as we were well fed and he seemed not to mind my talking, I held forth. Now you are all right, I said, I'm not a fool and I know the genuine article—phrase we have in England—when I see it, but I think there's nothing I've hated so much in my time and so reasonably as the love of the mountains. And as I talked I got enthusiastic. Now follow me, I said: take a chestnut, cover it with sugar. He was a shy fellow and looked quickly round, but I make no difficulty of an incident like that and I carried straight on. No, no, I said, cover it with sguar, more, boil it in sugar, say that you are a bad cook, five, six, ten, twenty times its own weight of sugar, boil it for two days, no two years, and you get my meaning, you have a fine piece of sugar left, but not a chestnut; after two years it would be a tragedy to go on calling a thing like that a chestnut. And a man's feelings are more tender than that, surely. So when a fellow produces thick syrup whenever he sees a hill, he may protest any fine origin for it that he likes, but most of us consider it simply sickening. We are right? Yes, he said. So I went on talking; for he did not understand: he had less experience of having other people's feelings himself than a child of ten.

We went to bed; at least we didn't go to bed, we lay on the floor that night for the hut was crowded out and the breathing was terrible. But who cares; throw off the cloak, make no pretence to be beautiful, cuddle down a bit, all fully dressed, all close together, and it's pleasant enough. No, I had forgotten; funny how one's mind goes on. He must have such feelings, but not the same I suppose; they'd get a different sort of reception in him; try to find out tomorrow; what a hope. So I lay on my back that night, Spartan. But next morning, early breakfast, it was just the same as the day before, the crowd did not count, we were in the heights again, miles away, and man's desires rose up over the sweat of the earth, and chased madly away, out of sight, in the air, where they dallied.

We went up one side of a mountain that day, down the other, over a fine snow col, and stood at about two o'clock in the afternoon by the front of a small tin cabane, miles away high up on the side of the mountains, difficult to get at, used ten or a dozen times a year perhaps, not more, at the top of the small steep armchair valley beneath our cliff; not a valley, a ledge, a slight relenting of the main sweep, existing for no good reason. I was excited. Toni went to bed and I was alone. I became a little frightened inside me, and I stood at the door of the hut. The sun streamed in at the window; the stones shone white before me; the little cabane dwarfed, crouching away; nothing moved; down on the left there was a faint sound of running water, but none visible; then the slope dropped steeply over into cliffs, then beyond that, far below, the valley, a little river in it, with trees and a few pastures, and beyond that the hills, the trees rose steeply up their sides in dark patches, and then more hills, grey-green hills. But up here there was not much green. And the boy still slept. And I couldn't get it out of my mind. Then after a time I got some water in the bucket and made some tea for him. Woke him up. He was quiet now; enjoyed the drink, and he even accepted my attention. Then there was nothing else to do, and we stood at the door of the hut again. The valley shimmered still in the warm sun of the late afternoon, but up here the shadow of the great ridge opposite was coming over us, and there was a slight cold breeze. And, up on the right, dominating the whole, part white in the sun, part black, hard and scintillating, stood the shape of the mountain. He gazed at it carefully, so did I. Then we went in, and went to bed early in preparation for the morrow. Toni looked a little tired. Well, we were here now, and I didn't like it.

Why we got up at that hour of the night I don't know. To miss the avalanches perhaps, the stone falls, but so far as I could see we couldn't miss them anyhow on this route, so what was the use? I expect Toni liked getting up. It was alright for him, he could take it. And as I laced up my boots in the early morning I cursed, and as I ate I was angry, and all the while under the warm shirt my muscles shivered slightly in the cold, and the shiver flitted on and over my mind, so that my heart beat quicker than it should before a climb. Then Toni got up, ready: I am always in a bit of a scramble with my things on an early start, and I went out after him. God, it was black. I am a rabbit at heart, I said. He said nothing. We set off along a tiny track. Panting and unhappy, I said, I yet shall do it. I shall follow this boy until I drop, nor will I ask for sympathy; though with his massive limbs he has no pity for me, me small, following after. Here, where a slight temporary difficulty on this patch of rock makes it impossible for me to keep to his heels, I will make a clatter with my ice-axe, rather louder than the ordinary, and attract his attention so that he will notice the labour of my breathing and go a little slower. No. Now I shall have to run a few paces to catch up with him. No. He has a heart of stone, this boy, he cannot respond. All my kindness, my special treatment is to no purpose. Panting and unhappy. And we picked our way along the head of the valley, crawled up a small rock slope, stumbled over the stones across the tongue of a short moraine; ach; then we stepped off on to the snow of the glacier. Ah, now my friend, let me not be angry. In the cold morning air I can forget. Well? You take no notice? You do not understand? My hatred and my forgiveness have nowhere to go? You have come here welded, set into something, I believe, and your weldedness, your one object, is to climb, apparently, this mountain. But aloud I said do you think we might rest a minute? And he assented.

So we turned and stood, looking outward over the valley, and we were high up and it was dark, and in the cold I shivered and was excited again, and Toni took off his hat, loosened his hair with his hands, and looked out over the dark beneath, over to the north far horizon, with me for a minute, then we went on; and the cliff rose before us, as we turned, bare and dark, standing like a ghost over the glacier. We went steadily up, not difficult, over the grey snow, crisp to tread upon, bending slightly, winding in and out, making our way. We were playing the part now and no mistake. An hour passed and another hour, the glacier steepened, we trod carefully in on the edge of our boots, now and then kicking slightly; the snow was perfect; if all would go like this—then the glacier stopped and the bergschrund lay before us, eight to ten feet wide, uniform, curving, the far side steep, so we stopped too, sat down in a dip on the top of the glacier and ate a little. It was lighter now. Then we unhooked our sacks, drew up our leggs, strapped on the crampons and drew them tight round the instep; and then we stood up again and felt strong like conquerors; but there was this damned bergschrund yet. Would it go? So I made myself firm while Toni scouted, and he walked along the edge of the bergschrund to the right a little and said I will try here, and he got on to a little bridge, looked at the wall above split by a vertical crack, thin, the right size, jammed his ice-axe at chest height into it, put a foot high up and lay back on it, then he pulled in a bit, slipped his right arm into the crack up to the elbow, held on so, and with his left hand, a twist, got the ice-axe out and jammed it in higher and so proceeded. Ten feet or more; then the angle eased slightly and the crack was not so good and the ice gave way to brittle snow, but the crack widened also with a thinner crack at the back, and he stood up, jammed himself, cut a wide foothold out on the right, and at last, about a quarter of an hour I should say, got on to it. And the snow sloped steeply up before him towards the rocks, but could we stand there? and he rested a minute, and then cut big steps hand- and foothold upwards in good hard snow. It was 80 feet before he took me up and I needed aid. There was no doubt he could climb. But the cliff looked steep up ahead. A groove and rib structure, the groove going up wide, open and parallel and about 50 yards between. From a distance it looked as if, when you got fed up with one groove, you would climb into the next on either side, but now you could see it better, this was none of your Chamonix stuff, and the rock had no holds on it: nasty. The grooves were backed with a runnel of snow or ice mostly and the ribs with verglas. If you came off you wouldn't hit up against anything outstanding by the look of it either, but shooting the bergschrund you would skate for miles; the odds are, I think, you would not stop on the glacier going at that speed, but would follow it to the mouth of the little valley, tip up over the end of the cliff edge and die.

The dawn had risen unnoticed away on the left, but it was still cold here. Toni was off again and it looked bad. Our groove was rather bare at first, but he kept his crampons on and as there didn't seem to be much in the way of holds, he was using a pressure technique, pressing against the little grooves sideways to keep the snow up, and with hands pressing sideways also to keep himself up, and the method was slow, and produced much scraping sometimes, and now and then it took convulsions for a moment or two when a position became untenable. I can watch a climber and tell what he is doing exactly. Poor old Toni, he didn't like it any more than I did; but luckily in those days he didn't know how much he didn't like it. Then at last, it seemed hours, at 100 feet he got a stance for his feet, stuck in a piton and took me up. Then it looked as if it might get better, but it got worse instead. And so it went on; some patches of ice were more good than bad, though needing hacked hand-holds all the way, and it took a time. I led one or two bits of that, but was not safe on the rest. At midday we had done 600 feet or so; several times he stood on my shoulders; then it got worse and we were getting tired, and towards evening we were not much above 1,200 feet from the foot of the rocks still, but there was the best ledge we had met; carefully roping we might both lie down; so we ate a good meal and felt better, and decided to stay there for the night. Stones had been dropping a bit all day, but it was cold and you hardly noticed them, and what could you do, anyhow? and now the sun appeared on the right, and at last unexpectedly we were warmed, and he sat and watched it set, and I began to think again of what we were doing for the first time that day. Why should he be noticing the sunset? But he was noticing it, watching about the weather maybe, the chances for the night; no, he wasn't looking like that; it was those other things, he could drag those same thoughts out of me still. What a sky it was! Restless, slowly spread her arms out towards us while the sun went down. Look at her. Ha! Red. Light. Straight. A vision. For the faithful a sign. Truth, naked, looking over the mountain. Toni, come down again, come down. But I said nothing. Toni. It was all he knew. It was so he had been taught. And when he was young, early, he had looked out of the window. How do I know that? How? I know it. I was there, I tell you, I was there at the time. The ascension to heaven. I couldn't get it out of my mind.

And I knew perfectly well what was going to happen. We were going to go straight up into the clouds, he and I, then we might or might not get down again.

We had arranged ourselves on the ledge and, close together, we would be able to sleep. We were well off, but I did not compose myself at once. His chances of survival for the next two years I thought, are about fifty-fifty: as for me, I have fitted in nobly, have played my part, fool, and have even applauded. I couldn't get it out of my mind. I couldn't get the Alps out either. Then I dozed off.

We slept fitfully through the night, waited for the dawn, a lot of cloud about, then we set out. There was little snow on the next bit. I wanted to get on. All this is by the way. I think we both braced ourselves up; we were cold, and there was more cloud drifting around than we liked. The next bit was not too bad either. Three hundred to four hundred feet, quite quickly, three pitons and they only for safety; perhaps we were over the worst; then a tiny ledge and the groove went on under snow, and we stood on the ledge leaning back against the last two rocks to put on our crampons; and that heartened us; I think it would hearten a cow, that particular manoeuvre. Not? You think? With your back against the rock, bent slightly, putting on crampons? Oh, but you know it would! It increases a man's virility, any man's, tenfold. But it did not last. It never does. The next 80 feet took hours, and then it didn't look too good up above. You know what it is when a cliff is too steep to start with and then the whole structure gets steeper, a little bulge. The steepest part was 120 feet or so above us, and a big drop now below; the ice gave out in little runnels 40 feet up, couldn't hold on any longer, north face though it was. He got up 40 feet, 60 feet, 70 feet, in about half an hour, scraped for a quarter of an hour, and at last, thank God, managed to get down again, found a crack to stick a piton in at 40 feet, and had a rest. I was shivering hard all that time, watching, and I too was tied to a piton. What to do now? But his blood was up, a light in his eyes, no talk of surrender, he got down ten feet, traversed out right, quite quickly, on next to nothing, got a piton in I don't know how, let himself down on a long loop and swung out for the edge of the groove, got the rib by the nails of his fingers, more gymnastics, stuck in another piton, and rested. The other side sounded harder; I couldn't see; it took a long time; I didn't go that way myself either, there was a sureness about hanging on to a rope and swinging, even a long swing, that was preferable in my mind to the long drawn agony of trying to climb a traverse that you couldn't. I don't know why I'm going into all this, it's not the point, but it sticks in my memory, all this detail. I landed up bump in the next groove, jammed, breathelss, into a shallow, square, little, overhanging crack, quite a rarity, that crack; and I was surprised; I doubt if there's another crack good enough to jam in on this side of the mountain, and I struggled a bit, I can do that on the rope, got a sort of hold near the top, something stuck, but I gave a grunt of joy, pulled like hell (I am a man with great reserves of strength, though I seldom if ever get the chance to use them) and something snapped and up I went. I was exultant, I felt a lighter man, and it must have been a full second before it dawned on me; my rucksack; the sound of falling; my poor benighted rucksack. Yes, it was making tracks for home. In the wigwam of her fathers she would repose. Now she must be nearing the glacier. There she would burst and her contents would fly from her; separate, they would make their way each to their resting place. The food; birds might have it. A pair of kletterschuhe;

by luck a man might find them, sometime. The camera; there would be no use for that now, not in this world. The sleeping things. Oh, the devil. What have I done, Toni? And as I came up towards him I almost began to speak to him of my feelings; but I stopped halfway, he was thinking already more of the cliff again than of me, and that was as it should be; for this groove we were in looked difficult and we were short of time, short of everything now.

We got up a bit, and another bit, or rather he did, then the mists came. Like the words of the prophet they stole over, among the ribs of the cliff, and covered us. Then the snow came. What a mess. We put on all that was wearable in Toni's sack, ate, tied on to a piton—we had pitons anyhow—and we scraped in the snow and went on. That did not mean much but we did what we could. So at the end of the second day we were getting tired and we had got nowhere. We got a scrap of a ledge and anchored ourselves, up against each other, ropes crossed. There was a wind up now, and the snow swirled round us, coming in gusts, eddying very beautifully, but appallingly cold. What sort of a job was this? Is there any way out of it? Hell. I for one would be frozen in two hours at this rate. No, I said, slow up; don't let your thoughts run away, silly. Do you know, I've just got it. I have been wondering why I was here. My function is that I am the barometer of this party; I go up and down. Oh no, I had forgotten. As regards pressure that boy doesn't oscillate; if you put him in space he wouldn't alter to speak of; he doesn't know how. Screwed up to a certain pitch throughout his conscious existence, for the last ten years or so, he has had no experience of any variation. If he had a barometer it would not move, unless it had burst perhaps, or unless, protesting, it had begun to vary like me on its own account. My going up and down, then, serves no purpose. My being here is no good. Toni . . . Then I looked at him more closely. One thing was certain. The boy was about done. There was nothing more one could say.

The wind was cold but not very strong. We had a tiny bit of food. I had arranged his ropes very carefully, and mine, and we put our feet in the sack and settled down. We had two balaclavas, four good gloves. The snow coated over them and froze. We rubbed each other at intervals. I did not think at all that night. It was too cold. That's all I remember about it. Our legs and our feet froze; later on it became difficult to move arms and legs, and the cold went right through our bodies. But we did it, we lasted the night, and the next morning we took our feet out of the sack, pulled ourselves up into a standing position, creaking, leaning on the stiff cold rope, and trod about as best we could, painful and cold, to get moving. It must have been nearly two hours before we felt fit to go on, and the groove above looked hopeless; but you never know on a cliff, and as we went up foot by foot, using plenty of pitons, leading alternately, clearing masses of snow, it seemed not impossible. We kept to very short pitches, he did the harder bits. Once, close above me, he was swept clean off by a small snowslide. I fielded him. He gasped, got a footing, and held on. Are you hurt? he said. Me, no me? Not me, no, I said. He said nothing. His face was rigid and he did not look quite full at me. We went on again. The wind hardened and set round more to the north, blowing right into the groove, colder than ever. Climbing at this rate we didn't get on much, we didn't even keep warm. But we went on steadily, rather desperate. The details of it will not come to my mind now; I doubt if they were ever taken into it. At about five o'clock it looked as if things were getting easier, but the weather was worse than ever, blowing really hard now. We hadn't a chance, though we must be getting near the summit. I looked at Toni and suggested a rest. The storm increased in violence. It might blow itself out at any time, but meanwhile it was not possible. Toni was not breathing properly, damn it. I supported his head. He looked at me but could not speak. Toni, Toni, I thought; Toni, why did you listen always to the sounds of the mountains and to those things; and if you had listened some time to me also, and to my voice. Then his eyes went wild a little, they were a little wild always, and then he cried, sobbed out aloud on my shoulder. Not long after that he died.

But murder, you say. There was no one else present, you say, no murderer. So? Nobody else? Have you forgotten the singing, have you forgotten the scenery, the wild scenery? And how are you here to tell the tale, you ask? How! Do you not understand?

But the boy himself, Toni, my friend? Did he die? Was he killed? Or I, or was I alone? Well, those are quite different matters, and really I must confess I don't know. But take it which way you like, that does not alter the facts; and make no mistake about it: that does not justify that very wild scenery; nor does it justify murder.

Published in the *Climbers' Club Journal*, 1939

A Great Effort

IN THE LAST three years three people have asked me how I climb. Hence this personal article. They said also that it was the state of mind and not the mechanics that they thought important, and that if each man would write of himself under this head then others coming after might know better what to imitate and what to avoid. A primary condition for this, of course, would be to lay aside any modesty that one had at any other times assumed.

It will be best to describe directly a given instance.

I will not weary you with the preliminaries. There were none. Everything had been in order, the customary had occurred. I had come here for the week-end to climb, had got up, dressed, eaten a good breakfast with a good appetite and having nobody to climb with had gone out for the day alone. I had considered carefully which cliff to visit and chosen a near one not to make too strenuous a day. This involved walking along a stretch of road, then a slope up towards the cliff.

The slope I took by stages. Three hundred yards then a rest, three hundred yards, then a rest. During the last war it was explained to me that the British soldier marched by stages and it has been my chief method since. It is easier. Some people prefer to go up hills at a steady ten miles an hour, as if they were an army tank cruising or Scott hauling sledges in the Antarctic. I do not. During each rest I gazed at the cliff, exploring from a distance how a route might go. Then when quite near the cliff I stopped again and looked up at it more slowly, heavy with the fresh air, and it looked at me, and it slid about in my eyes as a cliff sometimes does, and was difficult to focus. I shall go there and there, I thought, and then perhaps coming to the steeper portion, I shall go there, or perhaps it will be too hard for me to go there then I shall not go there but will go there instead by what appears so far as can be seen from here to be a dirty and a bare sided finger crack, but which may not be so, or otherwise examining the rock closely when we are there, rubbing the nose against it, there may be some third or fourth way, not guessed at from a distance. But first I thought, husbanding my energies, I will rest here for a little time where stability can still be assured without effort or trouble by sitting down. So in the middle of the mountains upon a pile of rocks I sat down. A certain tendency to inertia in the mind can have great force.

Do not mistake me, the choice of cliff and pastime had been free, it was unhampered by any conditions either of expediency or friendship, there was no particular unhappiness on me at this time beyond the normal. Yet I sat down. And as I lifted my head, stones, blocks of rock, sky, cliff faces lay round the field of vision arranged in various ways.

Then later I got up and walked to the foot of the cliff meditating carefully where to start. Then tied the rope on, flung the loose end down the slope and arranged it so that its coils should open without snags. This took some time, due to a complex cluster of small rocks in the way which needed re-arranging before I could be sure that the rope would come clean across them. Then I moved on to the rock itself.

Now perhaps you looking on might remark of these actions that none of them had been done in any rapid or decisive mould. You would be right. Perhaps that is why there was no great resultant from them. After 20 minutes I had advanced about fifteen feet and was trembling slightly, not too sure of my position. The rock now before my face was ordinary rock, surfaced at an angle of 60 to 70 degrees, fairly smooth. Heaven was above, the earth a few yards beneath, and I remember nothing of either. As for myself the fore part of my right foot was planted well on a square ledge, the heel overhung into the air and demanded a constant muscular effort at the calf; my left foot was three feet higher and one and a half feet to the side put against a small sloped piece of grooving. In appearance there, had anybody been passing, I was about to step up. In practice I had been trying to do this for ten minutes but had not yet succeeded. It seemed simple, the need was clear, holds were there, but they were small and I am not a man in any way to make a move until satisfied that it is safe, so that to remain in this statuesque and silly position was my only choice for the time being. Every minute or two, when my right leg began to tremble, I pulled the left leg down from its unserviceable height, bent myself this way and that a little to relieve the strain, then put the leg back again, using the action also as a gesture of purpose.

But any man must be to some degree hard-pressed before he gives up on a point where his heart is set; so I began to struggle. Oh, good heavens, good heavens, I thought, what on earth am I to do; this is not very good, you are being a coward, an arrant coward and this cannot, must not, continue. I have time and again pointed out to you that you are being very silly but you do nothing, you do nothing except stand there with that fixed and ridiculous stare a few feet from the foot of this wretched precipice. But I still accomplished nothing. Then I began to struggle again. I thought, what is wrong, there is something missing, there is no spirit, I am heavy and unable to move; perhaps if I launch out and become sufficiently frightened; in fact I am sure that once over the border there would be no holding me. So I made several attempts to launch out, but nothing happened. Then I thought perhaps if I eat my sandwiches that will improve me, but no no for shame, it is not yet half-past eleven, how can I eat them now, yet there can be no harm in it, give yourself a change, I said, eat them all and that will be a load off your mind, then you will not have the temptation to eat again until you get home. So standing still on my footholds and feeling firmer than I had done for some time, I got the tin of sardines out of my pocket, twisted the lid off in the usual way but carefully because of the position and ate the fish one by one with my mouth. This took some time. Then I drained the tin, put it back in my pocket and turned to the rocks once more. Now how will it go I thought, every excuse is exhausted. And I tried again. No, it is not good, I said, it is no good: here I am fifteen feet from the ground on easy rocks as I said before it is after lunch but in my own bones there is no more energy than there ever was and my whole soul is as flat as a carpet, what am I to do? Perhaps if I were to recall former victories or to picture glory, but how can you do that when you are alone, perhaps if I shouted and sang, but you know you were never able to shout and sing: now if there were an onlooker, that would make an effort worth while, perhaps—is there anyone in sight? no, not a soul, not one in the whole valley: there is no representative of the human race, none to praise, nobody to look surprised at cowardice or to laugh at folly, to provide me with a gibe or comparison or stage: there is a sheep, but the sheep do not know about these things, a little bird but she is away out of sight already. So I stood on waiting, unable to move. It is difficult to describe what it feels like to be so, to describe that extreme desolation that may be left behind in the human brain when it is without anything working in it to spur it on. I stood on that hold for a long time. Then quickly, with the sweat standing out on my skin and my heart beating, I moved up on to the next holds and then the next and then I did not see what to do and the movement stopped again.

The view had changed. There was heather now in front of my eyes, and some of the thin dust that goes with it. I took a handful of heather in my right hand. It seemed firm but when bent back it snapped and broke off. A bad material. I made a final effort. Look at yourself I said, and do you know what this is, that it is schizophrenia, the split mind: I know but I do not care what I said: it is stupid: what could you do if you did get ten feet higher up, the rocks have not started yet to become difficult, take yourself off from this climb: oh, this climbing, that involves an effort, on every move the holds to be spotted and often there are none, then every limb placed, the body set into the one suitable position found but with trouble, then with the whole organism great force must be exerted, before anything happens, and this is to be done while the brain is occupied sick and stiff with its fears: and now you have been doing this for well over an hour and a half and the strain must be telling: get down therefore.

My mind made up, it only remained to go, not always an easy thing to do. But as it has often been remarked God may be merciful and is so sometimes when you least expect it; and on this occasion it happened that feeling in behind the heather I almost immediately found a good enough spike of rock for my rope and was able to get back down again in no danger. Then I walked a little way up the hillside slowly, rested and walked home.

But the resilience of man is great, and his ingenuity. So I was not done yet and on the way back setting to work I soon picked up my pride in this way, by thinking, today the victory has been to the devil, but tomorrow is not to him yet, also by thinking: it has been said that the secret of life is in detachment from it, good.

Published in the *Climbers' Club Journal*, 1941

FOUR POEMS BY J.M.E.

Struck there, see, as I call the name

Struck there, see, as I call the name,
His lips, his cheek, wrought, driven in flame,
And happiness and sight
Here in the pigeon-breasted night.

Watch. His slow fingers part his hair
In sheaves, in fine pages of the air.
They stir and they mark
Among the mouldings of the dark.

Plunged in thy furnaces they cleave
Through the feather-covered chest and heave,
And thy panthers fight
With suave coat muscles of the night.

And suddenly stark.
The glitter gone in the curving dark
The eyes numb, the blanket of the head,
As the living, yet as strangely dead.

The body gone and the mind may grope
For the you down its granites again
                          on its own slope

No, but come to me
                    come quite.

So, even darkly,
                    we could share the night.

1936. Published in *Samson*, 1960

Now here we are, my sister

Now here we are, my sister, here
In this rather bare garden, and two hours still to go.
Two hours. I shall get alone in it.
I will not know what to do. Two hours: and the garden
By the look of it, is dead. The flowers and the soil,
No good to me, the fencing. I'm dropping
And there's nobody to touch. Nobody. Perhaps
If I could drop myself away, right far away. Oh yes,
My sister, come: what was it? We'll be a hero?
Yes? Out in the Arctic? Siberia? In the
Days of the Emperor. Mile after mile, day
After day, was so weary, I kept on
And on. Then, oh my sister, you remember?
The snow. I saw it. Another and another came, a snowflake,
A great heavy snowflake, down she came carefully,
Swinging like a dancer, majestically down, like
A pearl shell in the sea, settled on a grey damp
Boulder, and there like a liner in the ocean, she
Lay down, she tipped up and sank. That was
The start of it, the snowstorm. Old men had not
Known worse, the heaviest in memory. They came
Quietly; the snows fell; day after day. Men
Died by thousands. The vultures were buried with their carrion,
And the flakes gathered in among the trees, They piled, they
Piled on the branches, a bough cracked, they fell, then they rose again,
Rose till they were covered, till the tops, till the forests
Lay white like the prairies. And still the air above
Was crowded, and the winds slid grey with their burden,
With the particles, the throng coming wistfully.

And I? It came delicately round me, I stumbled into it, it
Grew about my thighs, it deepened and deepened to my neck, then
Deepened over me, and the world—I, shut away from it.
Was I to give up, to lie down? No
Pushing it aside and thrusting, fighting it.
But it clings like stuff and coats the back of me,
And it waits about my head like a rider, and it paws
And settles back again, and it dips, then it suddenly advances
It is on me like a terror in the night, like a sheet, like

A thick, like a glove coming over me. Then I go
And I look
Then a horseman comes, from the West.

Then the clearing.
And she?
No, no, she is not here. You recollect the plague,
The people dying? She lingered on, she lay
Month after month, became so thin, and as
We looked her dark eyelashes long were poised, and
They stood like the mourners, like the flesh, and when
The evening came clear-eyed, whitening the waters, they were like
The reeds on the lake. Then when the first snows fell she sighed
And they lifted her away from us and went, and we sat for
A while, but she, like the day, like the year, had left
No relic.

                              1937. Published in *Samson*, 1960

The Climbers

The climbers. They. They and their hills.
    They come rowdily
At week-ends. They talk: of God: the
    Universe:
They talk of women. They tumble from
    their beds in the morning:
They blow in and out, and have their phrases.
    They wrap themselves:
They sweat: they cleave along their paths and
    hurl themselves,
At their special places, their few tracks among
    the mountains.
Sometimes they stop. Then the wind wanders
    over them, and breathes:
It walks in their pores and tugs a little. It
    drags the hair spaces.
They see the clouds above. They make a
    heart of it. They see the strange lights
Go pacing up and down upon the ridges, and
    colours

That flit thick upon the turf in patches.
They then set to again, attack. They launch
   themselves,
Their chosen problem; and the clatter back
Down the screes of the hillside—and the
   stones: they roll a little:
They shift and settle down again: one by
   one, in position
On the hillside, on the turf of the hillside,
   and the climbers go.
They cast a look back perhaps, behind them,
   where the rock
Grows black in the evening: it shakes itself
   away
With a gesture: away: the final: by the
   colours of the sky. The climbers,
The rapid beats, they lag perhaps: they sigh
   for a moment, then
Set to again. The climbers: they: with their
   special places in the mountains.
And what do they know of the mountains?
   They glance perhaps at the grass
Of the hillside. They go, returning to their
   well-lighted
Places: their shelter: they huddle carefully.
   They; needing
A home. And at our cottage they swear at us,
   the kitchen, the dirt
And the damp, and the staining. Our home?
   Home—there can be no home here for us,
Among the mountains. The strong grass:
   it jerks to and fro:
It gazes at us: the hillside: through the
   walls of the house,
Through the stone; the sky, the clouds
   drifting over us.
We need no windows—the hillside: where
   the moss grazes
Quiet round the stones. We shut the door.
We group by the fireplace. Yet they are
   there: the short grasses:

They wave, they flutter on the hillside. they
    are cold perhaps
In the evening: but they jerk, they flutter in
    the night air.
No.

Published in the *Mountaineering Journal*, September 1937

Lines for Harmony

So I asked him—Why do you climb?
He said, I will tell you why,
                I will tell you a story:
My tale is about three men.

                There were two of them stood there talking
A man wise, and another a climber
                And the climber he said this—
"I climb but I don't know why.
                I had a dream.
I was drifting up a precipice,
                there were no holds nothing beneath,
But I was caught there, straining,
                dark.
Then the cliff let go and I cleared
                but my footstep trudged on up,
Up high, and alone
Then a thing came swaying, swinging down,
                hung light in the air above;
A thing young, a form;
                and I looked up, smiled,
I rose, looked down,
                and the sun shone white—
On snow."
He said, "—and another dream.
—For they watched as I went, so my hand grew great
And I trod the cliff far up.
                And they watched, watched, so that I watched
                too,

And my hand grew greater, huge,
At my back,
but I must, I must
See down for a hold: I was bent;
my eyes
Stared cramped by my knees,
and a crevice, I gazed, it was filled
With the little fronds of moss,
that were green and straight,
And they watched me, watched,
from the forests that are in the head.
And the hand grew more,
And I feared;
my eyes went small; I died.
There was grist there; and I pondered."
And the wise man said,
"I have plucked it deep,
Have thought from many masters,
the crush of emotion
How it effervesces, breaks,
how it talks in the night.
But I too pondered.
And I fell into a sleep and I dreamt;
And the dream passed on,
and it had been a dream,
That I had dreamt.
Then the bright night passed it on."
"Yes," said the climber, "Yes, but mine?
You can say?—"
But the wise man had gone on, thinking.
And there, a little further, had met a man,
the third,
With a rope and a rucksack, walking.
And he asked, "You too are a climber?"
"No," said the third, "I climb as you see;"
But not now I am a climber."
And the wise man said, "If I might come and speak—?"
But he, he stopped, he sat down by the roadside,
Put a hand to his eyes; for he wept.
So the wise man turned,
stepped back;

For indeed there came
    the great climber,
And they two stayed,
    pointed thoughts at
Many subjects.
    For the dew stood wet
Among the stones of the wall,
And it seemed well to wait
    a little.

But the third man had gone on.

And I said, "But what was the meaning
Of the story, story of the three men?"
But he said, "No,
    I told a tale
Of one man,
    and three armies."

    Published in the *Mountaineering Journal*, January 1938

SELECT BIBLIOGRAPHY

1.

Menlove's published writings (guidebooks):
Cwm Idwal (Climbers' Club 1936)
Tryfan (with C. W. F. Noyce, Climbers' Club 1937)
Lliwedd (Climbers' Club 1939)
Clogwyn Du'r Arddu (with J. E. Q. Barford, Climbers' Club 1942)

Articles, poems and reviews by Menlove appeared variously in *The Climbers' Club Journal*, *The Wayfarers' Journal* and *The British Mountaineering Journal* between 1932 and 1941. His major prose pieces have been very frequently anthologized.

2.

Background reading:
The Mountains of Snowdonia, ed. H. R. C. Carr and G. Lister, 2nd edition, Crosby Lockwood, 1948.
The Black Cliff, P. Crew, N. J. Soper and K. J. Wilson, Kaye & Ward, 1971.
Lliwedd, H. Drasdo, Climbers' Club, 1972.
The Mountain Men, A. Hankinson, Heinemann, 1977.
Beyond a Boundary, C. L. R. James, Hutchinson, 1963.
A Woman's Reach, Nea Morin, Eyre & Spottiswood, 1968.
Mountains and Men, C. W. F. Noyce, Geoffrey Bles, 1947.
Samson: The Life and Writings of J. Menlove Edwards, C. W. F. Noyce & Geoffrey Sutton, published privately, 1960
Climbing Days, Dorothy Pilley, 2nd edition, Secker & Warburg, 1965.
Mountain Holidays, Janet Adam Smith, Dent, 1946.
In This Short Span, Michael Ward, Gollancz, 1972.
Snowdon Biography, G. W. Young, G. Sutton and C. W. F. Noyce, Dent, 1957.

3.

Articles on Menlove have appeared in:
Mountain Life 6 (1973)
Mountain 25 (1973)
Crags 23 (1980)
Climber & Rambler (November 1983)

4.
Film:
A Great Effort, directed by Jim Curran (1976)

5.
Obituaries and reviews
The Climbers' Club Journal (1958) and *The Alpine Journal* (1958) both carried obitu-
aries of Menlove. The review of *Samson* by Francis Keenlyside in *The Alpine
Journal* (volume 65, 1960, p. 253) is of particular interest.

INDEX